PROLEGOMENA TO HOMER

[1795]

F. A. WOLF

PROLEGOMENA
TO HOMER

===== 1795 =====

TRANSLATED

WITH INTRODUCTION AND NOTES BY

ANTHONY GRAFTON, GLENN W. MOST,

AND JAMES E. G. ZETZEL

PRINCETON, NEW JERSEY
PRINCETON UNIVERSITY PRESS

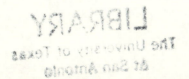

COPYRIGHT © 1985 BY PRINCETON UNIVERSITY PRESS

PUBLISHED BY PRINCETON UNIVERSITY PRESS, 41 WILLIAM STREET

PRINCETON, NEW JERSEY 08540

IN THE UNITED KINGDOM:

PRINCETON UNIVERSITY PRESS, GUILDFORD, SURREY

LIBRARY OF CONGRESS CATALOGING IN PUBLICATION DATA WILL

BE FOUND ON THE LAST PRINTED PAGE OF THIS BOOK

ISBN 0-691-06639-6

PUBLICATION OF THIS BOOK HAS BEEN AIDED BY A GRANT FROM

THE ANDREW W. MELLON FOUNDATION OF PRINCETON UNIVERSITY PRESS

THIS BOOK HAS BEEN COMPOSED IN LINOTRON BASKERVILLE

CLOTHBOUND EDITIONS OF PRINCETON UNIVERSITY PRESS BOOKS

ARE PRINTED ON ACID-FREE PAPER, AND BINDING MATERIALS

ARE CHOSEN FOR STRENGTH AND DURABILITY

PRINTED IN THE UNITED STATES OF AMERICA

BY PRINCETON UNIVERSITY PRESS

PRINCETON, NEW JERSEY

D. M.

JOHN ARTHUR HANSON

† 28 MARCH 1985

CONTENTS

PREFACE

Classical scholars have written few classics, but F. A. Wolf's *Prolegomena to Homer* is certainly one of them. Its literary impiety enraged traditionalists. Its vision of a primitive Homer captivated poets. Its elegant, fine-spun arguments convinced everyone that grammatical technicalities could be interesting. It thrust classical studies to the center of the German intellectual stage and made Wolf himself "the Coryphaeus of Philologians, the Ishmael of criticism."[1]

Wolf continues to receive praise, blame, and—above all—lip service. New summaries and critiques of his arguments appear regularly, but most of them are one-sided, and many are derived from earlier secondary works rather than from the text of the *Prolegomena* itself. It is not hard to account for this. The *Prolegomena* is a substantial and technical book written in a peculiar and difficult Latin and filled with obscure and often outdated details. Furthermore, its original context—the body of early modern scholarship and criticism on which Wolf drew—has largely been forgotten. Hence the few who today read Wolf himself tend to do so in an unhistorical way.

This edition is meant to make the *Prolegomena* accessible to modern readers. The introduction sets Wolf's ideas in their historical context. The translation provides a guide to the Latin text of his work. The editorial notes and the biographical entries in the *index nominum* clarify Wolf's allusions to texts and individuals. The subsidia offer selections from J. G. Eichhorn's *Einleitung ins Alte Testament*, which was the model for Wolf's work on Homer, and from Wolf's polemical *Briefe an Herrn Hofrath Heyne*, in which he explained the origins of his ideas about Homer and glossed several passages in the *Prolegomena*.[2] The bibliographical essays, finally,

---

[1] MS Diary of George Ticknor, 12 September 1816; quoted by Carl Diehl, *Americans and German Scholarship, 1770-1870* (New Haven and London, 1978), 71.

[2] Wolf reprinted in this pamphlet his teacher Heyne's review of the *Prolegomena*. This essay, translated in full in the subsidia, gives a detailed summary of Wolf's arguments as a contemporary expert saw them. Accordingly, we have not included a further summary of the book in our introduction.

offer an orientation to modern discussions of Wolf himself and the
fields in which he worked.

Classical scholarship was the core of the modern humanistic disciplines when they were created in nineteenth-century Germany
and passed on to the rest of the Western world. It is our belief that
studies and editions like the present one can help us to recover a
sense of what these disciplines were at a time when they still had
a central and formative role in education and culture.

ACKNOWLEDGMENTS

This translation is the fruit of a long and pleasant collaboration. The research for the introduction was done for the most part by Anthony Grafton, and an early summary of the argument appears in his article *"Prolegomena* to Friedrich August Wolf," *Journal of the Warburg and Courtauld Institutes* 44 (1981) 101-29. We are grateful to the editors for permission to reprint some sections here, and to audiences at the Warburg Institute; Oxford University; the University of Chicago; the annual meeting of the American Society for Eighteenth-Century Studies; the Max-Planck-Institut für Geschichte, Göttingen; Princeton University; and the California Institute of Technology for their helpful comments and criticism. The present form of the introduction reflects the views of, and includes substantial contributions by, all three translators.

The text, notes, and subsidia are the joint work of the translators. We are grateful to J. B. Trapp, whose trenchant comments on an earlier draft produced material improvements. For advice and criticism of a more general kind we owe thanks to J. Levine, H. Lloyd-Jones, A. D. Momigliano, T. K. Rabb, R. S. Turner and N. G. Wilson. For her consistent support we are especially grateful to Joanna Hitchcock of Princeton University Press. For editorial skill and forbearance we owe much to Robert E. Brown. And for superhuman patience in the face of adversity we are greatly indebted to Professor Trapp, who asked for a lecture and bore up splendidly when he found himself inundated by "Wolf & yet Wolf & yet Wolf."

ACKNOWLEDGMENTS

A NOTE ON CITATIONS

The following works and periodicals are cited by abbreviation only:

ALZ   *Allgemeine Literatur-Zeitung*

GGA   *Göttingische Anzeigen von gelehrten Sachen*

Grafton   Anthony Grafton, "*Prolegomena* to Friedrich August Wolf," *Journal of the Warburg and Courtauld Institutes* 44 (1981), 101-29

Peters   W. Peters, *Zur Geschichte der Wolfschen Prolegomena zu Homer*, Beilage zum Programm des Königlichen Kaiser-Friedrichs-Gymnasiums in Frankfurt am Main (1890)

Pfeiffer, *History*   Rudolf Pfeiffer, *History of Classical Scholarship from the Beginnings to the End of the Hellenistic Age* (Oxford, 1968)

Pfeiffer, *Geschichte*   Rudolf Pfeiffer, *Geschichte der Klassischen Philologie von den Anfängen bis zum Ende des Hellenismus*, 2d ed. (Munich, 1978)

Reiter   Siegfried Reiter, *Friedrich August Wolf. Ein Leben in Briefen* (Stuttgart, 1935)

Villoison   Jean Baptiste Gaspard d'Ansse de Villoison, *Homeri Ilias ad veteris codicis Veneti fidem recensita* (Venice, 1788)

Volkmann   Richard Volkmann, *Geschichte und Kritik der Wolfschen Prolegomena zu Homer* (Leipzig, 1874)

Wolf, *Briefe*   F. A. Wolf, *Briefe an Herrn Hofrath Heyne* (1797), as reprinted in Rudolf Peppmüller's edition of the *Prolegomena* (Halle, 1884 = Hildesheim, 1963)

Wolf, *Kl. Schr.*   F. A. Wolf, *Kleine Schriften in lateinischer und deutscher Sprache*, ed. G. Bernhardy (Halle, 1869).

References to the *Prolegomena* are made by chapter and, when applicable, footnote number.

In correcting and amplifying Wolf's citations of the scholia on Homer, we have used the following editions:

G. Dindorf, *Scholia Graeca in Homeri Iliadem* (Oxford, 1875-77)

G. Dindorf, *Scholia Graeca in Homeri Odysseam* (Oxford, 1855)

H. Erbse, *Scholia Graeca in Homeri Iliadem* (Berlin, 1969-83)

H. Schrader, *Porphyrii Quaestiones Homericae ad Iliadem Pertinentes* (Leipzig, 1880-82)

If no indication of source is given, the scholium in question is to be found in Erbse's edition of the *Iliad* scholia or Dindorf's of the *Odyssey* scholia; those found elsewhere are noted "A Dindorf," "B Dindorf," or "Porph." with the page and line number of Schrader's edition. References to Eustathius include both the line of Homer being discussed and the page and line of the *editio Romana* of Eustathius.

PROLEGOMENA TO HOMER

[1795]

INTRODUCTION

1. F. A. WOLF (1759-1824)

Wolf was the son of a village schoolmaster in the Harz. After attending the secondary school at Nordhausen and reading widely on his own, he went in 1777 to the University of Göttingen, the most up-to-date institution of learning in Germany. The dominant scholar there was Christian Gottlob Heyne, who had done much to modernize classical studies by connecting research on ancient art with direct study of the ancient texts, by subjecting Greek mythology to a historical and comparative approach, and by reading Homer, in the manner of the English traveler Robert Wood, as a primitive poet rather than a highly civilized one.[1] Heyne was amused by Wolf's presumption but taught him much, and found him a post as a schoolmaster, a capacity in which Wolf excelled.[2] In 1782 Wolf published an edition of Plato's *Symposium* with German commentary, displaying his mastery of the historical method of Göttingen (he treated Greek homosexuality, for example, not with reproach but as a normal feature of a society different from his own), and prominently praising the "philosopher-king" of Prussia and his reforming minister von Zedlitz.[3] The book had its intended effect; Wolf was made professor of philosophy and pedagogy at the best-endowed and best-attended Prussian university, Halle.[4]

Wolf's Halle years (1783-1807) were his finest. His lectures were so famous that Goethe hid behind a curtain to hear him teach. His

[1] On Heyne (1729-1812), see now *Der Vormann der Georgia Augusta*, Göttinger Universitätsreden, 67 (Göttingen, 1980), which gives a good overview of his manifold activities as critic of poetry, interpreter of myths, student of archaeology, and creator of the modern philological seminar. The most recent account in English is D. Constantine, *Early Greek Travellers and the Hellenic Ideal* (Cambridge, 1984).

[2] Reiter, 2:339-44.

[3] *Platons Gastmahl: Ein Dialog*, ed. Wolf (Leipzig, 1782); Wolf's *Vorrede* is reprinted in his *Kl. Schr.*, 1:131-57, his *Uebersicht des Inhalts* in *Kl. Schr.*, 2:593-620; his *Einleitung*, however, is omitted.

[4] Reiter, 2:344.

Philological Seminar produced original scholars and competent *Gymnasium* teachers. His editions of classical texts—above all his Homer and his commentary on the legal and historical aspects of Demosthenes' *Oration Against Leptines*—established him as the dominant Greek scholar in North Germany and won him the offer of a chair at Leiden, still the center of classical studies in Europe. His program for studying all aspects of ancient culture in conjunction with one another, a program as broad as Heyne's and more modern in presentation, fascinated the young Wilhelm von Humboldt and became the creed of classicists of the next generation.[5]

When the Prussian defeat at Leipzig in 1806 forced the University of Halle to close, Wolf moved to Berlin. There he helped Humboldt convince the Baron von Stein to found the new university at Berlin. At first he kept his powers as a teacher. "Boeckh instructs me," wrote the young Jewish scholar Leopold Zunz, "but F. A. Wolf attracts me."[6] The American George Bancroft also found Wolf to have a "genius" that Boeckh lacked.[7] But as Wolf aged he lost the drive to work. He wasted his time and wit boasting of his early triumphs, and bit every back that was turned on him. He never provided the second volumes to finish off the many works he had begun at Halle. After 1820 he did not write, and in 1824 he died.

The *Prolegomena* fell just in the middle of Wolf's creative years. Like all his work, it was written quickly, but it drew together threads of Wolf's own research and writing that went back to his student days with Heyne. At the same time, it derived much of its substance from previous traditions of scholarship and criticism. It is to these that we now turn.

[5] Grafton, 102-9; cf. Ada Hentschke and Ulrich Muhlack, *Einführung in die Geschichte der Klassischen Philologie* (Darmstadt, 1972), 80-88; Axel Horstmann, "Die Forschung in der Klassischen Philologie des 19. Jahrhunderts," in *Konzeption und Begriff der Forschung in den Wissenschaften des 19. Jahrhunderts*, ed. Alwin Diemer (Meisenheim am Glan, 1978), 32-40. On Wilhelm von Humboldt (1767-1835) and his role in the reformation of the German universities see P. Sweet, *Wilhelm von Humboldt: A Biography* (Columbus, Ohio, 1978-80).

[6] M. A. Meyer, *The Origins of the Modern Jew* (Detroit, 1967), 158. On August Boeckh (1785-1867), Wolf's most independent pupil and the most original student of Greek history and literature of the first two-thirds of the nineteenth century, see esp. E. Vogt, "Der Methodenstreit zwischen Hermann und Böckh und seine Bedeutung für die Geschichte der Philologie," in *Philologie und Hermeneutik*, vol. 1, ed. H. Flashar et al. (Göttingen, 1979), 103ff. and B. Bravo, *Philologie, histoire, philosophie de l'histoire* (Wrocław, 1968).

[7] M.A.DeWolfe Howe, *The Life and Letters of George Bancroft* (New York,1908),1:92.

2. HOMER AND THE PHILOLOGISTS

Classicists knew long before Wolf that Homer's text had been composed and transmitted in unusual ways. Ancients of high authority, Josephus and Cicero, suggested that the *Iliad* and *Odyssey* had been composed without writing and only put into coherent, written form by Pisistratus some centuries later (*Prolegomena*, chs. 18, 33). That explained, as Obertus Giphanius remarked in his Homer edition of 1572, why "some contradictions are found in Homer."[8] And it implied, as Isaac Casaubon pointed out a decade later, that it would be impossible to have Homer's poems "in a sufficiently correct form even if we should have the most ancient manuscripts, since it is probable that they were written down quite differently from the way they had been composed by him" (*Prolegomena*, ch. 39, n. 42). Others quoted Homeric verses not to be found in any manuscript or edition. Some authorities, notably Diogenes Laertius, suggested that the Athenian collectors of the first full texts had added to them verses of their own devising, verses meant to magnify Athens in the eyes of the rest of the Greeks.

More seriously, both Plutarch and the twelfth-century Byzantine commentator Eustathius of Thessalonica revealed that Aristarchus and other Hellenistic textual critics had treated the text quite roughly in their turn. Giphanius noted that Aristotle seemed to have produced the first critical edition of the *Iliad*. "Many Grammarians," he continued,

came later, who vied with one another in polishing up this poet. But the greatest of these, in fact and reputation, was Aristarchus. Hence his edition was always highly prized, and so much so, indeed, that it is apparently the only one that has come down to us. His judgment was so accurate and so expert in Homeric poetry that he noticed many spurious verses in the Homeric corpus and marked them with the obelus; though Plutarch, in the book on poets, does not accept all of his obelisms. This is why many verses are cited by the ancients, such

[8] *Homeri Ilias seu potius omnia eius quae extant opera*, ed. O. Giphanius (Strassburg, 1572), 1:15.

as Aristotle and others, which are not found in our texts today. For they used other recensions, we that of Aristarchus.[9]

As a case in point Giphanius discussed the four lines in which Phoenix described his desire to kill his father. Aristarchus had excised them as immoral, though they were perfectly acceptable in the view of Plutarch, who recorded them.[10] Such willingness to bowdlerize was thought deplorable. In the 1760s L. C. Valckenaer, discussing the same passage, argued that the ancient scholars had "rioted impudently" amid the ruins of Homer.[11]

The texts themselves, finally, in their idiosyncracies of language and content, offered further purchase to the textual critic's crowbar. The most prominent of these—the frequent violation of the metrical canon prohibiting hiatus—convinced the most expert Hellenist of the eighteenth century, Richard Bentley, that the Greek alphabet had changed between the time of the poems' composition and that of their being frozen in written form. A consonant mentioned by grammarians but not found in Greek manuscripts, the Aeolic digamma, must have stood between many vowels that appeared next to one another in the vulgate Homer. Bentley actually set out to restore the lost digammas to the text—and thus to restore the text itself to a state earlier than that represented by any surviving manuscript:

> I shall bestow on the world (though it does not deserve it of me), a new edition of Homer, e'er it be long, in which that Poet will make another sort of figure than he has hitherto done. I shall then show how ill he has been used by dull Commentators and pretended critics who never understood him. . . . In short, by the happy discovery I have made that Homer frequently made use of the Aeolick ᴍᴍ Digamma everywhere in his poem I shall render multitudes of places intelligible which the stupid scholiasts could never account for but by Licentia Poetica.[12]

---

[9] Ibid., 1:16.

[10] Ibid., 1:sig. kkk viii[v] ad 9.457.

[11] L. C. Valckenaer, *Diatribe in Euripidis perditorum dramatum reliquias* (1767), ch. 24 (ed. Leipzig, 1824), 274.

[12] Quoted by R. J. White, *Dr. Bentley. A Study in Academic Scarlet* (London, 1965), 235 n. 2. On the digamma see e.g. R. C. Jebb, *Richard Bentley* (New York, n.d.), 146-51.

And this plan, though never carried out, was discussed and debated for the next century.[13]

From the 1740s on, moreover, evidence of what ancient scholars had done to Homer began to multiply.[14] The growing interest in things Byzantine and in classical Greek poetry led many philologists to work on that amalgam of fragments from Hellenistic scholars and Byzantine schoolmasters, the commentaries or scholia on the poets. These might be dull and trifling; the great Demosthenes scholar J. J. Reiske called them "emptier than a nut with no meat, futile, footling, trivial, foolish." But they were fashionable nonetheless. Scholars wrote dissertations "On the excellence and utility of the Greek scholia on the poets"; "On the method by which the old scholiasts on the Greek poets, and above all Homer, can be used to sharpen the sense of elegance and grace." They lectured on scholia as well as on the texts that these were meant to illustrate. They published descriptions of and specimens from the Venice, Leiden, and Leipzig scholia on Homer. In 1788, this activity culminated with J.B.G. d'Ansse de Villoison's publication of the vast corpus of Venice scholia on the *Iliad*, still the richest single source for our knowledge of the working methods of ancient Homeric scholars. One of his avowed intentions was to enable critics to restore the text as nearly as possible to its original, primitive form:

These Scholia, never before published, shed much light on Homer's poetry, illuminate obscure passages, explicate the rites, customs, mythology and geography of the ancients, establish the pure and genuine text, and examine the various readings of various codices and editions and the emendations of the critics. For it is clear that the Homeric text, which the Rhapsodes recited from memory and everyone used to sing aloud, was corrupt at an early date. For the different Rhapsodes of the different areas of Greece necessarily removed, added, and changed many things. Josephus asserts, at the outset of his first book *Against Apion*, that Homer did not leave his poems in written form. And an unpublished Scholiast to

[13] Heyne accepted Bentley's arguments and used his working materials, which were lent him by Trinity College, in preparing his own great edition of Homer; see *GGA*, 19 December 1795, 2025-36 = Wolf, *Briefe*, 262-70. Wolf by contrast rejected Bentley's views on the digamma; see *Kl. Schr.*, 2:1070-71.

[14] For more details see Grafton, 115-19.

Dionysius Thrax seems to agree with this view when he relates that the poems of Homer, which were preserved only in men's minds and memory and were not written, perished in the time of Pisistratus, and that he offered a reward to anyone who would bring him Homeric verses, and that many thereupon, being greedy for money, sold Pisistratus their verses as Homeric. The Critics left these spurious lines in the Edition, but marked them with the obelus.[15]

Many scholars would have agreed, as Villoison did, with the Englishman Thomas Burgess, who described the transmitted text of Homer as a *rifacimento* "not so radically altered as Berni's Boiardo, or Dryden's and Pope's Chaucers, but apparently more so than Hughes's Spenser."[16] And many hoped, as Villoison did, that the Venice scholia would enable them to undo the *rifacimento*. Bold plans like these—plans far more sweeping and ambitious than anything Bentley or Valckenaer had had in mind—were not uncommon in the 1780s.

3. HOMER AND THE CRITICS

New information does not generate new questions of this kind; the histories of science and of scholarship both show the converse to be true. Villoison's hopes for the usefulness of the scholia—and the wide interest his huge, highly technical edition of them provoked—owed much to views of Homer that sprang up largely outside the professional tradition in philology, and in particular to a new sense of the poet's historicity that grew out of the criticisms of him voiced during the Quarrel of the Ancients and Moderns.

To be sure, criticizing Homer had been popular at least since the time of Xenophanes: but in general his disparagers had tended to

---

[15] Villoison, xxxiv. The chief source of novelties in Villoison's edition was the great Codex A of Homer: Venice, Biblioteca Marciana, Ms gr. 454 (tenth century), which preserves in its margins rich remnants of Alexandrian scholars' work on the text of Homer. Villoison also published the scholia (less rewarding from the standpoint of textual criticism) of Codex B (Venice, Biblioteca Marciana, Ms gr. 453), and others as well. For a modern discussion of Villoison's and other early editions of Homeric scholia, as well as the manuscripts, see the *Prolegomena* in vol. 1 of the edition by H. Erbse (Berlin, 1969-83). See also the Bibliographical Essays, below.

[16] Quoted by Villoison, vi n.

focus upon defects of his own knowledge or moral character, and
had sought neither to excuse nor to explain these defects by reference to his age. But in the course of the seventeenth century, the
fact that modern natural scientists had obviously begun to surpass
their ancient counterparts induced a number of writers to question
the validity of transhistorical models and criteria in other domains
as well: if Greek physics could be superseded, then why could not
Greek poetry be as well? Modernists tried to show that Homer's
deficiencies were characteristic of his primitive culture, and even
his defenders tended to excuse them by pointing to those same
primitive conditions. Thus, in the third volume of Charles Perrault's *Parallèle des Anciens et des Modernes* (1692), the spokesmen of
modernity criticize the impropriety of princes who do their own
cooking and princesses who do the laundry, and of a King Odysseus
before whose palace stands a pile of manure, as historically symp-
tomatic violations of taste—"the Princes of that time strongly resembled the peasants of this time"[17]—but even the defender of
antiquity can only vindicate the extravagance of Homer's epic similes by conceding that "the taste of the Greeks, and of the Greeks
of the time of Homer, was quite different from our own" (3.62).
In the same book, apparent weaknesses in the construction of the
Homeric epics are explained with reference to Aelian's claim that
Homer had in fact composed his poems in separate pieces, and
that it was only much later that these were stitched together into
their present form:

> As for myself, I am convinced that Homer had no other in-
> tention than to write the war of the Greeks against the Trojans
> and the various adventures that occurred during the siege of
> Troy, all in pieces and sections independent of one another,
> as Aelian says; and that with regard to the arrangement of the
> twenty-four books of the *Iliad*, it is the work of people who
> came after him and who, in order to link them together, re-
> moved from each one of these books the invocation and the
> summary that apparently had been there, leaving them only
> in the first book, whose first line says, "Sing, goddess, the wrath

[17] Charles Perrault, *Parallèle des Anciens et des Modernes en ce qui regarde les Arts et
les Sciences*, ed. H. R. Jauss and M. Imdahl (Munich, 1964), 3:98 of the original
edition. For subsequent quotations from this edition, reference is made in paren-
theses in the text to the original volume and page number.

of Achilles, son of Peleus"—a request applicable only to this first book, since all the other books do not speak at all, or hardly at all, of this wrath. (3.45-46)

The same passage of Aelian was to play an important role in Wolf's *Prolegomena* (chs. 25, 33).

The Quarrel of the Ancients and Moderns made one central point clear to French and English intellectuals—as well as to their German readers. If Homer was to remain interesting, he had to cease being an ideal ancient sage and become a historically plausible ancient poet: a representative or even a collective name for the Greek people in their most primitive stage of development. His poems had to become assemblies of popular or semipopular lays rather than grand embodiments of Aristotelian precepts. This was, as Vico pointed out, the only way to transform Homer's apparent poetic vices into clues to his real historical position: "Thus Homer, lost in the crowd of the Greek people, is justified against all the accusations leveled at him by the critics, and particularly [against those made] on account of his base sentences, vulgar customs, crude comparisons, local idioms, licenses in meter, variations in dialect, and his having made men of gods and gods of men."[18]

Such views soon came to the attention of the professional scholars, and the more original of these tended to adopt them. To Bentley, for example, it seemed obvious that Homer had not been an educated poet who consciously set out to instruct and entertain his posterity:

> To prove *Homer*'s universal Knowledge *a priori*, our Author [Anthony Collins] says, *He design'd his Poem for Eternity, to please and instruct Mankind.* Admirable again: *Eternity* and *Mankind*: nothing less than all Ages and all Nations were in the Poet's foresight. Though our Author vouches that he *thinks every day de quolibet ente*, give me leave to except *Homer*; for he never seems to have thought of Him or his History. Take my word for it, poor *Homer* in those circumstances and early times had never such aspiring thoughts. He wrote a sequel of Songs and Rhapsodies, to be sung by himself for small earnings and good cheer, at Festivals and other days of Merriment; the *Ilias* he

---

[18] Giambattista Vico, *The New Science*, rev. trans. of the 3d ed. (1744) by Thomas G. Bergin and Max H. Fisch (Ithaca, N.Y., 1968), sects. 882-89, pp. 325-26.

made for the Men, and the *Odysseis* for the other Sex. These
loose Songs were not collected together in the form of an Epic
Poem till *Pisistratus's* time.[19]

As the eighteenth century wore on, the study of dead languages
and classical texts was much criticized as a waste of time and talent.
After all, the philosophes argued, there was much useful, scientific
knowledge to be had in modern languages. Servile imitation of old
books—themselves the products of a society less advanced than that
of modern Europe—was foolish in an age of enlightenment. At the
same time, literary tastes turned more and more to the primitive
and the exotic. The direct, vivid, popular songs of Celts and Bed-
ouins were in favor, even if they had to be forged to meet the
desires of the public. The only way to keep Homer interesting and
to make classical studies look useful in their own right was to claim
that up-to-date, comparative research established Homer in the
enviable position of the Greek Ossian. Blackwell and Gravina, Wood
and Merian labored to knock Homer off his Ionic pedestal, to strip
him of his austere classic robes, and to deck him out with the rough
staff and furry cloak appropriate to a storyteller at a tribal
campfire.[20]

The new evidence of the scholia seemed to Villoison and others
to confirm and enrich the literary critics' view of Homer. The scho-

[19] [Richard Bentley], *Remarks Upon a Late Discourse of Free-Thinking, in a Letter to
F.H.D.D. by Phileleutherus Lipsiensis*, 8th ed. (Cambridge, 1743), 25-26; partly quoted
in *Prolegomena*, ch. 26, n. 84. Valckenaer followed a similar line in his lectures on
Greek literary history; Leiden University Library, Ms BPL 450, fol. 7ʳ: "Quoniam
autem non satis clare tradi solet, quo modo et quo potissimum tempore poemata
Homeri in eam, qua nunc prostant, formam devenerint, ea res paulo enucleatius
est tradenda. Ilias proprie non est unum poema, sed variorum poematum in unum
corpus collecta farrago. Similiter et Odyssea. Ista poemata separata suis nominibus
singula olim insignita, et ab ipso Homero et post ejus mortem a Rhapsodis tanquam
totidem cantilenae fuerunt decantatae. Aelianus . . . hujus rei auctor est luculentus."
Cf. J. G. Gerretzen, *Schola Hemsterhusiana* (Nijmegen and Utrecht, 1940), 295. But
in his "Collegium in Homerum" he professed more conventionally Neoclassical views
(ibid., Ms BPL 451, fol. 7ʳ: "Ilias Homeri primitus continuum fuit et unicum poema;
quod cum in centenas partes fuisset distractum, has partes sic collegerunt Grammatici, ut ex uno poemate, 24 libros condiderint"; fol. 8ʳ: "Id velim semel observetur,
scripta Homeri reliquis humanis longe esse diviniora, et in his nihil reperiri temere
aut inconsiderate positum. In singulis verbis, quo diligentius spectentur, eo major
adparebit significationis vis . . ."). These texts suggest that Valckenaer already felt
some of the tension between historicist and classicist modes of analysis that was to
bedevil Wolf.

[20] See in general Kirsti Simonsuuri, *Homer's Original Genius* (Cambridge, 1979),
which provides ample reference to older secondary literature.

lia showed that professional scholars in later periods of antiquity itself had found Homer's poetry alien and offensive to their canons of taste. And they proved that the ancients had known a far greater number of editions and variant readings of the text than any modern critic had suspected. Both sets of facts seemed to lead naturally to the same conclusion: that Homer had been a primitive oral bard, whose poems would inevitably shock more cultivated readers and undergo hundreds of changes and corruptions as they were preserved and transmitted by memorization. That, in turn, can explain why Villoison saw as the natural companion to his edition of the scholia an anthropological study of the Greeks he had met in his own travels. For what the scholia seemed to teach him was that the Greeks of Homer's day had closely resembled the warlike illiterate islanders of the eighteenth-century Aegean.[21] This program was quite reasonable in the light of the belief, widespread in eighteenth-century thought, that geography and climate gave a permanent form to every nation's character.[22]

The need to show that Homer's text had taken form by gradual accretions over centuries, the wish to trace the outlines of his original lays, the hope to find a Homer as pure and bardic as Lowth's David—these were the factors that made the evaluation and application of Villoison's new material seem an urgent task. No wonder then that long reviews of Villoison appeared in every serious German periodical.

4. WOLF'S IMMEDIATE PREDECESSORS

Yet the marriage between textual and literary criticism proved far harder to consummate than Villoison had expected. He and the other scholars who first worked through the Venice scholia did so in the hope of using the new data they provided to discover or recreate the original Homer. But as soon as they began to work in earnest, an older and much more limited set of questions reimposed itself at the expense of more novel and ambitious ones. Their attention was diverted by the vast fund of new information offered by the scholia about the lives and writings of the ancient Homeric

[21] Villoison, liv.   [22] Cf. Grafton, 104.

critics, the critical signs by which they had expressed their opinions about individual verses, and the history of all extant Homeric scholia and commentaries. These were the kinds of information that eighteenth-century scholars had traditionally looked for in scholia. And the first serious students of the Venetian ones, Villoison, Siebenkees, and Harles, confined their close attention to details of this kind even though they knew that broader problems could not be solved by doing so.[23] The distance between Wolf and these earlier grazers in the same pastures was well expressed by Schütz in 1796. Wolf's predecessors, he wrote, were industrious compilers of facts; but Wolf had gone beyond them when he "established new results by historical reasoning and ingenious conjectures."[24]

Heyne, certainly, never lost sight of the wide questions. But even he did not see how the scholia could help answer them. He admitted that the new data proved one point beyond doubt: "We will not regain the Iliad, as it came from Homer's mind and lips—that is clear; no more than the books of Moses and the Prophets can be restored as they came from the authors' hands. [We will not even gain the text] as it was in the first copies, when the Iliad was first written down in the script that was at that time incomplete."[25] He also admitted that the Venice codex was the best subsidium yet found for reconstructing the alterations that the text had undergone as the alphabet changed and the Alexandrians had their way with it: "in this regard the Codex is more precious than gold." But he insisted that the new information made no essential difference to the text: "Where Homer used to be corrupt, incomprehensible and interpolated, he remains in that state."[26] And he went further. Though the new scholia made clear what the methods and principles of the Alexandrians had been, this knowledge was not very much worth having. True, "it is pleasant to watch the human spirit, which continually goes on working above and below the earth, in all its efforts—even in grammar."[27] But on the whole, little pleasure could be derived from contemplating the melancholy paper battlefields on which the Alexandrian critics had shredded one another's recensions and interpretations. They had read Homer unhistorically; they had lacked taste and judgment in poetic matters.

[23] Grafton, 118-19.
[25] *GGA*, 4 April 1789, 561-62.
[27] Ibid., 563.
[24] *ALZ*, 30 January 1796, col. 271.
[26] Ibid., 562, 564.

A scholar might find it well worth his while to master all the Alexandrians' "techniques for splitting hairs,"[28] but they would not lead him further in his search for the true, the primitive bard.

Heyne went through the new material more from a sense of duty than from a genuine commitment or interest. His boredom emerges clearly from the comments on individual scholia that he scrawled down as he worked through them for the first time: "The Grammarians have many pointless subtleties on these words" (to 1.225); "The Grammarians are copious in their explication of a point clear in itself" (to 2.250).[29] His fundamental lack of faith that the new material could help solve the big historical questions about the original form of the poems is equally clear from his introductory lecture of 1789 on the texts of the Homeric poems:

> Homer's main works were the Iliad and Odyssey. Homer never wrote them down; the art of writing was still insufficiently sophisticated to be usable for anything more than matters meant to be recorded on public memorials. There were only 16 letters, and for writing materials at first only metal, stone, wooden tablets. . . . Also it was the custom of the time to teach only by speaking, to learn only by hearing. Poems were sung above all, repeated many times, finally learned. . . . In the early days there were only individual bits of the Iliad and Odyssey, Rhapsodies. These were sung separately. The division into 24 books is a work of the scholiasts. . . . Homer's poems were collected and recorded in writing at a later date; it is not clear who did it. It is ascribed to Lycurgus . . . also to Pisistratus or his sons Hippias and Hipparchus, finally to Solon. All may well have had a hand in it. . . . Given the way in which Homer has come down to us, many wrong readings must certainly have crept in. Aristotle made the first critical edition, *ekdosis ek narthēkos* ["the edition from the unguent casket"]. A whole series of editions was produced in Alexandria. They were also called *diorthōseis*. The most famous were those of Zenodotus, Aris-

[28] Ibid., 564-66.
[29] Göttingen, Niedersächsische Staats- und Universitätsbibliothek, Ms Heyne 8 (a heavily annotated copy of books 1-10 of the *Iliad* in Wolf's first edition): "Multae inanes Grammat. argutiae super his vocibus . . ." (on 1.225); "Copiosi Gr. in dilucidanda re per se clara . . ." (on 1.250); cf. "Multa commenta in B quomodo Helena ignorare potuerit fata fratrum" (on 3.236).

tophanes of Byzantium, and Aristarchus. . . . All these tried to
distinguish what was genuine from what was spurious, but
often by false principles. Thus the text was falsified anew.[30]

Heyne's lecture is characteristically learned and sensible. Yet to
compare it with the *Prolegomena* is to see the gulf that separated
Wolf from his predecessors in Homeric studies. Heyne provides a
skeletal list of people and events. When accounts disagree he is
indecisive and uncritical. And when it comes to the effects exerted
on the texts by Greek scholars and revisers, he is merely negative.
The Alexandrians appear not as central characters in the story but
as intruders; their work is not explained in terms of their needs
and interests but criticized for being vitiated by "false principles."
The text itself has merely become falsified to an even greater extent
with the passage of time.

Wolf by contrast wrote the first "history of a text in antiquity."[31]
He tried to show what the rhapsodes, the *diaskeuastai* [revisers], and
the Alexandrians in turn thought they were doing to and with the
original poems. He imagined with as much vividness as his sources
permitted what it was like to be a professional reciter in a society
passing from orality to literacy; what it was like to be a professional
textual critic in a world without manuals of the *ars critica*, criteria
for assessing the age and independence of manuscripts, and printing presses. Far more than Heyne's lectures—or than any of the
other responses to Villoison's edition—the *Prolegomena* was the history of the Homeric text, at once philological and literary in inspiration, that Villoison had dreamed of helping to create.

[30] Translated from the notes taken by Wilhelm von Humboldt, described and
published in part in his *Gesammelte Schriften* (Akademie-Ausgabe), vol. 7, pt. 2 (Berlin,
1907), 551-52. Heyne had not held these views before the Venice scholia appeared.
In his 1783 preface to Pindar—a text Wolf would later quote against him (*Briefe*,
261)—he remarked: "I have often been surprised by the fact that Homer and
Pindar—Herodotus too—though very ancient writers, are preserved far more intact
and pure than many writers who lived after Christ's birth. And those employed in
defending the authority of the Hebrew writers will use that argument if they wish"
(*Pindari Carmina* [Göttingen, 1798], 1:26).
[31] Sebastiano Timpanaro, *La genesi del metodo del Lachmann*, new ed. (Padua,
1981), 34.

5. THE PROBLEM

In one sense Wolf was naturally cast to be the renewer of Homeric
scholarship and the historian of the Homeric text. His interest in
the fundamental problem of Homer's literacy and level of culture
went back to his student days. As early as 1780 he had submitted
to the publisher Nicolai a plan for an essay arguing that "it was
impossible to prepare so great a work as the *Iliad* without writing."[32]
His interest in the work of rhapsodes and Hellenistic critics went
back almost as far. In his 1783 edition of Hesiod's *Theogony*, he
argued that the Homeric and Hesiodic poems, given their originally
oral character and the many additions and changes they had suffered, must be far more corrupt than later classical texts: "I little
envy the facility—not to say credulity—of any who still seem to
think that they read Homer and Hesiod as whole and pure as, for
example, the Romans Virgil or Lucretius."[33] He lamented that there
was insufficient information to reverse these changes and, even
more, that "the method of applying criticism to the most ancient
poets has not yet been sufficiently established by editorial rules and
examples that a new interpreter knows for certain what he should
do or dare."[34]

Wolf published school editions of the *Odyssey* (in 1784) and *Iliad*
(1785), and reprinted with the latter an older treatment of the
fortunes of Homer and the Homeric text, L. Küster's *Historia critica
Homeri* of 1696, in which he found sound historical reasoning as
well as useful information.[35] By 1786 his general vision of the
development of Homeric scholarship in antiquity was largely fixed.
In an appendix to a pupil's dissertation, he felt obliged to argue,
in the teeth of the evidence, that the poet Antimachus of Colophon
(late fifth century B.C.) could not have been the Homeric textual
critic also named Antimachus, since "the Greeks knew neither the
profession nor the term of grammarian in the age when the poet
lived."[36] From then on he would consistently treat textual criticism,

[32] Wolf, *Briefe*, 295-96; Wolf claimed that he began work in 1779. See ibid., 293.
In Reiter, 2:340, he pushes the date back to late 1778.
[33] Wolf, *Kl. Schr.*, 1:166.   [34] Ibid., 1:168.
[35] Ibid., 1:196; cf. *Prolegomena*, chs. 33, n. 6; 34, n. 15.
[36] Ibid., 1:281; cf. *ALZ*, 1 February 1791, cols. 246-47.

as his teacher Heyne did, as a discipline born of Hellenistic literary and scholarly life, one neither conceivable nor practicable in the city-states of classic Greece.

Yet Wolf's longstanding interest in the questions does not explain his ability to make the historical discoveries that Schütz praised. Already in the first sketch for the *Prolegomena*, the long review of Villoison that Wolf published in the *Allgemeine Literatur-Zeitung* in 1791, his approach had taken on its definitive form.[37] He showed little interest in Villoison's wealth of paleographical and codicological material. He made no effort to interpret the subscriptions at the ends of individual books in A, which gave crucial information about the sources from which the A scholia were compiled, and which had been of central interest to another early student of the material, Siebenkees.[38] What Wolf did was simply to make the scholia the pretext for a long essay in which the history of the Homeric text, the origins and development of scholarship in the ancient world, and the general history of Greek culture were inextricably interwoven. Like Villoison, he saw the early oral transmission of the Homeric poems as the chief source of early variants and the chief stimulus for the development of textual criticism: "There is no doubt that the fate of Homer and other older Bards—several of whom disappeared after Herodotus' time—namely, the fate of having been transmitted for a period by memory alone—must have given the first instigation and origin to philological criticism."[39]

Unlike Villoison, however, Wolf insisted that the ancient critics had not had old enough materials to give their critical work a firm foundation. They had no manuscript older than Pisistratus, far less the text of one of the rhapsodes. And even more unlike Villoison, he urged that criticism must by its nature have developed at a slow pace until literary conditions became more favorable in Hellenistic times: "the first steps in it were made in a gentle and inconspicuous manner, until a whole series of Critics of Homer could emerge under the Ptolemies."[40] Wolf drew far more distinctions than Villoison had. He argued that one must never assume that a given technical term or scholarly activity had had the same meaning in two different periods. Villoison had thought that Aristotle's *ekdosis*

[37] *ALZ*, 1-2 February 1791; cf. Volkmann, 41-43.
[38] Volkmann, 42; cf. Grafton, 117-18.
[39] *ALZ*, 1 February 1791, col. 246.
[40] Ibid.

(recension) of Homer, and those attributed to different cities, were more or less like those of the later scholars of the Alexandrian Museum: scholarly editions. Wolf by contrast warned that the term could have been "something different in the case of the famous *ekdosis ek tou narthēkos* than in those of Zenodotus, Aristophanes, etc."[41]

Above all, where Villoison heaped up without structure or order texts and data from all periods of Greek literature, Wolf moved systematically through the scholia, assembling what he took to be characteristic corrections attributed to the ancient readers and critics: the rash Zenodotus, the thoughtful Aristophanes of Byzantium, and the latter's pupil Aristarchus, who had been superior to his teacher in "precise, truly grammatical investigations." Wolf did not argue that one could reconstruct the full Homeric text of Aristarchus or Zenodotus from the proposals for emendation recorded in the scholia.[42] But he showed that the new material could give some body and coherence to the shadowy outline of the history of the Homeric text, that it could be used to supply some of the knowledge scholars had long wanted and, in greater measure, to define for them what could not be known.

Wolf's review adumbrated the chief novelty of the *Prolegomena*: the effort to construct a coherent history of the text in antiquity. It is Wolf's ability to do this, already visible in 1791, that needs to be explained, rather than the interest in oral poetry that he shared with many others.

6. WOLF'S MODEL: J. G. EICHHORN

In fact, Wolf's success can be explained in simple, undramatic terms. He had a model for his history; but it came from theology rather than from traditional forms of Homeric scholarship.

Since the Reformation, the textual history of the Bible—especially that of the Old Testament—had received much attention. The Hebrew text of the extant manuscripts and the printed editions had undergone radical changes since the days of Moses and David. The alphabet in which it was written was not the original one. The

[41] Ibid., col. 247.
[42] *ALZ*, 2 February 1791, col. 257; cf. cols. 253-55.

word divisions, the vowel points, the accents, the marginal apparatus of variant readings had apparently been introduced by the
Masoretes, the Hebrew grammarians of the Near East, during the
first millennium A.D. Some Protestants inferred from these facts
that the Septuagint was more reliable than the Hebrew. After all,
it had been translated with divine help from good manuscripts.
The Greek and Hebrew texts disagreed because perfidious Jews
had deliberately altered their manuscripts. Others denied patristic
and Jewish evidence alike and claimed that the extant Masoretic
text of the Pentateuch went back to Moses, vowel points, variants,
and all. Catholics, on the other hand, tended to claim that the Latin
vulgate surpassed both the Hebrew and the Septuagint.

Fueled by *odium theologicum* as well as *philologicum*, the debate ran
long and hot. By 1678 the Oratorian Richard Simon had produced
a *Critical History of the Old Testament*, which used the patristic evidence, the Talmud, and the Jewish scholarly apparatus and commentaries to reconstruct the state of the Biblical text century by
century from its origins to his own time. His object was to show
that no version was complete and reliable. Hence one had to rely
on Mother Church, which was guided by infallible Tradition, to
compensate for faulty Scripture.[43]

This tradition of Biblical research and controversy was still active
in the eighteenth century; and Wolf had it in mind as he worked
on Homer. His review of Villoison explicitly compared the Alexandrian scholars to the Masoretes.[44] In the *Prolegomena*, he likened
the Venice scholia to the apparatus of the Masoretic Bible. "Let the
masters of Oriental literature, proud of their Masorah, cease at last
to deplore the ill fortune that makes us rely [on such late manuscripts for the text of Homer]. . . . We too now have a sort of Greek
Masorah" (ch. 4). And he made clear that his efforts to reconstruct
the methods of Alexandrian scholars were exactly similar to what
the Orientalists had already done for ancient Jewish scholars
(though they had been hindered by the comparative poverty of

[43] See in general D. C. Allen, *The Legend of Noah* (Urbana, 1963); Paul Hazard, *The European Mind*, tr. J. Lewis May (New York, 1963). *The Massoreth Ha-Massoreth of Elias Levita*, ed. C. D. Ginsburg (London, 1867) remains fundamental.

[44] *ALZ*, 1 February 1791, col. 246: "To that extent Homeric criticism seems to have had the same sort of beginning as Masoretic criticism. Only the former was incomparably more rash, to a degree that we would find unbelievable without the evidence we have now obtained."

their sources): "The Orientalists would rejoice, I believe, if it were certain in even three places what Gamaliel or another Jewish teacher of the early period read in Moses and the Prophets: in Homer we know what Zenodotus read in some four hundred passages, what Aristophanes read in two hundred and what Aristarchus read in over a thousand" (ch. 42).

As these statements suggest, the *Prolegomena* was directly modeled on one of the most controversial products of the German Biblical scholarship of Wolf's time: J. G. Eichhorn's *Einleitung ins Alte Testament*, which began to appear in 1780. Like Wolf, Eichhorn studied at Göttingen under Heyne and Michaelis. He returned there as professor in 1788.[45] His works on the Old and New Testaments fascinated literati of widely different stripe. Coleridge filled the margins of his copies with approving, detailed notes.[46] Wolf thought the volumes on the New Testament exemplary. He cited those on the Old Testament in passing in the *Prolegomena*, and recommended them to his friends and students.[47] But the connection between his work and Eichhorn's is far closer even than his explicit remarks suggest.

Like Wolf, Eichhorn treated his text as a historical and an anthropological document, the much-altered remnant of an early stage in the development of human culture.[48] Like Wolf, he held that the original work had undergone radical changes, so that the serious Biblical scholar must reconstruct "the history of the text."[49] Like Wolf too, he saw the true history of the text as its ancient history, before the standardized manuscripts now extant had been prepared. With the work of the Masoretes, he wrote, "properly ends the history of the written text; for the chief work was accomplished, and the Hebrew text continued now, some insignificant

---

[45] E. Sehmsdorf, *Die Prophetenauslegung bei J. G. Eichhorn* (Göttingen, 1971), is the best treatment of Eichhorn's formation.

[46] See E. S. Schaffer, *"Kubla Khan" and the Fall of Jerusalem* (Cambridge, 1975).

[47] See *Prolegomena*, ch. 15, n. 25; F. A. Wolf, *Vorlesungen über die Alterthumswissenschaft*, ed. J. Gürtler and S. Hoffman (Leipzig, 1839), 1:305; H.K.A. Eichstädt, *Opuscula Oratoria*, 2d ed. (Jena, 1850), 607 and 634-35, n. 13.

[48] J. G. Eichhorn, *Einleitung ins Alte Testament* (1st ed., 1780-83; English translation of chs. 1-147 by G. T. Gollop, which we cite where possible, privately printed, London, 1888), ch. 2.

[49] Eichhorn, *Einleitung*, ch. 2, is entitled "History of the Texts of the Books of the Old Testament."

changes excepted, true in all its copies, to its once-for-all established pattern, as is clear from Kennicott's 'Collection of Variations.' "[50] Like Wolf, Eichhorn paid much attention to the development of the literary language in which his texts were couched, the history of the alphabet and writing implements by which they were recorded, and the growth of a canon of books accepted as genuine. Like Wolf, though from the opposite standpoint, he compared the Bible's growth and fate with Homer's.[51]

Eichhorn's and Wolf's conclusions about the early formation of their texts had almost as much in common as their methods. True, they differed on many points of detail.[52] Yet each found errors and inconsistencies of thought and language everywhere in his masterpiece, and each saw these as the clues that could enable one to identify the original substrates that Moses on the one hand, Pisistratus on the other, had reworked. In *Prolegomena*, chs. 30-31, Wolf shows how to use literary and linguistic evidence ("unusualness and ambiguity of their diction," "unusualness in words and phrases," "a disparate color in thought and expression," "the sinews and the Homeric spirit are lacking") to challenge the authenticity of passages and whole books. In the *Einleitung* Eichhorn had shown how to use literary and linguistic tests (differences in preferred subject matter, different names for God) to cut Genesis up into the original narrative sources that Moses had conflated.[53] Wolf's history of the conditions under which his text was passed down was more richly imagined than Eichhorn's had been; Eichhorn's efforts to

[50] Ibid., ch. 134 (2d ed., Leipzig, 1787), 1:260-61. This was the conclusion most scholars of the late eighteenth century drew from the vast apparatus of variants assembled by Kennicott and de Rossi. Virtually all of these were merely "secondary scribal changes, parallelisms, normalizations, harmonizations, or free associations"; see M. H. Goshen-Gottstein, "Hebrew Biblical Manuscripts . . . ," *Biblica* 48 (1967), 243-90, at 250-55. It seemed reasonable to infer, then, that all extant manuscripts of the Hebrew Bible derived from a single tradition of editorial work that reached final form in the Masoretic Text.

[51] Eichhorn, *Einleitung*, chs. 11, 12, 14.

[52] Wolf thought alphabetic writing to be a late invention in both Greece and the Near East, Eichhorn thought it to be an early one—and stuck to his view in the editions of the *Einleitung* that came out after the *Prolegomena*, even though he admitted the brilliance of Wolf's arguments. See Eichhorn's note to ch. 405 of the *Einleitung* (vol. 2, 3d ed., 1803), 237. Wolf thought Homer and the Bible were formed by learned collectors from oral sources, Eichhorn that they were formed from written ones.

[53] See the subsidia below.

reconstruct the submerged originals were more ambitious than Wolf's.[54] But the general similarities are clear.

Even clearer are the similarities between what Wolf and Eichhorn made of the early histories of textual scholarship in the Greek and Jewish worlds. Eichhorn ransacked the Masorah for evidence about the methods of its creators as ruthlessly as Wolf later attacked the Venice scholia. His conclusions, set out point by point in heavily documented chapters, resemble Wolf's far more closely than anything in strictly classical philology. If Wolf showed great resource in cataloguing the means by which Alexandrian scholars expressed their opinions of the received text of Homer, Eichhorn had already done the same for the critical remarks that filled the margins of the Masoretic text (and which, like the Alexandrian signs, assumed that the received text should be respected).[55]

Moreover, Eichhorn provided both formulations and solutions for technical problems that the scholia posed Wolf. We will give two examples. First, Wolf argued that the Venice scholia did not fully explain the methods Alexandrian scholars had used in collating manuscripts and assessing the worth of variants: "But the one thing that must be asked first, what novelty he [Aristarchus] brought to the totality of the poems, how conscientiously he dealt with ancient manuscripts, how he used the recensions of Zenodotus, Aristophanes, and the others I mentioned above;—these and other things can not today be perceived by certain or even probable arguments" (ch. 47). Wolf explained this gap in the information offered by the scholiasts historically, in terms of the cultural situation of the ancient grammarians. Exact details of a critic's reasoning about variants simply had not interested them: "The ancients apparently never worried about *our* problem." Eichhorn had already solved a parallel problem in a parallel way: namely, why the Masoretes did not bother to preserve the older, unpunctuated manuscripts of the Bible from which they copied their own more usable texts:

Truly the manuscripts of the ancient pattern were worthy of preservation for the sake of their critical value. But at that time

[54] Eichhorn's internal analysis of the books of the Bible appears after his general history of the text; similarly, Wolf meant to attempt a fuller internal analysis of Homer in a second and separate volume of *Prolegomena*.

[55] See the subsidia below.

criticism was regarded in a different point of view from that of our days. The Jews believed themselves to have furnished manuscripts better, and containing more information, than those of their ancestors, and to have imparted to the former all that was valuable in the latter; they were flattered also at beholding the manuscripts of their creation adopted and preferred. How probable then, under such circumstances, is the disuse and neglect of the older manuscripts.[56]

Second, Wolf argued that in the Venice scholia the opinions of individual scholars were irretrievably mingled and confused, since the Alexandrians had not considered it worthwhile to keep them separate: "From the time when the Aristarchean reading became the transmitted text ... new emendations and annotations were composed and attached to it in particular, with the omission, in general, of the first authors of the readings, except perhaps when they disagreed among themselves" (ch. 47). Hence no single recension—even the best-attested, that of Aristarchus himself—could be reconstructed line by line or word for word. Eichhorn had made exactly the same point about the Masorah: "We must regret that in the Masorah the earlier and later recensions of the Jews are mixed together, that each Jew did not publish the results of his critical work separately or designate his own contribution more precisely—in short, that we can no longer distinguish the old Masoretic recension from the new one."[57]

In each of these cases, moreover, Eichhorn must have been Wolf's model; for each of his solutions combined existing methods and traditional materials in a novel way. Michaelis had given Eichhorn the techniques for studying Masoretic scholarship and the conviction that the Masoretes had made changes in the text. But Michaelis's view of the Jewish scholars' work lacked sophistication and consistency. As a translator, Michaelis had freed himself from the established Lutheran view that the Masoretic text was perfect, at the cost of refusing any sympathy to the Masoretes, "whose names we do not even know" and whose arguments were often "Jewish whimsies."[58] As a teacher, however, he had assured his students

---

[56] Eichhorn, *Einleitung*, ch. 133, 1:260.

[57] Ibid., ch. 158, 1:309.

[58] J. D. Michaelis, *Vorrede*, in his *Deutsche Uebersetzung des Alten Testaments*, vol. 1 (Göttingen and Gotha, 1769), sigs. b[v], b3[v].

that the Masoretic text was fundamentally sound, at the cost of pretending that the Masoretes had not differed very much in principle from modern Biblical critics:

> What did the Masoretes do that is any different from what the [modern] critics who abuse them do? Both record variant readings, with this difference: modern critics record many, they recorded few; modern critics sometimes add the name of the manuscripts, they record from manuscripts that are not named; modern critics do so from manuscripts, the oldest of which is newer than their newest ones; for none of our manuscripts were written in the eighth century, but the Masoretes took their notes in the sixth, seventh, perhaps, and eighth centuries, from manuscripts that were already old. Therefore as modern critics are superior in two respects to the Masoretes, who were too sparing with their marginal readings, so the Masoretes are superior to modern critics in one respect.[59]

This formulation was undoubtedly more balanced than the hypercritical one of Michaelis's preface to Job. But it was no more historical and could not have served any better than the other to shape Eichhorn's thinking.

Eichhorn's approach came, in fact, from his other teacher, Heyne. Heyne held in theory that one must bring imaginative sympathy to every past person and phenomenon—even to past scholars. Though he did not apply this sterling principle in his dealings with

---

[59] Göttingen, Niedersächsische Staats- und Universitätsbibliothek, Ms Michaelis 39, caput iv (separately paginated), 14-16: "Keri et Kthib cum variae sint lectionis a sexto inde seculo usque ad octavum (ut suspicor) a Masorethis ex bonis codicibus, et vetustioribus [MS: ex bonis et codicibus, vetustioribus . . .] certe, quam omnes, quos nos habemus possumusque consulere, excerptae, male illi agunt critici, qui infesto in Keri sunt animo. Quid enim factum aliud a Masorethis, quam quod ipsi, qui illos reprehendunt, critici faciunt; utrique lectiones varias notant, hoc discrimine, nostri multas, illi paucas; nostri nonnunquam addito codicum nomine, illi ex codicibus non nominatis; nostri ex codicibus, quorum vetustissimus recentior est illorum recentissimis, nostrorum enim codicum nullus seculo VIII scriptus, Masorethae seculo jam VI. VII. forte et octavo, ex codicibus, qui jam tum antiqui, enotarunt. Ergo, ut duabus in rebus nostri masorethis, lectionum marginalium nimis parcis, ita una in re masorethae nostris praestant." Michaelis also insisted that repetitions in both Moses and Homer were natural features of early narrative writing rather than signs that two or more pre-existing sources had been conflated. See his *Einleitung in die göttlichen Schriften des Alten Bundes*, vol. 1, pt. 1 (Hamburg, 1787), 300-301—a rebuttal of Eichhorn's chief predecessor, Jean Astruc. Cf. in general J. C. O'Flaherty, "J. D. Michaelis: Rational Biblicist," *Journal of English and Germanic Philology* 49 (1950), 172-81.

the Homeric scholiasts, he did so with aplomb in the prefaces to
his editions of Tibullus and Pindar. Here he argued that one could
appreciate the talents and achievements of early textual critics only
"if one considers the times in which [they] lived."[60] What Eichhorn
did was to apply Heyne's method, more consistently than Heyne
himself, to the material Michaelis had made available. Only in the
Einleitung could Wolf have found so full an application of the principles in which he had been trained to material and problems anal-
ogous to those he faced.

The thesis that Wolf imitated Eichhorn explains why one of the
chapters he sketched for part 2 of the *Prolegomena* compared at
length the textual histories of the Old Testament and Homer, and
the origins of the Masorah and the Venice scholia:

> Our Hebrew text derived from a paradosis: so, clearly, did our
> Homeric vulgate. In each paradosis a choice was made among
> readings, which we may none the less rework. In each text the
> paradosis itself has undergone some mutilation and corrup-
> tion. . . . The Masorah is full of all sorts of absurdities and
> feeble, superstitious inventions; this mass of scholia has no lack
> of similar contents. True, Greeks rave in one way, Jews in
> another . . .

It explains why Wolf advised his students, if they hoped to understand Greek textual criticism, to approach it through that of the
Jews:

> One who wants to penetrate more deeply must concern himself
> with the history of the Masoretic manuscripts. True, these came
> into being much later than Greek criticism. But there is much
> similarity with the earliest Greek criticism. It is at least clear
> that they were much less bold than the Greek scholars. Yet one
> must not think that we have the Old Testament in its original
> form.[61]

It explains why Heyne, in claiming for himself the chief arguments
of the *Prolegomena*, remarked that "Much [of his teaching] has al-

[60] *Albi Tibulli Carmina*, ed. Chr. G. Heyne, 3d ed. (Leipzig, 1798), xlvi-xlvii; cf.
Grafton, 124 and n. 141.
[61] Wolf, *Vorlesungen über die Alterthumswissenschaft*, 1:311.

ready been applied to the oldest Hebrew writers";[62] for surely this was a reference to the analogies of structure and substance that run between *Prolegomena* and *Einleitung*. And most importantly it illustrates how a poorly paid, ill-populated, and culturally marginal field (like classical scholarship in eighteenth-century Germany) can draw on the achievements of a more central and prestigious one (in this case, theology). Wolf's main achievement, then, was the annexation for classical studies of a sophisticated set of methods formed by a contemporary in another field of work. And this too is a normal pattern in the history of both science and scholarship.[63]

7. THE IMPACT OF THE *PROLEGOMENA*

Nevertheless, from the very beginning the *Prolegomena* was taken to be a work of great importance and high originality. By 1816 it seemed clear to one observer that the book had effected a "revolution in philology" and had "become a canon" in its own right.[64] For almost a century thereafter it was *the* book that any aspiring classicist had to master.

Wolf himself had expected to make a stir. "The die is cast," he wrote at the start of one arrogant and defensive footnote: "I have certainly not come to it unprepared" (ch. 26, n. 84). But perhaps even he did not anticipate the vehemence and variety of the responses he evoked. Nay-sayers abounded. J. H. Voss, who had made Homer come alive in modern German, denounced the *Prolegomena* as impious.[65] Melchior Cesarotti, who had rendered Homer in Italian blank verse and interpreted him in accordance with the principles of Vico, dismissed Wolf's work as derivative.[66] J. L. Hug, who rendered due tribute to Wolf's learning and acuity, nonetheless set out to show that he had dated the origins of writing in Greece far too late.[67] And some of those who accepted Wolf's ar-

---

[62] *GGA*, 19 December 1795 = Wolf, *Briefe*, 262.

[63] For an exemplary analysis of a case that offers many parallels to this one, see Timpanaro, *La genesi*.

[64] George Ticknor, *Life, Letters, and Journals* (Boston, 1876) 1:105-6.

[65] Volkmann, 75-77.

[66] See M. Cesarotti, *Prose edite e inedite*, ed. G. Mazzoni (Bologna, 1882), 183-98, 396.

[67] J. L. Hug, *Die Erfindung der Buchstabenschrift* . . . (Ulm, 1801); cf. Volkmann, 110-15.

guments did so in ways more irritating than any direct attack. If Herder liked seeing Homer portrayed as a poet of the people, he angered Wolf by claiming that view as his own childhood discovery.[68] And if Wolf's Göttingen teacher Heyne praised his old pupil's erudition unreservedly, he angered Wolf even more than Herder did by implying that the doctrines of the *Prolegomena* had been learned from Heyne's lectures.[69] Wolf always insisted that his work had not had a fair hearing.[70]

On the whole, however, Wolf had more supporters than opponents. Schütz lavished praise on the *Prolegomena* in the Jena *Literatur-Zeitung*.[71] Böttiger praised Wolf's thesis to the literati and wrote essays in support of its main arguments.[72] Wieland greeted the book enthusiastically, as a fusion of the learning of the seventeenth-century polyhistors with the subtlety and good taste of the philosophes: "I have always wanted to see the vast learning of Salmasius, which I know from his *Exercitationes Plinianae*, united in one mind with the elegance of my idol Hemsterhuys. I have now found them truly united in Wolf."[73] Friedrich Schlegel took it as the model for his own studies in Greek poetry, and his brother August Wilhelm popularized it in his lectures and in a famous review of Goethe's *Hermann und Dorothea*.[74] Schelling went even further, rightly suggesting that Wolf's work would stand as the model for future workers in the natural sciences as well as in philology: "The earth is a book made up of miscellaneous fragments dating from very different ages. Each mineral is a real philological problem. In geology we still await the genius who will analyze the earth and show its composition as Wolf analyzed Homer."[75] And Goethe took it as an invitation to carry on with an epic of his own.[76]

More important still, the young scholars who would dominate the new profession of philology in the Humboldtian universities

[68] In his essay "Homer ein Günstling der Zeit"; for Wolf's reaction to it see esp. *Goethes Briefe an Friedrich August Wolf*, ed. Michael Bernays (Berlin, 1868).

[69] *GGA*, 21 November 1795, 1857-64 = Wolf, *Briefe*, 240-45.

[70] Wolf, *Kl. Schr.*, 1:237-39.

[71] *ALZ*, 29 and 30 January 1796, cols. 257-72.

[72] Volkmann, 101-2; cf. Peters.

[73] Peters, 36.

[74] Volkmann, 77-79.

[75] F.W.J. Schelling, *On University Studies*, tr. E. S. Morgan, ed. N. Guterman (Athens, Ohio, 1966), 40.

[76] See *Goethes Briefe an Wolf*, ed. Bernays; Humphry Trevelyan, *Goethe & the Greeks* (Cambridge, 1941), esp. 225-39.

took Wolf's side. K. F. Heinrich, who had studied with Heyne at Göttingen and always viewed him with respect and affection, took Wolf's *Prolegomena* as the model for his own efforts to trace the history of the text of Hesiod's *Shield of Hercules* (1802). And he treated Wolf as an exponent of a new form of higher criticism, one that could reveal "the lack of historical and critical sense in ancient times." Wolf's discoveries gave proof that "in our time the humanities too have begun to be illuminated with a more brilliant light."[77] Gottfried Hermann went even further. Wolf had "restored Homer to us, in more than one sense." Where Ruhnken and his followers had hunted for interpolations in the texts of Homer and Hesiod, Wolf had reconstructed the "art and method" of the rhapsodes who recited and thus preserved the earliest Greek poetry. He offered critics a fundamental tool, the need for which Ruhnken had not even envisaged: a systematic, historical explanation of "how it was possible for these [Homeric] hymns to be disfigured by so many large additions."[78] B. G. Niebuhr described the *Prolegomena* in 1827 as "those wonderworthy investigations in which the higher branch of criticism reacht its perfection." By the time this statement appeared, in a programmatic article in the first volume of the *Rheinisches Museum für Philologie*, the *Prolegomena* had obtained a firm place in the philological curriculum and Wolf himself, now dead, an even firmer one in the philological pantheon, as "the hero and eponymus of the race of German philologers."[79]

True, Wolf's arguments underwent hundreds of minor revisions. Boeckh remarked in 1834 that "younger scholars everywhere are now trying to undo that great reform of philology, which the *Prolegomena* seemed to effect"—and proceeded to use recent findings on Greek social history both to qualify and to defend Wolf's views.[80] Some attacked Wolf's achievement as a whole. Wilamowitz and

[77] *Hesiodi Scutum Herculis cum grammaticorum scholiis Graecis*, ed. K. F. Heinrich (Breslau, 1802), *Prolegomena*, xxxx. Heinrich uses Wolf's favorite terms to denote the ancients' lack of scholarship: ἀνιστορησία, ἀκρισία.

[78] *Homeri Hymni et Epigrammata*, ed. G. Hermann (Leipzig, 1806), v-vi; Volkmann, 103-6. Cf. Friedrich Creuzer's exclamation "Welch ein Buch!"—the only words he could find to describe the impact of the *Prolegomena* on his teaching of Greek literature in 1801 (quoted by Gisela Wirth, *Die Entwicklung der Alten Geschichte an der Philipps-Universität Marburg* [Marburg, 1977], 247, n. 313).

[79] B. G. Niebuhr, "Die Sikeler in der Odyssee," *Rheinisches Museum* 1 (1827), 257 = "On the Sicilians in the Odyssey," *The Philological Museum* 1 (1832), 176.

[80] A. Boeckh, "De ὑποβολῇ Homerica," *Gesammelte kleine Schriften* (Leipzig, 1874), 4:386.

Pasquali tried to show that he had learned everything of interest from Heyne; Bérard tried to convict him of simple plagiarism from Merian and Villoison.[81] But most scholars have continued to see him as the man who "opened the eyes of his contemporaries and of posterity to the unique *historical* position of the Homeric poetry"[82]—and thus opened a new age in the history of classical scholarship.

But if, as we have seen, Wolf was in essence merely transferring results from theology to classical philology, further questions immediately arise. Why did his book become the manifesto of the German historical spirit, the charter of classical scholarship as an independent discipline, the model for historical investigations in other fields from medieval German to theology itself? Why did contemporaries—and even Wolf himself—come to see the *Prolegomena* as the source rather than the tributary of theological research, the fountainhead of Tübingen rather than an offshoot of Göttingen?[83]

Part of the answer no doubt lies in what historians of science like to call "external and institutional factors." In the first decades of the nineteenth century, the German universities were radically reformed. Some of the most powerful reformers, Humboldt above all, wanted to have a reason to make classical philology, the field that French philosophes had scorned, a central area in the arts faculty and in secondary education. All the disciplines in the arts faculties had to define their goals and methods and prove their utility. The *Prolegomena* made the decision to concentrate on classics look intellectually respectable. It offered classicists the right to claim for their field a new intellectual weight and legitimacy. If Wolf had not written such a book, it would no doubt have been necessary to invent it—and to create much ballyhoo about it.[84]

[81] See esp. Pasquali's articles on Homer and on Wolf in the *Enciclopedia Italiana*; for a recent summary and extension of such views see G. Broccia, *La questione Omerica* (Florence, 1979).

[82] Pfeiffer, *History*, 214 = *Geschichte*, 263.

[83] For such views on Wolf's part see John Russell, *A Tour in Germany . . . in the Years 1820, 1821, 1822* (Boston, 1825), 286; for a contemporary who shared them see K. A. Varnhagen von Ense, *Tagebücher* (Leipzig, 1861 = Bern, 1972), 1:106; 2:68. For Wolf's impact on the study of early German epic see M. Thorp, *The Study of the Nibelungenlied* (Oxford, 1940), esp. 13-30.

[84] See R. Steven Turner, "The Prussian Universities and the Concept of Research," *Internationales Archiv für Sozialgeschichte der deutschen Literatur* 5 (1980), 68-93.

But factors like these cannot explain why Wolf's book and no other was chosen to play the important institutional role that fell to it—or why its originality came to be so much exaggerated by its admirers. To answer these questions one must identify those qualities of the *Prolegomena* itself that enabled it to be seized upon and exploited.

Form and style were clearly vital to the role the book played. Wolf and his readers agreed that he was a wonderful writer, concise, polished, and witty. "Of his style in Latin," George Bancroft recalled, "no praise could seem to him excessive."[85] The *Prolegomena* was his masterpiece in prose composition. Wieland could not find enough adjectives to express his delight: "Every word is weighed on the jeweler's scale, and is absolutely precise and very Roman. I feel that I am not reading an Ernesti-style Ciceronian Latin. It is more solid, richer in content and fact. This is how a Varro might write. One sees even in the Latin the man of genius, who thinks for himself, who knew how to create for himself a style that was peculiar to him but still genuinely Roman."[86] More than thirty years later Wolf's chief reviser, Karl Lehrs, was still fascinated by "the unsurpassably beautiful form of the book, the *Geist* that breathes through every word."[87]

Much that Wolf said was novel only in form. But novelties in form can of course make an idea take on new relevance. The account of the rules of textual criticism which occupies the beginning of the *Prolegomena* merely summed up the results of the most original eighteenth-century New Testament scholars. They had known perfectly well the rule *recentior non deterior* (the later manuscript is not necessarily the worse one). But they had not crystallized it in the striking, if slightly illogical, image that Wolf devised: "Newness in manuscripts is no more a vice than youth in men. In this case too, age does not always bring wisdom. Insofar as each follows an old and good authority well, it is a good witness" (ch. 2). That is why Wolf, not Bengel or Griesbach, came to be seen as the one who revolutionized textual criticism. It was in his formulations that the new ideas of what an editor should be and do caught the attention and won the assent of Lachmann.[88]

[85] George Bancroft, *Literary and Historical Miscellanies* (New York, 1855), 165.
[86] Peters, 40.
[87] Karl Lehrs, *Kleine Schriften* (Königsberg, 1902), 25.
[88] See Timpanaro, *La genesi del metodo del Lachmann.*

Wolf, in short, had something of the same quality that made Francis Bacon the great prophet of seventeenth-century science: the ability to coin sharp metaphors and striking similes, to put his own stamp and perspective on concepts that he was hardly the first to devise. On a more mundane level, he could write about philology without being boring. His arguments soar along in a series of aesthetically pleasing intellectual flights above the close-packed references in his footnotes, and so have an appeal usually denied to technical treatises.

Contemporaries found more than pretty images in Wolf. Wieland was impressed above all by the precision joining that made his argumentative cabinetry so solid: "Wolf has made every step forward in his argumentation so cleverly, but also firmly, that one follows him confidently despite all his asseveration of merely conjectural probability."[89] And it is true that Wolf makes a great show of rigor, elegance, and system, a greater one than his predecessors had.

One example will show Wolf's dexterity at the delicate task of drawing and linking inferences. His friend Merian had argued to the Berlin Academy in 1789 that Homer's failure to mention writing in the poems was evidence that he had not known it. Here is the beginning of his argument: "This is one of the cases where negative arguments have much weight; the probability necessarily falls on their side when there is no counterweight in the other scale of the balance. To know whether the Homeric heroes and Homer himself knew and used writing, you can only consult Homer. His silence on this point is therefore very meaningful."[90] He goes on to argue that Homer, who described so many other crafts in such detail, would have described writing too if he had known it. In contrast, Wolf starts by distinguishing between two different sorts of argument from silence: "There is doubtless a sort of silence that has no decisive weight and is not to be drawn to either side. On the other hand there is another sort that is distinct and, so to speak, articulate, which has always had the greatest weight with all prudent men" (ch. 19). The tone and movement of his argument thereafter

---

[89] Peters, 37.

[90] J. B. Merian, "Examen de la question, si Homère a écrit ses poëmes," *Mémoires de l'Académie Royale des sciences et belles-lettres . . . MDCCLXXXVIII ET MDCCLXXXIX* (Berlin, 1793), 517-18.

waver artfully where Merian had ignored qualifications and distinctions. Like Merian, Wolf shows that Homer nowhere describes
the art of writing in itself; unlike Merian, he admits frankly that
that is not by itself proof that Homer did not know the art. Like
Merian, he tries to show that the two passages in the *Iliad* which
seemed to mention writing did not do so; unlike Merian, he builds
up to a coherent argument that the whole culture described in the
Homeric poems was oral: "The word *book* is nowhere, *writing* is
nowhere, *reading* is nowhere, *letters* are nowhere; nothing in so
many thousands of verses is arranged for reading, everything for
hearing; there are no pacts or treaties except face to face; there is
no source of report for old times except memory and rumor and
monuments without writing" (ch. 20). Only then does he conclude
by returning to his starting point: "When all these silences are
gathered and assembled in a single array, does it seem possible that
they can be accidental? Or is one who is silent in this fashion playing
the part of one who speaks and bears clear witness? Though I am
not very credulous, they would be enough in themselves to persuade me fully" (ch. 21). In every detail Wolf brought out subtleties
that Merian had missed or only half-seen. Both pointed out that
Eustathius took the "deadly message" carried by Bellerophon not
to be a letter written out in script, like those of his day.[91] But it
took Wolf to argue that Eustathius normally read Homer anach-
ronistically, and that his noticing an archaic form of sending a
message was all the more striking for its uniqueness in his work.

What made Wolf's arguments so attractive, then, was above all
the care with which he joined them and stated the amount of weight
that every link in the chain could bear. To make an argument from
silence was nothing new; to classify one's argument as a particular
and reliable form of that problematic species was new and striking.
The *Prolegomena* really was a good model from which to learn the
niceties of philological argument. That is what Lehrs had in mind
when he praised Wolf's "true critical sense, which holds just the
right boundary between what can and what cannot be known."[92]

But if these characteristics made Wolf attractive and instructive,
two others explain why he seemed uniquely so—and how he dis-
placed his predecessors so completely. On the one hand Wolf did

[91] Ibid., 515-16; cf. *Prolegomena*, ch. 18.
[92] Lehrs, *Kleine Schriften*, 25.

everything to make his theses seem original and bold. He compared himself to Caesar crossing the Rubicon and Cappell defying Lutheran orthodoxy (ch. 26, n. 84; cf. ch. 3). He insisted that earlier generations would have been horrified by his analytical hypothesis and his view of Homer. As we have seen, all this was true only in part; yet Wolf's attitudinizing was taken at face value. Wieland found his preface to the *Iliad* "a bold song of triumph";[93] Goethe marveled at his having dared to "dethrone this heathen Moses."[94] Clearly Wolf managed to write himself into his book in the most up-to-date and flattering of personae, and a very resonant one in the 1790s: that of the typically German revolutionary of the spirit tearing down established dogma.

At the same time Wolf took great care not to write his exact results into the book. Wherever possible he stated his meaning by negation or approximation. He characterized Homer as neither primitive nor civilized, "as different from the singers in their forest gatherings as he is from the poets of learned periods" (ch. 12). He defined not the spirit in which Homer was to be read but the ones in which he was usually misread: "The method of those who read Homer and Callimachus and Virgil and Nonnus and Milton in one and the same spirit, and do not strive to weigh in reading and work out what each author's age allows, has not yet entirely been done away with" (ch. 12). He defined the method of Aristarchus and Zenodotus as something not to be confused with that of Valckenaer and Bentley (ch. 46). And above all he refused to give definite answers to the main Homeric questions, even though he liked at times to pretend he had them. These evasive qualities did not escape his admirers. But they did not make them cause for censure. Ticknor merely remarked that Wolf's "rules of criticism, in his Prolegomena" were a canon even "though not carried out and exemplified."[95] Lehrs, even less critically, wondered at "the wealth of ideas together with such—almost too much—concision, so that he reveals himself completely only after repeated readings to one who works independently in this field."[96]

---

[93] Peters, 40. [94] Peters, 34.

[95] Ticknor, *Life, Letters, and Journals*, 1:106.

[96] Lehrs, *Kleine Schriften*, 25. Wolf's compressed, allusive style was as prominent in his conversation as in his writing. See Schleiermacher, *Hermeneutics*, ed. H. Kimmerle, tr. J. Duke and J. Forstman (Missoula, Montana, 1977), 182: "Wolf—especially Wolf, who was such an artist in conversation, but who said more by intimation than

Yet Wolf's deliberate ambiguities were both more reprehensible and more responsible for his success than Ticknor and Lehrs realized. They allowed him to bring off two crucial tours de force. In the first place, he was able to sit on both sides of the fence—that is, to continue to maintain the beauty, the artistry, the coherence of the poems he was chopping into bits. He did so by a means as simple as it was illogical: he wrote his contradictory views of the poems into the *Prolegomena* as a sort of unresolved internal dialogue. "The Homer that we hold in our hands is not the one who flourished in the mouths of the Greeks of his own day, but one variously altered, interpolated, corrected and emended from the times of Solon down to those of the Alexandrians. Learned and clever men have long felt their way to this conclusion by using various scattered bits of evidence; but now the voices of all periods joined together bear witness, and history speaks." So ends chapter 49; and what could be more dramatic, more decisive? But chapter 50 begins by recognizing all the force of the internal evidence to the contrary: "But the bard himself seems to contradict history, and the sense of the reader bears witness against it." Wolf hints at a resolution of the dilemma, suggesting that Aristarchus—or Aristarchus and Aristophanes—was responsible for the poems' polish and coherence. But he does not explain how Alexandrian revisers could produce non-Alexandrian poems, of much of which they did not themselves approve. Yet just because Wolf is so deft, so artful, so compact of sense, his readers tended to go away satisfied, thinking he had offered them definite results instead of pretty enigmas.

In the second place, Wolf's deliberate ambiguity had a preservative effect on the bulk of what he wrote. He made clear that he was terribly modern; he invited the reader time and again to join his revolution; but he did not spell out its exact nature. Wolf's delicate arguments were thus kept from decay like flies in amber, tantalizingly half-visible, by the layers of ambivalence in which he wrapped them; and they went on seeming modern and relevant

---

by explicit statement, and even more by innuendo—would not deny that these were being understood by his listeners in an artistic way, so that he could count on the audience always knowing what he meant." Cf. also Milman Parry's perceptive remark: "Wolf was strong by his very vagueness. He made possible the large number of different theories concerning the composition, which appeared in the 19th century." Quoted in A. Parry, "Introduction," *The Making of Homeric Verse. The Collected Papers of Milman Parry* (Oxford, 1971), xvi, n. 2.

for a century while more explicit books, like Eichhorn's, showed their age within a single decade.

In the end, Wolf himself did not provide the grand synthesis his work promised. A second part of the *Prolegomena* was fragmentarily outlined (pt. 2, chs. 1-2) but never completed, and he never made a detailed internal analysis of the Homeric corpus. The definitive Homer edition of 1804-07 bore on the title page the bold words *Homeri et Homeridarum opera et reliquiae*—but as a frontispiece it had the traditional bust of Homer.[97] This incompleteness, far from diminishing Wolf's achievement, augmented its effectiveness. The *Prolegomena*, a partial and fragmentary treatise demonstrating the partial and fragmentary nature of a classical text whose canonical unity and perfection have not ceased to dominate our imaginations, opened up a discipline that has not yet been entirely closed off in our own time: classical philology.

[97] Cf. Wolf, *Kl. Schr.*, 1:211-12.

A NOTE ON THE TEXT AND
TRANSLATION

This translation is based on the third edition of the *Prolegomena*, prepared by Rudolf Peppmüller (Halle, 1884 = Hildesheim, 1963), for part 1, and on the second edition, prepared by I. Bekker (Berlin, 1876), for the fragments of part 2. In four passages of the text we have corrected errors in Peppmüller's edition, in each case accepting the text of the first edition (Halle, 1795). The correct readings, by chapter, page, and line in Peppmüller, are *illo* (14.42.21), *vocabulo* (18.56.11), *nonnullis plus tribui* (35.121.8), and *antiquioris* (48.189.1). We have made a number of equally minor corrections of typographical errors in the notes.

The two chapters of part 2 that we have printed at the end of the text were omitted by Peppmüller because of their obviously fragmentary state. They are clearly alternate rough drafts for the beginning of part 2; we have tried as far as possible to indicate similarities and differences of phrasing between them in the translation. We have not translated the many variant readings and corrections given by Bekker in brackets; and we cannot at all points work out Wolf's literal sense.

In one significant respect we have diverged from both Wolf and Peppmüller. The latter attempted scrupulously to preserve even Wolf's errors and obsolete references. He confined himself to a series of bracketed comments and additional notes, correcting some references and pointing out some mistakes, and his comments are not always either accurate or clear. As our purpose has been to make Wolf's work accessible to the modern reader and not to turn it into an introduction to Homer for the present day, we have proceeded very differently. In the text, to be sure, we have not changed Wolf's wording, although we have added translations of his quotations where they seemed to be needed and have given up-to-date references in square brackets to the texts cited. In the footnotes, however, we have felt free to make more significant alterations. We have substituted for Wolf's vague references to secondary sources the full title and date of publication of all works cited; we have changed his obsolete references to primary sources wherever possible to their modern equivalents; we have checked and silently corrected his references to the Homer scholia; if the passage in question is not to be found in Erbse's edition of the scholia, we have added in brackets the correct reference to Dindorf or Porphyry (see the note on citations above for the precise form of reference used). We have also drawn attention in brackets to places where Wolf's (or Villoison's) reading of the scholia is dubious.

On the other hand, it is important to note that we have made no effort to rectify Wolf's sins of omission. In some cases, he omitted relevant passages; in many more, others are now known that were not available to him. Peppmüller added references to some of these, but we have neither repeated Peppmüller's addenda, which are themselves often obsolete, nor included any of our own. The reader who wishes to obtain more modern discussions of the topics discussed by Wolf, particularly in the chapters on the Alexandrian critics, will find in the editorial notes (designated by letters) and the bibliographical appendices references to the standard modern treatments of these subjects, and these in turn will supply supplementary information.

Wolf's Latin is both vivid and idiosyncratic. As Wieland casually but perceptively remarked, Wolf's style is not that of a purist Ciceronian, but rather something like that of the polymath Varro. Like Varro, Wolf had a taste for oddity in expression. He used a number of archaic and recondite words (e.g. *purum putum* in ch. 2, *tetricos* in ch. 3, *amussim* in ch. 4, *cascis* in ch. 13, *dicterium* in ch. 16, n. 28). He sprinkled his Latin with Greek words and phrases (e.g. ἀοιδός in ch. 2 and passim; Μουσόπνευστον in ch. 3, ἀκρισία in ch. 13). At the same time, he wove into his prose a great many allusions to classical poets, especially Horace (e.g. ch. 35: "in tam antiquis et occulto crescentibus rebus," from Horace *Odes* 1.12.45f. "crescit occulto velut arbor aevo / fama Marcelli"; ch. 43: "regulas . . . quas nunc docti indoctique sequimur," from *Epistles* 2.1.117 "scribimus indocti doctique poemata passim"). We have pointed out a number of these allusions in the notes. What is more, he combined these classical and humanistic affectations with his own distinctively modern ones. Time and again, he translated modern ideas and idioms directly into Latin (his library included, to George Ticknor's surprise, a heavily used Latin-German lexicon). And the effect of such phrases as *diplomatica fides* ("diplomatic standards of accuracy," ch. 38) or *fungorum modo succrescebant* ("they sprang up like mushrooms," ch. 41) is distinctly unclassical. Had we tried to capture all these peculiarities in English, we would have produced a strange and unreadable piece of work. Instead, we have abandoned any hope of maintaining the full color of Wolf's style, in favor of attaining some degree of modernity and readability.

Wolf's technical vocabulary presents two distinct sets of problems. For a number of scholarly activities and concepts, Wolf used standard Latin and Greek terms. These we have tried to translate as consistently as possible, including the original term in brackets where it seemed advisable. *Emendatio* we have translated as "emendation" whether it refers, as is more common in modern usage, to the correction of a single passage, or, as is more common in Wolf, to the correction of an entire work. *Recensio* and διόρθωσις have both been translated as "recension" here. By the former Wolf usually means the thorough examination of all witnesses to a text (he defines the term and describes the process in chapter 1). But the meaning of the latter is much less clear, and Wolf lets it be taken as equivalent to either emendation or recension, as the context requires. We use "recension" not as a perfect equivalent but as the conventional one. For ἔκδοσις, ἐκδιδόναι, *edere* and the like we have used the vague "make public" instead of more precise English words like "edit" and "edition," which evoke inappropriate associations. Finally, we translate the word *ars* (as in *ars critica, ars grammatica, ars poetica*) as "art," again for the sake of convenience rather than accuracy. Its real meaning lies somewhere between the English "technique," "science," and "textbook"; it refers to the systematic organization of knowledge or instruction in a given field.

More difficult than these terms are certain others, less standard but no less crucial, which Wolf uses in a characteristically slippery and ambiguous way (see the Introduction above). He has at least three terms for the author of the *Iliad* and *Odyssey*: the Greek ἀοιδός, literally "singer," which we have generally translated as "poet" or "bard"; and the Latin *vates*, "bard" and *poeta*, "poet." For the poems themselves he apparently does not use *poema*, but prefers the Greek ἀοιδή, "song," or the Latin *carmen*, which can apply to anything from a magical incantation to a children's song to a written lyric poem. We have not tried to preserve this blurring of oral and written forms of composition, and have simply translated "poem" in all cases. Again, Wolf explicitly takes the Greek *rhapsodia* as referring to the portion of the Homeric corpus that a rhapsode could perform at one sitting, not to the modern books of the *Iliad* and *Odyssey*; but he also uses the term to denote precisely those books. We have not kept that ambiguity, but have used "book" where that is clearly meant and "section" where it is not.

*   *   *

To prevent confusion, we should point out that two sets of footnotes appear in this translation. Those signaled by superscript arabic numerals and without lemmata form part of Wolf's own work. Those signaled by superscript roman letters and preceded by lemmata from the text in italics contain comments and explanations by the present editors.

PROLEGOMENA
TO HOMER

OR

CONCERNING THE ORIGINAL

AND GENUINE FORM

OF THE HOMERIC WORKS

AND THEIR VARIOUS ALTERATIONS

AND THE PROPER METHOD OF

EMENDATION

BY

FRIEDRICH AUGUST

WOLF

CHAPTER I

Two principal kinds of emendation are normally applied to the
books of the ancients, to free them from the many and varied flaws
and stains that they have contracted on their long journey into
barbarism, and restore them more nearly to their ancient and original form. The one entails more effort and, I might almost say,
misery; the other, more leisurely delight. Each, if rightly applied,
is useful; but one is more useful. Take someone, even someone
poorly equipped with the best aids, who gives us a writer restored
to a more correct form, either by conjecture or by the use of a few
manuscripts; even if he removes just thirty warts, and leaves a
hundred, no one will deny that he has rendered service to literature.
And this used to be the way of things, especially in the days when
manuscripts had not long begun to be printed, and it was widely
expected that new aids would soon appear. Many have imitated
this custom from then on, down to our own time, even for those
writers who abounded with critical evidence and aids of all sorts.
In fact, few authors of new recensions are so diligent and willing
to work that they collect all the variant readings from what are
often obscure and scattered sources, and especially from old exemplars, and then compare these with the standard text so that
they can set about a consistent emendation of it. On the contrary,
they generally stop short only when a difficult thought or an error
obvious at first sight presents itself, and then they consult variant
readings or an old exemplar. But these oracles are usually unre-
sponsive except to those who consult them regularly. A similar
method is applied by those scholars—sometimes very learned and
expert—who hold that every emendation should depend on the
credibility of a selection of manuscripts, or who edit texts, as they
are called, in accordance with one exemplar, as if those manuscripts
had been destined by the fates to save their author.

A true, continuous, and systematic recension[a] differs greatly from this frivolous and desultory method. In the latter we want only to cure indiscriminately the wounds that are conspicuous or are revealed by some manuscript or other. We pass over more [readings] which are good and passable as regards sense, but no better than the worst as regards authority. But a true recension, attended by the full complement of useful instruments, seeks out the author's true handiwork at every point. It examines in order the witnesses for every reading, not only for those that are suspect. It changes, only for the most serious reasons, readings that all of these approve. It accepts, only when they are supported by witnesses, others that are worthy in themselves of the author and accurate and elegant in their form. Not uncommonly, then, when the witnesses require it, a true recension replaces attractive readings with less attractive ones. It takes off bandages and lays bare the sores. Finally, it cures not only manifest ills, as bad doctors do, but hidden ones too. This method certainly has a place for natural talent and the art of conjecture, but as the credibility of every ancient text rests entirely on the purity of its sources, we must strive above all—and can hardly do so without talent—to examine the properties and individual nature of the sources from which each writer's text is derived; to judge each of the various witnesses, once they are set out by classes and families, by its character; and to learn to follow their voices, and gestures, so to speak, with cunning, but without bias.[b] Indeed, in many cases both the critic, and anyone

[a] *A true, continuous and systematic recension:* Wolf here gives a classic description of the duties of the editor of any classical text. He himself never carried out a *recensio* of the sort he called for; and the manuscript tradition of Homer would not have allowed him to employ the ideas and techniques brilliantly sketched here. Wolf's formulation nonetheless had a great impact on later editors, notably Lachmann. On all these points see the study—itself classic—of S. Timpanaro, *La genesi del metodo del Lachmann*, new ed. (Padua, 1981), 30-34.

[b] *With cunning, but without bias:* Assessing the *fides* (credibility) of different sources and types of sources had long been a problem of interest to German scholars; see A. D. Momigliano, *Contributo alla storia degli studi classici* (Rome, 1955), 84-91. For a work comparable to the *Prolegomena* that starts from a similar standpoint cf. Griesbach's famous *Commentatio* on the Gospel of Mark, first published in 1789-90 and reprinted in 1794: "It is above all important to know the sources from which historical writers have drawn the things which they have put into their own commentaries, in order to interpret correctly their books, to evaluate justly the trustworthiness of the authors, and to perceive and judge skilfully the true nature of the events that they have recorded" (tr. B. Orchard in *J. J. Griesbach: Synoptic and Text-Critical Studies, 1776-1976*, ed. B. Orchard and T.R.W. Longstaff [Cambridge, 1978] 103; original text ibid., 74).

who would undertake a historical investigation, must emulate the prudent custom of a good judge, who slowly examines the testimony of the witnesses, and gathers all the evidence for their truthfulness, before he ventures to put forward his own conjecture about the case. And indeed, it is impossible that one who relies on a few codices of the common sort and practices conjecture, however cleverly, can often arrive at the genuine text. In resolving questions of law, no amount of talent can make up for a want of wills and documents. Similarly, the acutest talent labors in vain on historical and critical questions, unless it is tempered and controlled by diligent use of manuscripts. In fact these two activities differ more in name than in kind, and they are bound by the same rules of judgment. It is proper that you should attach more weight to talent than to costly parchments.[c] But even genius badly needs to have access to as many codices as possible, so that its judgment about the true reading may rely on their testimony and its divination may find aid of many kinds. The more often, then, that the manuscripts of any author undergo collation, the more a true and consistent recension takes place. For those authors who still suffer from the lack of useful materials, I am inclined to think that the multiplication of forms of their texts harms rather than helps these studies, which are more than tedious enough in themselves. Such authors can presumably be given a sort of review (*recognitio*), not what is truly called a recension (*recensio*).

CHAPTER II

But in general no one disputes any of these points. In Homer, however, the oldest poet, doubts clearly exist as to whether so much weight should be given to the authority of such recent manuscripts. For none of them is even so old as the latest Latin writers. Those that date before the twelfth or eleventh century are few and far between. This doubt may carry the implication that these sources cannot enable us to restore Homer's work to the genuine, pure

[c] *It is proper that you should attach more weight to talent than to costly parchments:* An echo of Richard Bentley's famous declaration (in his commentary on Horace *Odes* 3.27.15) that "We attach more weight to reason and to the nature of the case (*ratio et res ipsa*) than to a hundred manuscripts"; see Timpanaro, *La genesi*, 31-32, nn. 40 and 41.

form which first poured from his divine lips. If so, I shall say later how willingly I follow this school of thought and line of reasoning. But when I consider the fates of ancient books,[a] sometimes unexpectedly favorable, and see that we have Herodotus, Plato, Xenophon, others of the same period, whom we have received from the hands of the same scribes, restored so nearly to their original luster—then I can find no reason, unless perhaps the texts of the ancient bards that have come down to us are worse than the rest, why we should trust the latter so much less than the former. Moreover, thanks to the Alexandrian critics, who flourished after [Herodotus, Plato, and Xenophon], we doubtless read a Homeric text more correct in many passages than the one that they themselves could read. Finally, it is surprising how many of the variant readings found in authors who quote Homer—variants of any significance, and which are not simply errors resulting from a faulty recollection [of the passage]—are found in almost identical form in those manuscripts. For newness in manuscripts is no more a vice than youth in men. In this case, too, age does not always bring wisdom.[b] Insofar as each follows an old and good authority well, it is a good witness. True, I attach somewhat more weight to the apparatus of scholia and glossaries than to bare parchments. But I have learned from many cases in point that only by using both sets of material together can we restore these poems to a form that is neither unworthy of them nor inconsistent with the canons of learned antiquity. And at this point we will have to stop. If we demand the bard in simon-pure condition, and are not content with what contented Plutarch, Longinus, or Proclus, we will have to take refuge either in empty prayers or in unrestrained license in divination.

[a] *But when I consider the fates of ancient books:* Wolf had long been interested in the peculiar fact that some of the oldest Greek texts seemed better preserved than considerably later ones. See his edition of *Platons Gastmahl: Ein Dialog* (1782), xv = *Kl. Schr.*, 1:142.

[b] *age does not always bring wisdom:* Wolf did not devise this principle, now summed up by the formula *recentior non deterior*. It had been clearly formulated by the German New Testament scholars of the eighteenth century, including Wolf's close friend J. S. Semler, and was given currency in the lucid work of J. J. Griesbach. For Wolf's debt to this tradition, see Timpanaro, *La genesi*.

CHAPTER III

Once I gave up hope, then, that the original form of the Homeric Poems could ever be laid out save in our minds, and even there only in rough outlines, it seemed appropriate to investigate how far the ancient evidence would take us in polishing these eternal and unique remains of the Greek genius. I thought this study the first and most necessary of the many tasks that their better illustration requires. Hence in this edition I set out to give a sample of that more accurate sort of recension the nature of which I sketched above. Scholars agree that this has not yet been done for Homer. For the previous editors, who did not have enough aids to work with, could not have formed such a plan even if they had wanted to. Hence for the most part, unless some rag of a scholium or a variant from Eustathius or a manuscript aroused them, they rested, sleeping peacefully, on the apparent clarity of his thoughts. So Homer's extraordinary reputation has brought him poverty and emaciation, while others have waxed fat on their faults. Had he presented the obscurities of Lycophron, it would be astonishing if troops of porters had not brought him light long since from all sides. I will not reproach any of those who edited the poet in the past for having made so little effort to collect the manuscripts and remains of scholia from libraries. That is more a matter of luck than of talent or industry. Yet some, like Bergler, spurned even the riches of that sort that they were offered. Others, like the Italian editors,[a] had the opportunity to use them in their vicinity. In these affairs, as I said, chance rules. But as to the fact that none of them collected the materials readily available in common authors, grammarians and lexicographers, or used them to establish the text— that, perhaps, can be imputed only to negligence and frivolity. For who can begin to study, for example, Apollonius Dyscolus, the Etymologicum Magnum, Hesychius, without seeing at once that they conceal many readings and dittographies? No one would need to have this pointed out to him. But it is less trouble to trust the suggestions offered, as it were, by one's divining rod in the course

---

[a] *the Italian editors:* Demetrius Chalcondyles published the *editio princeps* (Florence, 1488); Aldo Manuzio issued editions in 1504 and 1517.

of editing, than to work consistently at one task with so many texts from so rebarbative a branch of learning. What is worse, every book of Homer reveals that the editors have not even worked continuously through Eustathius—who is universally acknowledged to be the best interpreter of Homer—or collected the useful things that he includes.

Barnes accuses Henricus Stephanus, not unjustly, of having used Eustathius in a slapdash way.[b] True, that most laborious of men was perhaps unwilling to cite what he had not used in correcting the text when he wrote his hasty notes. For in those days one's labors could safely be concealed; now, as customs have changed, we are compelled to reveal them. Thus from the second Aldine edition on, I believe, several of the early editors did not completely neglect this grammarian, though they did not mention him. For I see that they, too, accepted some readings which they could hardly have found anywhere else. But I do not find consistency in the collation. Not even the Roman edition—the one that contains the text along with Eustathius' commentary—clearly shows that. Admittedly, Barnes boasts that he has "plundered Eustathius' inmost treasures." But both other scholars and Valckenaer,[c] one of the few who had read Eustathius through with real care, have pointed out how unreliable he is in these and other claims. Yet even Barnes— in other respects an incompetent man, and one without rigorous training—should not be deprived of his title to praise: that he was the first to derive anything from ancient writers which his successors could use, and that he also drew some good corrections from these sources. Clarke, who later expunged Barnes's many rash corrections, was an expert grammarian, but he consistently reveals a genius ill-adapted to work of this kind and to any sort of serious critical work. He disregarded the authorities for readings, which should of course be sought in old manuscripts, and contented himself for the most part with the small collection of variants given in the Appendix of the former vulgate editions and by Stephanus and

[b] *in a slapdash way:* For an account of the manuscript evidence used by Eustathius and the editors from Chalcondyles down to Alter, see T. W. Allen, ed., *Homeri Ilias I: Prolegomena* (Oxford, 1931), 248-66.

[c] *Valckenaer:* Valckenaer published an edition of *Iliad* 22 with important scholia from MS Leiden Voss. gr. fol. 64 in 1747 (reprinted in his *Opuscula Philologica*), under the title *Hectoris interitus. Carmen XXII Homeri*; his criticisms of Barnes appear there in the preface, 10.

Barnes. He rarely turned aside to Eustathius or the scholia where others had run into problems, or he himself needed support for his opinion. He [treated] the rest of the text lightly, and gently, and with astonishing moderation—sometimes even in Barnes's purest nonsense he finds nothing wanting but "a sufficient reason." Ernesti[d] set out to reprint Clarke's edition in quite a different spirit and with a different store of learning, though he did so not on his own initiative but at the request of his publisher. I consider him more admirable for the work he did on this project, which was not his own, than for what he did on some of his own projects, which he was more eager to bring to completion. In it he did signal service to the text of Homer both by collating many manuscripts and by deciding what was the correct reading, which he did most acutely at many points. But he also saw, and pointed out in his preface to vol. 5, how much work would have to be done before the poet could be published in a perfectly pure and correct form. He thus did not hold anything remotely like the wrong-headed view of those who even today seem to consider the text, which took its present shape little by little and as chance determined, as genuine and, almost, as literally inspired by the Muses. They follow the example of the Buxtorfs, who used to claim the same thing for their Hebrew text. They prohibited the application of any conjecture, almost of any human reason, to it, revering as literally inspired by God even those passages that scholars now consider entirely corrupt.

CHAPTER IV

Ernesti, too, would have been completely astonished that such excellent and extensive materials survived for editing Homer as have appeared in the last seven years. At this point, we must devote a few words to the appreciation of Villoison's outstanding service. He was the first to publish the two Venetian manuscripts of the *Iliad*, with a mass of scholia that provides a far greater supply of material both old and relevant to determining the fate and textual

---

[d] *Ernesti:* In the preface to vol. 5 of his Homer (1759-64) Ernesti remarked that "there is still much concealed in manuscripts that could be of value to the Poems of Homer," and urged scholars to collate more manuscripts and print their results. He admitted that his own edition did not rest on an adequate foundation of manuscript evidence.

condition of these poems than all the rest of the manuscripts put together, and which surpasses in its critical and grammatical riches not only Eustathius but all the scholiasts of all the poets. A certain partiality in praising the book may perhaps be forgiven in one to whom a long and laborious course of study has endeared it. But even a superficial comparison between it and the similar materials that had previously been published will make anyone form the same opinion of it. Some of those who felt differently had not read scholiasts recently; others, encouraged to expect too much by the editor's first claims[a], resented the fact that they received less than they had hoped for. Some, apparently, since they had heard that the names of Zenodotus, Aristarchus, Crates, Alexion, and many other Alexandrians were often mentioned there, and that the readings of editions of which only the faintest record had come down to us as well as many scholars' individual works were cited, thought that it would provide us with their very commentaries and *diorthōseis*, assembled into a single work. At last the book appeared, famous because scholars had waited so long for it, less than half as long as Eustathius. And it provided only excerpts from the works of critics and commentators. They were not made with the method that one of us would now use when taking notes: sometimes they were rather full, sometimes rather short. They were stuffed with readings, but these were not taken from the earliest sources, and were not adequately equipped with explanations of the arguments in their support. They contained much that related to Homeric learning and literature; little that helps to form a sense of poetic qualities; nothing at all that depicts the poet's age in terms of its own opinions, customs, and general tenor of feeling and thinking— not to mention the further stock of learned and unlearned trivia, with which these scholia too reveal the date of their origins.

Therefore, now that knowledge of Greek and Latin literature has begun to be constricted to fit popular taste,[b] it is greatly to be

[a] *Encouraged by the editor's first claims:* Villoison promised in his *Anecdota Graeca* 2 (1781) to publish an edition of the *Iliad* "with the critical signs and the golden scholia from both manuscripts [i.e. Veneti A and B]."

[b] *Therefore, now that knowledge of Greek and Latin literature has begun:* This is an implicit criticism of Heyne's review of Villoison in *GGA*, 4 April 1789, 553-67. Heyne had remarked there that Villoison's work had "unfortunately come too late for our times, since the hands that should work on it are becoming fewer and fewer (and even of those who devote themselves to Greek literature, most prefer to stick to subjects that edify the mind and heart)."

feared that a work which completely lacks the things we normally look for most eagerly will find only a few distant admirers and a bare handful of readers. Nor can it, as they say nowadays, be read. It demands to be worked over with diligence, to be scrutinized, to be collated attentively with all the other aids that time has spared. The more carefully one does this, the more clearly one understands the extent of the damage that this sphere of learning has suffered, and how few fragments have slipped through to our time, like a few bookshelves from a great library. I shall say more about this matter later, if I discuss the sources of the Homeric text. True, we will not obtain the complete annotations or recension of even one of the famous ancient critics; for various reasons, I think it unlikely that these survived in their true form to the fifth and sixth centuries. And everywhere in the vulgate text there are readings rightly suspect, which no annotation attacks on our behalf. Others are completely bare [of notes], though we may learn or suspect from other sources that they were explicated in different ways by the ancients. Others, on the other hand, are overwhelmed by a mass of commentaries even though they needed no explicator. But even if you find these and worse faults, there remains a great supply of learned, acute, clever annotations, either the results of sensible study or the relics of a very ancient time. Hence anyone can see that once this treasury is opened, it brings a greater aid for the accurate interpretation of Homer, both critical and historical, than we have for any of the other poets on whom the same Alexandrians worked. Therefore let the masters of Oriental literature, proud of their Masorah, cease at last to deplore the ill fortune that makes us rely for the authority of the Homeric text on such recent manuscripts and that, since most evidence of the ancient recensions has been damaged or destroyed, makes the process by which our text was formed almost completely obscure. If we put together all our excerpts from all sources, we too now have a sort of Greek Masorah, one far superior to the other in both age and variety of learning, and far better preserved. And by comparing both of these farragoes, the Greek and the Hebrew, we will finally be able to gain a more profound knowledge of the beginnings from which the emendation of manuscripts and the art of criticism developed, as well as of many other things critical to an understanding of ancient literary scholarship. This study also often helps us more in under-

standing the poet than I can show here. What is especially remarkable, and adds extraordinary value to the Venetian manuscripts, is that we have received in them a norm and, as it were, a
rule, by which we can determine definitively the quality and condition of our manuscripts and of those that will be collated
hereafter.

This I have now learned by using the variants that Alter, a most
learned man and one of unwearied industry, published from five
Viennese manuscripts. But these readings, when compared with
the Venetian and other materials, leave me little hope that the *Iliad*,
at any rate, will ever receive much that is new and remarkable from
manuscripts. For even the better Viennese manuscripts do little
save confirm what was already known from other sources. For they
make clear which readings seemed preferable to some grammarian
or scribe of later days. Authorities of this kind have little weight
in themselves, nor does a large number, especially if they are not
specifically named. Hence I think that this apparatus of readings
will be enlarged a good bit more if scholars work through more
unpublished glossaries and scholia than if they enrich us with the
readings of ten or twenty new manuscripts. But why would that
too not be worthwhile for Homer's benefit? The critical illustration
of other ancient books—sacred ones to be sure—has recently called
forth such efforts, has reached so far beyond the borders of Europe,
has cost so much money, that poor Homer would have been content
with a third as much. Now he too awaits his Kennicott, to make
clear at last what is definitely lost and what we may still hope to
scrape together, as it were, from the rubbish.[c]

CHAPTER V

I shall be delighted if I prove to be wrong. But even when I thought
I should content myself with the materials already prepared, when
I looked only for printed texts of the *Odyssey*, at the very time when
the poet was first being fitted out for the use of students in this

[c] *For the critical illustration . . . :* Wolf refers to the vast sums solicited and spent on
procuring collations of the manuscripts of the Hebrew Bible, to little clear effect,
by Kennicott. See W. McKane, "Benjamin Kennicott, an Eighteenth-Century Re-
searcher," *Journal of Theological Studies*, n.s. 28 (1977), 445-64.

city, the very haste with which I worked in a sense forced me to adopt this plan: that by gathering whatever seemed likely to be of any use in founding the text, I would actively prepare myself for the task of recension. Whatever I have done in the meantime, though some tasks kept me quite busy, was spare-time work. I never let Homer escape my thought for long. For I saw that I would not only have to gather a vast amount of material, but also master it and work through it from the beginning; for when I first edited Homer I had hardly encountered learned interpretation. Therefore, starting with Eustathius, I worked carefully through his grammatical content. Then I extracted the readings which he revealed that he had found either in his vulgate texts, or in their margins, or elsewhere. I then added, beyond the other scholia then published, a substantial number of variants and critical notes which two late friends of mine had copied down from the Pauline manuscript[a] of Leipzig, and which Ernesti had omitted from his recension. A little later I made a direct study of the lexicographers, scholiasts, and other ancient grammarians; then, as my time allowed, all the rest of the writers who might conceivably preserve any vestige of the Homeric text. Meanwhile, I did not ignore the Greek poets, especially the Alexandrians. I was hunting for imitations of Homer, not in order to learn how flowers smell when transplanted into foreign soil—though I do not look down on that elegant study, in its proper place—but to learn where they showed, by a choice of words or a turn of style modeled on the prince of their art, what they had read in the best manuscripts of him, or what they thought should be the reading. This investigation was by no means farfetched; I found it extremely profitable, especially in the case of those poets who could be called poets or schoolmasters with equal justice. Then, after exploring all the recesses of Greek and Latin letters that revealed anything of use for the task I had undertaken, and after assembling a large apparatus of readings and critical notes, I was enriched by the Venetian and Viennese materials. The opening of this new field required new efforts from me even in the areas that I had considered complete. For I saw that I had to repeat a good part of the journey I had made, in order to compare the first harvest with my new riches, and, if by

---

[a] *Pauline manuscript:* Allen's Li.

chance I had wrongly rejected as chaff something useful in the past, to evaluate it more correctly by comparison and retrieve it. The farther I went in this work, the more extraordinary I began to find the pre-eminence of the Venetian scholia. Without them we would be quite unable to know the authority for many readings and verses. Nor was this a problem only for those of us who are engaging in these studies at so late a date. For when I then reviewed Eustathius for a second and a third time,[b] I saw that since he had no knowledge of the ancient manuscript Ven. 453 [B], he was little better off than any of the recent editors with their commonplace manuscripts. But he admired in Homer only the beauty of the poetry, taking little interest in the early portion of his afterlife and following rhetorical rather than critical commentators. On this side of things he deserves less praise than he commonly enjoys, and owes a vast amount [of what praise he gets] to the loss of the more learned scholia.

Finally, I set myself to find everything of any use that the manuscript exemplars could supply, and I continued the work, begun by Ernesti, of collating the early editions down to that of Stephanus—a job far more laborious than fruitful. For these printed texts have few distinctive readings, and even those which are good and deserve to be in the text cannot carry a great deal of weight, insofar as we do not know their sources. Some manuscripts, on the other hand, especially the Venetian, often deserve credit because of the testimony of the scholia even where the other texts do not agree. I often ended up reaching by a roundabout path the corrections which that excellent book had offered me in vain at first sight. For the general harmony between my text and the Venetian came about spontaneously; I did not seek it. I constantly resorted to clearly attested ancient authority, seeing no value in the common, frivolous method which assesses the truth of the text by its elegance or similar surface qualities, and embraces new and old readings with little distinction. I decided that the early editions rarely deserved attention, and that even the Venetian manuscript or Eustathius did not deserve it except where they mention their sources. Therefore, if I had searched for nothing but variant readings in the work of this very wordy man, from whom I accepted only a

b *For when I then reviewed Eustathius* . . . : Cf. Wolf's review of Villoison, *ALZ*, 2 February 1791, col. 251.

very few of those which are peculiar to him, the smallest part of my emendation would have cost me the most tedium and the greatest expense of time.

CHAPTER VI

But I do not regret at all[a] the effort that I expended on the study of the old grammarians. On the contrary, I feel that it aided me enormously both for this work and for general mastery of the Greek language, and that no one can do useful work on editing any Greek writer unless he has collected the grammarians' rules through a similar course of reading and tested them against correct principles. One who is used to spending the time needed for his tasks, working without pause and in an eager frame of mind, will not find the effort unpleasant. Certainly, I believe that one who ridicules[b] the grammarians' minutiae can argue more easily about the barbarism of Homeric times and their savage—or learned—style of speech, about fabulous history and mythical folly, or about the qualities of epic poetry, in the manner of a philosophical investigation, on the basis of Aristotle's rules. Of course those learned in that sort of reading are wearied by ignorant and trifling hair-splitting. But first of all, modesty forbids you to despise anything before you know it very well. And—not to mention how many things they alone have preserved for us from ancient memory—those same triflers often explain the literal sense of passages quite well. For native knowledge of the language, which they had not yet entirely lost, saved them from many errors which nowadays we wrongly shield with the pleasures afforded by novelty in interpretation. In Homer, moreover, work of that sort possesses a unique pleasure and value. For by mastering and criticizing[c] the variant readings and technical

[a] *But I do not regret at all:* A deliberate understatement. Wolf boasted more brashly about the work of this kind he had done in his announcement of his edition of Homer, in the *Intelligenzblatt der Allgem. Literatur-Zeitung*, 22 February 1794 = *Kl. Schr.*, 1:588-89.

[b] *Certainly, I believe that one who ridicules:* This seems to be a swipe at Heyne (see introduction, p. 13f.

[c] *For by mastering and criticizing:* The importance of mastering the Greek lexicographers, grammarians, and scholiasts had long been stressed by Dutch and German scholars; see the Introduction above. Wolf characteristically emphasizes the insight that such work can give into the cultural history of the ancient world.

rules offered by the grammatical books and scholia, we are summoned into old times, times more ancient than those of many ancient writers, and, as it were, into the company of those learned critics, whose judgments and teachings once nourished the young Cicero, Virgil, and Horace.[1] We barbarians, who have been so slow to learn, can, so it seems, thoroughly rework those [judgments and teachings] without absurdity even though they were written about the Greek—that is, their native—language. There is no ancient prose writer or poet who offers us critical work at the level offered by our friend Homer. But since a great many things from the writings of those critics have been passed down, as it were, from hand to hand, different ones arriving in different times, and the oldest of all arriving in part in the most recent times, anyone who wanted a more correct text clearly had to collect all the remains of that kind. If I have done that diligently, and ignored no passage that could help me give this recension a higher polish, I feel that I did no work beyond what the job itself required. By no means, then, will I complain about the vast amount of trouble I endured in preparing such a varied stock of equipment, in reading through so many writers, in reading and, in part, repairing the scholia, and in collecting and studying so great and, in so many cases, so useless a farrago of glosses and readings. What I did, whatever its value, I did willingly, and for my own use. And I would not even say this about my studies by way of preface if I did not have to render account of a project in which I could not use the work of others. I am far from boasting of my industry; I do not wish to be praised, if I have not shirked the necessary effort, but to be blamed, if I have either worked at it in an inappropriate way, or omitted anything that could have helped toward a true emendation.

CHAPTER VII

And indeed, my single primary intention was to correct the text of Homer by the standard of learned antiquity, and to display him in a text the wording, punctuation, and accentuation of which, remade from the recensions that were once considered best, might—if one

---

[1] Many passages in Cicero, Seneca, and others, together with the whole method of grammatical and liberal education among the Romans, show that this is not an overstatement.

may properly hope for so much—satisfy some Longinus or other ancient critic who knew how to use the materials of the Alexandrians with skill and tact. As to what sort of task and project this is, and what methods I followed in it, that is matter for a commentary, not a preface.[a] For I wish not only to repel the slanders of the ignorant, but also to make absolutely clear the reasoning behind my plan. Hence many things now entangled in vulgar errors must be restored to the truth; others, obscured by the loss of so many books, must be illuminated by historical conjectures drawn from afar; and everything must be confirmed by examples chosen in accordance with the common understanding. But to make clear the main rules by which the emendation of Homer is governed, it is necessary to investigate with the greatest application the changes in the transmitted text, by examining those sources and currents of them that either flowed forth in the past or are visible even today. Given the infinite supply of matter, I shall use due proportion, as follows: I shall briefly cover the most important and useful points, and shall not display the entire path that I have entered on, but only its outermost limits and its general plan. Hence, when I have dealt with the condition of the vulgate text and the need to reform it, I shall give the outlines of an inquiry, by which the internal critical history of these poems may be brought down to our own time through *six ages* of uneven length and character.[b] We set the *first age* from *their origins*, that is, from the time of the refined poetry of the Ionians (around 950 B.C.) to *Pisistratus*, the Athenian tyrant, to whom the ancients ascribe the arrangement of the two corpora that now prevails; II. from *Pisistratus* to *Zenodotus*, who was the first of the grammarians to open one of the more famous paths of Homeric criticism; III. from *Zenodotus* to *Apion*, who—according to Seneca—was celebrated throughout all of Greece because of his art of interpreting the poet; IV. from him down to *Longinus* and

---

[a] *As to what sort of task and project this is . . . :* Wolf never produced a commentary on Homer. The preface to his final edition of 1804 gives his most detailed account of his methods as an editor (*Kl. Schr.*, 1:236-78).

[b] *Through* six ages *of uneven length and character:* The *Prolegomena* as Wolf left them end with Crates, in the midst of the third of his six ages. It has been suggested, not implausibly, that he stopped here because he had reached the end of the material on ancient grammarians systematically collected in Harles's new edition of volume 1 of Fabricius's *Bibliotheca Graeca*, the major relevant reference work (1790). See V. Bérard, *Un mensonge de la science allemende* (Paris, 1917), 255-59. Here, as elsewhere, Bérard attaches an unnecessarily cynical interpretation to Wolf's conduct. He was rightly rebuked for doing so by F. Nicolini and M. Pohlenz.

his pupil *Porphyry*, both of whom contributed in some respects to the text and interpretation of Homer; V. from *Porphyry* down to the man responsible for the first edition, *Demetrius Chalcondyles* of Athens; VI. in these last three centuries, during which Homer has occupied in diverse ways the wits of scholars and the workshops of printers.[2] This will be the first part of the Preface. The second will deal with the principles on which the emendation of Homer rests, and with its most important and peculiar rules, and with giving an account of our project.

[2] This one final age—from which literary history rarely departs in other writers— offers so great a crop of books of every kind that it is an enormous task to survey their titles. The new editor [G. C. Harles] of Fabricius' *Bibliotheca Graeca* [ed. 4, vol. 1, 1790] recently did a full and accurate job. But even he left something for others to change and add to in evaluating the tools of criticism and the list of editions. But we must warn our readers again not to expect anything more than a sketch for a more elaborate treatise, and at that one dealing more with the technical uses of critical material than with literary matters. Therefore we shall inquire into the oldest sources above all, not these recent ones of printed books. The changes that the latter have wrought in the text, if compared with those wrought by the former, hardly deserve investigation from a busy man. Certainly this area of ancient letters includes a great deal of which you must carefully see to it that you are aware—but in such a way that you are happy to forget it as soon as you know it or have committed it to paper; at least so that you conceal whatever you have collected to no end. But if I repeat anything that others have already collected, I shall use our common matter in a new way. In this respect the narrow limits of this short book worry me greatly, for their result is a brevity which is inappropriate to such subjects and will at some points have the appearance of immodesty. But I have had to obey necessity even at the cost of some inconvenience.

PART I

<hr>

CHAPTER VIII

Now it may at first seem surprising that I maintain that so much work must be spent on correcting Homer, when serious faults occur so rarely in him. Compare Apollonius Rhodius, as he was read before Brunck, or the texts of Quintus Smyrnaeus, which even now are very corrupt; clearly, the poet who is older by so many centuries must seem remarkably pure and correct. But what sort of book do we call "pure" in the critical sense of the word? Clearly not one which can be read without displeasure, and in which nothing violates elegant usage and the other laws of correct writing. Granted that there is nothing of that sort in the vulgate text, it should not on that account be considered pure and correct throughout. On the contrary, sometimes the very fact that it contains nothing of that sort may make it appear all the more devoid of genuine purity. No doubt some will consider this statement ridiculous. But if above I properly related the text of ancient writers to the consideration of *historical facts*, then in establishing the text no appearance of plausibility drawn from one's sense of elegance, but pure and sufficiently old exemplars must take the first place. It is one thing to combine the laws of history with usage, learning, and taste when examining the credibility of the best witnesses; a very different thing to be propelled by this volatile sense [of taste] as by a gust of wind, so that we believe that any pretty and appropriate reading which crops up is also the true one. A more severe judgment, which must be made on the basis of the collation of the oldest authorities, often has the clear result that the most offensive readings have all the marks of truth, while others with a distinctively plausible and witty sense have little or no credibility.

But what is to be done if [passages in] the vulgate texts, which go against the agreement of the older manuscripts, are not even attractive? But I do not wish immediately to produce examples of that sort, some of which I have previously expelled from the text for sufficient reasons: for example *Il.* 2.451 ἑκάστου, 7.337 ἐν πεδίῳ, 8.563 σέλας, 10.328 βάλε, 12.343 Αἴαντε, 13.346 τετεύχατον, 14.168 τόν, 16.463 μέν inserted before ἀγακλειτόν, etc. In these cases the Venetian and other manuscripts that have since been collated confirm the correction. Rather, I shall support my case at first with examples where the errors are revealed not by deformity of speech or thought, but only by the testimonies and authority of manuscripts. Who, for example, would dare to change *Il.* 1.91 ἐνὶ στρατῷ to Ἀχαιῶν, 2.865 Πυλαιμένεος to Ταλαιμένεος, 3.220 ζάκοτόν τινα ἔμμεναι to ζάκοτόν τέ τιν᾽ ἔμμεναι, 4.435 ἀκούσασαι to ἀκούουσαι, 5.159 υἱοὺς to υἷας, 6.380 and 385 ἐϋπλόκαμοι to ἐϋπλόκαμον, 7.284 Ἕκτορα to Ἕκτορι (a verse which Ernesti corrupted by a double error), 8.4 ἅμα to ὑπό, 9.680 ἄμ᾽ Ἀργείοισιν to ἐν Ἀργ., 10.256 νηυσί to νηΐ, 11.466 αὐτή to φωνή, 12.9 τῷ κ᾽ οὖτι to τὸ καὶ οὖτι, 13.791 Πολυφοίτην to Πολυφήτην, 14.506 ὑπὸ χλωρὸν δέος εἷλε to ὑπὸ τρόμος ἔλλαβε γυῖα, 15.510 αὐτοσχεδίην to αὐτοσχεδίη, 16.510 αἰνῶς to αὐτόν, 17.266 τόσση ἄρα Τρώων ἰαχὴ γένετο to τόσση ἄρα Τρῶες ἰαχῇ ἴσαν, 18.63 ἴδω τε to ἴδοιμι, 19.393 ζεύγνυσαν to ζεύγνυον, 20.308 παῖδες παίδων to παίδων παῖδες, 21.33 κατακτάμεναι to δαϊζέμεναι, 22.59 ἐλέαιρε to ἐλέησον, 23.362 ἵπποισιν to ἵπποιϊν, 24.526 ἀχνυμένους to ἀχνυμένοις? Who, I say, could dare to change these passages and many like them so radically, given that it is scarcely clear on internal grounds which readings are better than which, unless either Eustathius and the scholiasts, or Greek writers who cite part of those verses, or many excellent manuscripts commanded that these changes be made? If you deny that this law holds, we deny in turn that there is any writer, of any nation or period, whom we cannot correct and interpolate elegantly by plausible conjecture.

　　Here I shall give only four examples of interpolated verses: *Il.* 1.265, 2.168, 21.480, *Od.* 2.191. The first two of these are clearly good and appropriate to their passages. The second, indeed, is clearly Homeric, [since it is] doubtless repeated from the beginning of the book [2.17]. The third is no less Homeric, and fits the general order so well that one might almost be sorry to see it expelled. The fourth, finally, is bad neither in meter nor in meaning, so long as you read δυνήσεται with Clarke. But even if all these verses seem quite Homeric, nevertheless they do not belong to Homer—unless, perhaps, whatever the testimony of manuscripts reveals to have been made up a thousand years later, perhaps in a spirit of rivalry, or whatever quasi-Homeric verses Rhodoman made in his *Palaestina* belong to Homer. For the first of them is not to be found in most of the best manuscripts, nor does any scholiast nor Eustathius anywhere acknowledge it; hence you may think that it was a late addition from the *Scutum Herculis* 182. The second has no greater authority from the best scholia and codices. For they call for the sharpest possible punctuation between 167 and 169.[a] If the ancient critics had found this asyndeton—which now, with the middle verse removed, offends the ignorant—to be harsh, they could easily have softened it thus: εὗρε δ᾽ ἔπειτα [instead of εὗρεν ἔπειτα]. Others have already expunged the third, which both Eustathius and several good codices reject, along with the first edition and the Roman. Nor does the fourth verse find support in Eustathius and other manuscripts, in which there appear a variety of versions of the ending, which obviously could not be brought along with the rest from *Il.* 1.562. Anyone would certainly find these verses and some others worthless, though by no means ridiculous, if Rhodoman had recently made them, or Barnes (for he now and then produces something *de ménage*, as he says). But if they are the work of wits buried centuries ago, will we not be permitted to reject them? I should like to learn by what right we may keep the rest.

CHAPTER IX

There is another, much more common variety of vulgate reading. These certainly do not lack the support of old manuscripts and recensions, and yet, either because of the poet's usage, or the symmetry and coherence of thought, or some other, similar reason, they must evidently be expunged and [the readings of] better manuscripts put in their place. But in this variety, as in the previous one, the lack of good sources sometimes makes it uncertain to what each reading should be attributed—whether to the negligence of the editors or to the authority of the codices that they used—and thus to the authority of the ancients themselves. Thus I do not

---

[a] *For they call for the sharpest possible punctuation between 167 and 169 . . . :* Schol. 2. 167b Erbse.

know the origin of the vulgate Πιερίη at 2.766, which has come into our editions; but I cannot defend it either on the basis of Hymn to Mercury 70ff. or that of any other passage. For what is mentioned there is not the "shepherd from Amphrysus" [Virgil, *Georgics* 3.2], but the herds sacred to the gods. However, several good codices[3] along with Eustathius[a] preserve a name almost unknown to geography, but for this very reason liable to corruption— Φηρείη or Πηρείη. And Stephanus of Byzantium and Hesychius,[b] doubtless on the basis of this passage, represent it as a region near Pherae in Thessalia. But for many more other readings witnesses exist, by no means obscure ones, whose number and quality, proven in other cases, still cannot give credibility to readings that have lost it for one of these reasons. The following examples from this class will show anyone with a thorough knowledge of Homer's genius and idiom what I mean at a glance: *Il.* 1.20 λύσαιτε φίλην τὰ δ᾽ ἄποινα δέχεσθε changed to λῦσαί τε φ. τά τ᾽ ἄποινα δέχεσθαι, 2.293 ἤν to ὄν, 3.42 ἐπόψιον to ὑπόψιον, 4.24 Ἥρη to Ἥρῃ, 5.227 ἀποβήσομαι to ἐπιβήσομαι, 6.51 ἔπειθε to ὄρινε, 7.277 μέσσω to μέσσῳ, 8.454 τὸ δὲ καὶ τετελεσμένον ἔσται to τὸ δέ κεν τετ. ἦεν, 9.632 φόνοιο to φονῆος, 10.88 εἴσεαι to γνώσεαι, 11.51 μεθ᾽ ἱππήων to μέγ᾽ ἱππήων, 12.382 χείρεσιν ἀμφοτέρῃς (or χειρί γε τῇ ἑτέρῃ) φέροι to χείρεσσ᾽ ἀμφοτέρῃς ἔχοι, 13.485 ἐνὶ θυμῷ to ἐπὶ θυμῷ, 14.414 ῥιπῆς to πληγῆς, 15.379 νόον to κτύπον, 16.732 ἔπεχε to ἔφεπε, 17.365 πόνον to φόνον, 18.531 ἱράων to εἰράων, 19.19 ἐτάρπετο to τετάρπετο, 20.35 κέκαστο to κέκασται, 21.493 ἔπειτα to ὕπαιθα, 22.326 μεμαώς to μεμαῶτα, 23.280 σθένος to κλέος, 24.793 κασίγνητοι ἔταροί τε to κασίγνητοί θ᾽ ἔταροί τε.

Some of the readings that I have now rejected have quite old and qualified witnesses, in some cases ones mentioned by name in

---

[3] Some of them, like the Venetian, have a beginning and, as it were, a sort of augury of the corruption, Πηερίη. In the scholia there is nothing on this verse, nor does the vulgate form appear in them except at one point, 23.383 [A Dindorf]. But I think that Valckenaer would not have held this authority weightier than that of Macrobius [*Saturnalia* 1.17.44]. See him on Ammonius, [*Animadversiones*] 3.12.

---

[a] *However, several good codices . . . :* Eustathius quotes Πηρείη as a reading found "in other manuscripts" and Πιερίη as that of "some of the manuscripts." Cf. Allen, apparatus ad loc.

[b] *And Stephanus of Byzantium and Hesychius:* Stephanus s.v. Πήρεια; Hesychius s.v. Πηρίη.

the scholia. But—not to mention that the very selection of different
readings which we are offered forces us to use our own judgment—
what compels us to swear by the words of the ancient critics, when
we find that they have sometimes preferred readings inappropriate
to Homer to better ones already accepted, or introduced them on
the basis of an unsuitable conjecture? "The heart of Zenodotus"
and "the liver of Crates" are objects of ridicule;[c] was Aristarchus
so penetrating in mind and judgment that it is improper to disagree
with him? Clearly, great names do not confer authority. If the poet's
own genius and usage, established by other passages, contradict
them, then it seems that there is no reason to ask or even to wonder
which—he, or critics many centuries later—has the greater authority. One wishes only that we knew for certain in individual
passages what each of the critics was the first to introduce into the
text, and in what state he received that from his predecessors.

Also relevant here are some entire verses, which even the unanimous agreement of the best texts cannot protect from the suspicion
that they are interpolated. From this group I shall produce several
below, and one particularly remarkable verse here: *Il.* 13.731, which
appears in all the codices yet collated save Vienna cxvii and—a
point that may surprise you greatly—appears in the Venice codex
itself without an obelus.[d] For it is easy to see that the sentence in
which Polydamas compares himself with Hector is awkwardly extended beyond the point by that verse. But Homer sometimes goes
into a bit more detail than a given thought requires, and he is not
to be judged by the cold rules of a correct eloquence. What need
of further argument? Eustathius omits the verse from its place.
And shortly afterwards he reports from the commentaries of the
ancients that it was forged by Zenodotus of Mallos.[e] Why, then,
should we accord this verse more authority than the verse of the
Isocratean Dioscorides, which Athenaeus cites at 1. 11a, which is
unsuitable and awkward after 9.119, or wherever else you stick
it on,

---

[c] *"The heart of Zenodotus" and "the liver of Crates"* . . .: Wolf refers to the second
passage by M. Furius Bibaculus ap. Suet. *De grammaticis et rhetoribus* 11.4 = Bibaculus
2.7 Morel.

[d] Il. *13.731* . . . *appears in the Venice codex itself without an obelus:* In fact the verse
does not occur there.

[e] *Eustathius omits the verse. . . . And shortly afterwards he reports* . . .: 957.11ff.

Ἤ οἴνῳ μεθύων, ἤ μ᾽ ἔβλαψαν θεοὶ αὐτοί
["Either (I was) drunk with wine, or the gods themselves
    harmed me"],

or this verse of Crates, in Plutarch, *De Facie in orbe lunae* 938D,
added after 14.246,

Ἀνδράσιν ἠδὲ θεοῖς· πλείστην ἐπὶ γαῖαν ἵησιν
["For men and gods; for he (Ocean) extends over the most
    land"],

or the similar ones preserved by others?

CHAPTER X

I am not certain if these examples of the worthlessness of the
vulgate readings will make the vulgate text lose something of its
favor with men of right judgment. In this field, examples are certainly more effective than the profound declarations of principle
that great scholars have often laid down about it. While one reads
those, one tends to approve of them; when it comes to action, idle
superstition returns. And in Homer, indeed, that superstition has
great advocates among the ancients themselves, among whom Lucian stands out for his ingenuity.[4] He reports that when he asked
the poet in the underworld about the verses considered counterfeit
by the critics, Homer answered simply, "they were all his." True,
one must take it that by this answer the kindly old gentleman only
acknowledged the verses that had been admitted into the text before his conversation with Lucian—for example, that Zenodotean
one which Lucian clearly accepts in another work.[5] Nonetheless,
we do not see why we may not defend all the other additions and
jokes and errors from other hands by the same excellent authority.
The witty storyteller forgot to put this one small question to Homer
as he departed: which of the many different recensions should one
accept if one would not take the trouble to read Homer with an
apparatus of manuscripts or to decide on these matters by oneself?
For it would be too rash and thoughtless to accept as correct and
genuine just the text that was by accident the vulgate in circulation

---

[4] *Verae historiae*, 2.20.   [5] *De saltatione* 23.

in one's time. Is there any difference between this and agreeing with the opinion of the one who is last of a large group to speak? Surely one who holds this opinion about the texts would have held a different vulgate to be valid had his life fallen in a different period. Indeed, if the text had been published at the outset from the very manuscripts whose faith he denies that we should follow, he would eagerly embrace exactly what he now despises and rejects.

But neither, finally, will anyone think that the errors of scribes or typesetters, which crept into the vulgate text in his own time, should be preserved so devoutly—as, for example, in many editions at 11.546 ὁμίλῳ has recently begun to be printed in place of ὁμίλου, at 12.340 αὐτά in place of αὐτάς, at 17.750 ἴσχεν in place of ἴσχει, etc. These minor stains, I believe, they are willing to see wiped away. We will therefore use this permission when similar errors lend themselves to an easy correction, even though they are some centuries older. But what shall I say of the cases which reveal that that "literal inspiration of the Muses" is spoiled[a] by human carelessness and ignorance, by barbarisms and solecisms, and by corruptions of thought and language that no one could accept with equanimity in any writer, much less in this best of all writers? I shall add a few examples of this kind as well—and especially examples of such a sort that a little stroke of the pen would be enough to restore them according to the dictates of the finer manuscripts. For at 5.416 ἰχώρ, with one letter removed, offers the absolutely correct reading ἰχῶ, which, according to Eustathius, was once accepted by all the best scholars, by analogy to the forms ἱδρῶ, κυκεῶ, and the like. For a great many passages in the medical writers show that the word found in the vulgate was never employed by anyone in the neuter gender. Nor was that the intention of those from whom we received it, in whose opinion an apostrophe was certainly to be added.[b] But Barnes removed this error long ago. In the same

---

[a] *that "literal inspiration of the Muses" is spoiled:* Wolf's term for "literal inspiration of the Muses," Μουσοπνευστία, is a play on the traditional Protestant theologians' term for the literal inspiration of the Bible, θεοπνευστία. For a similar attitude in a theological work that stands as a parallel to Wolf's, see Griesbach's *Commentatio* on Mark, cited in editorial note b to ch. 1 above: "Those who argue that Mark wrote under the influence of divine inspiration [*e theopneustia*] must surely regard it as being a pretty meagre one!" (op. cit., 135; original text ibid., 102).

[b] *an apostrophe was certainly to be added:* Wolf is defending the epic accusative ἰχῶ against the vulgate ἰχώρ. He took this as a corruption of ἰχώρ', the normal accusative of ἰχώρ with its final alpha replaced by an apostrophe.

book, at 394, the same editor should have corrected the absurd κεν from his manuscripts. If this is accepted, the sentence wrongly imitates the structure of verse 388, although it is rather of the same kind as what immediately follows at verse 395ff. For [the thought] is this: τλῆ Ἥρη, ὅτε μιν κρατερὸς παῖς Ἀμφιτρύωνος ὀϊστῷ βαλὼν ὀδύνῃσιν ἔδωκεν ["Hera endured, when the strong son of Amphitryon struck her with an arrow and caused her pain"].[c] Elsewhere, on the contrary, the deletion of the particle κε had corrupted the construction, as at 17.629. A similar error of one small letter occurs at the end of 6 [529] in ἐλάσαντες, a nominative which has nothing to depend on. It would be extremely awkward to take it back to ἀρεσσόμεθα, or, from the words which follow [that], αἴ κέ ποθι Ζεὺς δώῃ, taking only the sense into account, to express some verb in the first person. So far I have been unable to find examples of such grammatical elegances in Homer, except for those that are suspect: as *Od.* 4.263, where Eustathius cites as from the ancients too the excellent reading of some codices, νοσφισσαμένην, which was changed, I think, by those who were offended by the occurrence in the same case of a series of words different in gender, as in *Il.* 22.109. For certainly none of the ancients could have accepted the vulgate in the vulgar way. At 10.57 they normally read κείνου γάρ κε μάλιστα πυθοίατο, where they think that πυθέσθαι is *obey*. Since not even the compilers of glossaries foist this interpretation upon us, it should certainly have been proved by one clear example. Eustathius foils anyone seeking the reading of his manuscripts with that wretched καὶ ἑξῆς ["and so on"].[d] In fact, if he had found that reading, he would not have omitted so unusual a meaning, or would have come back to it elsewhere. This he does not do anywhere. For although at p. 1013.55, on 15.224, he remarks on πυθέσθαι constructed with the genitive in such a way as to show that he has mentioned the phenomenon elsewhere, that pertains to its meaning not *obey*, but *know* or *hear*, about which he had clearly spoken at p. 655.42. Therefore, Eustathius must also be added to the witnesses for our correction. He confirms our reading more clearly at 11.11,

---

[c] "*. . . and caused her pain.*": The sentence that begins in 5.388 is a contrary-to-fact condition; the one that begins in 395 contains a statement with a temporal clause. Wolf here rewrites 392-94 by combining 392-93 with the end of 397 to show the logical similarity.

[d] *Eustathius foils anyone . . .* : By failing to quote his text of 10.57 (he quotes parts of 10.53-56).

where in the vulgate the verb ἀύειν was connected with the dative. I doubt very much whether that was normal in the similar verbs γεγωνεῖν, κέκλεσθαι, κελεύειν, or indeed in that one; and I do not see that Homer normally used it so. And a trained sensitivity to meter can teach us that this is not the only awkwardness from which the verse suffers. The form γεγενοίμεθα at 13.485, which was transferred from there to the dictionaries of dialects, was from another kind of false analogy. We have given the reading of several codices, γε γενοίμεθα, as both usage and sense required. Evidently we should have waited for a greater number of codices so that we could correct the worst readings and easiest errors of some scribes, so that at 16.380 we could change ἀνά to ἄρα, at 18.405 ἔσαν to ἴσαν, at 20.409 πᾶσι to παισί. In addition to these, there is the very easy and very common confusion of moods, especially the subjunctive and optative. The debased Greeks themselves in later centuries did not do very well at maintaining the proper distinction between them. True, I have remarked about fifteen examples of this confusion which both the meter and all the manuscripts prevent us from correcting by the rule. But in a great many more cases there is no doubt that the older manuscripts, which agree with the grammatical and metrical rules, must be followed. At least no one but an ignoramus would wish to see an extension in the very common practice of disturbing the succession of moods when symmetrical clauses are joined, or of adding a present indicative to the particle ἄν or κε—especially when it is so easy to make the change, and that has the status of an argument for many people.

CHAPTER XI

And these specimens of corrections in the vulgate text, selected from a great quantity without special care, and suggested not by genius but by better manuscripts, may persuade anyone that by consulting purer sources the true form of the Homeric text can be reconstructed even today. Nor has the poet's great age snatched this hope from us. For it is a mistake to think that all historical credibility is weakened or the integrity of texts corrupted by simple length of time, and that whatever has been done or written most recently must therefore also be held most true and genuine. I do

not speak about events; time itself effectively undeceives the credulous about the things that they saw done almost before their eyes.[a]
But texts suffer no corruption when laid away in chests in a place
safe from moths and worms.[b] Why, then, if they are copied carefully
and not too often, can they not last a very long time without serious
harm, even if the autographs are lost? But for the faults that normally arise from frequent and careless copying, the remedy is at
hand in the art of criticism, which compares codices of different
workmanship with one another. But can we trust that this good
fortune, which is the lot of almost all texts, is that of the Homeric
ones?

We certainly can—unless these [Homeric] texts have undergone
certain peculiar corruptions and more, and more serious, changes.
But the very fact that their emendation was begun and practiced
by the Greeks at a very early period shows that the ancient Greeks
themselves already lacked exemplars of adequate purity, from
which those who wished could copy new ones. The very first recensions, the products of an art of criticism that was not yet sophisticated, disagreed on many points to an extraordinary extent,
and the vulgate form of the text was finally introduced in a more
learned phase of Greek history by various grammarians after Aristotle. But we do not even have that pure form of the Aristarchean
text, the one of which the ancients most approved for a long time,
but one reedited and reworked according to the views of different
critics in the generations just after Christ's birth, and finally
smirched with new blotches by the barbarous times that soon broke
in. Must we not gather from these facts, as I boldly asserted long
ago,[6] that the purity of Homer is very different from that of Lucretius or Virgil? As to the different state of those original editions
and the Alexandrian ones, it suffices for the present to touch on
the one fact that in Hippocrates, Plato, Aristotle, and other writers
of that time we read not only variant forms of individual words,

---

[6] On Hesiod *Theogony*, p. 57 [*Theogonia Hesiodea*, ed. Wolf (1783), 57 = *Kl. Schr.*,
1:166].

---

[a] *time itself effectively undeceives . . . :* Wolf echoes the familiar humanist adage that
"Truth is the daughter of Time."

[b] *safe from moths and worms:* The phrase comes from Horace *Sermones* 2.3. 119; it
was a topos in the Renaissance and after for the perils that awaited manuscripts
improperly preserved in private collections.

but also a number of remarkable lines, of which no trace survives either in our text or in Eustathius and the oldest and most learned scholia.[7] And so far I feel that I will receive a ready assent from all those who have learned to trust their own eyes. But what if the suspicion of some scholars is probable—that these and the other poems of those times were not consigned to writing, but were first made by poets in their memories and made public in song, then made more widely available by the singing of the rhapsodes, whose peculiar art it was to learn them?[c] And if, because of this, many changes were necessarily made in them, by accident or design,

[7] In the book *On Joints* which is, if not by Hippocrates, certainly from the period of Hippocrates or just after, there is mentioned a long discourse by Homer on cattle, and this one verse is quoted: Ὡς δ᾽ ὁπότ᾽ ἀσπάσιον ἔαρ ἤλυθε βουσὶν ἕλιξιν ["As when spring has come, welcome to cattle with twisted horns" ch. 8 = 4.98 Littré]. We find nothing like this anywhere in him today. Better known are the verses that Plato and Aristotle cite from their Homer, not ours. Those, indeed, include some for which one cannot now find a suitable place by conjecture. But I take it as established that the four verses quoted by Plato in the *Alcibiades* 2 [149D] found their home in *Il.* 8 at the end, and that they were not assembled from several passages. Therefore I inserted them there [549-52], but not without brackets, since I reckoned that the Alexandrian critics had rejected them, along with the vulgate line 548, for good reason. No trace appears in our scholia of those lines and the similar ones that Greek writers continually ascribe to Homer. But in general the scholia offer almost nothing of the kind that is unknown from other sources. Eustathius has many more, and ones which the writers for their part do not mention. One who considers this, however ignorant he may be of the history of the text, can hardly suspect that everyone who cited such verses under Homer's name was suffering a lapse of memory, or that we are wrongly assigning to the *Iliad* and *Odyssey* lines that perhaps occurred in other works ascribed to the poet. Thus Barnes—arbitrarily or, perhaps, by divination—assigned the hemistich found in Aeschines *Against Timarchus* 128, Φήμη δ᾽ ἐς στρατὸν ἦλθε ["Rumor came to the army"], to the *Thebaid*, although it is explicitly reported to be in *Homer's Iliad*, and even *to be repeated several times in the Iliad*. At one time I thought this meant the *Little Iliad*. Certainly no verse or sentence like this one occurs anywhere in either poem as we have it. But neither is there anything in the orator's words that smells of an error. For we must try anything rather than believe either that Aeschines was so forgetful or ignorant in letters, or that so great a change took place in many passages in Homer. But the fact that none of the old commentators mentions that hemistich, not Eustathius, not any of the scholiasts, seems less surprising. They do not have the remarkable verses which Plutarch, in two passages [*Quomodo adulescens poetas audire debeat*, p. 26F, and *Quomodo adulator ab amico internoscatur*, p. 72B], shows that the Alexandrians struck out of Phoenix's speech, 9.458ff., and that I restored, following the example of others and the judgment of Valckenaer, *Diatribe in Euripidis Perditorum Dramatum Reliquias* (1767), p. 264. But all of this makes clear how right Giphanius was long ago to feel that the version of the text that Alexander the Great used did not survive in ours. That could be gathered from Aristotle alone.

[c] *But what if the suspicion of some scholars . . .:* See below, ch. 26, n. 84; ch. 39, n. 42. Valckenaer also told his students that the Homeric poems were "farragoes" of what had originally been individual songs performed by Homer and the rhapsodes. See the Introduction above.

before they were fixed, so to speak, in written form? And if for this very reason, as soon as they began to be written out, they had many differences, and soon acquired new ones from the rash conjectures of those who rivaled one another in their efforts to polish them up, and to correct them by the best laws of the art of poetry and their own usage? And if, finally, it can be shown by probable arguments and reasons that this entire connected series of the two continuous poems is owed less to the genius of him to whom we have normally attributed it, than to the zeal of a more polite age and the collective efforts of many, and that therefore the very songs from which the *Iliad* and *Odyssey* were assembled do not all have one common author?[d] If, I say, one must accept a view different from the common one about all these things—what, then, will it mean to restore these poems to their original luster and genuine beauty?

I have summarized in a few words the points which I will discuss, a little later and more precisely, elsewhere. For since I see that in these things I must uproot the solid opinion of almost all antiquity, in order that my arguments may be weighed more honestly, I shall now treat only their strongest points, briefly and with a light hand. If I learn that scholars do not accept them—that is, that they are weakened by contrary points and arguments—I shall be the first to reconsider them, "but may the Gods make all these things idle."[e] For I think that in this sort of literature the true student must not be afraid of anything that goes against common opinion; and where history is silent or mumbles, he must be very willing to allow himself to be beaten by those who know how to interpret obscure report and uncertain traces of transmitted events with more subtlety. For in this earliest period, in which the origins of the Homeric text must be sought, we have only the faintest illumination. This we must use with skill, or we will necessarily misjudge much of what happened in later times.

[d] *And if, finally, it can be shown . . .:* Here Wolf makes an even more radical claim. He was never able to work out its implications in detail, though both Heyne and a large number of nineteenth-century scholars did attempt to do so, without lasting success.

[e] *"but may the Gods make all these things idle": Il.* 4.363.

CHAPTER XII

Our very entrance is blocked by the serious question recently raised—or rather revived—about the origins of writing among the Greeks. But the brilliant audacity of Wood[8] above all has made it possible for me to return to this without causing much offense and, if I am able, to dispatch it. For if our forefathers had heard that serious doubts were raised as to whether Homer, the greatest of writers, used the art of writing, they would have cried out that the lovers of paradoxes no longer had any shame. Now we have begun to examine the natures of ancient monuments more profoundly and to judge each event by the mental and moral habits of its time and place, while keeping the strictest law of history—that we do not call into doubt things which are true and supported by honest witnesses, and that we do not take as established things which are passed down in any way whatever or adorned with the name of some author or other. Thus these poems, too, when they have been studied with some care, reveal a marvelous abundance of nature and talent, less art, no recherché and subtle learning at all. To be sure, one who feels no art in them would have to have a dull

---

[8] In his very famous book, *An Essay on the Original Genius of Homer*, 2d ed., 1775, in the chapter on the poet's language and learning [237–92]. That, like the book as a whole, contains many shrewd and fine observations—save only for the almost complete lack of that subtlety, without which a historical argument can persuade but cannot convince. Hence we have recently seen several scholars criticize that chapter above all and support the common opinion: Wiedeburg, in *Humanistisches Magazin* 1:143ff. [apparently a wrong reference copied from the work cited next], and Harles in Fabricius' *Bibliotheca Graeca*, 1:353, with exceptional zeal. I would not prefer to their judgment the levity of those who have simply repeated the brilliant Englishman's opinion—or, as he calls it, his conjecture—or have been brought to it by their own errors, like the author [Charles Davy] of the tract *Conjectural Observations on the Origin and Progress of Alphabetic Writing* [1772], 99. Though the latter set out to remove the art of writing only from the time of the Homeric heroes, not from Homer, the former thought that it only became a truly common practice around 554 B.C. But the *philosophe* Merian gave a learned and eloquent account of Wood's arguments, and a fresh, acute defense of them, in a dissertation included last year in the French publications of the Berlin Academy [see the translators' introduction, p. 31f.]. My friend opportunely presented me with it just as I was about to send this sheet to the printer. A quick reading of it at just the right time induced me to compress and shorten my arguments further and to omit entirely several arguments that I had made for the same thesis. For this is written for the learned, who will read Merian as well, and with whom one gains little advantage in such a case by dilating on individual circumstances.

sensibility and deaf ears; for their art is such that the most learned imitators have not been able to attain it, even in meter. Nonetheless, it is clear that all that art is in a sense closer to nature, and derived not from the rules of a science set out in books, but from a native sense of what is correct and beautiful. In this and other respects that poet is as different from the singers in their forest gatherings as he is from the poets of learned periods.[9] This more accurate estimate has, as it were, set him back into his place and stripped him of the considerable excess baggage with which scholars had loaded him down for his honor's sake, since they did not want the best author of the fairest art to be ignorant of anything that was ascribed, in their own period, to the cultivation of the arts and the elegance of social life. Hence he has blossomed with a new elegance and grace in the eyes of those who are competent and expert.

"Not in the eyes of all," some say; and we find it easy to believe them. For the method of those who read Homer and Callimachus and Virgil and Nonnus and Milton in one and the same spirit, and do not strive to weigh in reading and work out what each author's age allows, has not yet entirely been done away with.[a] True, they ridicule the follies of the Reimanns; but they take it very ill when the god of poets is thought to have been ignorant of the very ABC of the sciences, when those who possess almost all of them in our day still do not dare to compose Iliads. That so great a genius, then, is to be deprived of the alphabet, and, along with it,

[9] This very noun *poet*, unknown of old to the bards, implies a *rather toilsome piece of work*. As to the common use of the noun we are happy to accept Plato's explanation in the *Symposium* 205B-C, which is greatly preferable to the one on the basis of which certain Frenchmen used in the recent past to teach about the nature of poetics. But the word seems even more recent than Hesiod, and was not generally received until music began to be commonly distinguished from the art of composing poetry. I shall investigate this matter elsewhere. But when I refer to Hesiod, I mean the entire period into which falls the composition of the works now attributed to Hesiod. For it is clear that they cannot be ascribed to one man; and many more circulated under his name among the ancients. In the *Works and Days* there are many passages distinguished by the patina of venerable antiquity. But the *Theogony* and the *Shield of Hercules* and the great majority of the works that survive in short fragments are certainly a full century later than Homer. Proof of this point lies in the fact that they contain a good many novel ideas and imitations of Homeric passages, and in particular a fuller and more orderly knowledge of lands and peoples.

[a] *For the method of those who read Homer and Callimachus . . . in one and the same spirit . . . :* This is directed against Heyne, who, in his vastly popular edition of the *Aeneid*, had treated the Homeric poems as the individual, deliberate creations of a single author—and thus as directly comparable to the work of later, more sophisticated poets. (Wolf did much the same when teaching Virgil.)

Of those instruments that boys now sling over their arm
as they come to school![b]

But I do not wish to make fun of those whom it is irrelevant and
immodest to undeceive here. For there are expert Latin and Greek
scholars among them. But I think many grant my view that exact
knowledge of the Greek language is not sufficient equipment for
understanding the poems of farthest antiquity in terms of the talent
and genius of their authors. And I claim the right to reject those
who lack this form of understanding as judges of all that I shall
say about the mentality of those times. But they will feel less anger
against me, I hope, since what I deny to Homer is less knowledge
of letters than practice and skill with them. Indeed, this entails a
consequence which they may employ to praise him in a new way.
We certainly admire the ancient navigators all the more because
they were able to direct their voyages without a ship's compass;
nor, perhaps, would every soldier today be able to believe that
Alexander or Caesar did such great deeds and took so many well-
fortified cities before the invention of gunpowder. Yet they had
something which offered a sufficiently powerful substitute for gunpowder. How much more remarkable will it be that there was a
poet who did not think that he should learn or that he needed that
art, without which it seems impossible to compose a fairly long
poem, even though it was known?

And in fact—to attack the problem seriously—in Wood's arguments many points are weak, many farfetched. He says that of the
philosophers, too, down to Socrates, the ancients had few written
works; that in Homer himself memory is treated as the sole cus-
todian of events; that she is the mother of the Muses; that the
Muses themselves are singers. As if the poet could have reworked
myths that had once been accepted and established,[c] or as if one
of those who used paper and ink could later have introduced into
the poem a new, paper-bearing goddess in place of Mnemosyne.

---

[b] *Of those instruments . . .*: Cf. Horace *Sermones* 1.6.74.
[c] *As if the poet could have reworked . . .*: This is directed not only at Wood but at
Heyne. Heyne held that the Greek poets radically reshaped the myths they inherited.
For his views see e.g. B. Feldman and R. D. Richardson, *The Rise of Modern Mythology,
1680-1860* (Bloomington, 1972), 215-23; A. Horstmann, "Mythologie und Altertumswissenschaft. Der Mythosbegriff bei Christian Gottlob Heyne," *Archiv für Be-
griffsgeschichte*, vol. 16, pt. 1 (1972), 60-85. Wolf makes clear that he is attacking
Heyne in his fourth polemical letter, translated in part in the subsidia below.

Such things remain even though objects and customs change—just as words remain in languages, while their meanings are changed in accordance with the changes of times and things. When Apollonius Rhodius uses the verb πεμπάζειν ["count on five fingers"] (2.975), no one, obviously, will believe that he counted on his fingers; nor, indeed, that Homer, who employed the same verb before, did so. For he counts up to 10,000, using reckoning by tens, and enumerates the Greek army of around 100,000 men. It would be the opposite error, but one of the same degree, if someone, on the basis of the customs of his own time, referred Homer's word εὐνομίη ["good order"] or even Hesiod's νόμος ["law"] to written laws, or ὥρη ["season," "hour"] to our modern division of the day, or—in the matter that now chiefly concerns us—inferred from the verb γράφειν ["write"] or the noun σῆμα ["sign"][10] that the art of writing was already practiced commonly at the time when those [words] were in use. One must not abuse this inconstant sort of language in such a way when examining the force of words, each of which has its own history, which depends not on words and utterances themselves but on the condition of the times and customs,[d] something known from other sources. Such investigations, indeed, can not be completed on the basis of words alone.

[10] It is established that γράφειν, like χαράσσειν and the like, belongs to the category of made up (onomatopoetic) verbs, and that its proper meaning is *dig* or *scratch*. Scholia to Theocritus, 6.18k [Wendel]: "The ancients said γράψαι for ξέσαι [carve]." Hesychius: "Γράψαι· ξύσαι, χαράξαι, ἀμύξαι." One clearly observes this usage in all the following passages: *Il.* 4.139, 11.388, 13.553, 17.599, 21.166; *Od.* 22.280, 24.229. In our language as well the verb for writing [*schreiben*] has the rough sound of a carpenter's chisel or some similar instrument. And in Homer that Greek verb does not have the meaning *paint*. Insofar as *siglae* and other abbreviations are called σήματα or σημεῖα, the period of the sophists reveals the first traces of them; to look for them in earlier times would be foolish. See J. Lipsius, *Epistolarum Selectarum Centuria Prima ad Belgas* [1605] 1:27 [pp. 23-28].

[d] *on the condition of the times and customs:* Eichhorn makes a similar point in his discussion of the Hebrew word *nabi'* ('prophet'); *Einleitung ins Alte Testament* (1st ed., 1780-83), sect. 9.

CHAPTER XIII

One who seeks ancient authority in the midst of all this uncertainty confronts the obscurities that often crop up around the origins of famous arts. How many arts are there—even of those discovered recently, that is, a few centuries ago—of the origins and development of which we can read accounts supported by good authors? But antiquity saw the origins and slow progress of many more things, the slender beginnings of which were witnessed by few and the utility of which to posterity was of concern to none. The mature race examined its origins only at a late date, when the memory of the first inventions had been obscured by the long time that had elapsed, and divergent reports had given rise to different opinions and new stories. Nor did historians employ that philosophical ingenuity with which we have investigated the progress and capacity of the human mind in inventing things, now that we have learned to take a wider view of the world, and to compare the habits and customs of different peoples that enjoy a similar level of material culture.[a] After all, this is the new light of our times, which was denied to, or of little interest to, the Greeks.

But very few of those who have made learned collections of the passages in the ancients on the authors of the Greek alphabet have apparently taken advantage of this light. Hence the most profound scholars have disagreed on many points and on some have followed implausible opinions. For after the chief proponents of the common opinion, Scaliger and Salmasius, there were those who attributed what they took to be so necessary an art to the old tribes of the Pelasgi, even somewhat before Cadmus, and that opinion is still accepted now by many outstanding men.[11] The common error lies

---

[11] J. Bouhier in his *Dissertatio* appended to de Montfaucon's *Palaeographia Graeca* [1708]; Wesseling on Diodorus Siculus [3.67 (1793-1807)], 2:558; Swinton, Jackson,

---

[a] *Nor did historians employ that philosophical ingenuity . . .:* J. B. Merian makes a similar point: "They saw even less clearly than we, because on the one hand superstition and blind faith obstructed their vision, and on the other hand reason, good philosophy, a sophisticated [art of] criticism, and the torch of Oriental literature offer us an illumination that they lacked." Merian, "Examen de la question, si Homère a écrit ses poëmes," *Mémoires de l'Académie Royale des Sciences et belles-lettres . . . MDCCLXXXVIII et MDCCLXXXIX* (Berlin, 1793), 529.

above all in this: they think that at the time when they see that
letters are recorded as first being introduced to the Greeks—at that
very same time their use spread through all of Greek territory and
provided the opportunity for writing books. They fail to investigate
the changes and degrees by which an invention of this kind had
to be developed from its initial state.[b] Therefore, they do not even
think that they must find out if these bards—many of whom, as
Homer himself bears witness, existed long before him—wanted to
use that very useful art, if it had been discovered. This error has
been magnified by the tales of certain Greek writers ignorant about
their own ancient past. There are reports of great scrolls of poems—
indeed, if it please the Muses, of prose; likewise of laws and regulations, as if they had been written down in the earliest times.
Given the ancients' lack of critical method, even the greatest scholars readily accepted this deceit.[12] To this extent, indeed, there is

---

Bianconi, Monboddo, Astle, Larcher, others. Though this opinion was not entirely
unknown to the ancients, there is no serious and reputable author among them
who relates that the inhabitants of Greece earlier than Cadmus used letters or any
other method for depicting sounds. To explicate the individual authors and stories
forms no part of my enterprise.

[12] I refer especially to the times when Greece was free, when the condition of
studies was very different from that which followed with the rise of Alexandrian
polymathy. Those earlier men lived in the forum, not in literary retreats; they were
busy smelling out the deceptions involved in false records and forged wills, and
more or less ignored the need to deal with forged books. For in the texts of this
kind that had appeared they investigated less whether they belonged to those to
whom they were commonly ascribed than whether they offered anything useful
and worth reading. Thus Demosthenes, in his *First Oration against Aristogeiton* [11]—
if that is really by Demosthenes—could produce a sentiment ascribed to Orpheus
from a hymn that was written perhaps two centuries before his own time. Therefore
one must not attach so much weight to Cicero and others, when they name the
authors of old books, as many moderns do, except where they assert that they have
gone into the matter carefully themselves or that they are following the verdicts of
acute critics. Many of the ancients themselves, from Dionysius of Halicarnassus on,
show how frivolously the most learned men used to deal with this whole area, and
what great errors they made about the easiest problems of this kind. And the point
would be even better established if the πίνακες ["tablets," i.e., lists of authors and
works] and other critical tracts of the Alexandrians survived. Instructed by these,
the best later writers often made a habit of bringing forward doubts about the
authority of the books from which they drew quotations and evidence. But they
very rarely do so with the care that we now regard as necessary in such matters.
Some even cite simply and with no suggestion of mistrust old books whose fraud-
ulence had long ago been exposed, as their own contemporaries bear witness. Indeed, there are even those who indiscriminately cite books by the common titles
and names which they themselves elsewhere deliberately expose as vulgar errors—
sometimes in the very same works.

---

[b] *They fail to investigate the changes and degrees . . .:* Cf. the similar considerations in
ibid., 530-38.

no point among these that cannot be given some color by stabs at argument and semblances of plausibility—if, that is, you may shape the chronologies and the credibility of authors as your own pleasure and cleverness dictate. "It is extraordinary," says Pliny, "how far the credulity of the Greeks extends. There is no lie so impudent that it lacks a witness."[c]

CHAPTER XIV

History falsified in this way is not acceptable. Therefore let us ignore the Phemius of the false Herodotus,[a] the Pronapides of Diodorus and others,[b] the invented grammar-masters of Homer, with their schools and books; and let us produce the facts that induce and almost force us to believe that even if all the letters had been imported into Greece before Homer, nonetheless they were hardly used with ease before the first Olympiads [after 776 B.C.]. To make this point we will not have to linger over the hidden beginnings of the art in its rude form, which require a long argument that cannot be divorced from the letters of the Phoenicians, Egyptians, Hebrews, and Latins.[c] But both consistent report and the form of the Greek letters convincingly show that of these peoples, the first that I mentioned either discovered this device independently or so improved and spread it to other peoples, particularly the Greeks, that they could be called and considered its inventor. But the time at which those three things were done is completely uncertain because of the many ridiculous things in the stories. We would know something for certain if those ancient Phoenician writers did not have to be relegated to the Phemii and Pronapidae, or if any author made it certain when this people began to use writing and for what sorts of affairs. But there is not even a trace of this kind, and there is no mention of the Phoenicians' using their art even in commerce and trade. One who, after sharing

---

[c] "It is extraordinary," says Pliny . . .: Natural History 8.82.

[a] the Phemius of the false Herodotus: See the Vita Herodotea of Homer, δ' (p. 194.36-195.2 Allen).

[b] the Pronapides of Diodorus and others: Diodorus 3.67; cf. Tatian Oratio ad Graecos 41.

[c] To make this point . . . .: This had been the standard way to treat the origins of the Greek alphabet at least since the appearance of Joseph Scaliger's Thesaurus temporum in 1606.

my surprise at this, carefully considers the many other indications of the lateness with which writing was developed will perhaps yield at once to this opinion: whatever some say about the antiquity of the common use of writing must be taken as the Greeks' invention, and should be evaluated in terms of Greek credibility.

The Greek race always had a reprehensible desire to trace each of its most notable institutions back to the earliest times, and to attribute virtually every useful component of later culture to the discoveries of its own heroes. That has rendered unknown the first cultivators of many other arts as well as this one. For just as they attributed to Atlas, Cepheus, and many of their contemporaries knowledge of the stars, distorting ancient report,[d] so the poets seem to have attributed the praise either for discovering or for improving and adorning this splendid art in an outstanding way to a variety of men whom they had heard praised for knowledge of very useful things, or whose services to the human race they wished to extol. Thus, since they did not make distinctions between these stages of development, Aeschylus attributed the device to his Prometheus,[e] others to Cecrops, others to Orpheus, others to Linus, many to Cadmus, some to Palamedes.[13] Later historians and schoolmasters thought they could not fairly do away with these disagreements except by somehow spreading the glory among all. In this regard one point seems to me especially worthy of mention: that Euripides, by transferring the entire discovery to Palamedes, would have been mocking the common judgment of the Attic theater in an extraor-

---

[13] So Euripides in a famous fragment of the *Palamedes* [578 Nauck], in Stobaeus, *Florilegium* c. 81 [2.4.8; 2:28 Wachsmuth-Hense]. For I thought it necessary to disagree with Hemsterhusius (on Lucian, *Iudicium vocalium* 5, [ed. Leipzig 1822-31, pp. 331-33]) about the meaning of those verses and similarly about the passage in Aeschylus, *Prom.* 460. He presses the language of the poets too hard [in trying to show that they do not see Prometheus or Palamedes as inventors]. Moreover, it does not seem possible that Tacitus, in the very important passage in *Ann.* 11.14, and Hyginus [277], and Dio Chrysostom [*Orat.* 13.21], all of whom ascribe the same discovery to Palamedes, derived that from Euripides alone. I omit the two declaimers in Reiske's *Oratores Graeci* (1770-75), 8:74 and 118 [Alcidamas, Radermacher B 22.16.22 and Gorgias, 82 B 11a.30 Diels-Kranz = Radermacher B 7.44.30], although they followed ancient reports in their arguments. All of them consider Palamedes the originator not of some few letters but of the whole invention.

---

[d] *For just as they attributed to Atlas . . .:* Such accounts were still treated as historical in the early eighteenth century; see Frank Manuel, *Isaac Newton, Historian* (Cambridge, Mass., 1963).

[e] *Aeschylus: Prometheus Bound* 459-61.

dinary way, if certain knowledge had then been available about the older development of the art and the gift of Cadmus. Euripides could not have been the first to do that; nor did tragedians invent in such a way. But if we are justified in relegating those forgotten stories to their authors the poets, will it be any part of an accurate judgment to award ready belief to one of them, drawn from the same sources, simply because it is more famous than the rest?

But the gift of Cadmus has a great witness: Herodotus. I see this; and I shall add another no less weighty, and certainly a little older. And I do not therefore cease to wonder whether the story or rumor itself has much authority. For I think it rash, when authors disagree so acutely, to agree with one or a few—especially in the case of a thing which, since it was commonly and rightly attributed to the Phoenicians, could very easily have drawn its name from the Phoenician founder of a very famous colony in Greece. The other of those authors, in fact, is Dionysius of Miletus, a recorder of mythical history.[14] I do not produce that fact because I look down on him on account of his subject matter; nor do I look down so much on the poets, on whom he entirely depends. But I do not understand why we—who are seeking the truth, not "Phoenician falsehoods"[15]—must consider him a more reliable witness in this regard than in the other things which he recounted. But Diodorus preserved this passage of his for us; we read Herodotus in full. And in fact this equally zealous lover of truth and eager teller of falsehoods follows his custom here too, when he indicates that he is offering, not something which is certain and commonly believed, but some sort of report which he accepts.[16] He could not have been

---

[14] In the great work Κύκλος ["Cycle"], passages from which are often cited by the grammarians. The one that we use here is from Diodorus Siculus 3.66-67.

[15] This is a proverbial description in Eustathius 1757.61 on *Od.* 14.289, for things that are surprising and unbelievable.

[16] 5.58: "The Phoenicians who arrived with Cadmus ... settling into this area, introduced many other arts to the Greeks, and in particular letters, *which the Greeks had not had before in my view*, etc." These words reveal that Herodotus was adjudicating between those who thought the device older than Cadmus and those who thought he had introduced it. But Larcher takes Herodotus to be following the latter opinion. He thinks that the omission of the article before "letters" means that he is reporting that Cadmus introduced only some of the letters. I wish that diligent man had not said this. For that omission is proper, given the sense that we follow; only the addition of the article would produce the one that Larcher prefers. I say nothing as to the great confusion that would ensue in the rest of the passage if it had to do with only a few letters. Most later writers have approved of Herodotus' views. Since their arguments are unknown there is no point in piling up names and passages. And

more candid; nor should it be thought that the fault of those who accepted this sort of rumor as certainty is identical to that of the historian himself, if his reasoning was perhaps incorrect, as happened to him both in other cases and with regard to his famous opinion about Homer and Hesiod, the first creators of the Greek theogony.[17] Therefore, Herodotus himself takes care that no one may be able to take a mythical event as established. I could make the point at greater length, producing similar examples of myths, in order to maintain that the famous name of Cadmus was irresponsibly transferred to a Phoenician discovery. But what has this to do with our inquiry? We grant that the barbarians of Boeotia had enough capacity for learning and free time that Cadmus could introduce letters, that he could reveal the marvelous art to them;[f] though Amphion, a whole century later, who is said to have moved stones by song to build the Theban citadel, could more easily have ordered the citizens to bring stones by an edict.[g] But even if a few men had already made experiments in writing for a few, or had already inscribed metals, which had just recently begun to be smelted, with short verses and epigrams, everyone can see without our instruction the vast distance between this crude sort of work and a fluent ability to use the art.

I am more surprised at Herodotus because he thrusts back to the vicinity of Cadmus' time the three epigrams that he copied out

---

almost all belong to a later period. Of the lost early ones, if we only had the historical digression that Ephorus wrote on exactly this point, the one which Clement of Alexandria uses as an authority in praising Cadmus, in *Stromata* 1.16.75.1 [2:48.10 Stählin], we could perhaps refute many more inventions. But I fear it is rash to join with Herodotus those writers who relate that the art had a Phoenician origin but not that Cadmus introduced it. Unless I am wrong, the passage from Sophocles' *Pastores* [514 Radt = 471 Nauck], mentioned by Hesychius s.v. Φοινικίοις, belonged to this class. And [Hesychius] soon after has this: "The Lydians and Ionians [took] letters from a certain Phoenician."

[17] 2.53. Wesseling wrongly takes the words "These are the ones who made a theogony for the Greeks" in the sense that they are described as the first two *to have expounded* the theogony *in verse*, not *to have founded it*. Clearly ποιεῖν [make] does occur in that sense. But the addition of a dative to the verb used in that sense would need illustration from examples, of a kind completely unknown to me. Athenagoras also agrees with the common view in *Apologia pro Christianis* 17, citing that passage and twisting it to agree with his opinion.

---

[f] *We grant that the barbarians . . .*: The Boeotians were proverbial in antiquity for their uncouthness and stupidity; see Pindar *Olympian* 6.90, "Boeotian swine," and the scholia on that passage (6.153a, c in Drachmann's numeration).

[g] *Amphion, a whole century later . . .* : Amphion and Zethus, the sons of Zeus and Antiope, were the mythical builders of the walls of Thebes.

in the same passage from the dedications of the Ismenian Apollo at Thebes,[18] and makes them three or four centuries older than Homer. He had heard this account, I think, from those who showed him the epigrams. He reports, as usual, what he had heard; and the unusual shape of the characters had convinced him, nor were minds then trained by judging things of this kind. But I cannot marvel enough at the fact that even today that deceit has aroused no suspicion in any of those accustomed to distinguishing the language of each period with subtle skill. Grant me, please, your close attention to the sound of those verses, and compare it with Homer; either you will find nothing spurious in the *Orphica*, or you will admit that they were made in imitation of the Homeric—that is, cultivated Ionic—language, and are very far from being as old as is claimed. I am unmoved by the fact that nothing extant is old enough to clear the matter up by comparison. For who, seeing for the first time a man who is grown up and of full size, would want to ask him what measurements he had when he was in the cradle? Therefore I not only do not criticize the forgetfulness or ignorance of those writers who passed in silence over these remarkable monuments of writing, as G. J. Vossius does,[19] but am led by this fact to wonder if Herodotus proved his opinion to the critics of his nation. And I think that the same conclusion must be drawn about the other inscriptions which some produce from the same temple.[20]

---

[18] I shall add them [from Herodotus 5.59-61] so that this page may make my meaning clear:

I.   Ἀμφιτρύων μ᾽ ἀνέθηκεν, ἰὼν ἀπὸ Τηλεβοάων.
     [Amphitryon dedicated me, coming from the Teleboans.]

II. Σκαῖος πυγμαχέων με ἐκηβόλῳ Ἀπόλλωνι
     νικήσας ἀνέθηκε τεῒν περικαλλὲς ἄγαλμα.
     [Scaeus the winning boxer dedicated me to you,
     far-shooting Apollo, as a splendid ornament.]

III. Λαοδάμας τρίποδ᾽ αὐτὸν ἐυσκόπῳ Ἀπόλλωνι
     μουναρχέων ἀνέθηκε τεῒν περικαλλὲς ἄγαλμα.
     [Laodamas the ruler dedicated this very tripod
     to you, sharp-shooting Apollo, as a splendid ornament.]

In the first verse I have agreed with some others in replacing the vulgate ἐών with ἰών, that is ἀνιών. Other conjectures are hardly appropriate—least of all the one made recently by several, after Bentley, ἀνέθηκε νέων. It would first be necessary to cite authors who use this active form [of the normally deponent verb νέομαι, "go"] other than some grammarians and the corrupt line 395 of the Homeric *Hymn to Demeter*.

[19] [*Aristarchus, sive*] *De arte grammatica* [2d ed., 1662] 1.10, p. 50.

[20] For example, Pausanias 9.11.1. The form ἑαυτῷ is enough by itself to reveal the modernity of those verses. And the epigram in Aristotle *Mirab. ausc.* 133 is no

82   PROLEGOMENA TO HOMER

Therefore, the only proper conclusion, in my view, that can be drawn from Herodotus is that the art of writing was known and practiced long enough before him that it could be attributed to the earliest times. You may think that this is enough to destroy Wood's view. For if it had begun to be practiced so few years before Herodotus, that most historical of writers would not have reached the judgment that he does. But I fear that the very familiar story of Cadmus must be referred to the time of the discovery rather than to the period in which knowledge of it reached the Greeks. For a vague report of such a discovery doubtless preceded exact knowledge among them; this was followed, after a long interval, by imitations by unpracticed hands, and these, finally, by common use and the writing of books.

CHAPTER XV

Here I do not doubt that many will suspect that those names conceal indications of advances of this kind, and that so many inventors of the art are not praised for no reason. And there was a time when I too accepted this argument, and did not dare to deprive the times of Orpheus of inscriptions and epigrams, at least. I was bothered by—among other reasons—certain monuments of writing older than Homer, which either are said to have existed once or are eagerly defended by scholars today.[21] But many historical traces diverted me from that path, along with a diligent and subtle judgment on the material culture of those times and on the monuments themselves. Therefore I stick to my opinion: I think that even if all those things preceded Homer in time (for I prefer to leave that point uncertain for the present rather than to digress from my

---

more ancient. Let others see if one must reach another conclusion about the inscriptions from other temples that the ancients continually report as from the farthest antiquity. I at least think that this whole area was the first one where holy deceit created havoc.

[21] As to the latter it will be sufficient to mention a single famous inscription, one of the Amyclaean ones discovered by Michel Fourmont [for whose forgeries see Sandys 2.390; 3.99, n.2]; as to the former, the stone stele of Theseus in Demosthenes *Contra Neaeram* 76; the votive offering of Cadmus himself in Diodorus 5.58; the brazen tablet in Pliny 7.58.210, etc., etc.

main path), nevertheless nothing is thereby established about the common use of the art. For a great effort had to be made before foreign characters could be adapted to native sounds and new characters furnished for the vowels and the letters that the Phoenician script had lacked. And only when this task was completed could the device finally be applied to inscriptions on stones and similar materials. But nonetheless, even if those preparations were sufficiently complete in the age of the *Iliad*, a long journey, and one made harder by many obstacles, had to be completed before that people, in a more learned phase of its history, could apply an art fitted out with manageable instruments, first to the writing of short pages and then to that of complete books.

I have summarized in a few words things which—as the times then were—several centuries could not, perhaps, have brought into effect. For a long time the simple life of those men contained nothing that could seem worthy of written record. Occupied in everything else, they did the things that their descendants write about—or, as we have heard about some peoples, they despised this craft, even when it had been displayed to them, as something that belonged to an unfitting idleness. But by long practice they became used to both passing on and receiving the poems they composed orally. Hence to reduce to mute characters poems that flourished mightily in song and recitation would have seemed, to the sensibility of the time, to be nothing less than to destroy them and to deprive them of their vital force and spirit. I shall discuss this point below when I explain the function of the rhapsodes. Now we turn our attention to the obstacles which an age not very adept at crafts must necessarily have set in the way of such a device, in itself not very accessible to the senses, so that it could not be quickly transformed from its rude beginnings to ready ease. And indeed, it is a great effort in itself to describe in detail the quantity and duration of the problems in this area that were caused by lack of tools. But I shall not entirely shirk that effort, for the sake of those who are so used to the ease of their pens and paper that they will think I am immoderately overstating the difficulties of this kind.

Let them, then, look over with me the things which, as ancient writers record, wretchedly held back the writing of the Greeks until about the sixth century before Christ, when *biblus* or papyrus first brought greater ease.[22a] But we abandon leaves and tree bark to the Sibyls, and to the fabulous Dares and to lovers, even though a trace of that custom may seem to persist in condemnation by leaves and in the Syracusan petalism.[b] Nor indeed did anyone teach that writing began at some point to be done on potsherds, simply because some forms of balloting were carried out with them at Athens. But there is no doubt at all that the first attempts were made on stones, on pieces of wood, and plates of metal. Certainly we believe the excellent authors who say that Solon and others inscribed laws on wooden tablets and boards. But let no one rashly believe that the Greeks consigned any writing that was not public to this substance—except those whom the Boeotians have persuaded about their leaden exemplar of the *Works and Days* of Hesiod, which Pausanias saw next to the spring on Helicon but apparently could not read because age had corrupted it in many places.[23] But as public monuments were recorded on wood and metals, so it would be quite credible that both kinds—especially private ones—were recorded on cloths, if only this sort of book had been normally used by the Greeks at any time. Since that is not the case, and that sort [of book] is ascribed to the Romans alone[24]—unless someone

[22] Many have already seen the falsity of the common opinion, which derives from M. Varro in Pliny 13.21.70, that papyrus was invented at Alexandria. To be sure Varro seems to refer to some more convenient way of making papyrus paper, of the sort used in his time. A point somewhat like this will be made a little later about parchment. On the other hand, the arguments by which Melchior Guilandinus ascribes the use of papyrus for writing to the time of the bards, in his *Commentarius in 3 Plinii capita de papyro* [1572] Membrum 2, pp. 17ff., are worthless. But we do find testimonies from the fifth century B.C. in the comic poets Cratinus and Plato, cited in Pollux at the end of bk. 7 [210-11], and in Herodotus, loc. cit. The first of these used βιβλιογράφος, the second χάρται, the third, less ambiguously, βίβλοι and, in other passages, βιβλία. And by that he gives sufficient indication that the use of papyrus was not new in his time.

[23] 9.31.4.

[24] This is how to interpret Pliny, loc. cit., which we have used in all our arguments about the instruments employed in ancient writing. It is pointless to summon as witnesses the other passages about [writing] and the individual books of scholars.

---

[a] *when* biblus *or* papyrus *first brought greater ease:* On the development of papyrus as a writing material (and the passage from book 13 of Pliny's *Natural History* which is Wolf's [and our] main source) see N. Lewis, *Papyrus in Classical Antiquity* (Oxford, 1974). For discussion of the passage before Wolf, see A. Grafton, "Rhetoric, Philology and Egyptomania in the 1570s . . . ," *Journal of the Warburg and Courtauld Institutes* 42 (1979), 167-94.

[b] *In condemnation by leaves and in the Syracusan petalism:* For the Athenian practice of condemnation by leaves see the scholium on Aeschines 1.111; for Syracusan petalism and Athenian ostracism see Diodorus 11.87.

wishes to offer Moses a supply of it so that he may compose the
Pentateuch[25]—we may not make up even a cloth *Iliad*. Therefore,
it is clear that the art remained rather crude and its use very uncommon until it was noticed that it could be practiced on sheep-
or goat-skins. But Herodotus records in the rich passage I have
mentioned several times that the Ionians invented that; and that
could have been the only device older than papyrus that offered
a convenient means for writing books. To be sure, the same author
mentions waxed tablets[26]—but scrolls and books certainly could not
have been composed of these.

CHAPTER XVI

But if in fact Ionia had begun to scrape skins and prepare them
for writing long before parchment was made, and the same people
that first refined poems produced a handier material for writing,
why are we trying to find out what sort of thing the Ionian bard
used for setting down his poems? Clearly [he used]

Οἰῶν πώεα καλὰ καὶ αἰπόλια πλατέ᾽ αἰγῶν
["Fair flocks of sheep and wide-ranging flocks of goats"].[a]

We would only wish that Herodotus had added the time at which
that Ionian custom began to be commonly practiced, though it
apparently was not very commonly practiced if indeed it yielded
readily to papyrus paper. And in fact—if only the other considerations allow—we will not interpret that in too farfetched a way
if we believe that this use of skins was introduced around the epoch
of the Olympiads [776 B.C.], and derived from the Orientals, among
whom, like certain other barbarian nations, it flourished mightily

---

[25] See above all Eichhorn, *Einleitung in das Alte Testament* [1787], 1:136 [#63],
2:213 [#405].
[26] At the end of bk. 7, in the history of Demaratus, king of the Spartans [239].
But he does not produce it there as something novel. And Hemsterhusius cleverly
guessed that the Cyprians used wax on skins, on Pollux 10 [1706], 1214.

---

[a] *"Fair flocks of sheep and wide-ranging flocks of goats"*: The first of these two phrases
closes *Od.* 11.402, 12.129, 24.112; the second appears in *Od.* 14.101 and 103. But
they never occur in the same line. Given that *Od.* 14.101 and 103 follow closely
after the phrase "so many flocks of sheep" (14.100 ad fin.), it would seem that Wolf
was quoting from memory and produced this conflation accidentally.

and survived for a long time. But even if you accept this, as the accumulated other considerations will force you to, nevertheless the very number of the letters shows that the device had not become handy and common even then. We waste no more time on the eleven or sixteen letters of Cadmus or the three or four of Palamedes, or any other inconsistencies in the historical interpretation of ancient myth-making. A more certain account attributed a rather prominent part in filling out the letters and devising new ones to Simonides of Ceos and Epicharmus of Sicily, the originator of ancient comedy, as late as the sixth and fifth centuries B.C.[27] It is reported that Ionian Samos then made public use of these letters, when set into a proper series with the rest by one Callistratus, before others did.[28] And several attest, and from reliable witnesses, that this Ionic alphabet of twenty-four letters was adopted by the Athenian people only under the archonship of Euclides, in Ol. 94.2, 403 B.C., and that before this time the use of the two long vowels was not common there.[29]

[27] See Hyginus *Fab.* 277; Pliny 7.56.192; Tzetzes *Chil.* 12.398 [50ff.]; the scholia in Villoison's *Anecdota Graeca* [1781] 2:187. Compare E. Spanheim *De Praestantia et Usu Nummorum Antiquorum Dissertatio* 2 [*Dissertationes* (1717), vol. 1)], 84-85; Goens on Simonides 4.1; A. Mongitor, *Bibliotheca Sicula* [1707], 1:181.

[28] Relevant to that was the bon mot of Aristophanes in the *Babylonians*, a play performed around 427 B.C., Ol. 88. See Suidas s.v. Σαμίων ὁ δῆμος [Σ 77]; cf. s.v. Ἀττικισμός [A 4360]; the Venetian B scholia to *Il.* 7.185; Tzetzes *Chil.* 12.398, 50ff. When the latter calls Callistratus a grammarian, that very stupid man is following the custom of the scholars of those days when they wished to praise those of older times as they deserved. More important is the fact that Spanheim (loc. cit.) revealed from that scholium, which was then unpublished: that the work of Callistratus was handed down by the authority of Ephorus. I suspect, moreover, that in the last part of his history, when this writer had come to the revision of the Attic laws made after the expulsion of the Thirty, he treated this entire matter at length, and that the passage from Clement in n. 16 above was excerpted precisely from there.

[29] Namely from Ephorus, Theopompus, Andron of Ephesus, perhaps many others. In place of these we must visit some muddy streams: Eusebius *Chronographia*, on Ol. 94.4; Cedrenus and the *Paschal Chronicle* on 96.4, with the scholia to Euripides *Phoenissae* 682, where an old variant is recorded based on the early style of writing, σῷ νιν ἐκγόνῳ and σοί νιν ἔκγονοι. There see Valckenaer [*Euripidis Phoenissae*, 1755] on line 688; G. J. Vossius, *De Arte Grammatica* 1.30 [above, ch. 14, n. 19], p. 113; C. Salmasius, *Add. ad Inscriptiones Herodis Attici* [1619], 232; J. Bouhier [above, ch. 13, n. 11], *Dissertatio* §66; P. Wesseling on S. Petit's *Leges Atticae*, 194 [in *Jurisprudentia Romana et Attica* . . . (1738-41), vol. 3]; E. Corsini, *Fasti Attici* [1751], 3:276. The passage of Syrianus on Hermogenes [*Staseis* (Venice, 1509) pt. 2] p. 17 quoted by this last [p. 277A] has an obscure reference of a sort that one would not expect at all from such compilers. It is enough that they all agree on the main point. But this reveals what it was that the Athenians called "the alphabet after Eucleides." The letters that had been used before were called "the old alphabet" or "Attic letters." True, the opinions of scholars about these differ; see the commentators on Harpocration, s.vv. Ἀττικοῖς γράμμασι [p. 65.7 Dindorf], etc.

The writing of the Greeks, then, reached completion and was reduced to order at a very late date: first, as I suspect for many reasons, in the city-states that held Sicily and Magna Graecia, then in Athens, that city later so fertile in letters. But we must again take care not to believe that the use of writing was so late or that it was established in all of Greece at that same time. In light of the fact that the Ionians gave their European kindred an example of more refined culture, both humane and civil, in so many things, and that they were proficient at an early date in various forms of art and commerce, it would be probable, even in the absence of historical testimony, that they were the first to perceive the utility of this outstanding device as well, and to have expended effort and ingenuity on it. Clearly, they did not have to await Callistratus of Samos in order to try to put something in writing; they used papyrus well before him. Indeed, before Simonides and Epicharmus there were lyric poets, both Ionian and Aeolic, who could scarcely do without that aid for making poems. Finally, in that city which held on to the old alphabet for the longest time,[b] in Ol. 39 [624-620 B.C.] a smaller number of letters was enough for the establishment of Dracon's laws. Indeed, would not the same number have been enough for great scrolls, if only the latter had been in normal use then, whether they consisted of skins or of Egyptian papyrus? And some years before Dracon's magistracy, thanks to Psammetichus, Egypt had been laid open to Ionian trade, so that they could have had a supply of papyrus. To give this conjecture historical credibility, Herodotus would have needed so few words, if he had not written for Greeks alone! Now the obscurity of two centuries, the eighth and seventh before Christ, is especially irksome. During them the nation blew into a fine blaze the sparks of that most refined humanity which it had previously received, and made wonderful progress toward complete excellence in the arts. The seeds of a good many practices were sown in those obscure times. And we can make a responsible conjecture and infer from some of the historical evidence that it was in those centuries just after the Lacedaemonian Lycurgus that the art of writing first found significant use in public and spread beyond inscriptions, with the result that we may more easily forego explicit testimonies.

[b] *in that city . . .:* Athens.

CHAPTER XVII

But these very pieces of historical evidence reveal that a far longer interval than anyone now thinks lay between these beginnings of the public use of writing and the time when writing and making books became common customs. In this connection, it is first of all vitally important that there is no record of any literary monument of that kind in the time of Lycurgus or immediately afterward, not a letter, not a poem, not a book of any kind, of which a copy or certain knowledge of a copy reached later ages. Unless, perhaps, we wish to heed the stories that I discussed in chapter 13 above and the writers who invent things ancient as their own customs and whims suggest; some among them cut their throats with their own sword.[30] But why look for private writing at a time when, amid zealous efforts to impose order on the city-states, even the laws were clearly not promulgated in written form? I refer to all the nations of Greece; I do not except the Ionians. For them I think I can accept as an authority the silence of those who often give precise lists of the ancient lawgivers, admitting to their ranks all to whom the honor of this appellation was attributed in any way. Certainly if those many Greek and Roman writers had seen written laws ascribed to the Ionians or the Aeolians in the once-famous books and collections of Aristotle and Theophrastus,[31] laws enacted before Pittacus in Ol. 48 [588-584 B.C.], no competent student of antiquity can think that they would have passed over them with such consistency, or failed to enlarge their list with a new name. From this it is clear that all those things which then took the place of laws, whether they were called νόμοι or θεσμοί or ῥῆτραι, were

[30] So Gorgias speaking as Palamedes [82 B 11a Diels-Kranz = B 7.44 Radermacher], who ascribes to him the invention of "the alphabet, the instrument of memory" [§ 30], mentions the use of correspondence as something very common in Palamedes' time [§ 6]. He is also deceitful when he denies in the same passage that a Greek could converse with a Trojan without an interpreter [§ 7]. If anyone finds such rubbish acceptable, I shall show him Ovid, the author of the *Epistolae Heroidum*, and many other, greater supporters, none of whom is so distinguished as that Mutianus, thrice consul, who had read in Lycia, to Pliny's amazement (13.27.88), a letter written from Troy by Sarpedon.

[31] See Fabricius, *Bibliotheca Graeca* bk. 3, [1793], 398 and 452. I omit the similar works of others on the Greek laws and those who proposed them, such as those of Callimachus, Heraclides Ponticus, Hermippus, etc., which were less frequently read.

published in Ionia and in nearby Greece no differently than they were among the Agathyrsi in the time of Aristotle, and previously among the Cretans and Lacedaemonians, who, it is known, also employed song and musical modes for this task. *The first of all the Greeks* to accept written laws were the *Locri Epizephyrii*, from *Zaleucus*,[32] whose prime Eusebius places in Ol. 29, 664 B.C., seventy years before Solon.

But only a faint report survives about the laws of Zaleucus, one corrupted by speech makers, and hence there is much that we do not know, including the sort of writing and the instruments by which they were set down. But what the Athenians' writing was like in the time of Solon—that is, their public writing to be sure— is shown by his laws, carved *boustrophēdon* on rough materials in Ol. 46.3, 594 B.C. That their private writing was more convenient at that time seems unlikely, for the same reasons for which Bentley denied that the *fabulae plaustrariae* of Susarion and Thespis (Ol. 50-61) were published in writing,[33] with no scholar opposing him. Certainly there is no mention or indication of Attic writers before

[32] Though there are only two suitable extant witnesses to this report (Scymnus *Periegesis* 312-15; Strabo 6.259-60), it is nonetheless clear from their words that it was established with complete unanimity of old. Thus Cicero seems to have read precisely that in the books that he mentions, *Att.* 6.1.18. The weight of this authority is greatly increased by the disease common among the Greeks, which I censured just above in Gorgias, and often elsewhere. For everyone who had ever been known for making laws normally received the same respect from them. Even myths—Ceres "the law-giver," Triptolemus, Cecrops—were not scorned. Elsewhere in this area, after the custom of early times, things that did not belong to one period or that had been changed and amended in various ways by the efforts of several were heaped at the doors of individuals. Was this not done in the case of Minos the Cretan, that of Lycurgus, similarly that of Moses? But all of them were commonly believed to have written, and the myths did not yield to the brighter light of history. Thus Clement, in *Stromata* 1.16.79.4 [2:51.22 Stählin], juxtaposes *Zaleucus, the first legislator* (for this is how he rightly describes the first man to write laws down; the earlier ones were rather educators and leaders to their fellow citizens), with Minos, in such a way that the latter is to be regarded as having done the same thing seven centuries earlier. And Clement's source was not obscure. For the Platonic Dialogue [*Minos*], 320C, explicitly ascribes to Minos "laws written on brazen tablets." This passage has somehow deceived even the best scholars of our time, although another one very like it in the same work has influenced no one. According to the same witness, tragedy should be dragged back from the period of Thespis and Phrynichus to that of Minos, and one should mock all those who made Homer much older than tragedy [320E-321A]. But the learned grammarian Apollodorus testifies, in *Bibliotheca* 3.1.2 that Minos "wrote laws." In fact he writes this, he does not give explicit testimony. Perhaps he did not even believe it. Many use this expression even for Lycurgus, who, as all antiquity cries out, left nothing in writing.

[33] In his *Apology* for the *Dissertation upon the Epistles of Phalaris*, 109ff. in Lennep's [Latin] translation. [*Works*, ed. A. Dyce (1836), 1:251ff.]

the time of the Persians,[34] the credibility of which is not weakened by the general condition of the period and the polity and by the silence of the most reliable authors. But I shall not pursue what I cannot establish without long digressions; I would even willingly admit that this art gradually began to be employed in private use at Athens somewhat before Solon; nor do I doubt that some clever men did that in other cities, specifically those of Ionia and Magna Graecia, in the eighth and seventh centuries, and that some poets either followed their example or initiated the practice on their own—if not Asius, Eumelus, Arctinus, and the others famous in the first Olympiads for epic poems, at least, surely, Archilochus, Alcman, Pisander, Arion, and their contemporaries. But if it is a question of *all Greece* and the rather more common use of the art *and the custom of writing books*, these are not to be removed from the period of Thales, Solon, Pisistratus, and those who are called the Sages—that is, that in which the language came to be freed from meter. This is shown us by the history of all the Greek arts, so that we seem to have no need at all for the testimony of that people, which forgot its own infancy.

I have nothing to say here about the cultivation of prose begun by Solon himself and many others at the beginning of the sixth century B.C., and about the causes for the new enterprise; and everything that can be drawn from passages in the ancients has been said; but I shall bring forward one point, which, although it rests on a conjecture, is nonetheless very useful for this question of ours, unless I am completely deceived. For it seems clearly necessary that at the time when the Greeks seized the impulse to tear away the chains of meter and create prose, the art of writing was sufficiently manageable, and a supply of instruments was ready which they could use for it without serious difficulty. This is not because I think that this supply had some power to create a new way of expressing thoughts—as some scholars, since they were sur-

34 Like the comic poets Chionides and Magnes, like the philosopher Anaxagoras, who moved to Athens at the age of twenty in Ol. 75.1 [480 B.C.]; Diogenes Laertius 2.7. Aristotle mentions the former of those poets as the first of the Attic writers of comedy. Suidas, with Eudocia, observed on the basis of ancient chronographers that he produced plays eight years before Xerxes. Hence Joseph Scaliger did well to enter him at Ol. 73 [488-484 B.C.] in his *Olympiad List* [*Thesaurus Temporum*, 2d ed. (1658) 2:318]. But the comedy of the Sicilian Greeks—which was set down in writing by Epicharmus even before the tyranny of Gelon, if I interpret the hints of the ancients correctly—preceded both of them by several years.

prised that poetry came into being so early and did not see the reason why it happened in that way, produced this as the principal cause of the thing: that the unlettered people shrewdly saw that the metrical arrangement of verses would be a splendid aid to their memorization.[a] But nonetheless, I do not understand how on earth it could occur to anyone to compose something in prose, unless he had available some storehouse for his composition other than his own memory. For the memory is overwhelmed and the mind wanders and goes astray in this free series of words, which is not bound by any fixed meter, not set off, as it were, by any limits in which the speech must round itself off completely. But the Homeric diction is very distant from the stridency of the rough tropes and images of primitive peoples, and it is quite pure in words and phrases. In its even and modest tenor it announces in advance, so to speak, the prose diction that will follow after it—which, however, we find that no one attempted for more than three centuries. Hence I tend to think that it was not the level of mental cultivation but certain other factors, and especially the difficulty of writing, that hindered prose from following poetic eloquence as quickly as nature would allow.

Therefore to attempt writing and to fit it to common use seem clearly to have been one and the same thing as to attempt prose and to set oneself to refine it. For it was not first created then; it lacked only cultivation and a certain symmetry, which could go no further in wood, metals, or stones than in familiar conversation, in letters, or in speeches. This, I believe, also enables me to show very elegantly why none of the ancients includes among the writers of prose those who had not yet used a portable material for writing— for example, Solon in his laws. Much less could Hipparchus have been admitted into their number because of the brief *sententiae* and moral precepts that he had carved on public monuments some seventy years after Solon.[35] Now if only those who set out to create

[35] The Ἱππάρχειοι Ἑρμαῖ were known previously from the comic poets, and now above all from the author of the Platonic Dialogue entitled *Hipparchus* [228-29]. See the further material in Meursius' *Atticae Lectiones* [1617], 5.7 [p. 257] and

[a] *This is not because I think . . . .:* This may be directed against Eichhorn, who had argued that writing was necessary to explain how "the old lofty language of poetry had subsided to nearly the level of prose, and become fettered by grammatical rules" (*Einleitung*, ch. 10; tr. G. T. Gollop [London, 1888], 41).

proper books are brought forward as the authors of the new way
of writing—like Cadmus of Miletus, Pherecydes of Syros, and
others, the contemporaries of Pisistratus (for all ancient report
clearly agrees on this)—then that serves as a powerful argument
that *the making of books*, among both the Ionians and the rest of the
Greeks, was not earlier than this very period.

CHAPTER XVIII

Up to now we have tried to test how much progress we could make
in this controversy by employing the testimonies of all of history,
not the authority of Homer and of his ancient commentators. Come
now, let us turn our attention to what these provide, setting aside
as is proper those who, careless of antiquity, speak of the works of
Homer, Hesiod, and their contemporaries as though these were
just any books in their library, or use the word "writing" through
a vulgar stylistic error, not a mental judgment. Thus I myself—I
who argue that those singers were not writers but singers—have
allowed that verb to escape me now and then without resistance,
lest the unusual repetition of another one several times prove offensive. This same explanation must cover a good many passages
in the ancients, like those which contain a reference to writing in
the laws of Lycurgus; no scholar has believed that these were first
promulgated in writing in ancient times. I would assign to the same
category the well-known passage in Apollodorus, in which he uses
the noun ἐπιστολή ["letter"] with regard to the murderous commands of Proetus in *Il.* 6.168—especially since reference to an
outworn custom would not have been appropriate there, and I
would deny that Apollodorus' opinion about this matter should be
sought in that passage, if the words themselves were not completely
inconsistent with the meaning of a proper letter.[36]

Pisistratus [1623, ch.] 12 [pp. 85-87]. But one must not infer from these inscriptions
that everyone in Athens knew how to read then. Even somewhat later that was
restricted to a few of the brave Cecropidae. Nonetheless that custom could have
enticed them to learn; I think it was no worse than our alphabet books.

[36] 2.3.1: "Proetus gave him a letter [ἐπιστολάς] to convey to Iobates, in which it
was written [ἐνεγέγραπτο] that he should kill Bellerophon. But Iobates, having
recognized [ἐπιγνούς] it, ordered etc. . . ." The two words in this passage that seem
to pertain to the writing of letters are, I maintain, such that if they are taken as
referring to notes or symbols, they are perfect, and have been used with care. For
ἐγγράφειν is both of uncertain force in itself and is the very verb that one finds in

To what, then, do those words apply? To what the most learned grammarians of Alexandria, as will at once be clear, more or less agreed on. What I am going to say will cause wonder; and I myself have often wondered at it, given the widespread lack of historical sense in antiquity. There was no learned Homeric commentator in Greece who thought that what is properly called the art of writing was mentioned in these verses or anywhere else in Homer's poems. If someone finds this a rash statement, let him please disabuse me of this error by some authority other than that of a certain recent scholiast, which I shall set forth at length in its place. From Eustathius and the older sources he will not be able to do it. Therefore, if any of the ancients whose materials Eustathius compiled for his own commentary had anywhere produced a contrary argument, how could it be that a man more expert in ancient words than customs—and who, perhaps, did not even retain his own sermons by memory alone—nowhere babbled about it in his extremely long commentary, and nowhere assigned the use of writing to the poet's heroes? For one cannot count the passage in which he feigns that the Pelasgi preserved the knowledge of letters from the flood—even though some antiquarians value it highly.[37] This is an inven-

---

the poet. Replace it with ἐγγλύφειν [carve], ἐγκολάπτειν [cut], ἐγχαράσσειν [engrave]; you will feel that the effort to change it is misguided. But he changed Homer's πίναξ [tablet] to ἐπιστολή [letter]. This too is fine, and so appropriate to a symbol of any kind that if he intended to describe the thing in general terms, not the manner of the thing and the obsolete custom, the Greek language had nothing more appropriate. For it is certain that the primary signification of ἐπιστολή is ἐντολή, command. From this also come the λόγων ἐπιστολαί in Sophocles [Tr. 493]. Cf. the commentators on Hesychius, 1:1390 [ed. Alberti, (1746), s.v. ἐπιστολαί]. But more relevant to this is the point made by Eustathius, p. 632.9 on 6.169, which will be more clearly understood later, that Homer's πίναξ is "what later men called ἐπιστολή." But the verb ἐπιγνῶναι, recognize—not read, which is ἀναγνῶναι, never the other—removes all doubt. Those who take it in a different sense will have to show us that the Greeks commonly used it in regard to a letter; and in order that they may show us quickly, we do not even exclude the times of Planudes and Eustathius. Otherwise they will have to concede to us that there was hardly any other, more expressive idiom for the mythographer to use if he wanted, as he normally does, to describe the thing itself briefly and in a prosaic style, not to play the antiquary in an inappropriate place.

37 On Il. 2.841, p. 358.6. Homer calls the Pelasgi δῖοι because of this great service of theirs. Is it not astonishing that Eustathius ignores this remarkable fiction at 10.429 and Od. 19.177? Or was it perhaps not in his scholia? Certainly ours do not offer it; nor does Diodorus Siculus 5.57, where he makes up similar stories about the monuments with inscriptions that were destroyed in the Flood. I pass over another point of a similar kind in this passage in Eustathius. The learned, who are well acquainted with him, will notice it even if their attention is not drawn to it. The others would simply believe it or, if they are less credulous by nature, would ascribe it to my partiality. I do not wish to undergo either danger here.

tion of historians making up old wives' tales, a twin to the one about Noah—the sort of thing that that age freely embraced. But we seek in Eustathius not the opinions of Eustathius but those of earlier grammarians, whose scholia he had before his eyes. And we will see a little later that he reports everything else from these scholia, both in general and above all on those verses where he treats a subject not in passing.

But so far as I can determine, neither Eustathius nor any of the scholiasts tries to learn whether Homer himself knew the art that was unknown to his heroes; thus they neither affirm nor deny the matter categorically. And how much weight would we attach to their words, should they be convicted of falsehood by events that not even the greatest antiquity concealed? No need of long discussions. This question doubtless exercised the Alexandrian critics as well. And if there is any authority that we can set—given this great loss of ancient books—against the ambiguous silence of our scholia, it derives precisely from their disputations. This is how one must take the remarkable passage in Josephus, where he clearly says, "It is said that Homer did not use writing in composing poems, and that they were first revealed to the public and spread by memory; afterward, being consigned to writing, they took on this form and tenor."[38] This is the only clear, authoritative testimony about

---

[38] *Against Apion* 1.2: "The Greeks learned the nature of letters late and with difficulty. For those who assign the earliest date for their use are proud of the fact that they learned them from the Phoenicians and Cadmus. It would not be possible to show any record that has been preserved from that time, either in temples or on public dedications." (G. J. Vossius finds this astonishing because of the noble epigrams in Herodotus. Those who have accepted what I wrote above [ch. 14] will now feel differently. Doubtless Josephus did not consider it worthwhile to waste time on refuting those stories and the like. And many others had done this before him, as this very passage shows. Now pay close attention to what he adds:) "Seeing that it later was considered a very difficult and controversial question, whether those who fought for so many years at Troy used letters. And the true position prevails, which is rather that they were not acquainted with the present way of using letters. In general, no commonly recognized writing is found among the Greeks older than the poetry of Homer. But he too seems to have been later than the Trojan War, and they say that not even he left his poetry in writing, but it was preserved by memory and assembled later from the songs. And it is because of this that there are so many inconsistencies in it." For the sake of beginners, I must point out, as Merian does, that the expression "they say" is used even for things that are quite certain, in a *report that is by no means obscure*, not for things that are reported by some or a few. The Greek expression for these latter is "some say." The nature of the Latin verbs *dicunt, ferunt, perhibent*, is just the same. Not that this is very helpful in itself. For rumor asserts [*perhibet*] a great many things that reason and three witnesses show to be false!

the question. But it is weightier because it was written against the most learned Homeric commentator, and no ancient defender of a different or contrary opinion survives. Therefore, however the overall credibility of Josephus may be assessed, that passage will have all the force that clear words have. Recently he was reinforced by a certain scholiast,[39] a coadjutor unworthy of any mention had he not gathered his tale, one soon corrupted by the stories of later grammarians, from the same Alexandrian remains. For it is clear that they did not draw it from Josephus. But each must work out for himself how much weight is to be attached to such a judgment of the ancients. Though I believe that it is very weighty, partly in itself, partly because they had in their possession more poems close to the Homeric age, let it take the place of an indictment, not a sentence, in this case. For since we have the very lines in which the poet is thought either to omit mention of or to bear witness to the art of writing, it is our part to decide which is true on the basis of the fixed laws of interpretation.

CHAPTER XIX

But some confront us, citing against us the fact that the meaning of silence is ambiguous in this sort of history. In this they clearly have a point, but it is not so strong as they think it is. There is doubtless a sort of silence that has no decisive weight and is not to be drawn to either side. On the other hand, there is another sort that is eloquent and, so to speak, articulate, which has always had the greatest weight with all prudent men, unless it is overcome by the authority of those bearing witness to a different conclusion or by reason, which overcomes all authorities. If, perhaps, Homer's silence is not of that kind, we will freely heed those who refer us to other poets, many of whom, we see, mention the art of writing nowhere, though they were clearly very practiced in it. Yet the condition of these and of the Hesiodic poems seems to be slightly different. For given the great length of the former, representations

---

[39] On the *Grammar* of Dionysius Thrax, in Villoison, *Anecdota Graeca* 2.182 [*Grammatici Graeci* 3.179]: "For the works of Homer were lost, as they say. For in those days they were not transmitted by writing, but only by training so that they might be preserved by memory, etc."

of a great many customs and remarkable arts are woven into them, especially of those that then had some element of the remarkable on account of their novelty; and in those of Hesiod a great part of the domestic economy is described. Hence one may quite rightly find it surprising that neither mentioned so very useful a device. But this argument would not be sound enough by itself, nor worthy that scholars should plume themselves so greatly on it. For they confess that they think Homer knew no art which is not found in his work, and this argument is rebutted by a variety of examples of arts to which he nowhere refers, but which are of such a nature that others which he often praises could not have existed without them.

Let us pass on to something else that involves the problem in question to a greater extent. The doubt was raised of old[40] whether Homer knew of the use of boiled meats.[a] For he does not have the verb ἕψειν ["boil"], or another of the same force; he sets only roast meats on his tables. But could he who sang, at *Il.* 21.362, *Od.* 12.237 and the like, about the custom of placing cauldrons on the fire, have been totally ignorant of the devices of cooking? Nor, I believe, did the ancients who raised the question doubt that. Homer knew no art of painting worthy of the name;[41] he mentions many woven things and products of related arts, no painting. For who could fasten this name on the reddening of ships or the pigments of the Carian woman,[42] even though those things were a sort of rehearsal for painting? Both poems indicate that the heroes practiced riding for neither military nor domestic ends. For we must ignore the authority of one particular passage, *Il.* 10.513ff., for several reasons; but the comparisons at *Il.* 15.679ff. and *Od.* 5.371 seem to make it quite impossible that riding itself was unknown to Homer. I have used these examples particularly because they reveal how great the difference is between things unknown and things com-

[40] A trace remains in Athenaeus 1.25D.

[41] So, rightly, Pliny 35.5.15f. This passage is not, as some think, opposed to another one in the same work, 33.38.115f., though that is perhaps drawn from a different writer. The history of the arts among the Greeks confirms the fact. We refer the reader to those who have written of it.

[42] *Il.* 4.141ff. "Black ships," "red-cheeked ships," "crimson-cheeked ships," are well known from many verses.

---

[a] *The doubt was raised of old:* Plato *Republic* 404B-C; Athenaeus *Deipnosophistae* 12B-C; Porphyry *De abstinentia* 1.13.

monly used, and how carefully and cautiously we must draw inferences about the development of the first inventions or customs. Imagine, then, that the bard somewhere spoke explicitly about the invention of Cadmus or Palamedes, or bore witness that exchanges of letters (which many consider the first essays at writing) were common; surely that does not make it clear that it was also customary for volumes of poems to be written.

But an accurate interpretation will easily prove that the two passages in Homer where something like writing occurs are no more to be taken as about writing than is the famous one in Cicero[43] to be taken as about modern printing. And in the one passage, *Il.* 7.175 ff., I think that all will soon agree that there is nothing that much helps either side. A method of drawing lots is described there, by a famous example to be sure, but in such a way that the entire tale cries out against any thought of letters entering one's mind. For the fact that the lot which left the helmet was shown by the herald, passing around, to everyone, so that they might acknowledge it, shows that the σήματα ["signs"] that the heroes use are χαράγματα ["marks"], or arbitrary symbols imposed on wood or some other scrap material.[44] Therefore the verb ἐπιγράφειν in line 187 must have the same meaning there as everywhere else: *dig* or *engrave*. The sense of the other passage, 6.168ff., was made more problematic by those who used not to learn Homeric customs from Homer but to import them into him, and to twist doubtful words to fit the customs of their own time. And certainly the matter of this passage persuades you, in a way, to expect a letter; so do the σήματα (who does not know the φοινικικὰ σήματα Κάδμου ["Phoenician signs of Cadmus"]?) and the πίναξ πτυκτός (a *folded tablet*,

---

[43] *De natura deorum* 2.37.93.

[44] Here I must record the explanation of a recent scholiast that I promised a little while ago [ch. 18], in Cod. Venetus B, on 185—a delightful fellow. We are finding it hard to seek out a single alphabet; he has as many different ones as there were peoples in Greece, and sees that as the reason why each of the heroes only knew his own handwriting. The shorter scholiast who has long been in print, informed by better sources at this passage, indicates more correctly that "not letters" but "certain lines" should be understood here. Best of all is the old scholiast of Cod. A on 187 [a conflation of Scholia Didymi on 175 and 187]: "Not with written words, but having engraved signs. For if they commonly knew letters, then the herald and the others to whom the lot was shown would necessarily have read it." Similarly, Eustathius, 674.35 on 7.189: "One must necessarily think that such symbols were not letters, but certain images or simply figures on an inexpensive substance, such as a rock or a piece of wood or something of the sort."

or, to put it more elegantly, *a sealed tablet*).⁴⁵ But on that account the agreement of the ancient interpreters was extraordinary. Here too they wanted the verb γράφειν ["write"] to be χαράσσειν ["scratch"] or ξέειν ["carve"], the σήματα to be εἴδωλά τινα ["certain images"], in accordance with their original meaning; the πίναξ, finally, to be a σανίς ["wooden tablet"] or ξυλάριον ["bit of wood"].⁴⁶ It is very striking,ᵇ I say, that they who elsewhere besmear Homer

⁴⁵ So, more or less, most of the best French translators, *des lettres bien sçellées*; Pope, *a sealed tablet*; others in similar ways; as if they had translated those Latin terms from Cicero in the text, or had taken the description of a folding tablet from Herodian *Hist.* 1.17. In him at 7.6, Poliziano rightly translates πυκτοὶ πίνακες as *litterae obsignatae* [a sealed letter]. Will we also have to listen to Pollux 4.18, where he cites in a single series the Homeric πίναξ and the more recent triptychs and polyptychs? And the tragedians? In them there occur σανίδες, πτυχαί, διαπτυχαὶ γραμμάτων [folding leaves with writing]; so in Euripides, both elsewhere and at *Hippol.* 856, *Alc.* 967. Indeed, to say nothing of the tragedians' custom of transferring modern customs into the heroic age, tablets could at any time have been folded as we fold paper. But the only point in question is whether they were furnished with alphabetical characters and true writing. That neither Pollux, nor Herodian, nor the tragedians tell us.

⁴⁶ Eustathius explains these things very accurately, 632.46ff. [on 6.168f.]: "The use of letters is recent; similarly the imprinting of rough signs on skins is a late discovery; and the use of papyrus is a discovery of the later period. But the ancients, like the Egyptians, made as hieroglyphic representations certain small creatures and other marks, to serve as an indication of what they wished to say. And so they, like some of the Scythians later, signified what they wished by inscribing or carving certain images and many sorts of linear carvings on tablets—that is, panels—both of various other sorts and in some cases from boxwood [ἐκ πύξων], from which come the ones called πυξίδες. . . . He says that signs were cut in the folding tablet in accordance with the oldest custom. . . . The folding tablet is what we call a writing tablet or book or tablet. . . . Someone might consider this too as evidence that letters were at one time carved on boards, which was practiced especially on marble blocks, with which the onomatopoeia of γράφειν is very appropriate. But if such a writing tablet were assembled from pine in a triangular form, like the later Attic axones, on which the laws were inscribed, then both the πίναξ in Homer and the δέλτος in later writers could be a literal description of it. . . . Also useful for the present passage is the ancient custom according to which the ancients cut on trees as on tablets the names of those they loved, as if Loves or mountain nymphs were doing it—for example, 'such and such a fair woman,' 'such-and-such a fair man.' . . . But from these things a proverb was later derived: 'Bellerophon by his own letters,' etc." Compare Eustathius on the *Odyssey* p. 1926.49 [22.277ff.], p. 1959.57 [24.229]. Anyone who knows Eustathius can see at once to what authors all that must be ascribed; and he himself cites his "Ancients." That is why the oldest scholiast remarks in Cod. A that the writing of syllables and words *seems* to be meant here, but that *it is not so*, the "symbols" are "images, not letters." Apollonius preserved the same point in brief in his *Lexicon*, s.v. γραπτῦς [55.22 Bekker]. And the passage in Pliny 13.13.88 is relevant precisely to this; there, when he had written that the use of *writing tablets* was found in Homer even before Trojan times, he added that Bellerophon was given *writing tablets* (i.e. *orders on tablets*), not *letters*. Though this description based on Roman customs would be of little use to us without the remains of the Greek grammarians.

ᵇ *It is very striking . . .*: Cf. the Introduction above for the importance of this passage.

so zealously with their modern wisdom, now suddenly appear so unlike themselves. For this is how we find the authors of the oldest scholia and Eustathius himself, from whom the long-standing agreement—if not of all[47] the interpreters, at least of most of the best ones—is apparent.

Therefore, though much in this passage is ambiguous, it may nevertheless seem to contain something hidden which, though neglected by the learned until now, induced and forced the ancients to see there too some sort of marks or symbols, not true written characters. To this category belongs in particular the verb δεῖξαι ["show"], the force of which is such as to drive even the fiercest opponent from his position. For if Homer was speaking of a piece of writing that was conveyed and delivered, either I am completely ignorant of his idiom, or I maintain that he would have used any verb other than that one. Not only do I maintain this, but I further deny that any poet, Greek or Latin, not even one completely enamored of violent phrasing, ever used a verb of *showing* or *displaying* for delivering a letter. I would be less troubled by σῆμα ἰδέσθαι ["see the sign"] for the reading of a text at line 176, though I would not think that this was properly Homeric either; now it is clear that both fall into the same category. It is pointless to add anything more. I shall ask one question: will it be more correct to torture and twist Homer's speech than to accept an interpretation of the ancients that goes against the custom of both their times and ours?

What sort of custom that was—what sort of symbols from Proetus were shown to Iobates—must be investigated elsewhere. We do not know what the ancient grammarians conjectured, except that a few of them, as more have done in modern times, seem to have reckoned them among the *hieroglyphs*.[48] But I may not find it hard to convince one who compares the passage in Apollodorus with our scholia that they considered the πίναξ πτυκτός a sort of wooden *die* or *token*, which had the deadly marks carved on it with rough

---

[47] Eustathius, p. 633.9 [on 6.168f.]: "Some say that 'signs' there could be a more philosophical term for letters. For letters are the signs of words and thoughts and things." One of these "some" is the scholiast of Cod. B, who explains "signs" in the common way as "letters"; not to mention Plutarch and other writers, who babble sometimes about Bellerophon's "letter," sometimes about his "letters."

[48] See for example C. G. Bachet de Meziriac on Ovid *Heroides* [4.5-6] [*Commentaire sur les Epistres d'Ovide* (1716)], 1:328. But a certain trace of this explanation is found in the passage from Eustathius that I quoted.

skill.[49] The poet's habits hardly allow us to think of a waxed tablet, for he would surely have adorned skillful work of that kind with some epithet or other addition.

CHAPTER XX

The explication of these passages, not fetched from extraneous opinions but carefully established on the precise meaning of Homer's language, shows, then, that no mention of writing is made in them. And, clearly, if the matter were different in the second passage, a suspicious man could not unreasonably think it interpolated or corrupted in some way. Since this suspicion would remove the very appearance of a common use of letters (by appearance I mean *the example of one epistle*) and would leave no trace of them in the poet, no support at all would remain to the opposite opinion—except from the great length of the two poems, which makes it seem incredible that they could either have been completed or passed on to posterity without the aid of that art. But learned and unlearned men know how weak that scrap of an argument is, and how it violates the first laws of history.

But not only is there no such testimony or trace of the device in Homer, no evidence of even the faintest beginnings of true writing or Cadmus' gift,[50] but, what is by far the most important point,

[49] The scholiast of Cod. A, on 169: "Γράψαι means ξέσαι [*scratch*]. Because he cut images, through which the father-in-law of Proetus had to know." This is a periphrasis of the verb that Apollodorus used, ἐπιγνούς [*having recognized*]; thus it is clear that both follow the same opinion. Eustathius, loc. cit.: "Euripides somewhere says, changing the Homeric 'signs' into 'tokens,' 'And to send tokens to foreigners, who will do you good' " (*Medea* 613). But it seems very likely to me, that already at that time relatives employed certain symbolic marks, by which they could share their views about *certain very important matters*, and particularly that this sort of *deadly sign* was perhaps invented in that age when killings and hostilities were usually avenged with terrible savagery. But these points must be dealt with more accurately in an investigation specifically devoted to *the tokens of the ancients*. In the meantime no one will be sorry for consulting the similar points in Merian [*Mémoires de l'académie royale*, Berlin, 1793], 523ff., including this very witty passage: "If there were really a letter written in alphabetical characters there—it would be extremely odd that an invention so useful, and ever since then so well known, had disappeared two generations later, in circumstances when its use would have been important in quite a different way. *Was it then only good for letters of recommendation that tended to get people eaten by the Chimera?*"

[50] I have always found it particularly hard to understand how it was possible, if that story about Cadmus were so old as they claim, that so many Greek poets

writing

early tech

everything contradicts it. The word *book* is nowhere, *writing* is nowhere, *reading* is nowhere, *letters* are nowhere;[51] nothing in so many thousands of verses is arranged for reading, everything for hearing; there are no pacts or treaties except face to face; there is no source of report for old times except memory and rumor and monuments without writing;[52] from that comes the diligent and, in the *Iliad*, strenuously repeated invocation of the Muses, the goddesses of memory; there is no inscription on the pillars and tombs that are sometimes mentioned; there is no other inscription of any kind; there is no coin or fabricated money; there is no use of writing in domestic matters or trade;[53] there are no maps; finally there are no letter carriers and no letters. If these had been in normal use in Ulysses' homeland, or if "folding tablets" had been adequate to

completely ignored it. The silence of the Latin poets and of Apollodorus, who collected everything notable from the mythic poets, shows us that all did this, not only the ones whom we still possess. This is all the more remarkable in that the remainder of the story of Cadmus provided the occasion for very famous legends. Therefore we might infer with certainty from that fact this much: that the obscure rudiments of that art were unable through many centuries to inspire any of the mythic poets to praise its author. But a proper explanation of this will be easy if the Greeks did not have those rudiments before the ninth century B.C.

[51] The verb γράφειν has been sufficiently discussed. In the older writers it never has the meaning which is normal from Aeschylus and Pindar on. The nouns derived from it, γραφή and γράμμα, are also later. The ancients observed this in the Homeric passage where the triple occurrence of σῆμα struck them. They thought the poet would have engaged in variation if he had known those [nouns]. Eustathius, loc. cit.: "The poet did not know γράμμα. If it had been in use in his day—just as if γραπτύς, which [occurs] in the *Odyssey* [24.229], had been—he would not have said σῆμα three times, persisting in the word because it was the only appropriate one." I find γράμμα first in Erinna [*AP* 6.352 = Gow-Page *Hellenistic Epigrams* 1797]. Nor do you find ἀναγνῶναι, *read*, or anything like that, where you would most expect it, though σήματα ἀναγνῶναι occurs in a different sense at *Od.* 19.250, 23.206, 24.346. Finally the word δέλτος is no older than Aeschylus and the author of the *Batrachomyomachia*, who was contemporary with Aeschylus, as even some of the ancients saw.

[52] See the passages in E. I. Koch's article, *Litterar. Magazin* [*für Buchhändler, Schriftsteller und Künstler*, Berlin, 1792] 1: 76.

[53] You may look for such things in Hesiod's *Works and Days*. But at *Od.* 8.163 someone φόρτου μνήμων ["mindful of his cargo"] is mentioned on a ship. Now let someone compare, if he can, the Romans who had the title *a memoria* [remembrancer]. We follow the old usage, as in *Od.* 21.95. Nor do we care about the explanation found in Eustathius [1590.7], "the secretary, or one who records in writing; or, also, to explain it differently, auditor, financial officer." Though these too sufficiently reveal the opinions of the ancient commentators. But our hawkers and retailers would laugh if they read this. I myself once heard a woman of this order, who was quite illiterate and unintelligent in other respects, make so long a reckoning of the wares that she had stored in various towns, that she could perhaps vie with the μνήμων of the Phoenician ship.

the inquiries of the suitors and Telemachus, we would doubtless have an *Odyssey* that was shorter by some books—or, as Rousseau concluded,[54] none at all.

CHAPTER XXI

When all these silences are gathered and assembled in a single array, does it seem possible that they can be accidental? Or is one who is silent in this fashion playing the part of one who speaks and bears clear witness? Though I am not very credulous, they would be enough in themselves to persuade me fully; and to defend the common opinion would seem the maddest obstinacy. But some, I think, will say that [those silences] can support the conclusion that letters were either very obscure or quite unknown in Trojan times, but not that the poet two centuries later was himself illiterate as well. If I wanted to block off this last retreat, I would have to embark on a long excursus about the whole method that Homer normally employs in describing the heroes' life. Only rarely do I find in him

[54] This very clever man's opinion certainly deserves to be copied out in full here from his *Essay on the Origin of Languages, Oeuvres posth.* (ed. Geneva, 1782), 16:240 [cap. vi]: "Whatever we may be told about the invention of the Greek alphabet, I believe it to be much more modern than it is thought to be, and I base this opinion chiefly on the nature of the language. It has often occurred to me that it is doubtful not only that Homer knew how to write, but even that anyone used writing in his time. I greatly regret that this is so directly refuted by the story of Bellerophon in the *Iliad*. As I have the misfortune, like Father Hardouin, to be a little stubborn about my paradoxes, if I were less ignorant I would be tempted to make my doubts include this story, and to impeach it as having been—without much scrutiny— interpolated by those who compiled Homer. Not only does one see few traces of this art in the rest of the *Iliad* [It is not surprising that he says that there are *few* traces when there are *none*; this is the language of those who are uncertain of their opinion (Wolf's note).]; but I venture to suggest that the whole *Odyssey* is nothing but a tissue of stupidities and ineptitudes that a letter or two would have sent up in smoke. Yet one can make the poem reasonable and even decorous by assuming that its heroes did not know the art of writing. Had the *Iliad* been written, it would have been sung far less; the rhapsodes would have been less in demand and would have appeared in smaller numbers. No other poet has been sung so much, except perhaps Tasso in Venice—and even that is done only by the gondoliers, who are not great readers. . . . The poems of Homer were for a long time written only in the memory of men; they were assembled in writing quite late and with much effort. It was when Greece began to abound in books and in written poetry that all the charm of Homer's poetry began to make itself felt by contrast. The other poets wrote, Homer alone had sung; and these divine songs did not cease to be heard with delight until Europe was covered with barbarians, who involved themselves in judging what they could not feel."

the sort of learned artistry affected by the poets of more cultivated times, when they take great care, in bringing onstage the mythical deeds of their ancestors, not to corrupt pure antiquity with modern customs, so that they may more easily deceive readers or audiences who are skeptical because of their expert knowledge of antiquity, and force them to join and to live, with their whole minds, as it were, with the things and people that they especially desire.[55] From this are also derived certain rituals among the poets, which sprang at first from a *belief* held by the bards and now maintain themselves by sanctified *custom*. Thus even today the creators of long poems feign the same inspiration from the Muses and Apollo in which the ancients believed, and pretend that, having been instructed by divinities in whose existence no one believes, they are *bringing forth a song*, not *speaking* or *writing* in the human way. Hence nowadays even those who cannot *pronounce* correctly also *sing*, and hope that they will have *hearers* for verses which are sometimes *written* for the printer alone, and are *read* by him only syllable by syllable. But these and the many other ways in which the method and art of modern poetry differ from that antique purity must be learned from other masters. Those who cannot judge Homer except on the basis of our own minds may despise these subtleties of ours, so long as they admit that we who favor other opinions are not being led to arrive at our different conclusion by thoughtlessness.

But neither would we ourselves find it credible that poets composed and handed down these poems with the aid of memory alone (for some of the things that history makes us believe are not credible), nor would I be surprised if someone imagined that Homer alone had a certain secret art of writing—if the custom of recitation, which was of old very widespread, and the whole history of the rhapsodes did not confirm our arguments and reasoning very solidly. But it contains a point that can wholly eradicate from the mind the doubts which hinder assent. For it teaches how it was possible

---

[55] This is why words deriving from this sort of social refinement are so rare in the best poets. This is why Virgil, even though he fails to attain the Homeric purity of nature in most respects and has beautified everything, never mentions writing and its appurtenances in the *Aeneid*. Yet in one passage he did not take care enough to avoid a trivial error, in the case of the Sibyl, *carmina in foliis describente notis et nominibus* [writing her songs on leaves with signs and words; a conflation of] 3.444-45 and 6.74. Go then, and add to Gorgias, Ovid, and the tragedians Virgil. He is a most weighty witness; after all, he continually imitates Homer.

that the singers either did not feel a need for the art of writing before it had been fitted to the Greek language, or left it with equanimity to wood and other intractable materials, when it had already begun to be refined.

CHAPTER XXII

At this point, let us quite forget the bookcases and libraries that nowadays preserve our studies, and be transported to other times and another world, where many of the inventions which we think necessary for the good life were unknown to both wise men and fools. In those days, not even immortality for one's own name was reason enough to make anyone seek out enduring monuments; and to believe that Homer sought them is wishful thinking rather than convincing argument. For where does he indicate that he is possessed by such an ambition? Where does he utter a declaration of this sort, so frequent among other poets, or cunningly conceal one? Indeed, he often proclaims that wicked and outstanding deeds are bequeathed to fame by means of his song, but he also affirms that the most recent song is most popular among listeners.[56] But, in general, that age, playing as it were under its nurse's eyes[57a] and following the impulse of its divine genius, was content simply to experiment with very beautiful things and to offer them for the delectation of others: if it sought any reward, it was the applause and praise of the contemporary audience—the most splendid of prizes, if we may believe the poets, and one more welcome by far than an immortality preserved in papyrus. And indeed, both the passages in Homer's poem in which Phemius and Demodocus are introduced singing,[58] and that delightful Platonic dialogue in which

[56] *Od.* 1.351-52.

[57] Cf. the splendid verses, Horace *Epist.* 2.1.93ff.; the place of a commentary on them is filled by the very acute C. Garve, "Betrachtung einiger Verschiedenheiten in den Werken der ältesten und neuern Schriftsteller, besonders der Dichter," in *Sammlung einiger Abhandlungen. Aus der Neuen Bibliothek der schönen Wissenschaften und der freyen Künste* (1779), 116-97.

[58] *Od.* 1.325ff., 8.62ff., 17.518ff., etc.

[a] *playing as it were under its nurse's eyes:* Wolf's image is drawn from a commonplace of eighteenth-century thought: nature as the mother or nurse of (especially primitive) man.

the rhapsode Ion describes his public performance, reveal the great admiration with which the bards and their songs were then received. Ion boasts that, by a form of art, he can cause whole theaters to be borne along by any given emotion, so that at times they shed tears, at times they look around with blazing eyes, at times they show a joyful countenance.[59] The same result was achieved by the bards themselves, to a far greater degree and thanks to an art which was closer to nature. Almost all the traditions about the rhapsodes are highly relevant to understanding the life of the *aoidoi* [poets], since the rhapsodes were their successors. Hence we must briefly discuss the noble order of rhapsodes, especially with regard to the points about which earlier scholars have shown little acuity.[60]

CHAPTER XXIII

The arguments of Salmasius and others about the rhapsodes have not made clear that we owe them our possession of the Homeric poems, and that their art paved the way for all the public discourse, both theatrical and oratorical, of the Greeks.[61] On the contrary, many have followed Plato and Xenophon in considering those whom I call an illustrious order the most trivial of men. This is the first of the three errors[a] which distort the truth in this matter: namely that the ancient methods and those of the Socratic age are

[59] Plato *Ion* 535E: "I look down upon them each time from the platform and see them crying and looking at me wildly and being astonished by the things I say"; and elsewhere in the same dialogue.

[60] It is generally held that S. F. Dresig wrote best on this subject, in *Commentatio critica de Rhapsodis, von alten Meister-Sängern, quorum vera origo, antiquitas ac ratio ex auctoribus et scholiastis Graecis traditur* [1734]. In fact he has gathered together just about everything that could be gathered together mechanically; but he has left the judgment on these matters to the reader. Whoever seeks this should consult at least J. Gillies, *The History of Ancient Greece, Its Colonies, and Conquests* . . . [6th ed., 1820], vol. 1, ch. 6 [pp. 248-88].

[61] Hence ὑποκρίνεσθαι is often used for the song of the rhapsodes, and they themselves are called ὑποκριταὶ ἐπῶν both by the lexicographers, Hesychius (s.v. ῥαψῳδοί) and Timaeus (*Platonic Lexicon* s.v. ῥαψῳδοί), and by Diodorus Siculus (14.109, 15.7). But the majority of authors use ῥαψῳδοί and ὑποκριταί, ῥαψῳδία and ὑπόκρισις as different terms, in their more literal usage. For literally ῥαψῳδεῖν referred to all the types of songs in which real performance was lacking—that is, the kind of performance which the orator too lacks.

[a] *This is the first of the three errors:* Cf. Wolf's fourth letter to Heyne, 9 January 1796, in the subsidia below.

confused with one another. I think that a second error has already
been resolved: namely, that from a false etymology of the noun
$ῥαψῳδός^{62}$ some have inferred that the rhapsodes' work consisted
of excerpting verses from a variety of sources and stitching them
together, just as certain holy men made the Homeric centos that
still exist—ridiculous pieces of nonsense about the most profound
of subjects. And this second piece of absurdity was embroidered
even more crudely by those who thought that the rhapsodes were
similar to the street singers of their own day, and imagined that
the things about which they had sung were depicted in a painting
and pointed out with a staff. The third error is most widespread,
and we must here refute it above all. They have attributed to Homer
as his unique practice what used to be the normal condition of
poems before the art of writing became familiar. They were certain
that he consigned the monuments of his genius to writing, and
they thought that he was the only poet, or one of few, who was
commonly sung and propagated by memory. The nature of the
case and the authority of the ancients entirely refute this line of
argument. For the art of the rhapsodes embraced not only the
poems of Homer, but also those of Hesiod and others, and the
whole epic genre, and soon the lyric and iambic ones as well.[63]
Indeed, this was for a long time the only way to reveal one's genius
in public, so that we read that even Xenophanes performed his
own poems as a rhapsode.[64] But many witnesses attest that a great

---

[62] Παρὰ τὸ ῥάπτειν ᾠδήν, *to sew together* or *weave together a song*. This is, to be sure,
the true etymology, but it must be interpreted in terms of the character of very
ancient times. For it is one thing to weave together shorter songs in a manner and
order appropriate for public recitation, that is, as the scholiast to Pindar *Nem.* 2.1d
[3.30.7 Drachmann] says, to apply "a certain sequence and sewing together," and
another thing to stitch together a cento. But some scholars in these later centuries
have been misled by a false analogy into thinking, on the basis of the meaning of
the word, that ῥαψῳδός and ποιητής designated the same person. For it is not so
customary to use ῥάπτειν and ὑφαίνειν for composing verses as for making crafty
plans. This is opposed too by Pindar *Nem.* 2.2, where, on that theory, the words
ῥαπτῶν ἐπέων ἀοιδοί ["bards of stitched songs"] would contain an extremely feeble
epithet. Nor is the phrase ῥάπτειν ἀοιδήν in the verses attributed to Hesiod in that
Pindar scholium [3.31.10-12 Drachmann = Hesiod Frag. 357 Merkelbach-West] to
be applied to that, but instead simply to the *rhapsodic song*. But here all these matters
can only be touched upon.

[63] Cf. Plato *Leges* 2.658D, *Ion* 530B; Athenaeus 14.620C.

[64] Diogenes Laertius 9.18. This passage has recently been just as poorly interpreted by I. Rossi, *Commentationes Laertianae* [1788], p. 184, as it had been by
T. Roschmann (praes. J. W. Feuerlin), *Dissertatio historico-philosophica de Xenophane*
[n.d. (1729)], 21.

many people devoted their efforts to the Homeric poems, the most outstanding of all, and that a sort of *family of Homer's sons* came into existence, which practiced this art, first in Chios, then elsewhere.[65]

But though the name of this art seems to be later than Homer, the actual art and profession were already flourishing in the most ancient times, and were much more illustrious then than later. For so long as only a few could embrace the majority of poems in their memory (since schools, in which boys could be taught them, had not yet been opened, and since there was only one type of learned person, the holy bards who were widespread in Greece), it was only natural that the men who brought the works of the bards to the notice of the public were also held in special honor. Yet the fact that Hesiod, like others of his contemporaries, is called the founder of the profession of rhapsodes shows that at first each poet publicized almost exclusively his own work.[66] But clear historical evidence proves that soon, from Terpander of Lesbos in the Thirty-fourth Olympiad [644-640 B.C.] down to Cynaethus of Chios, who particularly excelled in his art in the Sixty-ninth Olympiad [504-500 B.C.], the same men sang not only others' songs but their own as well, and that almost all rhapsodes were also competent poets. And I think this is why so many poems of those times were eventually assigned to false authors and in the end circulated as anonymous, after the names of the rhapsodes who composed them had been lost to memory, since they came in time to be repeated by more and more others.

---

[65] I speak of family in the sense in which sects or schools of philosophers are called families, not as though there were a lineage and progeny of Homer. Let us leave this interpretation to the vanity of the Chians (Strabo 14.645), from which perhaps the Homerids themselves were free. For if in fact they had derived, not their art, but their familial origin from Homer, then they would certainly have transmitted rather more reliable information concerning his birth and life than they did. Nor is there any proof in the passages of Pindar, Acusilaus (at Harpocration s.v. Ὁμηρίδαι [= FGrHist 2 F 2]) and Hellanicus [ibid. = FGrHist 4 F 20] which might support that common opinion; and far less in the usage of the noun in Plato, Isocrates, and other authors. For once that distinguished family had become extinct, the name was transferred indiscriminately to singers, interpreters, or lovers of Homer, as in Aelian *N.A.* 14.25. For the rest, how quickly this whole matter became obscure is shown by the dissent of the ancient grammarians in the passages cited from Harpocration, Suidas, and the Pindar scholia.

[66] Nicocles in the Pindar scholia, loc. cit. [3.31.13 Drachmann] and Athenaeus, loc. cit. We would have more certain information about this whole matter if the writings of Dionysius of Argos, Timomachus, Hippostratus, Aristocles, Menaechmus, and others cited by these two authors had survived.

CHAPTER XXIV

Now even if very few arts and crafts were practiced in Homer's age by designated individuals, nevertheless the art of the poets was no less specialized[a] at that time than that of the builder or potter, of the doctor or seer,[67] and it had the greatest possible public and private distinction. For whether they remained within their own towns or wandered through various places, the assemblies of the peoples and the banquets of kings, they were considered dear to the gods and venerable to men. The rhapsode enjoyed the same respect, the same way of life, until his profession, gradually changing together with men's interests and characters, diminished and cheapened to a trivial job when money was offered as a prize at contests.[68] But this we will discuss elsewhere: now we should consider whether the rhapsodes sang from a book or from memory, and what method they used to learn poems without any books.

Here no one but a perfect stranger to ancient Greece would doubt that they declaimed everything from memory: this was the practice of all ancient bards, since they worshiped the three muses, Melete, Mneme, and Aoide.[b] Indeed, as late as the age of Socrates, when rhapsodes above all sought written texts of Homer,[69] the recitation itself was not performed from a written text.[70]

Does it seem surprising that an individual memory could have a capacity great enough to embrace all Homer? To me at least that

[67] Cf. *Od.* 17.383ff., Hesiod *Works and Days* 25-26, *Hymn to Apollo* 165ff., etc.

[68] Ion at Plato *Ion* 535E: "If I make them cry, I myself shall laugh, because I shall obtain money; but if they laugh, I myself shall cry, because I shall lose money."

[69] Xenophon *Mem.* 4.2.10.

[70] I feel silly to be teaching such things. But many people have not even grasped this; in fact, they have sought support for their opinion from Plato's *Ion*, where nevertheless it is said that *to have a strong memory* is most necessary for a rhapsode (539E) and where nothing else is mentioned that refers to the use of written texts. Add to this finally the fact that there is nothing which pertains to written texts in the words by which the recitation of the rhapsodes is signified. The Greeks say of this ᾄδειν, ψάλλειν, μελῳδεῖν, μνημονεύειν, ἀπαγγέλλειν, διατιθέναι, and similar words, but nowhere ἀναγιγνώσκειν or ἀναλέγεσθαι.

---

[a] *the art of the poets was no less specialized:* Wolf considered this reconstruction of the rhapsode's craft one of his most original achievements. See his fourth letter to Heyne in the subsidia below.

[b] *Melete, Mneme, and Aoide:* Cf. Pausanias 9.29.2.

does not seem very large, and I suspect that good rhapsodes occasionally mastered much more. For even after an encyclopedic culture, based on the reading of books, and the affairs of a highly refined life had overwhelmed men's memory, there were men at Athens who had received a liberal education and who knew all of the *Iliad* and *Odyssey* by heart.[71] Why then doubt that those who earned their living by doing a diligent job of memorization could achieve as much, particularly at a time when the smaller range of knowledge gave a sort of elbow-room to their talents, and a reputation for wisdom could be won by quite different pursuits? Indeed, Plato[72] and other ancient philosophers judged that this faculty of our soul ought not to be measured in terms of the period when the availability of aids could impede its cultivation, and that the discovery of letters had helped the branches of learning but had hindered those who would learn them. In fact, the very invention that had been called the medicine of memory might not unjustly be termed its injury and ruin instead. This warning was perfectly true, as is clear from consideration of the illiterate and of peoples who have no share in our learning. For we need not supply individual examples of unusually strong memories, such as that of Hortensius the orator, who, according to Cicero [*Brutus* 301], could deliver word for word without a text everything that he had prepared privately, or those of poets, both those who compose extempore, who are called *improvvisatori* in Italian, and many others who can, we know, especially when they are forbidden the use of writing, both compose many thousands of verses in their heads and repeat these quite often once they have been imprinted upon their memory. Of course, we are not speaking about rare miracles of nature, but rather about *a class of men, who had time throughout their lives for this one art, so that they could either compose poems in order to make them public afterward by singing, or learn them from others once they had been made public in this way.*

And yet we find generally similar classes of men among other peoples as well: among the Hebrews, what they call *the schools of the prophets*; then again, more akin to us, *the bards, the scalds, the Druids.* Caesar and Mela report[73] that the Druids had their own course of training, in which some pupils remained for up to twenty years,

[71] Xenophon *Symp.* 3.5.   [72] Plato *Phaedr.* 274E.
[73] Caesar *Bell. Gall.* 6.14, Pomponius Mela 3.2.18.

"so that they could learn by heart a vast number of verses which had not been committed to writing."[74] How I wish that the Greeks had transmitted to us even that much about their own bards and rhapsodes! For I judge it to be quite certain that they too had their own course of training and a particular devotion to their art. Come then, let us use comparisons with similar things to reconstruct the method of rhapsodic teaching, obscured as it is by the shadows of antiquity. If I am right, it was the same as that which was employed on the tragic and comic stage, in the various kinds of choruses, and finally in elementary and advanced schools, before the ability to read and write became widespread. Indeed, the words themselves provide evidence about the nature of the method. For the poets there is a technical term, one drawn from the thing itself, διδάσκειν δράματα [to teach dramas], in Latin *docere* [to teach]; for the actor, μανθάνειν [to learn], *discere partes* [to learn roles]; from here are derived διδάσκαλοι, ὑποδιδάσκαλοι, ἀντιδιδάσκαλοι, διθυραμβο-διδάσκαλοι [teachers, subteachers, counterteachers, dithyramb teachers], and other words of this sort.[75] No doubt, just as actors learned gesture, the other movements of the body, and the whole art of dance by watching their teachers' demonstrations, so too they learned the words not, as today, from scripts, but by listening while the poet himself sang before them. And that is why rhapsodes seem customarily to have taught one another face to face, so that practice and frequent recitation might soon furnish skill. There is, of course, no reason why we should think this method inconvenient or more troublesome for the memory than our own: certainly, anyone would admit that theirs must have been much more effective for achieving the best pronunciation and the true meaning and sound of words and of whole sentences. Moreover, the listeners' ardent zeal, com-

---

[74] Similar things have often been reported elsewhere, most recently about the nation of Ossian by W. Thornton, ["On Teaching the Surd, or Deaf and Consequently Dumb, to Speak,"] *Transactions of the American Philosophical Society* 3 [(1793), 310-19, here] 314ff.: even now there are in that nation old men who preserve such an abundance of ancient songs in their memory that they could exhaust even the fastest scribe by dictating for several months.

[75] A number of scholars have made brief observations drawn from Harpocration and Hesychius s.v. διδάσκαλος; more material is provided on the didascalia by Casaubon on Athenaeus 6.235E [cf. J. Schweighaeuser, *Animadversiones in Athenaei Deipnosophistas post Isaacum Casaubonum*, vol. 3 (1802), 369-73]. But since then no one, so far as I know, has investigated this matter carefully, and it still awaits clarification, together with many other things that pertain to the dramatic contests of the Greeks.

bined with their deep love for national history in the ancient epics, doubtless made this work easy and pleasant. All these considerations, based upon the genius and character of those times, leave no room for doubt about how what historical arguments prove to have happened could indeed have happened.

CHAPTER XXV

When I reflect upon these things, it seems to me a grievous mistake to believe that a Homer who did not use writing must immediately and entirely have been transformed and made unrecognizable [in the process of transmission]. Had this happened, it would have been the result of desultory performance, not that of *rule-bound* and well-organized formal teaching. Nevertheless, the ancients themselves ascribed the origin of variant readings to the rhapsodes, and located in their frequent performances the principal source of Homeric corruption and interpolation. And this judgment, which began with the Alexandrian critics,[76] is clearly supported by consideration of the nature of the case. For even the most tenacious memory, when deprived of written texts, wavers on occasion, and gradually deviates further and further from the truth. But in the first place, the recitation itself, since it was performed with lively impulse and emotion, must have weakened the memory and occasioned many changes, particularly in those words which almost seemed to end the verse spontaneously and did not have that elegant artistry which could repel extraneous additions. For all the sentences and words are woven together with such simplicity of thought and language, flow along in such little clauses and short phrases,[a] that it is extremely easy to change, subtract, and add at any point. Finally, it would have been a miracle if those rhapsodes who possessed a more noble inspiration and were themselves poets had not thought that here and there they could say something better, that some things had to be phrased more clearly for the sake of the listeners, and other things had to be brought into co-

---

[76] Preserved by Josephus in the final passage which I cited above in ch. 18.

---

[a] *in such little clauses and short phrases:* For these terms of analysis see Cicero *Orator* 213, 223.

herent form by stringing a number of poems onto one thread. For their greatest concern had to be, not to preserve these poems unadulterated just as the bard had uttered them at first, but rather to be understood and to be heard with pleasure by all. And thus the family of Cynaethus is expressly alleged to have corrupted Homer by various means, and particularly by interpolating their own verses.[77] Hence for my part I would believe that, if an exemplar of Homer, recorded as it was recited by such rhapsodes and left unpolished by later critics, were still extant, it would have the same appearance as our larger *Hymns of the Homeridae* have.

This word, *hymns*, introduced by Hemsterhuys and other scholars,[b] suggests a further remark about interpolation by rhapsodes, which should show clearly how great the poetic ability of these men was and how little such interpolation was intended to deceive. The former indeed would be highly probable even if we had no evidence, unless you think that their genius was so frigid that an almost daily contact with the best poets could not kindle it to something similar. But even if the historical record for this period has many gaps, Pindar and Plutarch report[78] clearly enough that hymns were composed by rhapsodes, by which they furnished preludes to the formal recitation of the poems of Homer and of others. And so, relying especially on the latter author, I speculated a long time ago, following Hemsterhuys, that the hodge-podge of hymns we possess was conflated out of such proems and fragments of proems, and

---

[77] Schol. on Pindar *Nem.* 2.1c,e [3.29.13-14, 31.17f. Drachmann], and thence Eustathius 6.39-40.

[78] Ps.-Plutarch *De musica* 1133C, speaking about the citharoedic modes and the more ancient rhapsodes: "*Having discharged their duty to the gods as they wished,* they passed at once to the poetry of Homer and the others. This is clear from the preludes of Terpander." From this one passage we learn that it was the custom to compose preludes not only to Zeus and the Muses, but to the other gods as well. Yet it would also be incorrect to infer from Pindar that *the beginning* was always made *from Zeus.* As is fitting for a lyric poet, his simile is derived from the most illustrious genre, i.e., from the custom at the most distinguished festivals and public assemblies. For the rest, just as Pindar says "a *prelude* to Zeus," so Thucydides 3.104, citing part of the longer *Hymn to Apollo* under the name of Homer, calls it a "*prelude* to Apollo"; and this is the name used by most other authors for the hymns. Indeed, the word ὕμνος has a broader sense, and often includes every type of epic verse. Whence arises this line at the end of three of the hymns (5.293, 9.9, 18.11), an obvious trace of that custom: Σεῦ δ᾿ ἐγὼ ἀρξάμενος μεταβήσομαι ἄλλον ἐς ὕμνον ["Having begun with you I shall pass to another hymn"].

---

[b] *Hemsterhuys and other scholars:* Cf. T. Hemsterhusius and J. F. Reiz, eds., *Luciani Samosatensis Opera,* vol. 1 (1743), 6.

I supplied a reason, perhaps not an improbable one, why they gradually became confused with the Homeric poems themselves.[79] For I believe that those audiences did not care about knowing for certain who had composed each and every thing, so long as it was worth listening to; but in the age of the Alexandrians, to whom this made a great deal of difference, nothing seems to have survived except contradictory and obscure reports, like the ones about many other anonymous works, some of which Herodotus already mentions.

Finally, very little has been transmitted with certainty concerning the method of formal recitation in the public assemblies and contests. On one point all agree: both epics of Homer were sung only bit by bit and in different orders, and each bit had its own popular name.[80] These names appear both in Aelian and Eustathius at the beginnings of the books, and in very many other writers, who everywhere produce Homeric passages in this way. But from the very beginning, these parts were rather long, and, as you can tell from Eustathius, they did not correspond to Aristarchus' demarcation of the books. Thus "The Story of Alcinous" comprised four or five books of the *Odyssey*;[81] such a work-load could easily be performed in a one-day festival. In other poems, like the "Catalogue of Ships" or the "Interrupted Battle," I think that the rhapsode's skill was tested, especially in the official contests, to see whether these would fit together well with the rest and produce an elegant joint. Nevertheless, there can scarcely be any doubt that in this matter nothing remained certain and constant through several centuries, since it depended partly upon the places and times of recitation and partly upon the genius and judgment of the rhapsodes.

[79] F. A. Wolf, ed., *Theogonia Hesiodea* [1783], 60. Cf. C. W. Mitscherlich, *Homeri Hymnus in Cererem* [1787], 101, and G. E. Groddeck, *De Hymnorum homericorum reliquiis commentatio* [n.d.(1786)], 21.

[80] For us, the authority of the ancient author excerpted by Aelian, *V.H.* 13.14, can take the place of them all.

[81] Cf. the correct note of T. Twining, *Aristotle's Treatise on Poetry, Translated: with Notes . . . and Two Dissertations* [1789], 365. I add the very similar example in Herodotus 2.116, where *Il.* 6.289ff. are cited as from "The Exploits of Diomedes," the title by which the grammarians refer to the fifth book of the *Iliad*. This fact, together with the course of the construction, argues strongly against the obelus of Valckenaer, who deletes the words ἐν Διομήδεος ἀριστείῃ ["in 'The exploits of Diomedes' "] [in P. Wesseling, ed., *Herodoti Historiae Graece et Latine* (1768)].

CHAPTER XXVI

This whole detailed investigation about the time when writing was first received among the Greeks, about the way in which poems were composed and made public in the most ancient times, about the rhapsodes, their sole guardians, is, as it were, a preliminary to a different and deeper investigation. Here suddenly the whole field of argument changes, historical evidence practically vanishes, and conjecture and inference tremblingly take its place. These do not seek after the testimony of Herodotus, Plato, or Aristotle himself, but rather follow out with rigorous judgment and compare with nature itself the conclusions that can be drawn from carefully thought-out principles. Conjectures of this sort the mob nowadays tends to defame by calling them hypotheses. A sad fate: but after much hesitation, having waited for someone else, more confident than we, to make the attempt, we need no longer be apprehensive for our own reputation. Instead, let us say at once, in all clarity, what the case is.[a]

It seems to follow necessarily from what we said above that works which are so large and are drawn out in an unbroken sequence could neither have been conceived mentally nor worked out by any poet without an artificial aid for the memory. Say that Homer had a genius sent down from heaven, capable of the most lofty cogitations, with which he could drain dry the knowledge of all things divine and human; say that he is for us, as Velleius says, the very greatest, without model and without rival[b]—and surely the splendor of his light will never arise again, unless the globe should see a second Greece come to birth—; say that he, who surpassed all others in natural genius, possessed at the same time—what is con-

---

[a] *Instead, let us say at once, in all clarity, what the case is:* After Wieland read Wolf's *Prolegomena*, he wrote on 3 May 1795, "Wolf makes every step forward in his argumentation so cleverly, but also firmly, that one follows him confidently despite all his asseveration of merely conjectural probability and feels that one's faith receives ever more foundation with each step forward." After reading this comment, Wolf wrote in reply, "I am bold enough to call this pure historical chains of reasoning and interrogations of witnesses," thereby indicating he was prepared on occasion to claim something more for his theory than merely hypothetical status. Cf. Peters, 37, 43.
[b] *Without model and without rival:* Cf. Velleius Paterculus 1.5.1-2.

trary to nature—every art in its most polished and most perfect form. Not even to a man like this can we attribute something that quite exceeds the grasp of mankind, something for the mere conception of which the space, the material, and the foundation were all lacking. For earlier epic poems were all fairly short, and the only way to make them public, even in his own age and long thereafter, was open recitation of the sort we have seen the rhapsodes of Cynaethus' time using. Furthermore, it is scarcely credible, and no authority attests, that a number of singers were ever brought together for several days or weeks to pour out such lengthy poems to listeners—which would have been the only way for such long poems, if not to be understood, at least to be heard through to the end.[82] Accordingly it is implied, I say, and necessarily the case, that a powerful and truly intractable force of nature would have prevented the writing down of the complete work, a task perhaps not too difficult in itself. In all these considerations we do not wish to detract at all from the bard's ingenuity; innumerable examples

[82] When Aristotle saw an "easily surveyed magnitude" in the *Iliad* (*Poetics* 23.1459a33), even though its length was proverbial among the ancients, he was judging of the poem as read, not as heard. But this is of small importance. Yet it is worth noting that A. Dacier reports [*La poétique d'Aristote traduite en François. Avec des Remarques* (1692), 393] that the *Iliad* can easily be read through in a single day. Reading this, I often consigned it to Apella the Jew [an expression of disbelief; cf. Horace *Sat.* 1.5.100-101]. Similarly Twining: "For a wager, indeed, I will not say what might be done, if we had *reading races* at Newmarket" (op. cit., 478). But if this most learned man has rightly interpreted the passage in Aristotle starting with the words, Εἴη δ᾽ ἂν τοῦτο [1459b20ff.], then that philosophical critic thought the *Iliad* and the *Odyssey* would be even more easily surveyed if they were shortened to a third of their present length. Indeed, this is entirely compatible with our arguments. Neither is this opinion generally unworthy of Aristotle nor is it contrary to his other doctrines, and it has been approved recently by another interpreter of this treatise, H. J. Pye, *A Commentary Illustrating the Poetic of Aristotle, by Examples Taken Chiefly from the Modern Poets* [1792], 458. And now that, to the great benefit of these studies, the summaries of the *Cypria* and the *Little Iliad* have been published [by C. G. Heyne, in *Bibliothek der alten Litteratur und Kunst* 1 (1786), Inedita 23-26 and 35-37], no scholar will agree with Dacier, who referred the word "of the ancients" to those songs (loc. cit.). But two things make the interpretation of this passage doubtful: first, that we are uncertain about the length of the other epic poems published just before Aristotle's lifetime; and second, that we do not know what "one hearing" was in a tragic drama. For the authority of Diogenes Laertius 3.56 ought no longer to be adduced, now that it has been emended by that great man who relegated those four names of festivals to the margin [D. A. Wyttenbach, *Bibliotheca critica*, vol. 2, pt. 3 (1782), 56; cf. H.K.A. Eichstädt, *De Dramate Graecorum comico-satyrico, imprimis de Sosithei Lytiersa* (1793), addenda to p. 29; modern editors do not question the authenticity of these words]; yet no other authority is available upon whom one might rely without the risk of error. Cf. Barthélemy in *Mémoires de l'Académie des Inscriptions*, vol. 39. But this is not the place to take refuge in conjectures, even if they promise to be of great benefit to our main argument.

make clear how little ingenuity can be enough for large volumes. Rather we are contending that the aid of hands was necessary for the writing down of such great works, and so were tools, by means of which they could be noted down in some way or other and at once passed on in their entirety to the public or at least to a few close friends. This Homer could not have accomplished "with ten tongues, a voice of iron, and lungs of bronze":[83] here he needed pens and a writing tablet. If as the only man of his time to have such equipment, he had completed the *Iliad* and the *Odyssey* in their uninterrupted sequence, they would in their want of all other suitable contrivances have resembled an enormous ship, constructed somewhere inland in the first beginnings of navigation: its maker would have had no access to winches and wooden rollers to push it forward, and therefore no access to the sea itself in which he could make some trial of his skill. I shall not recall how neatly every step forward in the arts of the Greeks is connected with steps before and after it, each one prepared for by the others, so that the earlier progress and sequence of causes makes clear why each one follows. For example, it was easy for the Greek genius to contrive a theatrical plot out of the epic songs by changing the form and, because of a certain natural disdain for the same old song, to entrust the events that had been narrated in them to stage characters so that they might be acted out before their eyes: but no nation was so ingenious as to make it possible for someone to appear at such a public show without spectators or for the length of a performance to exceed 15,000 verses. Similarly, if Homer lacked readers, then I certainly do not understand what in the world could have impelled him to plan and think out poems which were so long and were strung together with an unbroken connection of parts. All too often I repeat the same things: but that "could" must be repeated over and over again, for its force, by the very nature of man, is so great and is such a foundation for our case that, unless it is removed, no one need be disturbed and worried by the many other difficulties which may beset our argument.[84]

[83] *Il.* 2.489-90.
[84] The die is cast: I have certainly not come to it unprepared. Two men of high scholarship who are still alive (and may they long remain so!) will perhaps remember my discussions with them about this matter in the years 1780 and 1781 [1779 and 1780; see Subsidia 2 below], both in conversations and in letters. But from that time on I was diverted into other concerns and rarely allowed myself to utter a word among friends by which I might disturb the silence and established opinion of

CHAPTER XXVII

I shall entrust to others the tasks of examining in detail and of magnifying to the best of their ability the difficulties presented by the marvelous beauty and written form of these epic poems and by the organization of their parts. For I myself have done both to the best of my abilities, taking great care neither to conceal anything

scholars. In my lectures, too, I imitated for many years the interpreters of Scripture, who, deterred by their dread of the law, teach not what they really think but instead what has been prescribed as acceptable to the Church since earlier times; nor did I publish anything concerning these doubts. Furthermore, I repeatedly set aside and destroyed whatever I had noted down for myself about these doubts, in case, once they had slipped from my memory and mind, further reflection, at a later time, might remove these scruples. Once, indeed, I became quite ashamed of myself and thoroughly wearied of my path, or rather of my wandering, when I read C. Perrault, *Parallèle des anciens et des modernes en ce qui regarde les arts et les sciences*, vol. 3 [1692, repr. 1964], 33f., where to bring antiquity into contempt he adduces a similar hypothesis advanced by one of his fellow-countrymen and intended for eventual publication. A little later I obtained the small treatise which he threatened, the work of a man who denies that Homer ever lived but teaches that both oeuvres were conflated from *tragedies and various street songs of beggars and wanderers, à la manière des chansons du Pont-Neuf*, and so on in the same manner, and who declares in the Introduction that he learned nothing at all worthwhile from Greek literature. This last statement is one of the few things about which everyone might easily believe him; everything else is dreams and delirious ravings. This small book, called *Conjectures académiques ou Dissertation sur l'Iliade*, by a man in other respects not obscure or witless, and known for other books in Germany as well [F. Hédelin, Abbé d'Aubignac], appeared at last once its author had died (1715 [repr. 1925, ed. V. Magnien, who indicates on pp. xxx-xxxi the many inaccuracies in Wolf's summary of d'Aubignac's book]). It had lain hidden for a long time in the hands of Charpentier and others, who had delayed its publication—it is uncertain whether they were motivated more by love for their friend or for the ancients. Repeated readings of this book, as I have said, made me weary of my own opinion, for d'Aubignac's capricious temerity and ignorance of antiquity had slipped into a sort of similarity with it; and I began in earnest to seek out arguments in support of the common theory, incoherent as it was. For I saw that no proper response had been made to d'Aubignac by Boileau, Dacier, and others. And so, having striven in various ways to meet the historical difficulties, I was soon harassed by them again, and forced again to yield. I am conscious that I have in no way indulged either vanity of ambition or novelty of opinion, and that I have strained all my sinews to avoid the snares of error. As witnesses to this I have many of my close friends, with whom I have shared this labor of mine through these last years, inciting them to seek the truth and to gather together carefully everything in the poems themselves that seemed to oppose me, and to collect it all within a single purview. And even now I am not discussing these matters in order to persuade anyone who is not persuaded by the thing itself, but rather, in case I have erred in anything or have distorted it into falsity, in order that I might be convicted of my error by those who are more sharp-witted than I am.

But I do not wish to seem to have adopted a Rudbeckian character, for I deem historical truth a sacred thing even in the most trivial matters [Olof Rudbeck, 1630-

from myself nor to proceed rashly. But this latter concern deserves the attention of many,[a] including those who follow a different method, and particularly those who can measure the strength of the human genius in this domain by their own genius and have disciplined their judgments of art by the study of ancient literature:

1702, was a Swedish polymath who, in his major work, *Atland eller Manheim* (1679-1702), attempted with extraordinary erudition to prove that Scandinavia was the cradle of civilization, identifying Sweden with Plato's Atlantis and deriving the language of the Lapps from Hebrew]. I can cite the authority of two great men, Isaac Casaubon and Richard Bentley, whose writings contain unambiguous traces of the same opinion. There are more in the writings of Casaubon; Bentley's single remark, an extraordinary one, is in the book he wrote in English against Collins, *Remarks upon a Late Discourse of Free-thinking, in a Letter to F. H., D.D. By Phileleutherus Lipsiensis,* of which I have the first edition of 1713 and the seventh of 1737 before me. The following passage occurs in section 7 in both editions in the same words: "Homer wrote a sequel of Songs and Rhapsodies, to be sung by himself for small earnings and good cheer, at Festivals and other days of Merriment; the Ilias he made for the Men, and the Odysseïs for the other Sex. *These loose Songs were not collected together in the Form of an Epic Poem, till Pisistratus' time above 500 years after.*" What could be clearer than these words? And the context of the whole passage proves that they were written as the result of careful thought, and not dashed off in the ardor of combat. Yet not even this statement by the prince of critics—so manifest and so memorable by reason of the time at which he proclaimed it, a few years after Perrault's notorious work—has been called into question by any scholar, either because it lay hidden in a book primarily for theologians, or because it seemed to many to have been uttered rashly. In fact, most have entirely neglected it: for example A. Baillet, *Jugemens des Savans sur les principaux ouvrages des auteurs, revûs, corrigez, & augmentez par Mr. de la Monnoye* [2d ed.] vol. 3 [1725, repr. 1971], 95-96, who recounts d'Aubignac's blind attack; while others, like Clarke, have reported it coolly or in a few words, and people like Pope have even perhaps derided it. But Bentley himself, who had set aside for his old age the critical recension of Homer, had planned (as I gather from certain indications) to shed light upon this matter in it on the basis of his scholarship. Hence I am quite amazed that nothing relating to this question is to be found in the critical books of the Englishmen who mention the plan of this edition. R. Dawes [*Miscellanea Critica iterum edita*, ed. T. Burgess (1800), 344] and others take pains to show that he was planning to restore the Aeolic digamma. Yet this report concerning the digamma has made me seriously wonder what inference I might make as to what Bentley thought about the antiquity of writing among the Greeks, and for what reasons, if he thought that Homer wrote, he could date this epic form of his poems so much later. I wish that those who have access to his Adversaria and Homeric notes, which are said in *Biographia Britannica,* 2d ed., vol. 2 [1780], 244 [s.v. Bentley, R.], to have come into Cumberland's possession, would inform us on these points. There is nothing about which I would rather learn Bentley's judgment: and who would not wish the same who knows the judge of the Phalaris controversy? You might wonder whether Homer would have owed as much to his emendation as do Horace and the comic poets.

---

[a] *this latter concern deserves the attention of many:* Such contrasts are not uncommon in theological writing; cf. Griesbach's *Commentatio* on Mark, loc. cit. (above, editorial note a to ch. 10): "Mark understood the purpose and use of the Gospels quite differently from most theologians of later times. And if he had intended to illustrate Matthew by an accurate commentary, he would indeed have produced one quite unlike any of the customary commentaries. Undoubtedly such a work would have

the Klopstocks, the Wielands, the Vosses. For we can make no progress toward the heart of this matter by using the ordinary French prescriptions and formulas for making epic poems. Nor is it enough to admire the marks of skillful artistry which now belong to each of the two bodies of poetry: that original and simple action which remains everywhere visible throughout the great variety of matters and incidents, one act selected from the whole history of the Trojan War, one hero selected, everything else shrewdly interposed for the sake of embellishment; in the one poem everything referred to the wrath of Achilles, in the other to the return of Odysseus; nothing overextended, nothing inverted, nothing confused, nothing left out.[b] No one can deny that it is proper to praise many of these things to the skies.[85] This is particularly true of the *Odyssey*, which in its admirably unified structure must be considered the most brilliant monument of the Greek genius. As for the *Iliad*, the battles of scholars concerning the main point and the principal argument of the plot have not yet been resolved. However this question is decided, and even if the exordium has the widest possible sense (I suppose that descriptions of a couple of battles which took place in Achilles' absence would have sufficed for these lines), nevertheless it will never be irrefutably proven that those seven verses promise anything more than eighteen books. The remainder

---

[85] Hence it is false to believe that, in the *Iliad*, the poet artfully used the whole war to ornament and amplify his plot. This belief is derived from the ancient grammarians, especially Eustathius 7.17ff., who makes extraordinarily silly assertions in support of this opinion, ones which are also contrary to Aristotle's in *Poetics* 23.1459a30ff. (though I do not consider this a capital offense). And yet some of those who hold this belief indicate quite clearly that the whole war is described in the *Iliad*. Anyone who has not learned from such teachers will admit that neither view is correct, and that the only artistry revealed is what most historians have sought for when they have treated brief parts of history in single works, or what Cicero recommends "for the sake of rapidity" to Lucceius, the man he hoped would record his own deeds, asking him [*Ad fam.* 5.12.6] "to separate this off as the story of our deeds and events from your extended writings, in which you embrace the unbroken history of deeds." Often enough it is necessary for a writer in this genre to go beyond the limited period and to weave in earlier events.

---

pleased the followers of Lessing and those who, by their study of *belles lettres*, have sharpened and polished their natural disposition and have learnt by long practice the right method of dealing with ancient literature; but it would not have pleased the authors of harmonies and tiresomely industrious commentators."

[b] *nothing confused, nothing left out:* Wolf's (partly ironic) praise of Homer's dramatic unity derives ultimately from Aristotle *Poetics* 8 and 23. Here he is implicitly attacking Heyne for accepting such views uncritically. See Wolf's fourth letter to Heyne in the subsidia below.

do not contain the wrath of Achilles against Agamemnon and the Greeks, but a new wrath, quite different from the earlier one and not in the least harmful to the latter: that is, an appendix to that first wrath which is the only one sketched by those verses. But if you subordinate all the deeds of the Greeks at Troy and all the books to a single theme, then the whole *Iliad* indeed pertains to the *glory* of Achilles more than of any other Greek or Trojan hero, and only its greater part pertains to his *unforgetting wrath*. Hence it might well seem surprising that, up to now, the following lines or better ones have not been found in any manuscript instead of that exordium:

ΚΥΔΟΣ ἄειδε, θεά, Πηληϊάδεω Ἀχιλῆος,
ὅσθ᾽ εἵως βασιλῆϊ κοτεσσάμενος ἐνὶ νηυσὶ
κεῖτο, Ἀχαιοῖσίν τε καὶ αὐτῷ ἄλγε᾽ ἔδωκεν,
αὐτὰρ ἀνιστάμενος Τρωσὶν καὶ Ἕκτορι δίῳ.

[Sing, goddess, the glory of Achilles, son of Peleus,
Who, so long as he lay among the ships in wrath against
The king, bestowed pains upon the Greeks and himself,
But, once he set forth again, upon the Trojans and godly
    Hector.]

It would be absurd to claim that such accuracy was too meticulous for the age of Homer: not even those who feel that the exordium of the *Odyssey* was placed at its front by Homer himself dare to claim this: for they would thereby make the poet so inarticulate that he could not even recognize and explain in words that art which he had first discovered by his innate genius, or at least had skillfully drawn from the natural order of the legend.[86]

But in fact it may also be doubted whether Homer attached the same value to the character of Achilles as do most professors of the art of poetry. For considering that he did not invent that sequence of great events, but received it by report,[87] these things

[86] Aristotle *Poetics* 8.1451a24: "either through art or through nature."

[87] For neither does the poetry of those times tell everything truthfully or on the basis of a corrupted truth, nor does it invent everything, as scholars once thought. But those who wish to separate the one from the other toil for the most part in vain. The Muses warned:

We know how to say many false things that are similar to true ones,
And we know, when we wish, how to declare the true ones.
[Hesiod *Theogony* 27-28.]

hardly seem to be lacking in verisimilitude: that the bravest hero, by withdrawing from the army with his troops, makes his absence keenly felt; and that he himself while unoccupied makes a great deal of work and trouble for Agamemnon and the Greeks; that he is soon called back when the Trojans attack even more boldly, but refuses at first, being a harsh and inexorable man, and hangs back, then yields his friend to the common danger, and finally, when the latter has been slain by Hector, returns to the fray himself for the sake of revenge, attains his desire, and commits atrocities against Hector by the law of war. If Thucydides or Xenophon had included the events of this year in their annals, they could hardly have described Achilles as being less longed for when he had withdrawn, or less honored or less obstinate when he was called back, or finally as less extraordinary, fierce, brave, and noble-spirited when his new wrath had expelled the old one. Or do you think it odd, and the result not of nature but of art, that among the many myths concerning that war there was one which could produce by its continuous narration a poem which would be harmonious and complete in its parts? Or, these things granted, do you suppose that the work would have come out very different even if four poets had woven its web? Well might you name that people happy, and most fertile in great deeds, for whom poems grow spontaneously that other peoples cannot produce by the most intense studies and skills! Perhaps you smile: yet the genius of the Greeks engendered many things which we would certainly lack if that people had not existed.

CHAPTER XXVIII

The *Odyssey* is surrounded by greater uncertainty and problems peculiar to it. Not because everything in it refers to the return of Ulysses—who would find this odd in poems that have as their theme Ulysses wandering and seeking his fatherland and restored home?—but because the fortune of Penelope and Telemachus and the domestic calamities of the hero are so conjoined with his foreign vicissitudes by a suitable chronology and plot that we are drawn *in medias res* from the very outset, we continually hasten toward the end and anxiously wish to see the hero return and enjoy rest and a tranquil kingdom after having endured so many labors. Hence no one who likes the ancient bard at all can set the *Odyssey* aside until he has read it through. But that art is the very thing which seems scarcely, if at all, consistent with a bard who is singing only individual sections, who, in order to prepare himself for planning such a work of art, would have sung to himself, like the Aspendian citharist,[a] even before a very select audience. Hence the voyage of Telemachus to Nestor and Menelaus, the retreat of Ulysses in the island of Ogygia, even that very lovely poem in which he is introduced narrating to the Phaeacians his own wanderings, and the rest as well, may seem to have been composed by Homer and sung for a long time in the same way, that is, separately and without regard for the shape of the whole. Later, in an age which was more polished and richer in the arts, someone noticed that by forcing these episodes into a single great continuous body by a few excisions, additions, and changes, they could be made as it were into a new and more perfect and splendid monument.

Perhaps the Greeks might have tried the same thing in vain with the other *Nostoi* [Voyages Home]. A number of ancient poems were extant under this name; even about their authors we know too little.[88] But no other man's wanderings lasted so long or extended over such disparate regions as did Ulysses', no other man's marvelous vicissitudes on land and sea and pranks of fortune had been made known by report. So it may justly be suspected that poems of this sort about anyone else were not available in such abundance. Both here and in the *Iliad*, therefore, it becomes unclear once more whether, if you plucked out from the whole four or five longer sections, each of three or more books, and separated them from one another, you could detect in them traces of that whole which we now all admire, or even the connecting links of that great structure which is sketched at the beginning.[b] I know how hard it is to forget Aristotle and the other literary theorists who drew their precepts from these parts long after they had firmly coalesced, but

---

[88] For those cited by Casaubon on Athenaeus 14.157F [cf. J. Schweighaeuser, *Animadversiones in Athenaei Deipnosophistas post I. Casaubonum*, vol. 2 (1802), 529-30] and by others are for the most part rather late, and they derived their material from those contemporaries of Homer's.

---

[a] *the Aspendian citharist:* Cf. Cicero 2 *Verr.* 1.20.53.

[b] *That great structure which is sketched at the beginning:* As in the preceding chapter (cf. note b), Wolf is echoing Aristotle's discussion of Homeric unity in *Poetics* 8, especially 1451a32-35, and criticizing Heyne's adherence to Aristotle's views.

would it not be pleasant to obtain an example of the most ancient poetry once in a while by contemplating the parts? I know that all agree no one produced a very long work of this sort before Homer.[89] I confess that whenever I return in spirit, so far as I can, to that ancient age, I find that these poems are not in the least displeasing when read in this way, nor do I miss the wisdom of old age in this extraordinarily talented youth. But I submit that it is not so much wisdom and preeminence in artistic skill that are foreign to the historical position and innate talent of Homer, but rather the planning out of a continuous story which is so long and so varied in its episodes. For that artistic, skillful conjoining,[c] even if it has deserved the highest praise, is not so shrewd and subtle that an immense natural talent, equipped with the necessary aids, could not have attained it even without a model. Nor, given the many sections once extant, was it so difficult to discover, so it seems to me, that we might not prefer to attribute it to the taste and efforts of a later age. And this reasoning will become even more probable if the thread of the legend appears to have already been spun out at some length by its first author.[d]

CHAPTER XXIX

But perhaps this is playing, not reasoning, especially in view of the great authority of the common belief. But suppose we took Aristotle's laws of the epic and threw them into disorder, insofar as they rely upon that belief, by using the testimony of all the ancient

[89] I know how daring this view of Aristotle is. But I belong more or less to the same school to which the author of that elegant book, *Parallelen*, 14ff., has recently professed adherence [Wolf may be referring to the anonymous *Parallele zwischen dem ächten Seelsorger und dem Mönche als Pfarrverweser. Ein Beleg zu B. Stattler's Reformationsartikel* (1792)]. In the end, what I have claimed to be true of poetry before Homer relies not upon conjecture alone but upon the authority of the ancients themselves, who provide a good many plots and names of their songs. An obvious example, in addition to Velleius Paterculus and the many others who praise him in much the same way, is Aristotle *Poetics* 24.1459b12-13. After enumerating a number of the virtues of the epic poem, he adds, "Homer makes use of all of these, both first and sufficiently." Thus Homer is for most authors both *the first* and *perfect in all regards*.

[c] *that artistic, skillful conjoining:* Cf. Horace *Ars poetica* 47-48.

[d] *to have already been spun out at some length by its first author:* For the phrase cf. e.g. Ovid *Metamorphoses* 1.3-4.

grammarians. None of the extant ones anticipated modern acuity with regard to the basic action of the *Iliad*. For all agree that the *Iliad* contains *the deeds of the Greeks and Trojans at Ilium*, and, if they add anything, *the brave actions of Achilles*. So, with particular clarity, the author of the book on the poetry of Homer who goes under the name of Plutarch;[a] so Eustathius consistently.[90] But the latter had previously singled out the first of these alone as the main theme of the poem, absurdly declaring in addition that Achilles was honored in it so greatly beyond all other heroes because Homer loved him beyond all others. Absurdly, I say, and following the ancient error which made the poet the inventor of practically all the material of his stories. But anyone who knows the sources of the grammarians would be thoroughly astonished that not even the Alexandrian critics had perceived the true direction of the plot of Homer, which our age discovered long ago, albeit by a different method. Fools, those Alexandrians of yours, he says, rooted to their words and syllables and born before the so-called philosophy of the arts was discovered. Yet not even the bard himself was a philosopher, he who supposedly concealed the great artistry of his basic plot by winding it through the labyrinth of its episodes. For it must have been concealed, since besides Aristotle and before him only a very few of the ancients had the faintest inkling of it.[91]

[90] As in Eustathius 7.47-8.2: "That, beginning with *the wrath of Achilles*, he will narrate the evils which arose from it, not only for the Greeks (even if more for them) but also, as it seems, for the Trojans." This, together with the other matters discussed there, pertains to the famous question of why Homer began his narrative with "the wrath of Achilles." Yet another problem arising from ludicrous superstition was why he prefixed to this splendid work the foul and ill-omened noun μῆνις ["wrath"]. Both of these, or rather this latter, which we have recently learned about from the scholia to *Il.* 1.1, are ridiculed by Lucian *Verae historiae* 2.20, where d'Aubignac's dreams are acerbically censured by M. Solanus [in I. F. Reitzius, ed., *Luciani Samosatensis Opera*], vol. 2 [1793], 117-18.

[91] A strange sort of effort is this: to defend it, one page is not enough. Most people will think they can adequately refute it on the basis of Horace. It is up to them to work out a way of doing this. We are now investigating *the common opinion of antiquity*, which must be learned from the ancient interpreters of the *Iliad*, from passages of orators and similar writers. Such people must compare all these materials before they pass a stern judgment against my audacity. But, in general, it would be most useful to have a single collection, drawn from all the scattered sources, of the ancients' rules of poetics and judgments on their poets. If I am not mistaken, these would show, when compared with the best poems now extant, *how late the Greeks learned to construct wholes in poetry*, and would show that not even Horace, who made a precept of this, established the same limits to his precept as our philosophers do.

---

[a] *who goes under the name of Plutarch:* Cf. Ps.-Plutarch *De Vita et Poesi Homeri* 2.4.

The authority of the Cyclic poets and of the others closest to Homer's age must be given special weight here. Little about them is certain,[92] even if Nonnus and other students of antiquity could still study the bulk of them closely. In that little which we do know, one thing is particularly noteworthy: that all the Cyclic poets either failed to notice these marks of Homer's artistic skill, or they either did not wish or were not able to imitate those that their contemporaries did notice. For let someone read those epitomes of the *Cypria* and of the five other poems which have recently [1786] been edited,[93] and try to discover in any of them a basic hero or a basic plot or a narrative which plunges *in medias res* as in the *Odyssey*.[94] Again, survey the remaining epic poems or arguments of poems of that age, the *Genealogies* of gods and heroes, the *Dionysiaca*, *Thebaids*, *Epigoni*, *Naupactica*, others: to be sure, you will find one hero in several of them (for many were quite brief), but in none a single or basic plot woven together with episodes in the manner of the *Iliad*. I base my case not upon conjecture but upon a great witness. For this is how Aristotle consistently speaks about Homer, this is precisely why he ranks him above all others writing in this genre. Apparently, then, none of them imitated their leader and prince in this regard, not even Pisander or Panyassis or Antimachus, who are counted the best after Homer, still less the more ancient poets and the Cyclic poets.[b] A new argument about these last can be drawn from the very idea of the Cycle, as we know it from the passage of the Lycian Proclus contained in Photius. For this Cycle was a collection of many epics, extending from the very

---

These matters will have to be particularly investigated by anyone who wishes to judge the dramas of the Greeks by the laws of ancient aesthetics. And if in these matters Aristotle was too often diverted from historical method, his perspicacity, by which he surpassed his age, is all the more to be admired.

[92] These are collected, or it is indicated where scholars have collected them, in J. A. Fabricius, *Bibliotheca Graeca*, 4th ed., vol. 1 (1790), 379ff., and C. G. Heyne's extremely full Excursus I, "De auctoribus rerum Troianarum (τῶν Τρωικῶν)," to Virgil *Aen.* 2 [*Publius Virgilius Maro varietate lectionis et perpetua adnotatione illustratus*, 4th ed., ed. G.P.E. Wagner, vol. 2 (1832), 378-400].

[93] In *Bibliothek der alten Litteratur und Kunst*, vol. 1 [1786], Inedita 23-46.

[94] For in the *Iliad* the order of events is natural, and the beginning of the first book brings the reader into the middle of the course of events in the same way as happens in most of the other books: e.g., in the various "exploits," in which it is also noteworthy that the heroes are clearly introduced as though they had not appeared before. Cf. especially *Il.* 11.

---

[b] *Still less the more ancient poets and the Cyclic poets:* Cf. Aristotle *Poetics* 8,23.

creation of the universe through the death of Ulysses, containing practically the whole of legendary history *in a continuous and natural sequence*. This alone makes clear that the Cyclic poets narrated their stories in the same order in which they had happened one after another, not following the design of our *Odyssey*.

But if this is so, how is it conceivable that, if they had all seen that Homer employed this technique, which is the cause of his exceptional perfection, they would either not have understood it, or, having understood it, would not have wanted to emulate it? For no one can rightly fear that they might not have been able to, that they all might have brought to bear talents unequal to such pre-eminence. And not even Hesiod, to whom the critics have never-theless accorded a distinguished place in the canon, may be thought to have sung anything in this manner. This is proven by the *Works and Days*, a work that can be compared neither with the Alexan-drians nor with Lucretius or Virgil and is not much better organized than the gnomic verses of Theognis;[95] it is proven by other poems as well, formerly attributed to the same man by doubtful hearsay. Finally, even the poets of more recent times show somehow that they have not disagreed with the grammarians about the artful coherence of the *Iliad*. How foolish would have been the plan of that man, generally called Quintus Calaber, to add his own works as a supplement to an *Iliad* broken off too early, if he had not had the examples of earlier times before his eyes! Indeed, we reproach him as being ignorant of the rules which schoolboys now learn from Batteux; but would we not make the same reproach if by chance we had an *Iliad* which ended with the return of Achilles and was supplemented by him from that point up to the funeral of Hector? The philosophy of art knows how to adapt and subject itself to events, often even to chance ones. If we did not read the Catalogue of Troops in *Iliad* 2, that philosophy would not, I think, complain that anything had been omitted; perhaps it would even

[95] The first examples of a genuine didactic poem, that is, of one in which a given art or doctrine or any given subject is treated in full by the continuous consideration of its parts, are found in the works of Xenophanes, Parmenides, and Empedocles on nature: if only those who have collected their fragments would publish them! This genre was neglected by the Athenians, who strove for a prose which might more usefully be cultivated for the purpose of instruction; later, the Alexandrians brought it to perfection, and from them it came to the Romans and received new ornaments from their genius. Hesiod and the gnomic poets offered a prelude to this genre, not the pattern for it.

have taught that that part was the task of a historian, not of a poet, and that it would be ridiculous to think that our knowledge of the heroes was defective because it was missing.[96]

CHAPTER XXX

But even if most of the ancients either did not investigate the artistry of the structure and composition of the Homeric poems or judged these less accurately than we tend to do today, nevertheless it is impossible to doubt that there is some artifice in them. But we may be uncertain whether this belongs to Homer or was derived from the genius of others, who were inspired by the theme of the poems and the ordering of the plot. If so, then the question is one which must be attacked not from the standpoint of what is in accordance with poetic laws or what we believe sheds honor upon the poet, but rather from that of what appears to be probable on historical and critical grounds. Even this question I merely pose, I do not treat it systematically: for it involves an immense subject matter, nor is it necessary to our theme. Still, two matters must be touched upon briefly here, which even by themselves would arouse the suspicion that different hands had made the framework in both poems.

Of one sort are a number of obvious and imperfectly fitted joints, which I believe that I have found, in the course of very frequent readings, to be both the same and in the same places: joints of such a sort that I think anyone would at once concede, or rather plainly feel, once I had demonstrated the point with a few examples, that they had not been cast in the same mold as the original work, but had been imported into it by the efforts of a later period. True, not even the most erudite readers have felt difficulties of this sort for many centuries, though I would think that no one of even average intelligence could avoid encountering them. Perhaps one reason for this was that the poems' continuous sequence deceived

---

[96] Here we are reminded of the ridiculous (or, as Aulus Gellius 3.11.4 says, "pretty trivial") arguments by which Accius tried to show that Hesiod was earlier in birth than Homer: he says, "Because Homer, when he said in the beginning of his poem that Achilles was the son of Peleus, did not add who Peleus was: beyond any doubt he would have said this if he had not seen that it had already been said by Hesiod," etc. Anyone can see the relevance of this.

their readers, thanks in part to their high reputation and in part to their own beauty, and thus banished any meditation on this matter; and that we are almost all naturally more eager to join together things which are disconnected than to disconnect things which are joined together.

Hence, when I first discussed these matters with certain friends, I recall quite well how much they distrusted my suspicions and opposed to them the precept and the silence of so many centuries. A little later, in one of those places in which I had suspected that something had been stitched on by an artist different from the author, the authority (for what it is worth) of an ancient grammarian unexpectedly came to the support of my conjecture. This passage is *Il.* 18.356-68, which is placed (to put it mildly) frigidly and ineptly between the affairs of the Trojans and Greeks on the one hand and the arrival of Thetis in Olympus on the other. A long disputation concerning these verses has been excerpted in the more accurate scholia from one Zenodorus; the chief point that I derive from this is that these verses were added not by an ordinary interpolation, nor by some grammarian or other, but by the first διασκευασταί [revisers] in order to bind together two sections.[97] And I think I can see a number of additions of the same sort in the *Odyssey*, one of which is so obvious that I suspect that very few of those to whose judgment I submit this example for examination will oppose me.

After *Od.* 4.620, where we are snatched away from the pleasant conversation of Menelaus more quickly than you might wish or expect, to return to it only in book 15, which describes the return of Telemachus, there follow four verses, extraordinarily harsh in

---

[97] Διεσκευασμένον τοῦτον τὸν τόπον ["this passage revised"]. We shall see a little later (ch. 34, n. 13) about this word διασκευάζειν, which M. Casaubon, *De Nupera Homeri Editione Lugduno-Batavica, Hackiana: Cum Latina Versione, & Didymi Scholiis: Sed & Eustathio, & Locis Aliquot Insignioribus ad Odysseam Pertinentibus . . . Binae Dissertationes* (1659), 36, interpreted wrongly. The scholium from which we have learned this is from Porphyry [so according to Villoison; but since Dindorf editors deny it to Porphyry: cf. H. Schrader, *Porphyrii Quaestionum Homericarum ad Iliadem Pertinentium Reliquiae*, vol. 1 (1880), 429, 433, and Erbse on Schol. to *Il.* 18.356b]; it was first provided to us from the Leiden codex by L. C. Valckenaer in "Dissertatio de Praestantissimo Codice Leidensi et de Scholiis in Homerum ineditis" [in his *Opuscula Philologica, Critica, Oratoria*, vol. 2 (1809), 95-152, here 139] (for Barnes's excerpted manuscripts had provided no certainty), and now has been published in its proper place from Ven. B [by Villoison]. But here we lack the more ancient A. [Wolf has misunderstood the scholium, which asserts only that Zenodorus considered the lines in question to be an interpolation.]

the unusualness ア _ ambiguity of their diction and entirely devoid
of the Homeric _ ality.

[δαιτυμόνες 〕᾽ ἐς δώματ᾽ ἴσαν θείου βασιλῆος.
οἱ δ᾽ ἦγον μὲν μῆλα, φέρον δ᾽ εὐήνορα οἶνον.
σῖτον δέ σφ᾽ ἄλοχοι καλλικρήδεμνοι ἔπεμπον.
ὣς οἱ μὲν περὶ δεῖπνον ἐνὶ μεγάροισι πένοντο.

The banqueters came to the palace of the godly king.
They drove sheep and brought man-strengthening wine,
And their beautiful-veiled wives sent them bread.
Thus they were occupied with the feast in the halls.]

Indeed, I have noticed a fair number of traces of this fault in the
whole remaining part of book 4: it would not be inappropriate to
perform a trial attempt for such cases by means of this easier test.
For no scholar will feel any doubt about the ambiguity of this
passage, a fault of which Homer is rarely guilty, particularly on
very familiar subjects. And I would suspect that the commentators
were already working on and disagreeing about it long ago, though
we lack most of their materials on the *Odyssey*. Indeed, Eustathius,
who used too abbreviated scholia on this passage, interprets δαιτυμόνες not as *guests*, as the usage of Homer and all other authors
requires, but rather as *hosts*, "those preparing the banquet"[98] (this
is unavoidable if, as the author doubtless intended, the next οἱ
refers to δαιτυμόνες), and then ἄλοχοι, equally in violation of
usage, as *maidservants*, that is, the concubines of the suitors: and he
refers the whole passage without any hesitation to the court of
Ulysses, not to that of Menelaus. On the other hand, most of the
more recent interpreters have not permitted themselves to be led
away from Menelaus so easily. Among them, Barnes, as he says,
humanely forgives Eustathius his slip, though I believe that in his
work of compilation Eustathius could not even have slipped in this
way. But he himself understands the ἄλοχοι as some sort of *wives
of the sons of Menelaus and his friends* and says nothing about the
other word.[a] Madame Dacier, following Eustathius on both points,

---

[98] Eustathius 1512.2 on *Od.* 4.621. And this theory may be considered to have
been generally transmitted in the past. Hence the shorter scholia gloss οἱ ἑστιάτορες
["the banquet hosts"], Hesychius at the end of the entry s.v. δαιτυμόνες offers
μάγειροι ["cooks"], and so too *Etymologicum Magnum* s.v. δαιτυμών.

---

[a] *But he himself understands . . . .:* Cf. Joshua Barnes, *Homeri Ilias et Odysseia et scholia*
(1711), ad loc.

nevertheless herself still lingers in Sparta.[b] And perhaps these and others are persuaded, not without reason, by the consideration that the phrase ϑεῖος βασιλεύς seems to be used in this context to distinguish someone from Ulysses, who is called by name [line 625]. But again, μῆλα ἄγειν recalls the suitors to mind, αἰὲ᾿ μῆλ᾿ ἀδινὰ σφάζοντες [always slaughtering throngs of sheep], and the μνηστῆρες [suitors] themselves (line 625) may seem appropriate in conjunction with slaves or servants preparing the meal. But whichever of these is true, and wherever the transition to affairs in Ithaca is made, it is made in a confused and most unpleasant manner: we do not hear Homer singing here. If I did not know how easily minor faults are obscured by the splendor of the great parts in a work of this scale, I would be amazed that none of the critics who emend these poets in accordance with the accepted stereotype has yet arisen to make this passage resemble 17.166 by deleting these four offensive verses, and thereby to add himself to the ranks of the first polishers of these poems. If the latter had once actually done this, as one may believe they often did elsewhere, or even had made line 625 the beginning of a new book, then I believe that that slight exercise of ingenuity would certainly have deluded the best minds of all the ages. Now the matter has turned out unexpectedly. For even if the Greeks put all their energy in the earliest times into hewing out, polishing off, and embellishing this poet, nevertheless they have left a Pylaemenes who forgets his death all too quickly, and many similar things which later critics tried to coerce into order and harmony with their obeli and emendations.[99] For they sought only what would be in harmony with the continuous movement and art of epic poetry.

[99] Sometimes infelicitously or inconsistently. As in the case of Pylaemenes, whose son Harpalion precedes him in death in *Il.* 13.658 after Pylaemenes himself has already been slain at 5.578-79. The scholiasts and Eustathius furnish us with several theories on this matter. If I am right at all, none of these is true; one is by far the silliest, that which proposes the correction μετὰ δ᾿ οὔ σφι πατὴρ κίε ["his father did not go after": Schol. to *Il.* 13.658-59]. Nevertheless, Barnes adorned this one with his own little verse. Others have recently accused the poet himself of forgetfulness: a remark that, I think, none of the old Aristarcheans would have approved. For different men can follow different traditions in these matters, or the same man can

[b] *Madame Dacier . . . still lingers in Sparta:* Madame Dacier translates the passage in question as follows: "C'est ainsi que s'entretenaient ces deux princes. Les serviteurs du roi arrivaient pour préparer le diner; ils amènent des moutons et apportent d'excellent vin, et leurs femmes les suivent avec des corbeilles pleines des dons de Cerês." *L'Iliade et l'Odyssée traduites en prose avec des notes* (1709).

CHAPTER XXXI

There once were philosophers who decreed that this universal framework of all things and bodies was not made by a divine mind and will but instead was born and developed by accident and chance. I do not fear that anyone will accuse me of like temerity if I am led by the traces of an artistic framework and by other serious considerations to think that Homer was not the creator of all his—so to speak—bodies, but rather that this artistic structure was introduced by later ages.[a] For we find that this was not done suddenly by chance, but that instead the energies of several ages and men were joined together in this activity. But just as it is extremely stupid to believe that things which cannot be done have been done, so too we must take care not to measure the bounds of nature and the universe by the sharpness of our own eyes and to believe that, because we ourselves have not seen something done, it therefore cannot be done at all. But we must move on to another kind of argument. Even if all the rest were explained away, this would raise a doubt about the entire form of these poems, one which could not be answered. Someone might say that nothing could be added to or subtracted from the form as it now is without violating the laws of elegance. I hear this, and in part I see it clearly, and I am grateful to those revisers. But it will surely be clear to everyone that they have applied their own skill in putting together

---

follow different traditions in different writings, but the same man cannot vary in the same one, and indeed within the brief space of a single work. Finally, something of the sort could happen to a late poet who was laboriously collecting stories, but not to a bard who lived within this tradition. Things were certainly better when certain critics used to expunge both verses, which is surely the quickest way to remove every discrepancy and difficulty. But they were deterred in other passages, either by carelessness or by base superstition, from rejecting everything which disturbed the complete and equable course of events. One example (lest I now pile up others) is provided by the very description of the plain of Troy, where some degree of discrepancy remains and has not been removed by them; but I would not be the cause of anyone's again undertaking a long voyage for the sake of this.

---

[a] *that this artistic structure was introduced by later ages:* This is a central point. Wolf is faced by the alternatives: *either* save Homer as a poet and destroy the *Iliad* as a text, *or* save the text as history and destroy the poet as its author. As Cesarotti writes, "[Wolf] . . . admires and exalts the *Iliad*, and sacrifices Homer without remorse" (*Prose edite e inedite* [Bologna, 1882], 197).

these works, once it has been demonstrated that both poems contain not only certain small portions, as I showed before, but also whole sections which are not by Homer, that is, by the man responsible for the larger part and the order of the earlier books.

It is clear that Aristophanes of Byzantium and Aristarchus (no overly audacious critics in this regard) were already uncertain at an early date about the authorship of the last part of the *Odyssey* from 23.297 on. The same uncertainty was also expressed about *Iliad* 24.[1] No one has yet explained the arguments for either side about either uncertainty. Moreover, the disputations of those ancients have not been transmitted to us in a sufficiently trustworthy manner, for it is most plausible that they used historical reasons and ancient reports to confirm the matter.[b] Nevertheless, something has been said by those who expressed uncertainties and nothing by those who wished to disperse them. In fact the former affirmed that they had detected many things in these two books that were unusual in Homer and unworthy of his genius, while the latter either sought to demonstrate their antiquity and beauty by citing Virgil and his contemporaries (as though Plato and Aristotle, who were far more ancient, had not cited them as Homeric) or claimed that they were necessary to fill out the form and measure of full-sized works. It is quite obvious what sort of argument this is and we are ashamed to refute it. For by it they prove only that they themselves would be prepared to add these supplements if they had not yet come into existence: though they do not demonstrate by their rules why the *Iliad* should end particularly in the hurried description of the funeral of Hector. They plainly achieve

---

[1] On the *Odyssey* cf. schol. on *Od.* 23.296 and Eustathius 1948.47ff. on *Od.* 23.296, and the notes on that passage of Clarke, Dacier, and Pope, where the opinions of Aristarchus and his new supporters, Casaubon and R. Rapin [*Comparaison des poëmes d'Homère et de Virgile*, 3d ed. (1664, repr. 1973), 49ff.], are refuted; on the *Iliad* cf. J. Jens, "Observationes de Stilo Homeri," [in *Lucubrationes Hesychianae* (1742), 290], and R. Dawes, *Miscellanea Critica* [2d ed., ed. T. Kidd (1827), 266], and against these Ernesti on *Il.* 24.1 [in S. Clarke, *Homeri Opera Omnia* (1759-64)]. But Dawes (loc. cit.) was the first to judge *Il.* 20 too, as a whole or in large part, unworthy of Homer. In the *Odyssey*, furthermore, a number of manuscripts give evidence of that suspicion, like the Clarke manuscript collated by T. Bentley [cf. S. Clarke, op. cit., Preface to vol. 2; and T. W. Allen, *Homeri Ilias*, vol. 1 (1931), 264], and Vindobonensis philol. 5 [Allen's Vi[1]] and 133.

---

[b] *they used historical reasons and ancient reports to confirm the matter:* Wolf is assuming that ancient scholars worked by the same methods as modern ones—a dangerous assumption, and one he himself forcefully attacks in ch. 38 (see ch. 38, note a).

what they wish for the *Odyssey*. Anyone with common sense can see that if the last part of this poem were missing, we would go away worried for Ulysses, who had conquered such great difficulties. For at that point we would be quite fearful for him because of the parents and relatives of the 108 slain noble youths, if an amnesty and peace were not brought about by a sudden intervention of the gods.

But what if it can be shown by all the arguments relevant to issues of this kind that that very part, together with some others necessary for the proper composition of the poem, is not by Homer, but instead was composed by some ingenious rhapsode in the age just after him? What if the same thing can be shown about the last six books of the *Iliad*? Certainly, every time I have come down to those parts in continuous reading, I have always sensed in them certain things of such a sort that, I would wager, they would long since have been detected and remarked upon by scholars if they had not merged so early with the rest. In fact I have sensed that many things, although now considered perfectly Homeric, would by themselves have sufficed to taint the *Hymns* with the suspicion of spuriousness if they were only read there. But I shall not try to sell this sense of mine to anyone as an argument, since a quite serious recent example makes me cautious. Out of joy at a new find, most people thought that Hymn[c] to be as similar to Homer as one egg to another; others, however, thought it unworthy of the bard, but quite ancient and the product of some Homerid. Pindemontius called it scarcely earlier than the Alexandrians; Ignarra, a Muscovite cento glued together at a later period out of ancient verses scraped together from Pausanias and elsewhere. Ruhnken, indeed, said (having given the best verdict on the subject) that the point can be sensed by the expert but cannot be explained to the inexpert. Yet both of these [sensing and explaining] are much more difficult in those poems, separated as they are from one another by the

---

[c] *that Hymn:* The hymn in question is the Homeric *Hymn to Demeter*. This is now accepted by scholars as being genuinely archaic and belonging to the seventh or sixth century B.C., but in the eighteenth century it was tainted with the suspicion of spuriousness. Cf. Ippolito Pindemonte, *Volgarizzamento dell' Inno a Cerere scoperto ultimamente ed attribuito ad Omero* (1785), and Niccolò Ignarra, *Emendationes hymni in Cererem* (1784). David Ruhnken's statement appears in *Epistola Critica I in Homeridarum Hymnos et Hesiodum, ad virum clarissimum, Ludov. Casp. Valckenarium* (1749), 8: "Nam revera haec saepe sentiuntur melius, quam verbis explicantur" ("For in fact these things are often sensed better than explained in words").

space of only one or two centuries. They deceive us by their appearance, which is uniform in general and extremely similar to the rest. For *in general* all the books have the same sound, the same quality of thought, language, and meter. Hence it will be necessary at some point to investigate with the greatest care what it is that imbues one person, out of the many who read those last books, with this sense, what is the unusualness in words and phrases, and of what sort (for even the first book of the *Iliad* has some *hapax legomena*), what is different and of a disparate color in thought and expression, what traces of another poet's imitation lurk in the things derived from Homer, but in such a way that the sinews and the Homeric spirit are lacking, what is jejune and frigid in many passages—for example *Il.* 21.273ff. and a large part of the supernatural occurrences in this book and the next, 22, where there are nevertheless many brilliant passages (in the same way there are also many brilliant ones in the *Theogony* and the *Shield of Heracles*); 23.88; 24.247ff., 602ff.; *Od.* 23.310ff.; 24.24ff. These and many other passages will have to be discussed elsewhere in detail and with the most intense care: for the matter is important enough to deserve it. But now I think it enough to have registered these passages, as I do not care how much weight they will add to the arguments given above.

CHAPTER XXXII

Let us go on to those things which the Greeks have transmitted by consensus about the most ancient history of these poems—in themselves slender and obscure remnants, not adequately understood even by the Greeks themselves, but for us now not entirely opaque.

First it is said that Homer's poetry was brought by the Lacedaemonian Lycurgus from Ionia to the Peloponnesus. We have four extant witnesses to this;[2] the first of them, both in age and in authority, is Heraclides Ponticus, who reports that the poems were

---

[2] Heraclides *De politiis Graecorum libellus*, in J. Gronovius, *Thesaurus Graecarum Antiquitatum*, vol. 6 [1699], 2821-34, here 2823B [Heraclides 10 Dilts = Aristotle Frg. 611.10 Rose (V. Rose, *Aristotelis qui Ferebantur Librorum Fragmenta* [1886, repr. 1967], 372.22-24): the ascription of these excerpts to Heraclides Ponticus is due to N. Cragius, *Heraclidae Pontici de politiis Libri cum Interpretatione Latina* (1593), and is now rejected by most scholars, who assign them instead to Heraclides Lembos, a compiler of the first half of the second century B.C.; cf. Rose, op. cit., 258-60, 370]; Dio Chrysostom *Orat.* 2.45; Plutarch *Lycurgus* 41D; Aelian *V.H.* 13.14.

obtained from the descendants of Creophylus. Although this Creophylus is a figure of legend, since he is numbered among the most ancient epic poets and among the friends of Homer, one might conjecture that his descendants were a family of singers or of rhapsodes, who at Lycurgus' request taught the poems to the Lacedaemonians or gave him upon his return a comrade who had memorized them and could sing them. Plutarch says that the poems had been written down and were in the possession of the family and were copied by Lycurgus. But this story has as little importance for this inquiry as the reason he adds for the legislator's taking the trouble to import them into the city. Historians add such things from their own wits, lest they seem to narrate events in an unadorned and jejune manner.[a] And I cannot believe Aelian either when he claims (how could he have known this?) that Lycurgus already knew all the songs from which the *Iliad* and the *Odyssey* were later composed. Hence, when we have discarded all the inventions which have been added onto the mythical report, this one bare fact remains: that before Lycurgus only a few songs were known to the Spartans, that several more were added in his age or by his efforts, and that the poet was ever afterwards held in the highest esteem there.[3]

Nothing is certain about [the history of] these poems for the three centuries immediately after Lycurgus except that they were made public bit by bit by the rhapsodes, as we said above. Even without the testimony of an ancient writer, then, one might well believe that it was the custom to recite them even before the time of Solon.[4] Solon's reputed innovation in recitation, "that the rha-

---

[3] Plato *Leges* 3.680C; Plutarch *Apophth. Lac.* 223A; Aelian *V.H.* 13.19.

[4] Dieuchidas at Diogenes Laertius 1.57(= FGrH 485 F 6): "He made a law that rhapsodes perform the works of Homer in a fixed order, such that, where the first one stopped, the next one started from there." The phrase ἐξ ὑποβολῆς ["in a fixed order"] means the same as ἐξ ὑπολήψεως elsewhere, "in such a way that one would follow another, or, where one had stopped singing, the other would begin with what followed; and thus one body of Homeric poetry would be put together": these are the words of L. Allacci, *De patria Homeri* (1640), ch. 5. On this subject cf. Fabricius, *Bibliotheca Graeca*, 1:356, and Dresig, *De Rhapsodis*, 35, who refutes him. In fact I approve the opinion of neither of these two scholars (though all the others have virtually followed them); yet I judge that Fabricius has strayed less far from the truth.

---

[a] *Historians add such things from their own wits . . . .:* Cf. ch. 31, note b. Where there is no evidence, Wolf says that there must have been, but that it has been lost; where there is evidence, he says that things could not in fact have been as the evidence suggests. Modern historical scholarship has not improved on Wolf's methods.

psodes perform in a fixed order," is such that he was clearly not the first to invite rhapsodes to Athens; rather he changed something in their customs. Now what exactly that change and that custom were must remain a matter of conjecture because of the brevity of Diogenes Laertius. For if perhaps it had previously been the custom that only one rhapsode sang at public festivals, then Solon could have made the affair more splendid by convoking several, who could have sung a greater number of books by following one another in turn. But I give little weight to this argument. For that scarcely reveals so important a transformation of custom as to be a noteworthy deed; nor can the words of Diogenes pertain to this, even if he often talks nonsense. Therefore, when I pursue the meaning of those words more closely and compare the ancient custom of the rhapsodes which I described above, it seems to me that Solon's innovation was this: earlier, single sections were sung without any order of plot or temporal sequence, that is, in one session first the bath of Ulysses (*Od.* 19) or the slaying of the suitors (22) was sung, then the visit to Hades (11), then the events in Pylos or in Lacedaemonia (3-4), and again, from the cycle of the *Iliad*, the funeral games (23), then the forging of Achilles' arms (18), then the embassy (9), finally the plague (1); after Solon, the parts were distributed to various rhapsodes in such a way that the one started where the other left off, and an unbroken and agreeable sequence was finally produced. Memorable indeed, this decree of the legislator who was at the same time a poet; had he not made it, I would perhaps not be writing this book. Nor do we read anywhere that he had the assistance of a written text: if there had been one at that time, Solon would not have had to teach the rhapsodes to do things differently. Moreover, this story must refer to Attica alone, not to all of Greece. For it is quite implausible that Solon was the very first to provide by this method the occasion for a more elegant systematic ordering of Homer's works, or that they had previously been sung, in Ionia and elsewhere, in so disconnected a manner as some have recently argued,[b] and were so confused and jumbled up that their whole uninterrupted course could be destroyed.

But if we had no help except bare conjecture, where but in Homer's homeland would we expect to find the first decision to

---

[b] *as some have recently argued:* For example, Villoison; cf. Introduction.

arrange his poems more elegantly? I add further the decision to use writing: the first attempts at this seem to have been made by that highly cultivated people at the time in which, as we showed in chapter 17, the making of scrolls began, that is, in the period of Pittacus or Solon. Perhaps the ancient and celebrated custom of singing, since it was enormously pleasurable and had evidently developed into an art, could make writing less desirable and therefore perhaps put delays in its path. Nevertheless, after writing had once begun to be attempted, it seems likely that hardly any song of earlier times existed which could so have incited the Greeks to write it down.

CHAPTER XXXIII

But there is no need now to grasp for conjectures. History speaks.[a] For the voice of all antiquity and, if you keep the heart of the matter in view, the consensus of tradition attest that *Pisistratus was the first to set down the poems of Homer in writing*[b] *and to have put them into the order in which they are now read.* This is reported later by Cicero, Pausanias, and all the others who mention this matter, in almost exactly the same words and as something generally very well known.[5] But the way in which certain more recent scholars have

---

[5] Cicero *De oratore* 3.34.137: "Who was more learned in that same period, or whose eloquence is said to have had a higher literary culture than that of Pisistratus? He is said to have been the first to have arranged the books of Homer, which were previously confused, in the way we now have them." Pausanias 7.26.13: "Pisistratus gathered together the epic poems of Homer, which were scattered and preserved by memory elsewhere." Josephus *Against Apion* 1.2.12: "They say that Homer too did not leave behind his own poetry in written form, but that it was preserved by memory and was put together later from songs," evidently by Pisistratus. Aelian *V.H.* 13.14: "Later Pisistratus brought together and published the *Iliad* and the

---

[a] *History speaks:* The reader should be warned that by this phrase Wolf refers to no writer earlier than Cicero and only to writers who connect Pisistratus with the textual tradition of Homer. Sources earlier than Cicero have much to say about Pisistratus but nothing at all about his literary activities. Wolf is also conflating Cicero's testimony, that Pisistratus put the books of Homer in order, with Pausanias' testimony, that he collected the scattered and in part orally transmitted poems of Homer, and Josephus' testimony, that Homer's poems were originally oral. Wolf exaggerates the similarity of these reports and makes no attempt to determine whether they might all have been derived from one source.

[b] *Pisistratus was the first to set down the poems of Homer in writing:* In fact Cicero seems to have thought that Pisistratus was the first to set in order the papyrus rolls that contained Homer's poems, one roll to each book. See B. Hemmerdinger, *Essai sur l'histoire du texte de Thucydide* (Paris, 1955), 17.

twisted this tradition around in interpreting it[6] is a lengthy and wondrous story. For as a rule they seem to give Pisistratus manuscripts of the individual books, left behind, or perhaps pawned by the poet, as Suidas reports, in the various cities through which he had traveled; they seem to believe (for they do not dare to assert this with solemn assurance) that, equipped with these manuscripts, he removed the confusion which had little by little been introduced by the stitchers of the poems, and achieved not so much the definition of a new order as rather the restoration of the original and genuine one. This is how they explain the references to the poems having been *confused, scattered, torn apart, sung here and there*, as

---

Odyssey." Libanius *Orat.* 12.56: "We praise Pisistratus for his gathering together the poems of Homer." Suidas s.v. Ὅμηρος [O 251]: "Later they were put together and set in order by many people, and especially by Pisistratus, the Athenian tyrant." Eustathius 5.33-36: "That the poetry of the *Iliad* is altogether one continuous and coherent body; and those who put it together, by the command, as they say, of Pisistratus . . ." Anonymous Life of Homer [T. W. Allen, *Homeri Opera*, vol. 5, Vita 5.24-26, p. 248]: "The Athenian Pisistratus placed in order his genuine poems, which had earlier been sung here and there." Anonymous Life of Homer [Allen, op. cit., Vita 4.8-16, pp. 245-46]: "Homer sang his poems while traveling through the cities; later Pisistratus brought them together, as this epigram, inscribed by the Athenians on Pisistratus' statue, makes clear:

Thrice the people of Erechtheus banished me, I who was a tyrant
   Just as many times, and thrice they recalled me,
Pisistratus, great in councils, I who gathered together
   Homer, who had formerly been sung here and there.
For that golden man was our fellow citizen,
   Since we Athenians colonized Smyrna. [*A.P.* 11.442]

[6] For most authors hasten through this matter as though it were one of small importance. Others speak absurdly about it as though it were a new edition. But no one has written more candidly on this subject than L. Küster, *Historia Critica Homeri, qua de Scriptis Ejus tam Deperditis, quam Exstantibus, Spuriis et Genuinis . . . Agitur*, 99 [in Wolf's 1785 edition of the *Iliad*], after citing that passage of Eustathius: "I confess that this opinion is not free of difficulties; yet to decide otherwise is precluded by the consensus of almost all of antiquity." This scholar, in his reverence for history, means that consensus that makes Pisistratus, not Homer, the author "of a continuous and coherent body." Frivolously, and spoiling Küster's opinion, Dresig, *De Rhapsodis*, 34: "*By the consensus of almost all antiquity* it seems necessary to concede that Homer himself wrote out in a single sequence the books of both poems and left them to posterity in uninterrupted order, not dispersed, but that while alive he published them only in the form of dispersed songs which he sang in the towns to earn a living." In Latin, we use the adverb *fere* ["almost"] for the sake of modesty, not to cover up a falsehood. Hence he ought to have informed us what that "consensus of almost all antiquity" might be. Not even Suidas agrees in that single passage which Dresig had in view, s.v. Ὅμηρος, [O 251]: "He did not write the *Iliad* all at once or in that continuous form it now has; but he himself wrote and published each book while wandering through the cities and left it behind for the sake of food." Thus in the end there is nothing left for Pisistratus to do except "to divide the poems into as many books as we now have." Hence the good man was ignorant of the fact that this division was introduced by the Alexandrians.

though they had been ripped asunder and jumbled up by the fault of the rhapsodes: and in general they leave only so much of this business to that man (who attained by it the greatest fame for erudition)[7] as nowadays the more negligent writers sometimes leave to the care of printers.

All this would be well if it were a question of a work of our own age, or if there had been written books before Pisistratus, or rhapsodes such as these men imagine them, or finally if any ancient authority existed for this interpretation. It would be quite inept to argue against me that, in general, when the ancients praise the beautiful composition of these poems, they praise Homer, not Pisistratus. It happens quite often in history that the voice of tradition is refuted by facts and that the consequences of those things which everyone held to be true are entirely different from what those who had reported them realized. But the ambiguity which they suppose to reside in this mention of confused poems disappears immediately upon comparison with those writers who have left behind a slightly different report, Josephus and Aelian—or rather, upon comparison of all of them. That the poems were now assembled for the first time, not reassembled, and that the art of arrangement was acquired now for the first time, not called back into existence by critical study—this is what I found in all these authors, and what anyone will find if he takes the trouble to read them attentively and does not, blinded by partisanship and rashly accepted opinions, prefer to be deprived of the light of truth.

And yet the constancy of this tradition was not entirely obscured, even in much later times. The very number of pieces of evidence, deriving from times in which the new form of these poems had long since affirmed itself, might well occasion wonder (the latter could have taken place among the Greeks within two or three generations at that time). Noteworthy in this regard is the story in

---

[7] I think that the report of the first library, founded by Pisistratus, pertains to this as well, even if it is preserved only by a rather late author, Aulus Gellius 7.17.1. For I cannot find any other writers besides Homer who might have been in it, except for some poets whose works were copied down just before at his own orders. Perhaps we should come to the same conclusion about Polycrates of Samos, whom Athenaeus 1.3A joins together with Pisistratus because of his zeal in buying books. Unless I am mistaken, those libraries were doubtless similar to the ones which are said to have been deposited in some temples, also in Jerusalem, and which consisted of a few writings and were hardly worthy of the name as it is used nowadays; perhaps another similar one was that at Smyrna, which Strabo 14.646 mentions together with a shrine to Homer.

the Leipzig scholia and Eustathius[8] that the "Doloneia," that is, book 10 of the *Iliad*, was composed by Homer as a single small work but was assimilated by Pisistratus into his oeuvre. But particularly relevant here are the absurd inventions of the grammarians, who took refuge in corrupt rumors and in their own wits when trying to explain the work of Pisistratus in ignorance of ancient customs. For the sake of amusement I will cite in the note a passage from a certain Diomedes, as Allacci first and Villoison more recently have published it from the manuscripts.[9] There the grammarians of the

[8] Eustathius 785.41f. on 10.1: "The ancients say that this book was put separately by Homer and was not counted among the parts of the *Iliad*, but was put into the poem by Pisistratus."

[9] Allacci, loc. cit., 93. Villoison, *Anecdota Graeca*, 2:182ff. [Scholia on Dionysius Thrax, *Grammatici Graeci* 3.29.17-30.17]: "That at some time the poems of Homer were destroyed, either by fire or flood or earthquake, and the books were scattered abroad this way and that and were destroyed; later one man was found who by chance possessed a hundred verses of Homer, another a thousand, another two hundred, another some other number, and this magnificent poetry was going to be abandoned to oblivion; but Pisistratus, the Athenian general, wishing to make a name for himself and to revive Homer's poetry, devised the following plan. He had heralds announce in all of Greece that anyone possessing verses of Homer should bring them to him for a reward calculated according to the number of verses; then all those who possessed verses brought them to him and received exactly the specified reward. He did not reject anyone who brought him verses which he had already received from someone else, but gave the same reward to the second man too; for sometimes he found one or two extra verses among them, sometimes even more; thus some people interpolated their own verses, which are now obelized. And after having brought them all together, he summoned together seventy-two grammarians *to compose the poems of Homer*, each one in private according to how it seemed best to him, for a reward appropriate for skilled men and judges of poetry, having given to each one in private all the verses he had gathered together; and after each one had composed according to his own judgment, he brought together all these grammarians, and obliged each one to show him his own composition in the presence of all. When these had been heard, not for the sake of competition but for that of the truth, and everything was fitted together with skill, they all judged, together and unanimously, that the composition and recension of Aristarchus and Zenodotus were the best; and again they judged that of these two compositions and recensions, that of Aristarchus was better. And since some of those who had brought verses of Homer to Pisistratus had inserted their own verses as well, as we said before, in order to obtain a greater reward, and these were already well known to readers: this did not escape the notice of the judges, but they let them stand on account of their familiarity and previous acceptance, but placed obeli beside each of the verses which were spurious, belonged to another author, and were unworthy of the poet. In that way they made clear that these verses are unworthy of Homer." This final passage about suspected verses which were left in place is not ill-informed: on this matter I shall have something to say below in my treatment of Zenodotus. Another scholium, whose beginning I have given in ch. 18, n. 39 [scholia on Dionysius Thrax, *Grammatici Graeci* 3.179.14-19], reports more briefly about Pisistratus as follows: "*He wished the written poetry of Homer to be preserved*. He proposed a competition at public expense, had heralds announce it, gave safe conduct to those who knew how to reveal the poems of Homer and wished to do so, and established a reward of one obol for each line of verse. In this way he brought together all the versions, and

latest period invent the fable that, after the works of Homer had been destroyed—they are uncertain whether fire or earthquake or flood consumed them—Pisistratus decreed that anything of Homer's lurking anywhere must be brought to him from all over Greece. In this way people were turned up everywhere, one to bring a hundred verses, another a thousand, and another even more. When these had all been received and collected, he himself gathered together seventy-two grammarians (you will remember Aristeas' story of the seventy-two translators of the Bible) and ordered them to bring this hodgepodge into the proper order. The most conspicuous place in this assembly of grammarians is reserved for Zenodotus and Aristarchus—a most abominable error, yet one that neither Eustathius nor certain more recent scholars have eschewed.[10] And the authority of this one fable may serve as a defense for those men who contend that Pisistratus did not collect and arrange the poems in their first written form, but instead restored ones that had been pulled apart, scattered, and torn to pieces.[11] We, who think that we know the difference between fable and history, recognize here the history which is hidden under the fable and which has to be excavated by a method similar to that used by scholars for the Jewish inventions about the seventy-two translators.[12c]

gave them to wise and understanding men." This is the one grammarian who explicitly confirms that *the first text was prepared by Pisistratus*. He says that previously, not writing, but *only the teaching* of the rhapsodes was used to preserve Homer. No one reports this so explicitly besides Josephus; yet all report the same thing.

[10] Following the great compilers of *Histoire universelle*, J. J. Barthélemy, *Voyages du jeune Anacharsis en Grèce, dans le milieu du quatrième siècle avant l'ère vulgaire* [1788], Introduction, 52-53, repeats this very error (which would scarcely have been forgiven in Anacharsis the Scythian), but with the names of the grammarians omitted, and also reports the rest of the history of Homer's works in the ordinary way.

[11] This is clearly reported by one small scholium edited in *Anecdota Graeca* (op. cit.): "It is reported that they stitched together under Pisistratus . . . the poems of Homer and put them together into order after they had previously been read here and there and by chance, since their order had been torn apart in the course of time."

[12] As, most sharp-wittedly of all, J. G. Eichhorn in *Repertorium für Biblische und morgenländische Litteratur* (1777), 1:266ff.

c *A method similar to that used by scholars for the Jewish inventions about the seventy-two translators:* For the connections with Eichhorn, cf. Grafton, and Introduction above. Wolf's technique here is fundamentally that of rationalizing eighteenth-century historical allegory; on this phenomenon cf. e.g. Frank E. Manuel, *The Eighteenth Century Confronts the Gods* (Cambridge, Mass., 1959), and Michael Murrin, *The Allegorical Epic* (Chicago and London, 1980) (pp. 189-96 on Wolf).

CHAPTER XXXIV

But if, as the ancients held, no one before Pisistratus thought seriously about gluing the works of Homer together, it is not credible
that they could immediately have reached the public complete in
all their parts and in the state in which we now see them, even if
the gluing had been elaborately worked out in advance. Pisistratus
could have thought it enough to put several sections into an appropriate order, leaving to the side those that impeded the general
plot, even if inconsistencies and gaps might exist here and there,
or scraps remain from the earlier form. One motive among others
for seeking out that uninterrupted sequence could have been the
very activity of continuous writing, in which each poem had to be
assigned its place. But polishing everything and, as it were, making
it absolutely smooth might have seemed too toilsome to manage in
this first attempt. But I have two reasons ready for being disinclined
to attribute this skill to Pisistratus alone. Both are quite clear and
manifest to anyone accustomed to the darkness of those times. First,
we previously inferred from those passages which are cited from
Homer by Plato and his contemporaries but do not appear in him
today that the Greeks lacked any firm text until the age of the
Ptolemies. Thus no one can guess, on the basis of the text that we
handle today, how it was first written down. In fact, if one rhapsode
after another had been summoned for the writing after Pisistratus,
its form would necessarily have varied and changed from time to
time until it reached the hands of Zenodotus and Aristarchus. The
commentaries of these men doubtless preserved more evidence
about this subject: now, since these are lost, the common opinion
speciously maintains itself. But there has been a change. Before
Villoison's gift, only one passage in the scholia mentioned a revision
more ancient than those of the Alexandrians: no one, as far as I
know, knew what this might refer to. Now the Venetian scholiast
has given us a clear account of both revision and revisers. In a
number of passages he reports that they forged something which
later critics thought to be unworthy of the bard and to require
excision.[13] Since the revision had previously been known only from

[13] The passage is in the shorter scholia on *Od.* 11.584; when it is compared with
schol. Ven. on *Il.* 2.597 and schol. on Pindar *Ol.* 1.91a [1.37.21-22 Drachmann], it

that one tenuous trace, and since even now its method has not been accurately explained, we cannot easily come to any firm conclusion about it. And yet, when those indications are compared with one another, they clearly show that the revisers are to be thought of, not as unknown authors of critical recensions (for such people other words were used), but as supervisors or polishers, who set their hand to the same task as Pisistratus, either together with him or a little later.[14]

But I think it entirely unclear whether the ancients themselves attributed this business to Pisistratus alone, or whether, as they often did, they made him the author of what had been accomplished at his urging and under his authority. To be sure, the Platonic dialogue entitled *Hipparchus* assigns to its eponym, the younger son of Pisistratus and, together with his brother, Pisistratus' successor in that tyranny which was so beneficial for Athens, a magnificent role in glorifying Homer. Perhaps he either aided his father especially in the labor of collecting and arranging or carried out his father's plan and shared it with lovers of literature.[15]

---

shows that Aristarchus suspected several verses there of being a reviser's interpolation. And if the note of the manuscript Vindobonensis philol. 133 deserves any belief, his suspicion created a large lacuna in the most beautiful part of the book. But, if I recall correctly, in this one passage Eustathius [1701.26ff. on *Od.* 11.583] mentions this matter; but his information is derived from this same scholium, and he seems not to have understood it better than any scholar had before the publication of the gift from Venice. Hence let us omit M. Casaubon, who tried to shed light on the scholium from the rhetorical notes of Eustathius, in which the σχῆμα διασκευαστικόν ["reviser's trope"] is mentioned [cf. ch. 30, n. 97]. But cf. now schol. Ven. on *Il.* 4.208 (to be referred to 3.396-418), 6.441, 8.73-74, and the one on 18.356 which I indicated a little earlier, 19.327 and 400 (to be referred to 8.185), 20.269-72, and 24.130-32.

[14] This word's meaning, which we are investigating, is generally unknown, and it is not listed by Stephanus and Scott. But it is sufficiently explained by the scholia to Aristophanes *Clouds* 552 [Dübner] and 591a [Holwerda], as well as by the passage in the same play's well-known Hypothesis [6, p. 4.16 Holwerda]. When these are compared it becomes clear that διασκευάζειν was understood by the ancient teachers as having the same meaning as the verb ἐπιδιασκευάζειν, so that among the tragic poets it would be practically synonymous with ἀναδιδάσκειν, i.e. "to stage a play repeatedly, one that has been emended by changing, adding, subtracting, that has been formed anew and systematically reworked." For, in general, those poets did this very often, and later others did as well, like Apollonius Rhodius. Nor did Plato do otherwise in his best dialogues: this is why it is not possible to determine when each one was composed, though in the case of dramatic plays it is usually known when they were published, at least on the basis of the didascalia. Therefore the word was used of the authors of a book themselves, or of those who polished the books of others, not of the critics of later ages.

[15] The passage in Plato *Hipparchus* 228B concerning Hipparchus is well known: "who produced many fine works of wisdom, and in particular was the first to bring

True, he commanded above all that Homer be sung in a new order by the rhapsodes at the quinquennial Panathenaic festivals.[16] But that could not have resulted in the report that he was the first to bring him to Attica. A lovely flowering of lyric and ethical poetry occurred in the age of these two men, together with new additions— namely, tragedy and comedy. Among so many poets there were perhaps some who could help Pisistratus and Hipparchus in this matter, especially since both of them were very well disposed both to the arts and to learned men. It is expressly reported that Orpheus of Croton, the author of an *Argonautica*, Onomacritus of Athens, who was later exiled from the city by Hipparchus, Simonides of Ceos, and Anacreon of Teos lived in the closest friendship with Pisistratus and Hipparchus.[17a] I would conjecture that one of these men offered them his help in arranging the poems. Pisistratus himself certainly had his hands full with his own affairs, while the

---

the poems of Homer into this land and compelled the rhapsodes at the Panathenaic festivals to go through them in continuous sequence just as they still do nowadays." It is quite remarkable that the very things which others attribute to the father and to Solon are here attributed simply to the son. But this discrepancy is greater in appearance than in reality if you follow our opinion or, what is practically the same thing, that of Küster [in F. A. Wolf, ed., *Homeri Carmina. Ilias* (1785), 101], and at the same time remember that this appears in a text composed to praise Hipparchus. For the rest, the doubts of an ancient critic at Aelian *V.H.* 8.2 (cf. above ch. 13, n. 12) and L. C. Valckenaer's assent in P. Wesseling, ed., *Herodoti Halicarnassensis Historiarum Libri IX* [1763], 398, have fully convinced me that this dialogue is not a genuine work of Plato's, but was written by an Athenian of the same tribe that counterfeited so many exercises for the orators. If this conjecture wins the approval of the more learned scholars (and it will someday deprive Plato of certain other lesser dialogues as well, and will return them to Demodocus and Sisyphus), no one will wonder why I have not called Hipparchus older than Hippias, as does J. Meursius [*Pisistratus. Sive, De Ejus Vita, & Tyrannide, Liber Singularis* (1623), 71f.], since I have submitted to the grave authority of Thucydides and, to a certain extent, to that of Herodotus as well.

[16] Lycurgus *Oratio in Leocratem* 26.102 [71.5-9 Scheibe-Blass-Conomis]: "Your fathers were so convinced that he was a noble poet that they established an ordinance that at each of the quinquennial Panathenaic festivals the rhapsodes would recite only his poetry and no other poet's, thereby proving to the Greeks that they preferred the very finest works."

[17] Herodotus 7.6; Plato, loc. cit.; Suidas s.v. Ὀρφεὺς Κροτωνιάτης [O 657].

---

[a] *It is expressly reported . . .*: When the *Scholium Plautinum*, a fifteenth-century Latin translation of what was probably originally part of Tzetzes' twelfth-century *Prolegomena to Aristophanes*, was discovered in the nineteenth century, it seemed (wrongly) to confirm two of these names, those of Orpheus of Croton and Onomacritus of Athens. So for example Friedrich Ritschl spoke of Wolf's "happy guess" (*Die Alexandrinischen Bibliotheken unter den ersten Ptolemäern und die Sammlung der Homerischen Gedichte durch Pisistratus, nach Anleitung eines Plautinischen Scholions* [Breslau 1838], 41).

poets had leisure and a considerable familiarity with the ancient works. Onomacritus' celebrated forgeries of Orpheus and Musaeus, for example, must be referred to the very beginnings of writing.

I think it rash to carve out the traces of history from every low haunt of fables: otherwise I would seek to derive color and plausibility for these speculations from the fact that those inventions of the grammarians and Suidas ascribe several associates to Pisistratus in his work.[b] But the passage most worthy of note is the one in Pausanias mentioned earlier. There, while discussing the variability of the name at *Il.* 2.573, he clearly mentions *Pisistratus' friends and helpers in putting the* Iliad *into writing.*[18] It is thus obvious that this subject, which we have revived, had not yet been completely obscured in the age of Pausanias.[c]

CHAPTER XXXV

Therefore it was under the rule of the Pisistratids that Greece first saw the ancient poems of its bards consigned to durable records. A number of nations have experienced such an age, one when letters and a greater civic culture were in their infancy. By comparing these carefully, much light may be shed upon the matters we are discussing here.[a] For—to touch in passing upon two nations entirely dissimilar both to one another and to the Greeks—scholars

---

[18] "Either Pisistratus himself, or *one of his comrades*, changed the name through ignorance."

---

[b] *I think it rash . . . .:* Here Wolf takes a far more conservative position than he had in the previous chapter (another example of his effort to stay on both sides of all fences). There he had written: "We, who think that we know the difference between fable and history . . ."

[c] *It is thus obvious . . . .:* The passage in question mentions Pisistratus and "his comrades" (quoted by Wolf in n. 18). It hardly sustains the interpretation Wolf places upon it in the text.

[a] *By comparing these carefully, much light may be shed . . . .:* Analogies like this one were a staple of eighteenth-century Homeric criticism. Merian (see ch. 13, note a), for example, described the crystallization of the poems of Ossian in similar terms (op. cit., 517): "Why should his [Homer's] case not be like that of the first poets of many other nations, whose verse passed from mouth to mouth and memory to memory—for example, the Celtic poets, whose Songs the Druids made the young Gauls memorize? When, later, writing comes into use among these peoples, and in proportion as the operations involved in it become easier, amateurs will use it to give a permanent form to the works that please them, or the parts of those works that win their preference." Herder made similar ideas accessible and influential in Germany.

agree that in our own Germany, which had celebrated civil wars and the deeds of its princes and generals in poems even before the time of Tacitus, Charlemagne at last collected these first fruits of rude genius and put them into books. So too the Arabs began only in the seventh century to gather into collections (*Divans*) the disorganized poetry of earlier ages which had been transmitted by memory, and the diversity of the early texts of the Koran itself shows that it had a fate similar to Homer's. Besides these and other peoples we should compare the Hebrews. Widespread literacy and writing of books were, in my view at least, a good bit more recent among them than is generally thought, and hence the corpus of writings, especially the more ancient ones, is less genuine. But experts on Oriental literature will decide about these questions and about those Arab collections.[b]

We return to the Greeks. After they had collected their Homer, they probably applied similar efforts to the rest of the more outstanding poems that were of about the same age. The silence of antiquity surprises me less in their case. For, once an example had been given, the work could not have been so very difficult; nor do we see an attempt to attain so skillful a structure in any other poem. Hence there were, I suspect, revisers both for all the other remains of Homer and for those of Hesiod; they connected together the individual sections or included in one volume, like the *Catalogue of Women* and the *Great Eoiai*, those books which the same authors had composed on an identical pattern. I suspect that this was accomplished not much later than the Pisistratids for the Cyclic poems and for many others that today are scarcely known even by name and would not have survived to the age of the Ptolemies if they had not been preserved then from destruction or from further corruption.

The false attributions of a number of works are probably also to be assigned to the same period, since everything that had approximately the same tone and subject matter was ascribed to one author, especially Homer and Hesiod, both of whom had in their glorious brilliance eclipsed all the lesser lights. Indeed, even quite

---

[b] *But experts on Oriental literature . . . .:* The analogy between Homer and the Koran had been made by Villoison and others before Wolf; see Grafton, 115, n. 87. In general Wolf seems to be calling for a comparative treatment of Homer and the Bible that is more openly radical in its conclusions than Eichhorn's.

significant discrepancies did not always shake the ancients' credulity. Thus it was not until Herodotus that anyone tried to expel two poems, the *Cypria* and the *Epigoni*,[19] from the Homeric corpus; others later did the same for the *Hymns* and other poems, until more or less everyone acquiesced in the judgments of certain Alexandrians. I would append some fresh examples of this if I could go where my subject invites rather than where it leads me.[20]

But before I enter into a new period, I should like everyone to bring together in his mind everything I have explained up to now, separating the fine-spun threads of my argumentation so that the strength of the individual arguments and their strength as a whole may become clear. To be sure, probability resides in the arguments when they are joined together and, so to speak, fused together just as beauty resides in members of the body when they are joined together. Nevertheless each individual argument must have enough force in itself to tip the scale. If, in some matters, I have attributed more to probability than the strict law of history requires, this is not my own fault but that of the paucity of witnesses—of whom, indeed, you would not expect to find such a large number in matters which are so ancient and which grew up in secret. But I certainly have not knowingly twisted any passage of an ancient author to

---

[19] 2.117. With reservations, I add the other passage, 4.32, where in the meantime I suspect in the words ἀλλ' Ἡσιόδῳ ["but to Hesiod . . ."] etc. the annotation of an ancient grammarian, not of Herodotus. On this matter cf. the end of ch. 23.

[20] I shall introduce here in a few words one thing, deserving a long explanation, from which it will be clear how far the doubts of the Greeks themselves had progressed even before the Alexandrians. This will simultaneously excuse our audacity somewhat and serve as a new argument that many of the most important matters have been obliterated by the confirmed opinions and doctrines of those ages from which our scholia derive. Among the questions of the Greeks which Seneca describes in *De brevitate vitae* 13.2 as being useless for living well, we have always read this one as well: "Whether the *Iliad* and the *Odyssey* were by the same author." Until recently there was no other trace of this question anywhere. But lo! Now more traces have come to light in the extraordinary Venetian scholia of Codex A, where this subject is mentioned as being very well known to the learned, and a number of times οἱ χωρίζοντες, i.e. those who denied that the same man was the author of both poems, are refuted by name. Cf. the scholia on *Il*. 2.356, 649; 4.354; 10.476; 11.147, 692; 12.96; 13.365; 16.747; 21.416, 550. Next to these verses the simple diple was placed because of οἱ χωρίζοντες, that is, as we read in the fragment of Aristonicus on the critical signs, "against those who say that the *Iliad* and the *Odyssey* do not both belong to the same poet" [A Dindorf, xlv.1-3]. But I infer from many indications that these were earlier than the celebrated schools of the grammarians. Perhaps, then, the first trace of that suspicion lies hidden within this mutilated passage of [Proclus'] Life of Homer [T. W. Allen, ed., *Homeri Opera*, 5:102.2-3]: "He wrote two poems, the *Iliad* and the *Odyssey*. Xenon and Hellanicus deprive him."

mean anything that someone unconcerned with this question would not consider its true and genuine sense. I trust that I shall be able to prove this to all scholars, even to those to whom I shall not be able to prove the logical consequences I have drawn from those passages—especially this final one, by which I have dared to deprive Homer of some of the renown for that artistic skill which they admire so greatly. No doubt only very few scholars will be convinced of this, even, perhaps, when they are overwhelmed by the weight of all the arguments. For in these matters one needs a certain sensibility which arguments do not provide. But as for me, whether I contemplate the progress of the Greeks themselves or that of other races, I find it impossible to accept the belief to which we have become accustomed: that these two works of a single genius burst forth suddenly from the darkness in all their brilliance, just as they are, with both the splendor of their parts and the many great virtues of the connected whole.

CHAPTER XXXVI

The second period, from the *Pisistratids* to *Zenodotus*, is almost as obscure as the first one. This is greatly to be regretted, for we must seek in this second period the origins of all forms of interpretation that the ancients used. For before a highly literate age set about it with more equipment, philosophers, sophists, and other liberally educated men gave examples of the interpretation of Homer. Soon the desire to increase the number of copies, which created the necessity of selecting the best texts from the variety that the rhapsodes had provided, paved the way for a more careful critical activity. But these matters must be discussed in somewhat more detail.

At first, and almost up to the time of Pericles, Greece still knew Homer and its other poets more from hearing than from reading. Even then, few people took the trouble to write, and reading was toilsome and difficult; hence they paid the greatest attention to the rhapsodes, and hung from their lips, captivated by the extraordinary sweetness of their song. Cynaethus is mentioned among the most famous rhapsodes of this age, around the Sixty-ninth Olympiad [504-500 B.C.]. A contemporary of Pindar, he emigrated from

Chios to Syracuse, or at least practiced his art especially there.[21]
And since the men of this profession spent all their time learning
the poet by heart, they might well be thought to have been his first
interpreters. But that is not confirmed by the certain testimony of
any author. For the passage from Plato which some scholars cite
could apply in this context to any stage actor.[22] That is why I do
not doubt that the most ancient philosophers are to be considered
the founders of Homeric interpretation and, at least at the beginning, of a pragmatic interpretation. For there was basically no obscurity in the words in those ages, since each of the best poets
normally used the same diction. But when the philosophers saw
that the poems were considered sacred and were celebrated by the
whole populace, and that the precepts for governing one's life
rightly were drawn from them, and when they nevertheless also
noticed in them many false, ridiculous, and unseemly fictions concerning the nature of the gods and the world, they began to correct
the fables by interpreting them and to accommodate them to the
physical and ethical beliefs of their own age, and finally to reduce
the stories and almost everything else to wrappings for an elaborate
philosophy. Already around the Sixty-third Olympiad [528-524
B.C.], in which Pisistratus died, Theagenes of Rhegium was taking
great pains in this area, and he was soon followed by Anaxagoras
of Clazomenae, Metrodorus of Lampsacus, Stesimbrotus of Thasus,
and others of the same period.[23] On the other hand, a few others,

---

[21] Schol. on Pindar *N.* 2.1c, e [3.29.14-18, 31.16-19 Drachmann].

[22] Plato *Ion* 530C: "No one could ever become a rhapsode who did not understand
the words of the poet. For the rhapsode must become an interpreter of the poet's
thought for the listeners." Ion's answer, that he can "say the finest things of all men
about Homer" and that in this regard he can compete with the best interpreters,
is pretty impressive. For the rest this pretty little interpreter offers nothing worthy
of such boasting: but even if he could do this, as F. Sydenham, [tr., *"Io," a Dialogue
of Plato, concerning Poetry* (1759)] thinks, we are not asking about the rhapsodes of
the age of Plato, but about the ancient successors to the bards. Cf. 535A.

[23] Plato *Ion*, loc. cit.; Xenophon *Symp.* 3.3.6; Diogenes Laertius 2.11; Tatian *Against
the Greeks* 21, 31. Cf. P. Bayle, *Dictionnaire historique et critique*, s.v. Anaxagoras, and
J. Burnet Monboddo, *Antient Metaphysics. Volume Third. Containing the History and
Philosophy of Men* (1784), 108n. Out of these four, Theagenes is cited twice in the
scholia [schol. on *Il.* 1.381 and 20.67ff. (Porphyry 241.11)], Anaxagoras also twice
[schol. on *Il.* 16.161, 17.747], Metrodorus once at *Il.* 10.252 [Porphyry 147.18; and
cf. schol. on *Il.* 21.444], Stesimbrotus thrice (schol. on *Il.* 11.636, 15.189, 21.76 [and
also on 14.325]) and twice in the scholia to Apollonius Rhodius [on 1.1126 and
1.1304], and in the *Etymologicum Magnum* [s.v. Ἰδαῖοι and s.v. Διόνυσος]. Plato
adds Glaucon, perhaps the Teian in Aristotle *Rhetoric* 3.1.1403b26 who had written

like Pythagoras, Xenophanes, and Heraclitus,[24] did not shrink from accusing Homer of impiety because of the many falsehoods that he invented or adorned with beautiful verses. In this regard, these latter authors seem to me to have done something very important, and worthy of the natural talent of that most liberal of races. For they were not deterred by the bard's sanctity (which everyone, and even, in a sense, they themselves believed in) from openly criticizing everything in him which they thought inconsistent with true wisdom and good morals. But even the former do not lack an appropriate excuse, whether they themselves believed in their allegorical and anagogical dreams or merely wished to be believed by others. For it is the nature of reason that we insert almost all our own opinions and those of our age into the books with which we have been continuously familiar since early youth; and if those books have long since been consecrated by popular usage, then veneration also hinders us from believing that they contain absurd and ridiculous things. Hence we soften and adorn by interpretation whatever does not seem tolerable in its literal sense; and the more eruditely and subtly we do this, the more scrupulously we seem to be doing it. And this has been the way of things at all times in those books which have been considered sacred.[a] If this is done so that knowl-

---

about the tragic or rhapsodic performance; unless we prefer Sydenham's correction (op. cit.) to Glaucus because of the B Schol. on *Il.* 11.636, where Glaucus is joined to Stesimbrotus. We know even less about Xenophon's Anaximander. For chronology makes it impossible that the famous disciple of Thales could have been the teacher of Niceratus; it could have been a son of the same name; but nothing of the sort is to be found about even this.

[24] Diogenes Laertius 8.21, 9.1, 9.18, and the commentators, ad locc.

---

[a] *And this has been the way of things at all times in those books . . .:* This striking passage is in part derived from and in part directed against Heyne. He too had held that the Greeks' misinterpretations of Homer were directly comparable to other cultures' misinterpretations of their sacred texts; he too had seen such misinterpretations as the result of the efforts of sophisticated readers to read their systematic and up-to-date ideas back into the unsystematic and archaic poetry of their forefathers, which they knew, revered, and wished to continue to admire. See the useful summary by his pupil J.H.J. Köppen, *Ueber Homers Leben und Gesänge* (1788), 246-47. Wolf departed from Heyne, however, in that he treated the Homeric texts as objects of misreading only (Heyne had seen Homer too as a misinterpreter of still earlier myths) and in that he tried to show the historical mode of reading to be the only true one (Heyne had continued to believe in the value of aesthetic analysis). Both men, however, agreed on one point: that Greek misinterpretations of their own myths were directly comparable to Christian theologians' misinterpretations of the Bible. This is indicated by their application to the Greeks of the formal terminology of Protestant hermeneutics: "accommodation," "allegory," "anagogy."

edge of them may remain useful for the people, I see nothing reprehensible in it. For only in a few passages can the majority of the illiterate be recalled to the true, that is, historical, interpretation. Nor were the most learned of the Greeks sufficiently acquainted with this latter; otherwise they would both have censured their Homer more leniently and have been less unanimous in attributing to him knowledge of all the most important subjects.

To pursue through all the ages the question of how and by whom these things were done, and to explore all the sources and currents of allegorical interpretation, would provide the matter for a lengthy history. Socrates, to be sure, that most sober of sages, only alludes to it playfully; Plato followed him, in some way, when he wrote philosophy in a popular manner.[25] But in that work in which Plato constructed a model of the best customs and of a city-state perfect in every respect, he makes clear that he cannot really find in Homer what this allegorical method reveals. That philosopher was the first—so it seems to us—to make imitation the essence of the poetic art, on the basis of several genres, especially drama. But he thought that imitation dealt with trivial and transient things (for he assigned stability and truth to his Ideas alone). He thus demonstrated that this art, since it was a third step away from celestial truth, was itself also vain, contemptible, and a vicious guide to life.[26] That is why he banished both Homer and the tragic poets, together with the whole flock of rhapsodes, choral dancers, and musicians, from his new city-state. His primary opinion of the poetic art was adopted by Aristotle in his own celebrated little book. True, Aristotle corrected it here and there, but even so, he did not explain it in such a way as to make it quite appropriate for every kind of poem: thus he completely excluded the genre of didactic poetry. Nor does any philosopher after Aristotle seem to have understood correctly the true meaning of this art or its historical interpretation. For while the Epicureans rejected all poetry and music and denied that any doctrine was concealed under Homer's fables, all the other sects reverted with great zeal to the ancient allegorical meanings—especially the Stoics Zeno, Cleanthes, and Chrysippus, whose writings

[25] The outstanding passage on Socrates is in Xenophon *Mem.* 1.3.7. N. Schow, *Allegoriae Homericae quae sub Heraclidis Nomine Feruntur* [1782], 223, cites more, derived from Plato; add to these, besides many others, Plato *Alcibiades* 2. 147B-D.

[26] Students should especially read *Republic* 2, 3, and 10, particularly starting with 603B, together with *Leges* 2 starting with 668A.

are the source for most of what Heraclides or Heraclitus, Cornutus, and Eustathius report. Aristarchus opposed himself to these men, since he thought that one must everywhere adhere faithfully to the words of the poet and that this doctrine of theirs was pure non-sense.[27] But not even the authority of Aristarchus dissuaded the philosophers from their nonsensical study: virtually none of them in the following centuries did not force upon Homer some ineffable secrets or at least the tenets of his own sect. Hence Seneca says wittily,[28] "None of these things seems to be in that author in whom all things are: for they disagree among themselves." In this context belongs the further question, discussed by Favorinus, Longinus, Oenomaus, and others, whether the poet was a philosopher. Porphyry's scholia and his separately published works make clear the manner in which he dealt with this question. It was from this time onwards that the Greeks really slipped back into the disease of seeking either anagogical or historical allegories everywhere. It was with these weapons that Proclus defended Homer against Plato; it was in this way that Simplicius found in fables the curtains spread before the true wisdom; it was in this way, finally, in the Middle Ages, that Eustathius' friend Michael Psellus explained both poems, and that Nicephorus Gregoras explained the wanderings of Ulysses—to name only these.

CHAPTER XXXVII

But, returning to the ancients (for we must conclude our digression where we began it), it is by no means certain how they discharged the other duties of the interpreter. On the basis of Plato's *Ion* and of that memorable passage of Aristotle in which he criticizes "the ancient Homerists" as a noble order of learned men who became bogged down in details with an obsessiveness almost worthy of the Masoretes, I conjecture that the ancients certainly did not waste their energy on this one thing alone, but also undertook to illustrate the poet's art and other matters.[29]

[27] Cf. Eustathius 3.23, 40.27f. on 1.46, 561.28f. on 5.395-400, 614.5f. on 5.842-44.
[28] *Epist.* 88.5.
[29] Aristotle *Metaphysics* N.6.1093a26-28. For, like F. Sylburg, [*Aristotelis Opera quae*

In the age of Pericles, the sophists seem to have done a little better in the interpretation of Homer, for they tended to introduce into their own teaching everything then considered worthy of liberal study and hence did not think that they should even neglect grammatical precepts and the teaching of the best poets. Thus we read that Prodicus argued subtly about the true meanings of words and their causes,[30] and again that Protagoras and Hippias of Elis plainly set out to discuss the matters which belong to learned interpretation.[31] It is useless to inquire how much success they enjoyed. For the first attempts at reducing such things to an art with formal rules are very difficult. The greatest geniuses may well stumble without reproach then on points about which beginners could not go wrong with impunity a century later. An example of this is Protagoras' precept about the use of the imperative mood of verbs: he censures the poet because he invoked the Muse less modestly than propriety would have demanded. But we see Hippias, even in his display speeches in Plato's dialogue of the same name, answering doubts and questions about the opinions, virtues, and vices of Homer and the other poets. This makes it perfectly clear that the "Problems" or "Uncertainties" and "Solutions" on which the erudite pupils of Alexandria later toiled so greatly[32] had already begun to become standard exercises in the schools of the philosophers and sophists.[a] This, indeed, must be the source of critical study, which those controversial questions in many passages could themselves have brought into being.

Two emendations of this sort by Hippias of Thasos have survived; for one of these we would not even be able to find the place

---

Exstant (1584-87)], I think that this passage is to be understood as referring to the explainers of Homer, not to his imitators. So too Eustathius 260.10 on 2.484-93 writes "the Homerists."

[30] Plato *Charm.* 163D, *Meno* 75E, *Cratylus* 384B.

[31] On Protagoras cf. Aristotle *Poetics* 19.1456b15. The scholia [on *Il.* 1.1] and Eustathius 10.32ff. prove that the grammarians later wrote against this. On Hippias cf. Plato *Hippias minor* 363Aff., Cicero *De oratore* 3.32.127, where knowledge of the poets is attributed to him; and on the Sophists in general cf. Isocrates *Panathenaicus* 18, 33.

[32] Porphyry on *Il.* 9.656 [141.13-16].

---

[a] *had already begun to become standard exercises in the schools of the philosophers and sophists:* Despite his many admonitions against doing so, Wolf here retrojects the terms and conditions of Alexandrian literary life into the fifth and fourth centuries B.C.

(so changed is our text) if Aristotle had not indicated it in passing.[33] It is *Il.* 2.15, where at that time for the words Τρώεσσι δὲ κήδε᾽ ἐφῆπται ["and troubles were hung over the Trojans"] the reading was more or less as in 21.297, δίδομεν δέ οἱ εὖχος ἀρέσθαι ["and we grant that he may achieve his prayer"]. It was thought impious that Zeus should promise with these words something that would never happen—as though for the rest Zeus acted differently with Agamemnon than Jehovah with Ahab (1 Kings 22). But Hippias, with a shrewdness worthy of the arts of Loyola, changed the verb δίδομεν to διδόμεν, an infinitive to be understood as an imperative, so that a transposition of accent would transfer the crime from Zeus to the Dream. The other passage is 23.328, which he corrected to read as it does today. If Hippias was the first to expel the previously accepted οὖ here, or his contemporaries propagated other similar readings in their own texts—like θηλυτεράων ["fertile"] for the Aristarchean τηλεδαπάων ["remote"] in 21.454 (as we have recently learned from the "city copies")[b]—then it is easy to see from these examples what truly disgusting corruptions clung to the texts of this period. But more can be suspected than known about these matters. Erasures in the manuscripts themselves, surviving even to this day, prove that the Homeric passages cited by Herodotus and other very ancient authors were also frequently changed by scribes to the vulgate form of the text. We would have a very different Homer, then, if we were to receive a copy of him from the library of some sophist or of pretty Euthydemus![34]

For since a book trade of a sort already flourished in those times, every educated man doubtless had plenty of copies, especially the schoolteachers, who earlier had dictated everything from memory to their pupils. This was the source of Alcibiades' celebrated wrath against a man of this class: when he could not find even one book of the *Iliad* at the latter's house, he is said to have struck him with his fist.[35] Consequently, at that time one could expect that a well-

[33] Aristotle *Poetics* 25.1461a21f. and *Soph. Elench.* 1.4.166b3-6, where cf. J. Pacius, *Aristotelis Stagiritae Peripateticorum Principis Organum*, [2d ed. (1597, repr. 1967)], 793. There are several things in that chapter of the *Poetics* that confirm our opinion about the antiquity of the Homeric προβλήματα and λύσεις.

[34] Xenophon *Mem.* 4.2.1.

[35] Plutarch *Alcib.* 194D, cf. *Apophthegm.* 186D; Aelian *V.H.* 13.38, where cf. J. Perizonius, ed., *Cl. Aeliani Sophistae Varia historia* [1701], 847ff., and compare what I pointed out above, ch. 25. Plutarch said, less ambiguously, "a Homeric book."

[b] *as we have recently learned from the "city copies":* Schol. 21.454c Erbse.

equipped school would have a text of Homer—if not of all his poetry, at least of certain parts. That is why another teacher soon went to Alcibiades to say that he had a Homer, and in fact one which he himself had corrected. Then Alcibiades replied, "Really? You know how to correct Homer, and yet you teach mere boys, and not adolescents instead!"

CHAPTER XXXVIII

This story gives us the opportunity to make some general observations about the birth of critical study, which in turn may enable us to form an estimate of the state of the recensions reported to have been made at this time. For no one, I think, will now find it surprising that the Greeks—at a time when, by extraordinary good fortune, they were men more of genius than of learning and were complete strangers to that polymathy for which monarchy later supplied the leisure—had already turned their attention little by little to an art entirely derived from the varied knowledge of literature and antiquity. Indeed, all the causes which played the greatest part in bringing the ancients to the art of criticism already existed at that time. Among these I would assign the first place to that older method of preserving songs by memory alone, the second to the errors and deceptions in transmitting the names of their authors, the third to the various slips easily committed by unpracticed hands in preparing the first texts. But even if this last cause would necessarily have created a desire for that art after a few centuries, nevertheless anyone who knows the Greeks will easily understand that their genius could not have descended so quickly or so eagerly to such minute concerns if their books had been corrupted only by the faults common to every text. Let it therefore remain the unique fortune of the monuments of Homer and his contemporaries that they in a sense forced philological criticism into existence, and had done so even before the name of critic or grammarian had passed into common use.[36]

---

[36] In this second period the term γραμματικός ["grammarian"] referred not to a *profession*, but to a *science*. For before the greatness of the arts, as Cicero said (*De oratore* 3.33.132), began to be diminished by the distribution of their parts, ἀγράμματος was said of the man who lacked the ability to read and write, while he who possessed it was called γραμματικός, the skill itself γραμματική, and this was the special province of the γραμματιστής or γραμματοδιδάσκαλος. This is the usage of

For suppose (what history does not permit us to imagine in any other way) that ten or twenty copies had been made by private men—for example, by rhapsodes—after that first attempt at writing: a number of variations would necessarily have been introduced into them at once, partly because of the various modes of recitation, partly because of the ingenious caprice of the scribes. For although the Greeks' conviction of the divine origin of Homer never vanished, nevertheless they never refrained from changing whatever they wished in his language or in his interpretation, from correcting, from inventing to suit themselves—and all with the greatest of ease—so that what he finally uttered might be absolutely worthy of divine inspiration. Nor is this so remarkable, when we see that a much more serious people, the Jews, held long enough to the same principle. Now if new copies were continuously being made from these, then unless an ignorant scribe faithfully transcribed whatever he seized upon next, those who were concerned with these matters, once they had compared several texts, could only have

---

Plato (*Philebus* 18D), Xenophon (*Mem.* 4.2.20), and Aristotle (*Topics* 6.5.142b31). And later many called this ἀτελεστέρα γραμματική ["incomplete grammar"], when τέλειος or ἐντελής ["complete"] grammar had come to occupy a large territory (cf. Sextus Empiricus *Contra math.* 1.44, 75); until Crates, criticism was subordinated to this as a part of it. But the name—either for this profession or for its particular branch of learning—does not occur before the Alexandrian age except in the dialogues of Aeschines and Cebes, whose spuriousness C. Meiners has now well established ["Iudicium de quibusdam Socraticorum reliquiis, inprimis de Aeschinis dialogis, de Platonis eiusque condiscipulorum epistolis, nec non de Cebetis tabula," *Commentationes Societatis Regiae Scientiarum Gottingensis per Annum* MDCCLXXXII, vol. 5 (1783), *Historicae et Philologicae Classis*, pp. 45-58]. Hence it is to the thing, and not to the name and profession, that Dio Chrysostom *Orat.* 53.1 is referring when he says that "criticism and grammar took their beginning" from Aristotle; and yet we cannot even confirm this adequately, given the loss of so many of Aristotle's exoteric books. And it is even less clear what Clement of Alexandria *Stromata* 1.16.79.3 [2:51.17 Stählin] reports about Apollodorus of Cumae, or what is reported about Autodorus [now recognized as a mistaken variant for the correct name, Antidorus] in the scholia on Dionysius Thrax, *Grammatici Graeci* 3.3.23ff., 7.23ff. and 448.6f. Hilgard. For we do not know the age of either one, if in fact they were different people. All that we can do, therefore, is to investigate the beginnings of the thing, not of the name. For learned treatments of the other areas of the history of grammar and criticism see, in addition to Valesius, op. cit., [pp. 144ff.], P. J. Maussac, ["Dissertatio Critica de Harpocratione Eiusque Scriptis," in J. Gronovius, ed., *Harpocrationis Lexicon*, vol. 2 (1824), 18ff.]; J. Wowerius, [*De Polymathia Tractatio, Integri Operis de Studiis Veterum* ἀποσπασμάτιον (1603)]; J. A. Fabricius, ed., *Sexti Empirici Opera* [1718]; and J.E.I. Walch, [*De Arte Critica Veterum Romanorum Liber*, 3d ed. (1771) (and cf. F. Früchtenicht [*praes.* J.E.I. Walch], *Diatribe de Arte Critica Veterum Romanorum* [1748], and J. F. Thauer [*praes.* J.E.I. Walch], *Diatribe Posterior de Arte Critica Veterum Romanorum* [n.d. = 1749]). Both dissertations, as was common in German universities, were evidently written by the *praeses*, Walch.]

approached the problem by judging and choosing what seemed most appropriate to each passage. They would thus produce a very different version of the text. But in those days a new text of this sort could not be brought to public notice (since the labor was private), nor could it check others from a similar undertaking— that is, emendation. As the number of manuscripts gradually increased in this way, that Pisistratean source, if indeed it was one source, was soon divided into several streams with different flavors, so to speak, and impeded the attempt to arrive at an accurate reading. Hence if some more intelligent person, one who was also a poet or at least no stranger to the poetic faculty (nor did anyone else, as far as we know, take such a task upon himself before Aristophanes of Byzantium)—if, I repeat, an intelligent student of ancient artistry had compared the best manuscripts which he had heard were preserved anywhere in order to prepare for himself and for his friends a new copy,[37] he would quite often have found it extremely difficult to judge what might really be the genuine reading, and would have had no readier and better aid than his own talent.

At this point we must thoroughly abolish the opinion by which we model the critics of that period to match the modern rules of the art.[a] I shall show shortly that not even Aristarchus himself must be judged by this standard. We certainly find that the early progress of the art was aimless and random, whether we consider its subject matter in the ancient variants of the rhapsodes and manuscripts, or the innate character of the Greek genius, or the condition of the times, or finally the remains of the art themselves. Perhaps many toiled to the limit of their ability to represent Homer with complete accuracy and in his own dress; but they had to toil even harder to make him appear nowhere inconsistent or unworthy of himself, often removing many verses, and elsewhere adding polish where there was none. Just as nowadays an elegant and ingenious man, but an amateur critic, would work on an ancient poetic mon-

---

[37] Ἰδίως γεγραμμένον, i.e. "written down on his own initiative," like the copy of both poems Athenaeus 14.620B says Cassander of Macedonia made. But as to this royal study I do not dissent from Fabricius, *Bibliotheca Graeca*, 1:361. If there had also been emendation, Athenaeus, by the custom of the Greek grammarians, would not have said γράφειν, but διορθοῦν.

---

[a] *At this point we must thoroughly abolish the opinion . . .:* Cf. ch. 31, note b.

ument of our language which he might have found in a mutilated form and equipped by many readers with marginal variants[b]—that, I claim, is more or less how those first emenders toiled in correcting and harmonizing their bards. They were still quite far from that severity which rigorously abstains from introducing anything not written by the author of the work himself: although even now those whose strength resides in their genius do not quite succeed in avoiding that reef. In short, this whole art arose rather from what our fellow countrymen call aesthetic judgment than from critical judgment,[c] or, if I may put it this way, from poetic rather than from diplomatic standards of accuracy. Many other arguments can easily be assembled from our whole booklet to complete this induction. And as we shall see, the method that even the best Alexandrians used in emending itself points toward the same conclusion.

CHAPTER XXXIX

And it would be possible to show what this is far more clearly if almost all those very ancient exercises in criticism had not been obscured by the following age, which was itself obscured in many ways thereafter. Nevertheless, the names of eight divergent texts earlier than Zenodotus, which the Greeks called διορθώσεις, have been transmitted to us. Two of these bear the names of very famous men, Antimachus, a poet of Colophon, and Aristotle, whose genius, splendidly and abundantly productive of great things, scorned no work of the more graceful Muses. And one might think these recensions more worthy than any others of being enumerated among those called in the scholia "those of individuals."[38] From these are

---

[38] Only in these two passages of the new scholia, on *Il.* 22.108 and 23.88. Here and elsewhere I apply the term "scholia" *tout court* to the Venice scholia.

---

[b] *Just as nowadays an elegant and ingenious man, but an amateur critic, would work on an ancient poetic monument of our language . . . .:* Wolf seems to have in mind the Swiss critic Bodmer, who had done pioneering work as an editor of medieval German poetry some fifty years before Wolf wrote. See M. Thorp, *The Study of the Nibelungenlied* (Oxford, 1940), 115-23.

[c] *What our fellow countrymen call aesthetic judgment . . . .:* In his contemptuous dismissal of the term and discipline of aesthetics—which Wolf treats as a specifically German aberration because the term had been invented by Baumgarten—Wolf is emulating his fellow philologist Ruhnken. See *Kl. Schr.*, 1:393, where Wolf quotes a letter in which Ruhnken denounces "the aestheticians, a race filled with hot air."

distinguished "the city ones" or "those by cities," "those from cities," whose authors are unknown. Two of these had been named long ago by Eustathius on the *Iliad*, together with the Aristotelian, as being of the greatest renown: those from Marseilles and Sinope. Recently four others have been added from the Leipzig and Venice scholia. If each of these is ranked in accordance with the number of its known readings, since we cannot determine a fixed order, then they should be arranged as follows: *Massiliote, Chian, Argive, Sinopic, Cypriote, Cretan.* From the Massiliote (which you could, in a way, call Ionic because of the origin of this city-state) we have received approximately twenty readings, from the Chian approximately twelve, and thereafter fewer and fewer; from the Cretan, one, as cited in a note of Seleucus'.

But since all antiquity, except those scholiasts, is silent on the subject of all these recensions, we do not know either by whom they were prepared, and whether they were made by public authority or at the request of private individuals, or even to what date they should be assigned. But no one will be surprised that I have placed them here, since others seem to have done the same; but a conjecture about their method and condition is necessarily more doubtful. For in all the passages where they are cited their antiquity is quite clear from the fact that they are either put before Zenodotus, Aristophanes, and their contemporaries, or at least are put together with them—not to mention other indications which you might notice here and there, even in the very careless language of the later Greeks.[39a] When I considered all these things it often

---

[39] Because only rarely is any one of the editions cited by itself, I shall list all of the passages here in a single series so that I shall not have to note the same passage three or four times. It will be clear to the reader that most of them are due to the excellent Codex A alone: on *Il* 1.97, 298, 332, 381, 423-24, 435, 585, 598; 2.258; 3.10, 51; 12.281; 13.363; 14.349, 418; 15.44; 16.127; 17.134-36; 18.39-49, 502; 19.56, 76-77, 86, 96, 117, 386; 20.62, 188, 308; 21.11, 86, 88, 162, 351, 454, 535; 22.51, 93; 23.77, 206, 870-71, 879; 24.30, 109, 192, 332. We hope that this labor of ours, here and elsewhere, will be welcome to readers who have hitherto badly lacked an index to these scholia. Here students should consider particularly worthy of attention those numbers that are underlined. For I have marked in this way those passages which offer something particularly notable in favor of either side, or which could illustrate my discussion of these recensions. In the Leipzig Codex there is nothing in this regard which we might lack in the Venice Scholia, except that in the former the note in Codex B on 5.461 is amplified by mention of the Sinopian and Cyprian and Antimachean recensions: the scholium says that in these three editions

---

[a] *the very careless language of the later Greeks:* A reference to the peculiar dialect of the Byzantine compiler of the Venice A scholia.

occurred to me that the very first who are truthfully called critics used these recensions, and I conjectured that their evidence and names were to be sought in the libraries of the Ptolemies. It is very well known how much greed and care these kings devoted to that treasure-house of theirs, buying books everywhere and acquiring the oldest and rarest copies of the Greek authors by entreaties, by force, and by other means. Hence if some heir of Antimachus, who loved to carry Homer around in his mind and coins in his pockets,[b] had perchance offered a manuscript written by the hand or polished by the genius of the poet of Colophon, he would doubtless have found enthusiastic buyers in the Ptolemies. So manuscripts of Homer seem to have flowed together little by little from various places and cities to Alexandria and even to private persons, where they would soon become legitimate material for more careful emendation. But it is not at all surprising if the only thing certain about most of them was the home from which they came, and not by whom they were written. In such cases of doubt the keepers of the library could note in their catalogues only that one manuscript had been brought from Chios, another from Marseilles, another from somewhere else. In exactly the same way Galen reports that books were taken by royal command from Greek ships[c] which landed in Egypt and that, once copies had quickly been made and sent back to their owners, the originals were deposited in the great library

---

ΤΡΩΙΑΣ, i.e. Τρῳάς, appeared with an iota adscript or subscript; but Lesbonax *De figuris*, p. 183 Valckenaer did not find this in his copy. But this Lesbonax did not see in this verse, any more than did Eustathius, the reading that was common until then, but instead the one for which Ptolemaeus Ascalonites is cited in the same Leipzig scholia as sole defender: "the common reading with which Ascalonites agrees too, Τρῶας like Κᾶρας." In the text at that point, ἀς was written above the last syllable of Τρώων by another ancient hand. We return to the Venice scholia. If anyone ponders the fact that in these scholia, through eight books, not even a single trace of those copies appears, he will be able to understand (a point which is of great importance in these conjectural questions) how incomplete the documents are which it is our fortune to use, and that nevertheless they contain material from which probable inferences can be derived.

---

[b] *Hence if Antimachus' heir . . . .:* Possibly a joking reference to Heraclides Ponticus, who went to Colophon at Plato's request to collect the poetic works of Antimachus. See *Antimachi Colophonii Reliquiae*, ed. B. Wyss (Berlin, 1936), test. 1.

[c] *Galen reports that books were taken by royal command from Greek ships:* Galen derived this report from the earlier Hippocratic commentator Zeuxis. For a modern discussion see W. D. Smith, *The Hippocratic Tradition* (Ithaca and London, 1979), 199-202.

under the rubric OF THOSE FROM SHIPS.[40] Nothing could resemble that title more closely than the one by which those editions are referred to: THOSE FROM CITIES.

But if these editions were distinguished in this way from those whose authors are known, a judgment on their authority is easier. Take care not to believe that they were made at public command or preserved publicly,[41] until it has been demonstrated by a plausible argument that institutions of this sort existed in antiquity in the cities of Greece—something that, at least in my opinion, is inconsistent with those times. But since formerly, as I said before, almost no one but a poet or a rhetor devoted himself to these critical studies, perhaps the evidence of these city *diorthōseis* was the same as what we have lost in the Antimachean and in the others of this period. But if their variant readings, which have so fortuitously been transmitted to us, include some rather good ones, and two or three even more excellent than the vulgate, nevertheless a much greater number confirm what I already suspected—namely, that the more accurate form of Homer emerged at length from the Alexandrian museums. And no one who has pondered the matter carefully will doubt that the critics of this city and their students tried to reach all sources composed in the past from which they thought they could derive a purer text.[42] Scholars skilled in this

[40] The well-known passage is in Galen *Commentary on Hippocrates on Epidemics III* [17.1.606 Kühn]: "They say that King Ptolemy of Egypt became so eager for books that he ordered the books even of all those who sailed in to be brought to him; he had these copied onto new sheets, and gave the copies to the captains whose books had been brought in to him when they had sailed in, but deposited the originals that had been brought in the libraries; they bore the title, OF THOSE FROM SHIPS. They say that one like this was found, the third book on epidemics, bearing the legend OF THOSE FROM SHIPS, ACCORDING TO THE CORRECTOR MNEMON SIDITES." But the whole passage must be read, especially what follows, which has been used by most scholars who have written about the library at Alexandria.

[41] Cf. the erudite Prolegomena in Villoison, xxvi.

[42] To this question the passage at Diogenes Laertius 9.113 is relevant: here, when Aratus, about to correct the poet, asks, "How can one securely obtain the poetry of Homer?", Timon of Phlius answers, "If he meets with the ancient manuscripts, and not the ones which have already been corrected." I. Casaubon, ad loc. [in H. G. Hübner, ed., *Commentarii in Diogenem Laertium*, vol. 1 (1830), 132]: "If what Josephus says is true, that Homer did not leave behind his poems as written texts, but that 'having been preserved by memory' they were written down much later, then I do not see how they could be had in a sufficiently correct form, even if we should have the most ancient manuscripts, since it is probable that they were written down quite differently from the way they had been composed by him." Later G. Ménage [ibid., vol. 2 (1832), 493], looking to Casaubon's intention, not to his words: "Casaubon correctly observed here on the basis of Josephus that Homer did not leave behind

sort of divination must judge whether or not those recensions which
are called in the scholia "the ancient ones," "the majority," "most,"
"all" include some earlier than the Alexandrians. Thus you could
immediately explain why there is so little explicit mention of them;
indeed in many passages both they and "the more or most elegant
ones" are clearly the work of grammarians known to our scholiasts
from the commentaries of Trypho, Didymus, and others.[43] It will
become clearer below that those compilers had no such ancient
resources in their hands. Hence it is not odd that we lack a fuller
knowledge of them. Indeed, for a number of books hardly a single
comment of this sort survives. And if we had ten or fifteen fewer
scholia, no place at all would be left even for these conjectures.

CHAPTER XL

So too, these same best scholia have now finally acquainted us with
the recension of Antimachus.[a] Indeed, the six passages concerning
him in Eustathius which were previously known could not yield
any information more certain than what Eustathius himself asserted

---

his poems as written texts, but that 'having been preserved by memory' they were
written down much later."

[43] On *Il.* 9.657 they are "many of the ancient ones," just as at 6.4 from the
commentaries of Aristarchus himself; at 5.83 once "the ancient critics," which will
perhaps remind one of Aristotle's "the ancient Homerists." "All" are cited by the
scholia on *Il.* 1.117, 123-24, 434, 522, 531, 567, 585, 598; 2.163, 196; 7.171; 9.394,
639; 10.346; 11.439; 12.68; 14.112, 259; 15.18, 114, 272, 307; 18.95; 21.106, 122;
23.548; etc. Elsewhere they are "most," and sometimes joined with them are "the
more elegant ones," i.e. those polished with greater learning and care; Eustathius
calls them "more accurate." Cf. 2.12, 53, 164, 192, 196, 415; 3.18, 51, 292; 4.213;
10.291, 341; 11.503; 12.318, 382; 18.499; 20.30; 22.251, 315; 24.97. Whether "the
common" or "more common ones," "the more careless ones," "the mediocre ones,"
"the bad" or "worse manuscripts" have the same reference cannot be determined
for a number of reasons, especially in Eustathius. But now just take a look at the
scholia to 2.53; 3.406; 5.797; 9.324; 15.50; 197; 17.214; 18.100, 376; 19.95; 20.255,
384; 21.587; 22.468, 478; 24.214, 344; etc. In these passages, sometimes the present
tense ("they write") is used, sometimes the pluperfect ("it had been written"). But
the scholiasts almost always use the pluperfect tense for the editions of Zenodotus
and for the others, the memory of which had long since been effaced. For the rest,
I think that "the popular ones" were hardly different from these "common" etc.
ones: 5.881; 8.349; 14.125, 235. For the "city ones" the term "popular" or "demotic"
was scarcely appropriate.

---

[a] *the recension of Antimachus:* For a modern discussion see Rudolf Pfeiffer, *History*
93-94 = *Geschichte,* 122-23.

he knew. That is why scholars readily pardoned my former error when I denied the trustworthiness of Eustathius and Suidas, who simply number Antimachus among the grammarians, and when I thought that one Antimachus was the poet of the *Thebais* and another the Homeric critic.[44] True, Antimachus is only cited once by name as a Colophonian in the new scholia, and there as one "of those after Homer" (i.e., as one of the poets after Archilochus, whose use of Homeric language made clear in what way they themselves had understood him). And there are more citations from his own poems than from his recension of Homer.[45] Nevertheless, when all his remains are collected, I think that the plain result is that everywhere the Colophonian poet alone, a contemporary of Socrates, is to be understood. For the rest, those examples scarcely inspire a great desire for this copy in us. Yet here too it must be remarked that no judgment can be made about the whole body on the basis of such minute scraps of bone, and that those very things which must seem to us corrupt and absurd were perhaps once common to a great many texts.

But we see a memorable object lesson about the role of blind chance in the preservation of these bits and scraps, in the fact that our scholia do not mention even once the recension generally attributed to Aristotle, "the one from the unguent casket." The authority of Aristotle is indeed cited in one variant reading, yet not in such a way that it would appear to be taken from that recension.[46]

---

[44] In my letter in K. A. Schellenberg, *Antimachi Colophonii Reliquiae . . . Accessit epistola F. A. Wolfii* [1786], 119ff. [= *Kl. Schr.*, 1:278-86]. What I wrote there was refuted by Villoison, p. xxiv; I dealt with the matter again in my review of his edition, in the *Allgemeine Litteratur-Zeitung* 31 (1791), 246f. I must summarize here what is necessary for my argument; the rest must be corrected and more diligently investigated.

[45] Passages of the latter sort, referring more properly to criticism, are in the scholia on *Il.* 1.298, 423-24, 598; 21.607; 22.336; 23.604 (where the transmitted αἱ at first sight spread the rumor of a double edition of Antimachus [but Villoison has emended it to οἱ]), 870-71; 24.71-73, to which add Eustathius 1234.40 on 21.397. These are the passages of the former sort: on 1.1; 2.2; 3.197 [Porph. 58.3]; 4.400, 439-40 (cf. on 13.299 and 15.199); 5.389 in the shorter scholia; 6.200 [Porph. 95.26]; 11.754; 13.499-500, 500; 16.134-36; 23.845; 24.23. Most of what these passages contain is unworthy of a learned poet, and from them you will not judge highly of the learning of Stesimbrotus, whose student he is said to have been. But there is not time to linger on them now.

[46] Cf. on 2.73 [Porph. 24.14], where in 1.187 ἄντα is written. More trustworthy is what is reported in the scholia on *Il.* 21.252, and in the scholia on Theocritus [1.34b] about *Od.* 16.176, on which cf. Barnes [Lehrs' emendation, Ἀρίσταρχος for the transmitted Ἀριστοτέλης, is generally accepted]; there are far more of this

Nor does any other source offer more certain knowledge of that very celebrated monument which, according to Plutarch, contained only the *Iliad*. Furthermore, when Plutarch and Strabo are compared, it becomes clear that many scholars, and Alexander the Great himself, took a hand in emending it.[47] If each of these writers followed reliable sources, Alexander first received that book from his Stagirite teacher, then brought it with him into Asia as a comrade on his expedition, read it together with Callisthenes and Anaxarchus in spare moments,[48] annotated it with his own hand, and deposited it as *the most precious work of the human mind* in a very elaborate Persian chest. It is most uncertain whether this manuscript later came to the library of the Ptolemies, and which critic used it for emendation; for it may seem to have been used. But we find that the same philosopher's "Homeric Questions" or "Problems" and "Poetic Questions" were used much more heavily and frequently by the interpreters. Much of the former work survives, particularly in the scholia of Porphyry, and in these it will be possible to find not, indeed, fragments and the very words of Aristotle, but at least his method of interpretation.[49] We who are solely occupied with the history of the text must omit these and similar matters. But we shall make one point again: the very title of those

---

sort in the works of Aristotle themselves. And one can well believe that those books of his which have been lost contained a considerable number of such things, and also examples of readings of the sort that is found in Aelian *N.A.* 15.28. In the Venice scholia to 2.447 and to 8.23-25, it will be obvious to everyone that the transmitted name of Aristotle should be changed to that of Aristophanes [Erbse obelizes Ἀριστοτέλης in the former passage and prints Ἀριστοφάνης in the latter].

[47] Strabo 13.594; Plutarch *Alex.* 668D. On Alexander's study of the poems of Homer cf. the learned G.-E.-J. de Clermont-Lodève, Baron de Sainte-Croix, *Examen critique des anciens historiens d'Alexandre le Grand* [1774], 113; but disagreeing about the edition "from the unguent casket" O. Giphanius, ed., *Homeri Ilias Seu Potius Omnia Ejus quae Extant Opera* [n.d. = 1572], Preface; L. Küster, ed., *Suidae Lexicon, Graece et Latine*, vol. 2 [1705], 8; and Burman, *Valesii Emendationes*, 155.

[48] On this cf. the passages in G. Ménage on Diogenes Laertius 9.58 [H. G. Huebnerus, ed., *Commentarii in Diogenem Laertium*, vol. 2 (1833), 454-55]. Callisthenes is well known.

[49] Cf. on *Il.* 2.73 [Porph. 24.14 = Aristotle frg. 142 Rose], 169 [Porph. on *Od.* 23.269], 183 [Porph. 28.1 = 143 R], 305-29 [Porph. 32.18 = 145R], 649 [Porph. 49.7 = 146R]; 3.236 [Porph. 58.10 = 147R], 276 [Porph. 60.2 = 148R], 277 [Porph. 2.113.12 on *Od.* 12.374 = 149R]; 4.88 [Porph. 70.19 = 151R], 93 [apparently a wrong reference by Wolf], 297 [Porph. 73.10 = 152R]; 5.741 [Porph. 44.29 on *Il.* 2.447 = 153R], 778 [Porph. 86.22 = 154R]; 6.234 [Porph. 96.28 = 155R]; 7.93 [Porph. 108.4 = 156R], 229 [Porph. 109.13 = 157R]; 9.17 [Porph. 132.31 = 158R]; 10.98 [Porph. 145.22 on *Il.* 10.194ff. = 159R], 153 [Porph. 145.15 = 160R], 252 [Porph. 149.4 = 161R]; 13.295 [Porph. 262.1 on *Il.* 23.269]; 19.108 [Porph. 236.7

books indicates that even before the foundation of the Alexandrian museum "problems" or "inquiries" and "solutions" were the hobby of the learned, and that all more precise interpretation of the contents arose from these.[b]

CHAPTER XLI

I have listed eight copies which were well-known to the earliest grammarians. A copy attributed to Euripides, mentioned (inaccurately) by Suidas alone,[50] does not belong in this company, although it leads one to suspect that many of the first attempts at this sort of criticism were forgotten at an early stage. A thorough search, indeed, would perhaps reveal other emenders of Homer who would snatch from Zenodotus the primacy awarded him by Suidas. But a number do not belong in this context: not Nessus of Chios, a pupil of Democritus credited with one metrical observation;[51] nor Aeschrion, to whom one improvement in accentuation is ascribed;[52] nor Lysanias the Cyrenaean who is twice mentioned in the scholia—even if he should be identified with the teacher of

---

= 163R]; 23.269 [Porph. 262.1 = 164R]; 24.15 [Porph. 268.1 = 166R], 559ff. [Porph. 277.5 = 168R]; and the scholium on 16.233 [B Dindorf]. I omit the passages where something is cited from the Constitutions, from natural history, and others, as on 11.115 [B Dindorf], and 16.149 [B Dindorf], and those derived from the Rhetoric, like Schol. on *Il.* 1.303, 481. In general, there is practically no help in any of these for removing the obscurity of sentences and words, even if some of them are ingenious enough and useful for the history of interpretation.

[50] Even in his manner of speech, which is not at all usual on this subject [E 3694]: Ἔγραψε (Euripides, the nephew of the earlier one—I am not sure which) Ὁμηρικὴν ἔκδοσιν· εἰ μὴ ἄρα ἑτέρου ἐστίν ["He wrote an edition of Homer; if, that is, it is not someone else's"].

[51] Cited at 9.378 [Porph. 137.14] on the word καρός which, as Ruhnken already noted in his preface to Hesychius [*Hesychii Lexicon cum Notis Doctorum Virorum*, ed. J. Alberti (1766)], vii, was subject to various interpretations at a very early date.

[52] There were a number of famous men named Aeschrion. See J. Jonsius, *De Scriptoribus Historiae Philosophicae* [1716], bk. 2, ch. 2, p. 147. Nor can it be shown that the one mentioned by the scholia and Eustathius on 11.239 [841.24] was the Mitylenaean, the friend of Aristotle and father of Lysanias (on whom see below [n. 53]). It is remarkable that his reading, λῖς, rightly preferred by Brunck, *Analecta Veterum Poetarum Graecorum*, vol. 3, pt. 2 [1776], 85, to the vulgate λίς, has for so long escaped the notice of editors in this one passage. But there are numerous equally ancient variations in Homer, some of them quite trivial.

---

[b] *even before the foundation of the Alexandrian museum "problems" . . . were the hobby of the learned . . . :* In treating these "problems" as a hobby of ancient scholars, Wolf follows Valckenaer; see Grafton, 115-16.

Eratosthenes,⁵³ as no other Cyrenaean of that name is known. I would be even more reluctant to include Telephus, the father of Philetas of Cos,⁵⁴ or others whose right to the title of grammarian is doubtful. Three references, however, do demonstrate that Philetas himself, who was both the teacher of Zenodotus and one of the best of the elegiac poets, made some contribution to the correction of Homer shortly after Aristotle's time.⁵⁵ Not even that much remains of Aratus' edition of the *Odyssey*. Antiochus Soter, the king of Syria, is said to have invited him to add to it an *Iliad* freed from *the corruptions of many*.⁵⁶ When this work was not completed, Rhianus, no mean poet himself, seems—if my guess is correct—to have taken up the task. The few surviving fragments make his recension seem more to be missed⁵⁷ than the frivolous attempts of Apollonius of Rhodes in this direction.⁵⁸

⁵³ Cf. Jonsius, loc. cit., the scholia on 9.378 [Porph. 137.12] and 16.558, and also Eustathius on that passage (1075.45). His place of origin, however, is only given in the first of these passages.

⁵⁴ Certainly I would rather assign the readings at 4.133 and 10.545 to the Pergamene grammarian who taught at Rome, whom Fabricius [vol. 1 (1790),] p. 525 rightly distinguished from the other. Nor is it easy to say to whom to assign the scholium on 1.420. I shall have occasion to disagree here and there with that most learned man, with whom I agree on much more significant matters.

⁵⁵ 2.269; 21.126, 252 [in Eustathius 1235.39; see Erbse's testimonia]; see also the scholia on 6.459, 22.308, Porphyry Q. H. 8 [293.9], Eustathius 1235.39. There is, however, no point in referring to Eustathius and his like when their sources are available in the scholia. The emendations and comments of that critic do not themselves whet our appetites; the first is very inept, nor are the other two particularly worth reporting.

⁵⁶ The subject is only referred to by Suidas [s.v. Ἄρατος, A 3745], and by the author of the ancient life of Aratus [Achilles, in E. Maass, ed., *Commentariorum in Aratum Reliquiae* (2d ed., 1958), 78]. To that latter one can also add another ancient life [ed. Maass, 148]. Wherever the scholia and Eustathius refer to Aratus, they refer us to his known poems. But it is worth remarking that the Homeric poems were already said "to have been damaged by many people" [Achilles 78.11] at a time when scarcely any of the critics, with the exception of Zenodotus, had deliberately undertaken their corruption. This too confirms what I said above about the rhapsodes and the first copyists and brings to mind the warning of Timon (above, ch. 39, n. 42) which in my opinion is correctly interpreted by Fabricius [vol. 1], 368.

⁵⁷ 1.97, 553; 16.559; 18.10-11 (not found "in the edition of Rhianus"); 19.41; 20.188, 331; 21.607; 23.81; 24.85. Two or three of these specimens are quite displeasing; the rest display the man's modest talent. Perhaps this recension—and the manner of reference to "the [edition] of Rhianus" or "the [edition] according to Rhianus" supports that name—was available to Aristarchus.

⁵⁸ Three of his readings are reported, 1.3 κεφαλάς in place of ψυχάς (presumably from 11.55; see the scholia there) and 13.657 ἀναθέντες for ἀνέσαντες; the latter is cited "from the (tract) to Zenodotus," that is "*to*" or rather "*against*" Zenodotus. The third reading, which is not bad, at 2.436 ἐγγυαλίζει, was shared by Apollonius with Aristophanes and Aristarchus. The word that the scholiast uses there, προφέρεται ["it is brought forward"], everywhere refers, unless I am mistaken, to single works of criticism, not proper editions.

Zenodotus of Ephesus was earlier than these three poets, but he came to the task of recension with more manuscripts and greater daring than any of his successors. We have defined the *third period* of this history as stretching from him to *Apion*; a period in which at last, by the efforts of the critics and grammarians who sprang up like mushrooms at Alexandria and Pergamum, *a text more consistent in form* was introduced. In many respects the appearance of Greek literature had already been changed as completely as had that of the cities themselves. In place of the agora, the speaker's platform, the stage, and the public festival appeared museums and libraries; in place of genius rich in its own resources appeared timid imitation, which undertook only modest tasks; in place of a very elevated spirit of poetry and eloquence appeared sober and sometimes chill erudition, reading spread over all areas of learning; in place of original ideas appeared thoroughness, care, and a certain polish of arrangement and poetic diction; in place, finally, of the magnificent native bloom of all the arts appeared garlands composed of the blossoms from everywhere.[59a] Among the studies aroused at just this time by the desire to imitate antiquity was the *art of interpretation and emendation*—a subject that had heretofore been sluggish—and none of the ancient poets supplied greater fodder for it than Homer. The same method was soon applied to other poets, particularly lyric, tragic, and comic, and also to historians, orators, medical writers, and to whatever genres were remarkable for importance of content and obscurity of language. To this end the grammarians explored the widest range of variegated philology; they began to collect a body of precise interpretations from their study of history, of chronology, and of the remaining areas of antiquity. At the same time, they began to examine the

[59] This subject is discussed with learning by Heyne, "Dissertatio de genio saeculi Ptolemaeorum," *Opuscula Academica*, vol. 1 [1785], 76ff.

---

[a] *In place of the agora . . . blossoms from everywhere:* While Wolf's picture of the sterility and preciosity of Alexandrian culture is certainly vivid, few would now leave such a negative assessment unchallenged. For a full survey of intellectual life at Alexandria, see P. M. Fraser, *Ptolemaic Alexandria* (Oxford 1972), pt. 2. The greatest modern study of the poetry of the period is that of U. von Wilamowitz-Moellendorff, *Die Hellenistische Dichtung in der Zeit des Kallimachos* (1924, repr. Zurich, 1973); for a brief but eloquent analysis, see Rudolf Pfeiffer, "The Future of Studies in the Field of Hellenistic Poetry," *Journal of Hellenic Studies*, 75 (1955), 69-73, reprinted in *Ausgewählte Schriften* (Munich, 1960), 148-58. As Wolf himself suggests in note 59, his picture of Alexandrian life is largely based on Heyne's brilliant essay *De genio saeculi Ptolemaeorum*; for a discussion of this see Grafton.

very nature and structure of the Greek language, to make it fit the laws of analogy and the usage of good authors, to set out the various categories of words, to define the distinctions of words with many meanings, of synonyms and homonyms, and of the dialects, and to undertake many tasks of this sort. After great subsequent alterations, wretched abbreviation, reshaping into one form after another, these works are still employed, often unwittingly, in scholarly study of languages.[60]

What is more, of the hundreds of men who, in the course of these centuries, brooded over the explanation, correction, and corruption of Homer, scarcely thirty are adequately known to us. The vast crowd of those who did one or another of these things incidentally, in the course of other tasks of the most diverse sorts, is not relevant here: the philosophers, mathematicians, astronomers, doctors, historians, geographers, mythographers, and rhetoricians. In countless cases the passage of time has stolen the very memory of their names. No period in the history of ancient letters has suffered a greater loss. Among the 250 writers cited in the Venetian scholia, those whom we know with any degree of accuracy are rare indeed.[61] A laborious, but often futile, harvest here awaits the grammarian: for even the most detailed and microscopic search will yield with difficulty a faint and blurred impression, not the precise portrait of the scholarship that filled the libraries of the Homeric critics

---

[60] It would be worth showing, with specific examples, in how many things we are even now dependent on the judgments and research of the Alexandrians. Almost all the standard chronology, for example, is the work of these Alexandrians, as are innumerable fine points of the ancient languages, and other things. That single *selection of classical authors* who are the best in each genre, which Quintilian in book 10 and in some fashion all antiquity follows, directed the studies of every age and the hands of the scribes to that which was best of a vast array. In the absence of that selection we would certainly not have these remains of the early period of Greece, and we might well have less excellent ones.

[61] As, for instance, Antigonus on 23.319; Antodorus or Autodorus [Antidorus] 23.638 (perhaps the same as the man referred to above, ch. 38, n. 36); Aretades 24.110; Aristeas 13.137; Clitophon 20.404; Demo, a woman interested in allegory, 2.205, 5.722 (see Eust. 1154.42 on 18.481); Eron of Delos and Hermon 10.274 [Porph. 154.23, emended from Eron to Hermon]; Hagnon 4.101 [A Dindorf]; Licymnius 2.106; Nemesion 10.397; Polycletus 21.126 [Porph. 291.11]; Sextus 11.155 [Porph. 163.18]; Staphylus 16.175; Xenon 12.435; and others who will turn up unsought. There are many extremely obscure names among these, some totally unknown, and some also corrupted by the scribes. But there are also some who seem extremely ancient, one or two pupils of Aristarchus, and perhaps a continuous commentator on Homer. Very few are found in the new scholia who can be assigned on secure chronological grounds to the period after Apion.

in the time of Apion. It is not my desire to display the empty
bookcases of those libraries by giving a list of the individual lost
works, nor loudly to bewail an unjust fate—or whatever we should
call the creator of such desolation and disaster among works that
seemed destined for the eternal use of scholars. We men of letters
ought often to cast our minds in this direction in order to learn
the conditions of our fame; we should seek from the wretched
fortune of so many famous works some consolation for our own,
whether they are to perish immediately or at some later date, condemned by the pen of a fierce censor. How many are the corpses
and tombs of books that lie together there, before our eyes!

CHAPTER XLII

I return to those learned men who still live in extant authors and
scholiasts. In most cases, however, that life is precarious. Even for
Zoilus himself, who is held up to the scorn of the ages in notorious
tales, it is quite uncertain what the particular subjects were that
occasioned his barking at Homer.[62] In the same way, we no longer
read even full excerpts of the toilsome discoveries of men who are
reported to have spent an entire life over one subject, or one word,
of Homer.[63] Some have acquired immortality (if that is what we

[62] If nothing of Zoilus survived besides what is preserved on 1.129; 5.4 [A Dindorf
on 5.7], 20 [A Dindorf]; 10.274 [Porph. 153.22]; 18.22; and Eustathius 1614.48
[Od. 9.60], one would have to say that he hated all poetry and was totally ignorant
of the archaic fashion of thought and speech. But in fact his failings were no greater
than those of others, except that he apparently added madness derived from the
bitterness and perversity of his mind. In our day, many people have written similar
attacks on the Old Testament with impunity. For the rest, the history of the Zoili,
even after Hardion ["Dissertation où l'on examine s'il y a eû deux Zoïles censeurs
d'Homère," *Mémoires de l'Académie Royale des Inscriptions et Belles Lettres* 8 (1733), 178-
87], has numerous problems. Without doubt the most famous of them was the
rhetor; but in the passage (6.271) where Strabo calls him that, I believe that the
words "the one criticizing Homer for being a mythographer" should be consigned
to the margin.

[63] As of Neoteles, an unknown writer who devoted his whole life (Valckenaer's
reading, "a whole book" is less good) [Valckenaer is actually correct] to writing about
archery in the age of the heroes, which is used on 8.323 [Porph. 123.12], 325, or
of Dorotheus of Ascalon "on the word κλίσιον" (on the passage *Od.* 24.207), cited
on 9.90 [B Dindorf]. The latter was certainly not earlier than Aristonicus or Tryphon, but lived long before Athenaeus, who cites him at 7.329D and elsewhere
from the same huge work, I think, as is mentioned on 10.252. In the same way
Neoteles too reappears at 24.110. It is thus one thing to think about a subject for
one's whole life, but quite another to work on that subject alone.

should call it) through one faulty correction, others through one interpretation, others through a single accent.[64]

Others have already pointed out that not even all those whose authority is cited by the scholiasts and Eustathius for a reading or an explanation offered a continuous emendation or interpretation of Homer (διόρθωσις or ἐξήγησις); both common sense and the manner in which they are mentioned often show that clearly. Many took specific portions of either task as their object in specific works. In these they might either remove hidden obstacles to the sense (this includes the ἐνστατικοί [problem-setters] and λυτικοί [problem-solvers])[65] or elucidate the manners of the heroic age, the gen-

---

[64] Although examples here are somewhat later than Zenodotus, I cite them all the more readily in order to clear a field that is crammed with so many obscure men: Leptines, 23.731, changed ἐν to ἕν, which he thought was ἕτερον; Attalus, perhaps the same as the commentator on Aratus, is responsible for the paroxytone form of ἰοδόκον at 15.444, where others write it as a proparoxytone, as Euphranor at 14.372 wrote παναίθησιν for others' παναιθῆσιν, as Eustathius 992.59 reports it from Apion, Euphranor's pupil [also in A]. Ptolemy II Euergetes, the king of Egypt and pupil of Aristarchus, gave the correction σίου for ἴου at Od. 5.72 [Eust. 1524.52]; Lesbocles, perhaps the Mitylenaean rhetor, offered the mild and superficial correction θεὸς δ᾽ ἴα (i.e. μία) at 19.90, where Hellanicus, rightly distinguished by Sturz from the early historian, gave the even more inept θεόσδια; Aristodemus of Nysa corrected 9.453 to τῇ οὐ πιθόμην οὐδ᾽ ἔρξα, even if the glory of this pious conjecture is given to some earlier Sosiphanes. Democrines, at 2.744, made the correction Αἰθιόπεσσι; Antigonus at 23.319 made the correction ἄλλος because of the unusual construction; Agathocles at 14.398 [Eust. 994.40] made the correction ἐξοφόροισιν, and one's admiration of him is not increased by what is found in the scholia on 1.591 [B Dindorf] and 18.240. Zopyrus, in "The Foundation of Miletus" quoted at 10.275 [Porph. 155.7] with the reading πελλὸν [better πέλλον] Ἀθηναίη, cited for his grammatical work at 24.139; Dionysius Scytobrachion [Eust. 380.30] inserted a new verse after 3.40. Archias gave the reading ἑσταότως at 19.79, cited alone by Apollonius, Lexicon s.v. ὑββάλλειν [156.29 Bekker]; and if [Hermann] Tollius is right [ch. 43, n. 83] (and I agree with him) in accepting it, it is remarkable that it is not cited under his name in the very large body of scholia, and that there Epaphroditus, a pupil of Archias, is given as the author of almost the same argument [19.77, Eust. 1172.21]. But nothing of this kind is surprising in the history of these remnants; indeed, Eustathius is the sole source for a number of them. Thus, the Etymologicum Magnum 513.48, alone reports the futile conjecture Χειμερίων for Κιμμερίων in Od. 11.14 under the name of Proteas of Zeugma—the same man, in all probability, whose frivolous interpretation is given at 18.410. In the same manner Demetrius "the boxer" is cited, or rather rebuked, once, by Apollonius [121.23 Bekker] for his interpretation of ὀπαζόμενος as πληρούμενος at 11.493. But among the critics named only once, none is more ridiculous than Agallias the follower of Aristophanes who conjectured, or rather saw in a vision, that the two cities made by Hephaestus on the Shield at 18.490 [A Dindorf] were Athens and Eleusis.

[65] See Joannes Wowerius, De Polymathia Tractatio, ch. 10 [J. Gronovius, Thesaurus Graecarum Antiquitatum, vol. 10 (1701), 1037-45], Jonsius, De Scriptoribus Historiae Philosophicae, bk. 2, ch. 17, p. 247f., L. Valckenaer, Dissertatio de Praestantissimo Codice Leidensi et de Scholiis in Homerum Ineditis [Opuscula Philologica, vol. 2 (1808-9), 145ff.], etc. I already cited above [ch. 40] the passage of Porphyry which shows that this

eral usage of Homeric diction,[66] or the rarer and less familiar words and expressions.[67]

The majority of these works, however, had long been the province of mildew and worms by the time the extant scholiasts wrote their commentaries.[a] Indeed, by that time the recensions and inter-

---

whole method arose among the Alexandrians from the debates and discussions of scholars. These, along with the solutions, soon began to be written down, and they made a sort of group commentary, perhaps designed for the Ptolemies to read when they were completed. More of these commentaries (which you might call "Vexed problems in Homer" using the biblical term) have now become known to us from the new scholia, but very few of them, as at 1.24, 2.12, are from Zenodotus of Ephesus (unless this is that lesser Zenodotus, to whom Suidas [Z 75] ascribed *Solutions of Homeric Difficulties*), and the vast majority are anonymous. Perhaps some of these are from the works of the three Peripatetics, Heraclides Ponticus, Chamaeleon, and Megaclides, as well as of others. Chamaeleon is cited three times, at 12.231; 23.94, 454, I suspect from his book "On the *Iliad*"; Megaclides is cited four times, 10.274 [Porph. 153.30]; 16.140; 22.36, 205, from his book "On Homer." Among the most famous "solvers," however, was Sosibius the Laconian in the time of Ptolemy Philadelphus; Athenaeus 11.493C-494B tells a charming story about him, which is the source of Eustathius' one reference to him [870.39, on 11.636], but he is never mentioned in the scholia. The story shows how interested Philadelphus was in such matters; Suetonius (*Tib.* 70.3) reports the well-known similar taste of Tiberius.

[66] Few works about customs are known, unless one includes those on tactics in Homer referred to in the preface to Aelian's *Tactics*, or on bird lore in Homer in the scholia to 2.305 [B Dindorf]. The only author of such works that we know is Polles, found in Suidas [M 1898], and other similar works were composed by philosophers and rhetoricians. Works of the other sort, on Homeric idiom, are more well known, such as Ptolemy Pindarion "On Homeric Style," Aristonicus' six books on nouns in the *Iliad* and *Odyssey* in which impossible combinations of letters occur (ἀσύντακτα), on which see Suidas [A 3924, Π 3034]. Note also Basilidas "On Homeric Diction" cited in *Etymologicum Magnum* 142.28 [s.v. ἀρίζηλος] and particularly Zenodorus "On Homeric Idiom" in ten books, cited by the scholia on 17.263 [B Dindorf, Porph. 214.4 on 16.174]; 18.22, 356; and Apollonius *Lexicon* s.v. ζῶστρα [81.25 Bekker]. I give more credence to these passages than to Suidas, who attributes a book of this title to the younger Zenodotus [Z 75]. I shall refer to other books on the same topic, if not always very clearly so, under the appropriate authors.

[67] Γλῶσσαι or λέξεις. From these, glossaries and lexica were gradually made even

---

[a] *The majority of these works . . . had long been the province of mildew:* Wolf refers, here and elsewhere, to the difficulty of reconstructing the sources of the Venice scholia. But he nowhere analyzes the prime source of information: the subscriptions at the end of each book of the *Iliad* in A. These describe the scholia as based on the works of four men, Aristonicus, Didymus, Herodian, and Nicanor. Only one of the four (Didymus) is expressly said to have dealt with the work of one of the great Alexandrian critics (Aristarchus). Wolf's failure to subject these texts to scrutiny is good evidence of his lack of interest in scholia—especially given that Siebenkees had already called attention to the difficulties posed by the subscriptions: "Why does the subscription never mention Zenodotus, whose recension seems to be used heavily in the manuscript? This seems surprising" (*Bibliothek der alten Litteratur und Kunst*, 1 (1786), 70-71; cf. Grafton, 117-18). Karl Lehrs made the subscriptions one of the points of departure for his revision of Wolf, the treatise *De Aristarchi studiis Homericis* of 1833.

pretations of the leading critics, *Zenodotus, Aristophanes, Aristarchus,* and *Crates,* no longer circulated among the learned in complete form, although a book might lurk in its pristine form throughout those centuries and the whole so-called Middle Ages in some library, a book that they commonly numbered among the lost or read in snippets.[68] In fact, in the time of Augustus and in the succeeding period—an age that had swiftly begun to reduce the learning of Alexandria to the meagerness of handbooks—the readings and emendations of those critics and others were excerpted with varying intentions by many hands and scattered through dictionaries, commentaries, and scholia. If only we had a single one of those books; if only we had even the Lexicon of Apollonius in its complete form! The small-minded grammarians of a later age who undertook the task of compilation often deliberately neglected anything that smacked of obscure learning or anything that did not suit the vulgate text of their time. Thus there is not enough left even of those major critics from whose authority our text was first derived to permit us to understand their abilities or their methods of emendation. But that is the subject on which I now wish to concentrate, reserving for a more suitable occasion those things that are relevant to a precise knowledge of the Homeric critics.

---

in this very Alexandrian period—which is wrongly doubted by some scholars. It appears that those works were first organized by subject, as in the *Onomasticon* of Pollux. Strato (or Strattis) quoted by Athenaeus 9.383B mentions the earliest examples of this sort, the Ἄτακτα or Γλῶσσαι of Philetas, the poet as is commonly thought. The latter title is given by the scholia to Apollonius Rhodius 4.982-92i Wendel [which actually refer to Philetas ἐν ἀτάκτοις γλώσσαις] and *Etymologicum Magnum* 330.40 [s.v. ἐλινός]; see Valckenaer in P. H. Koppiers, *Observata Philologica in loca quaedam Antiphanis, Theocriti, Pauli Apostoli, Eratosthenis, et Propertii* (1771), 36 [= Valckenaer, *Opusc. Philol.* 2:334]. Among the words discussed in this work were μέροπες, οὐλοχύται, μῆλα and others including δαιτυμών, which concerned us above, ch. 30. Philetas' successors in this genre, ignorant and inept men for the most part, are frequently cited in the scholia. We will, however, have occasion to return to them later.

[68] When one is studying antiquity, one must never forget that the ancients did not have those aids to literary learning which public enlightenment and trade procure for us. When Eustathius set about writing his Παρεκβολαί, he may have thought that the best and most ancient scholia were to hand, while the more ancient and better ones of the Venice manuscript, unknown to him, were perhaps nearby. One should therefore try to discover in what period any ancient book ceased to be commonly known, not when it ceased to exist; and the more ancient a writer is, the more easily one should imagine happening to him what I suggested in the case of Eustathius. It is a superficially slight problem, but one that once had great influence on the very methods of literary scholarship.

But even if I must crave the pardon of the learned as I embark on a subject in which the evidence preserved in torn and tattered remains must often forsake even the most ingenious conjecture, I still think that it will be of some use if I can reduce widely scattered materials to a brief synopsis and offer my judgment about the most important subjects. In this way our resources, which are in themselves of no small value, will be augmented. The orientalists would rejoice, I believe, if it were certain in even three places what Gamaliel or another Jewish teacher of the early period read in Moses and the Prophets; in Homer we know what Zenodotus read in some four hundred passages, what Aristophanes read in two hundred, and what Aristarchus read in over a thousand.

CHAPTER XLIII

The reputation of the most ancient of these critics, Zenodotus of Ephesus, whom Suidas identifies as an epic poet and the first emender of Homer,[69a] has always been remarkably ambiguous. Some attribute the first scholarly study of these poems to his ge-

[69] Suidas [Z74]. After Küster [ed. Suidas, 1705] and Fabricius [vol. 1], 362 no one should ask how to interpret "first" in that passage. But as Suidas also reports that there was another Zenodotus [Z 75], an Alexandrian contemporary and adversary of Aristarchus, it is necessary to distinguish the work of one from that of the other. The scholia on Aratus *Phaen.* 33 [p. 374.3 Maass], and Eustathius 957.10 [on 13.730; also schol. T] and 1006.3 [on 15.56] add a third of the same name from Mallos, perhaps the same as the one called a disciple of Crates in the scholia on 23.79. In my own opinion, the second and the third are the same, but some call him "of Mallos" after his place of origin, and others, following the custom of the age, call him "Alexandrian" from his home; he will then be one of those disciples of Crates who, as frequently happens, made their own their teacher's dispute with Aristarchus. But as in the large number of passages in the Venetian scholia he is always referred to (with the sole exception of this one passage) simply as "Zenodotus" and grouped with or placed ahead of Aristophanes and Aristarchus, and as everything attributed to him shows a consistent method and character, I have no doubt that we should nearly always assume that the Homeric commentators are referring to the *Ephesian critic*. Whatever survives of *the other, from Mallos,* in the occasional observations directed against Aristarchus, is transmitted without his name. In half a dozen passages of the scholia I have had temporary doubts, but closer inspection has confirmed my original opinion, which is also confirmed by other writers, Strabo, Athenaeus, Apollonius Dyscolus, etc.

[a] *the first emender of Homer:* It should be repeated that in the notes to this and the succeeding chapters we have corrected, but not attempted to extend, Wolf's citations of the ancient critics. In the case of Zenodotus the most recent study is that of K. Nickau, *Untersuchungen zur textkritischen Methode des Zenodotos von Ephesos* (Berlin, 1977); for a more general assessment see Pfeiffer, *History,* 105-22 = *Geschichte,* 135-51.

nius,⁷⁰ but others including the medieval scholiasts, violently accuse him of frivolity and stupidity. Many of his readings are, indeed, so improbable, and result from such rashness of judgment, that even a beginner today would be ashamed to make such emendations;⁷¹ the number and the temerity of his atheteses are so great that many have thought that he made Homer almost unrecognizable. Often he deletes the most memorable and best lines, sometimes he conflates whole speeches. He abbreviates some passages, he expands others, and in general he treats the *Iliad* as if it were his own composition.⁷² If he were the first to behave this way, one might

---

⁷⁰ The verses of Ausonius in the *Ludus Septem Sapientum* [11f.] to this effect are famous:

Maeonio qualem cultum quaesiuit Homero
  Censor *Aristarchus* normaque *Zenodoti*.

["Such a finish did Aristarchus the censor and the regulations of Zenodotus seek for Phrygian Homer."]

I believe that he is also referred to by the same poet at *Epist.* [13.29 Peiper = 11.29 Prete], where along with Varro and other Latin critics are placed Crates, Aristarchus,

Quique sacri lacerum collegit corpus Homeri.

["And the one who put together the mangled body of sacred Homer."]

This is not an appropriate place for Pisistratus, and even less for Cynaethus, as one scholar has recently suggested.

⁷¹ I will give here a few readings as a sample from the huge number surviving; they are not selected as illustrating the worst tendencies of Zenodotus' text. At 1.68 he gave ἐκαθέζετο, where the scholia say "Zenodotus does not permit Homer to speak Greek"; 1.80 κρείσσω, a form which he used on other similar occasions, as at 249 γλυκίω. Also 351 χεῖρας ἀναπτάς; 3.56 Τρῶες ἐλεήμονες (see on 453 and 7.390), 273 Ἀρνῶν ἐκ κεφαλαίων [κεφαλέων] in the *Etymologicum Magnum* 507.15; 5.53 χραίσμεν θανάτοιο πέλωρα; 6.112 Ἀνέρες ἔστε θοοὶ, καὶ ἀμύνετον ἀστεῖ λώβην; 8.128 Ἐρασιπτόλεμον (although leaving 312 Ἀρχεπτόλεμον), 501 ἐπεὶ Διὸς ἐτράπετο φρήν from 10.45 (on which see the scholia), 562 Μύρια δ'ἐν πεδίῳ [Wolf has here misread Villoison, whose text read Μύρι' ἄρ'ἐν]; 9.641 Ἀθρόοι ἐκ Δαναῶν; 10.306 Αὐτοὺς οἳ φορέουσιν ἀμύμονα Πηλείωνα; 11.27 Ἐρίδεσσιν; 12.34 ὡς ἤμελλον [Wolf's ἤμελλεν is a typographical error] (on which the scholia note ἐστὶ δὲ βάρβαρον), 75 ἄγε τὼς ἄν, 153 λάεσσιν, 444 ἐπεὶ θεοῦ ἔκλυον αὐδήν; 14.177 καλοὺς καὶ μεγάλους; 15.134 Αὐτὰρ τοῖς ἄλλοισι θεοῖς μέγα πῆμα φυτεῦσαι, 439 τέκεσσι, 716 οὐκ ἐμεθίει; 16.202 μητιάασθε, 697 ἕλες; 17.51 Χαρίτεσσι μέλαιναι, 153 κύον ἔτλης, 582 Ἕκτορα δὲ φρένα δῖος Ἄρης ὤρυνε [Villoison; A reads ὤρυνεν, Bekker ὄτρυνε] μετελθών; 18.385, 424 ἡμετερόνδε. I call these readings, not corrections. Who could believe that all these were first introduced into the text by Zenodotus?

⁷² I will give here a list of both sorts of verses, first those to which he affixed a critical sign because he suspected them (see above, ch. 33, n. 9), then those which he did not even put in the text. The scholia distinguish clearly between the two types, using for the first the verbs ἀθετεῖν, περιγράφειν, περιαιρεῖν, and for the second sometimes Ζηνόδοτος τούτους οὐκ ἔγραφεν, οὐδ'ὅλως ἔγραφεν, and sometimes οὗτοι οὐκ ἐφέροντο παρὰ Z. Of the first type are: 1.4 5, 46, 47, 63, 80, 117, 143, 159 [Wolf is wrong], 160, 208, 209, 225-33 inclusive, 396-406, 488-92; 2.220-

marvel at the extraordinary rashness of the man's mind: if he followed the example of others, that too would show the violence and eagerness with which the earliest criticism attacked the monuments of antiquity. But it is scarcely believable that Zenodotus thought up on his own everything that is attributed to his authority; thus at least a large portion of the Zenodotean readings are none other than those of many earlier copies. Since this judgment is not

23, 227, 228, 231-34, 528 (cf. Eust. 276.40), 553-55, 579, 580, 612-14, 641, 642, 673-75, 686-94, 724, 725; 3.18; 5.187, 249, 250, 906; 7.195-99, 255-57, 443-64, 475-82 (Eust. 692.21); 8.1 [on 7.482] (a verse which he then placed between 52 and 53), 493-96; 9.692; 11.548-57 (ὡς—ἤιε), 794, 795; 14.114, 304-6; 16.93-96, 140, 432-58, 668 with the following verses [—683], unless he otherwise rearranged the whole passage; 17.260, 261; 18.39-49; 21.538, 539.

The verses which are said to have been totally removed by Zenodotus are the following: 1.491 [on 488]; 2.674 [on 673]; 8.284, 371, 372, 385-87 (see on 5.734, 735), 528, 535-37, 557, 558; 9.23-25, 416, 688 with some of the following verses, such as 694 [only 694; Wolf's error]; 10.240, 253, 497; 11.13, 14, 78-83, 179, 180 (compare 16.379, 699; for there are no other verses to which the scholia in that passage can be referring), 356, 515, 705; 12.175-80 [or 181; the scholia are unclear], 450; 15.18 with the whole "punishment of Juno" [—31], 33, 64-77; 16.141-44 (schol. on 19.388 ["Zenodotus athetized"]); 17.134-36; 19.77; 21.195; 24.269. Lines under the numbers indicate that there is something remarkable, notable either for its good or bad qualities. There are some good things to be found in each category, particularly the latter, and I have marked in my text [i.e. the edition to which the *Prolegomena* were to serve as preface] those accepted by Aristarchus. But in many other cases it is hard even to guess what he found fault with.

Zenodotus' most ridiculous attempts, however, involve transposition and the supplements he invents for lacunae which he created at will. Thus, after he condemned 3.335, he rearranged the passage in the order 333, 336, 337, 338, 334, changing the final words of the last to βάλετ' ἀσπίδα θυσσανόεσσαν [Villoison's emendation for A's τερσανόεσσαν]. He then deleted 423-26, and supplied the verse

Αὐτὴ δ'ἀντίον ἵζεν Ἀλεξάνδροιο ἄνακτος

between 422 and 427. Similarly, he put 10.522 before the two verses which precede it, where the scholia rightly comment Πρῶτα δὲ ἰδόντα ἔδει κλαίειν. Elsewhere he makes some ridiculous conflations of verses. He reduced two excellent lines, 1.219f., to a single verse:

Ὣς εἰπὼν πάλιν ὦσε μέγα ξίφος, οὐδ'ἀπίθησε.

In the same book, in place of 446f., he had:

Ὣς εἶπεν· τοὶ δ'ὦκα θεῷ ἱερὴν ἑκατόμβην

[εἶπεν here is Wolf's emendation for the transmitted εἰπῶν; εἰπών Bekker]. The third repetition of the same verses at 2.60ff. so offended him that for 65-70 he substituted these two:

Ἡνώγει σε πατὴρ ὑψίζυγος, αἰθέρι ναίων,
Τρωσὶ μαχήσασθαι προτὶ Ἴλιον. Ὣς ὁ μὲν εἰπών.

See Eustathius 173.9. He offers similar nonsense at 16.89ff. and elsewhere. But in many of these instances, particularly in those where he completely omitted something, anyone might suspect that part of the blame is to be placed on the poor quality of the ancient manuscripts, not on Zenodotus' invention alone.

only likely in itself but is also clear from a number of credible arguments,[73] we shall have to evaluate the first of the critics cautiously, so as to avoid attributing to him faults which were perhaps shared with every learned man of that age.

The faults and errors by which Zenodotus seems to distort the entire system of Homeric and Greek speech must be judged by different standards in his case from those that apply to an age overflowing with grammatical rules. In an age before the language had begun to be minutely examined in accordance with precise rules, even a talented man could slip, or be inconsistent in an area which is subject less to talent than to rules. No one of intelligence, moreover, can fail to recognize how much the art of grammar itself, in its early stages, falters in details and how prone it is, in attempting to adjudicate between the custom of the authors and the logic of rules, to wander unawares from either standard. Some learned men would contemptuously summon Varro and those of his contemporaries who investigated the system of the Latin language to their own classrooms so that they might easily and precisely learn the things that once they had sought in vain. Those learned in the Hebrew tongue in particular—men who ought to be aware of the

---

[73] All trinities are perfect, as they say. Aristotle *Rhetoric* 2.2.1379a5 cites 2.196 using the plural Διοτρεφέων βασιλήων. It is possible that the philosopher changed the number for the sake of his argument; but now we learn from the scholia that Zenodotus had the same reading. It is more noteworthy that he is reported to have used, in two or more passages including 2.144 and 14.499, the nonsensical and virtually unknown word φή for ὡς: φὴ κύματα μακρὰ θαλάσσης and ὁ δὲ φὴ κώδειαν ἀνασχών. But the scholia [on 14.499] show that this same creature appeared in the work of post-Homeric authors, specifically Antimachus [fr. 121 Wyss] and Callimachus [fr. 737 Pfeiffer]. Are we now to think it a coinage of Zenodotus? In the same way, concerning the verses rejected by him, it is reported once that 17.134 and the two following verses were missing in the copy of the Chians. It is easy to multiply examples. Zenodotus used σφωίτερον as a second-person singular at 1.216 [Lehrs, cited by Erbse, says that Zenodotus took it as a plural]; we will see below that other Alexandrian poets used it, and no one will say that they were deceived by Zenodotus alone. They say that he wrongly altered Ὀϊλῆος to Ἰλῆος at 14.442; but we will shortly show that that form too was used in antiquity. At 2.484 he gave Μοῦσαι [Ὀλυμπιάδες] βαθύκολποι, using an epithet which, we are told [in the scholia], Homer generally gave only to barbarians. But Pindar *Pyth.* 1.12 supplies support for this reading, although we do not know how trustworthy the ancient manuscripts are. But the ancients should have looked into that before complaining of the remarkable ignorance and temerity of Zenodotus: Ἡμεῖς γὰρ [δὲ Homer] κλέος οἶον ἀκούομεν, οὐδέ τι ἴδμεν ["For we hear only the report, but know nothing"; *Il.* 2.486]. We know nothing other than what was once read in Zenodotus' recension; we know very little about his judgment; but common sense compels us to believe that he got many of his errors from earlier sources, which could deceive even the most learned of poets, of the stamp of Antimachus or Callimachus.

minimal scope of their own knowledge—tend to scoff at Philo Judaeus, Origen, and Jerome as men whose knowledge of a language that was still alive was far removed from the precision demanded by the grammarian's calling.[74]

We must, therefore, wrench our minds back to that period of the Greek language in order to judge properly and fairly the first authors of the subject. A careful examination of the readings of Zenodotus clearly reveals that many of the customs and rules of speech were not yet fixed at that time, rules which now even an amateur observes. Examples of this are not using duals in place of plurals,[75] the use of the article in Homer,[76] the meanings of many words, the distinctions among dialects, poetic constructions, and much else of the same sort.[77] There is in addition a perfectly re-

[74] Who is unfamiliar with Scioppius' continual attacks on the *sewage-grammar* of the Romans? [C. Scioppius (1576-1649), grammarian and polemicist.] Nor were Scaliger and others any milder in their complaints about the ignorance displayed in early work on the Hebrew language. Ernesti, *Opuscula Philologica* [1764], 296ff., provides a reply that is brief but apposite for our purpose.

[75] See on 3.279, 459 where Zenodotus wrote ἀποτίνετον (the manuscript has ἀποτίνετε—but it is better to correct the errors of the scholia in silence), 6.112, 11.348, 13.627, 15.347, 18.287, 23.753. Note also 24.282, where Crates and Eratosthenes are brought into connection with this mistake, "wishing to confuse the duals in Homer." More poets of the Alexandrian and succeeding periods could also be adduced, who perhaps ascribed this confusion in Homer, which they themselves imitated, to deliberate choice or to the license of the age of the bards.

[76] The precise rules on this subject which we employ are, as in a great many matters of this sort, those of Aristarchus, who taught that Homer "customarily lacks the articles." See Apollonius Dyscolus *De synt.* 6.5 Uhlig, Plutarch *Quaest. Plat.* 1010D and many passages of the scholia. It was unavoidable that for Zenodotus, who sought the usage of his own time in Homer, many readings should appear to need alteration. Thus for him Ὀϊλεύς easily became ὁ Ἰλεύς: see on 2.527 [Zenodotus not named]; 12.365; 13.203, 694, 712; 15.333 [Zenodotus not named]; 23.759; *Etymologicum Magnum* 346.41 [s.v. ἐξάδιος], Eustathius 101.19 [on 1.264; Zenodotus not named], and elsewhere. The single passage 11.93 ought to have led him to the truth; but Hesiod and Stesichorus are cited as using this form as well, so that it should not be considered a critical trifle. Because of the same need for the article, Zenodotus thought it necessary to write ὧλλοι where ἄλλοι is used for οἱ ἄλλοι, *the rest*. See the passages cited [by Wolf] in F. W. Reiz, *De Prosodiae Graecae Accentus Inclinatione* [2d ed. by Wolf, 1791], with *Etymologicum Magnum* 821.39 [s.v. ὧλλοι], and the scholia on 2.1 and 10.1. In the latter passage others are said to have written the same, as Brunck's Apollonius (1780) now does with considerable consistency. The article could be added or removed with equal ease with many other words; at least there is no metrical consideration in writing στῆ δ᾽ ὁ γέρων, ἀνὰ δ᾽ ὁ πτολίπορθος Ὀδυσσεύς or δὲ γέρων, δὲ πτολίπορθος Ὀ. in *Il.* 2.278 [the reference is to the second example; the first is not Homeric].

[77] We should add here a miscellaneous collection of comments for which Zenodotus is often criticized and branded with the *diple* in the scholia. At 11.730 he is said to have confused δόρπον with δεῖπνον [the reference to the *diple* is Villoison's supplement], at 13.610 μάχαιραν and ξίφος [Villoison's supplement], at 18.247 and

spectable form of error, when a grammarian departs from his own province to twist the consistency of usage in accord with some idea of analogy, and thus pretends to rule over the very master of the language.[78] Finally, one must call to mind over and over that the copies which he used were perhaps filled with faults and errors of the sorts which we pointed out above.[79] Zenodotus, therefore, is

---

19.14 φόβος and δέος [in the latter the *diple* is Villoison's supplement]. At 1.56 and 198 he wrote ὁρῆτο for ὁρᾶτο, and 530 κρητός for κρατός; in these passages he is criticized for confusion among dialects. At 3.459 he is criticized for failing to recognize the infinitive with imperative meaning; at 14.162 for taking ἑαυτήν as a single word ("Aristarchus says that he does not know the difference"; see Reiz on Hesiod *Theog.* 470); at 1.393, 15.138, 19.342, 24.528, 550 for giving ἑοῖο for ἑῆος; at 2.302, 3.280, 14.274 for changing μάρτυροι to μάρτυρες, ignoring the clear example at *Od.* 16.423; at 3.244 and 11.142 for neglecting the true meaning of the pronouns σφός and ἑός, which was indeed the only one recognized as legitimate after him; at 14.469, because he added an accusative to the verb γεγώνειν, in which he could not be consistent, because such phrases as Δαναοῖσι γεγωνώς, Τρώεσσι γεγωνώς and many others refused such alteration; at 3.71, 92; 7.114 because he wrote such forms as ἀμείνων, γλυκίων, and others without their final letter, as ἀμείνω, γλυκίω, a proceeding which is completely absurd and contrary to analogy; at 2.36, because he always attached singular verbs to nouns in the neuter plural, according to common practice, which he seems to have followed wrongly in other areas as well. Examples are his expulsion of anacolutha, such as his terrible emendation at 6.511, ῥίμφ' ἑὰ γοῦνα φέρει, cited also on 14.405, 17.700, 18.148; so also his linking of the sections of a sentence with participles in the manner of prose, as 2.187 Σὺν τῷ βάς or 14.169 ἐπιθεῖσα where the scholia give an intelligent comment. He is also criticized for not knowing that Homer "places in parallel words of identical meaning"; at 16.666, 21.17 and elsewhere, for not preserving the figure κατὰ τὸ σιωπώμενον, which is known also from the Latin scholiasts; etc. These examples show clearly how much we owe to the grammarians subsequent to Zenodotus, who organized all these matters that pertain to grammatical precision and interpretation in accordance with the proper principles. Many of the examples, indeed, are extremely remarkable in a critic, particularly one who himself wrote verses; this is particularly true of the unmetrical lines at 2.520, 658; 6.34; 13.172. One does not find such things in the three epigrams which survive under his name in *A.P.* 7.117, 315, *Anth. Plan.* 14 [Gow-Page, *Hellenistic Epigrams*, 3631-45].

[78] This appears to be the source for most of the errors given above, particularly those committed by Zenodotus in declining pronouns. When the scholiasts point them out, their peculiarity makes one think on first reading that they are creating monstrosities. For at 2.239 and 19.384, they report that he gave ἑοῦ in place of the genitive of the pronoun ἕο, at 8.377 and 22.216 νῶϊν for the accusative νῶϊ, at 1.336 σφῶϊν for the accusative σφῶϊ, at 12.366 σφῶε for the nominative of the second person σφῶϊ, and likewise in the third person at 1.8, 10.546 σφῶϊ for σφῶε. A further cause for astonishment in the last case is provided by the fact that it was approved by Seleucus and thought worthy of refutation by Apollonius Dyscolus *De Synt.* 227.16 Uhlig. We learn from the same source something that assists in explaining the variants at 24.486, *Od.* 19.358 [a manuscript variant, not in the scholia] and elsewhere and in Ammonius s.vv. ἐμεῖο and σοῖο [167, 445 Nickau], namely that Zenodotus altered the possessives ἐμοῖο and σοῖο to the pronominal ἐμεῖο and σεῖο. See Apollonius 223.16 Uhlig. What he says there, that "these readings are ascribed to Zenodotus," shows clearly that already in the Antonine age scholars only knew the Zenodotean readings from the excerpts of others.

[79] See above, ch. 37. One should particularly ascribe to this source the faults of

not to be treated as solely responsible for all the absurdities which are attached to his name.

"But he is responsible for some interpolations; he altered Homer in accordance with his own desires and his ignorance of both archaic language and heroic manners." That, in any case, is the accusation of the scholiasts, and no one should doubt it even though they nowhere make an adequate distinction between what he imported on his own into the text and what he merely found that was common long before.[80] On the other hand, the same sources report a number of marvelous things of his; some of them carry the approval of

the most ancient writing, which was continuous and incomplete in as much as it did not have distinct forms for all the letters, and also the nodding of the scribes in manuscripts written for sale, which Strabo mentions in the well-known passage 13.609. Many things are doubtless to be ascribed to the second type, which having once been transferred from manuscript to manuscript have now acquired the status of *variant readings*. Of the first type are the variations of long and short vowels, for which see on 11.104, 14.45, 18.198, 21.127, 22.236 (on which see Valckenaer [*Opusc. Philol.*, 2:55f.]), and variations of the sort μ'εἰρόμενος, μειρόμενος 7.127 (see also on 9.612), ἐξελόμην, ἐξ ἑλόμην 9.130, ἐξήλατον, ἐξήλατον 12.295, etc.

[80] Frequently, they speak in such a manner as to seem to make Zenodotus himself the author or emender of his own reading; but frequently too, as if they even had his copy in their hands. As when they report at 9.131 that he gave 19.245f. badly corrected, as follows:

Ἐκ δ'ἄγεν ἑπτὰ γυναῖκας, ἀμύμονα ἔργ'εἰδυίας,
ἕξ, ἀτὰρ ἑβδομάτην Βρισηίδα καλλιπάρηον.

There, and at a few other places, they say "Zenodotus writes," in the present tense, which properly refers to books which are commonly available. Of the same sort is "Zenodotus (σύνοδος in the manuscript) adds," for example at 13.808, a verse to which he added:

Λίην γάρ σφιν πᾶσιν ἐκέκριτο θάρσεϊ πολλῷ,

just as he added to 14.136 the equally inept

Ἀντιθέῳ Φοίνικι, ὀπάονι Πηλείωνος.

Or "Zenodotus made it," as at 22.378, which he read as:

Ἀτρείδη τε καὶ ἄλλοι ἀριστῆες Παναχαιῶν.

Or "his order of verses was," as at 4.123, which he placed after the verse which follows it, or as 14.394 which, with the following verse, he placed after line 399; or finally "he changed the text" as at 2.681. And if we followed Zenodotus' reading there, a reading in itself not at all bad,

Οἳ δ'Ἄργος [τ'] εἶχον τὸ Πελασγικόν, οὖθαρ ἀρούρης,

[τ' is wrongly omitted by Wolf], we would have lost the *peculiar device* of Clarke and Madame Dacier. [Clarke, ad loc., commenting on the text Νῦν δ'αὖ τούς, ὅσσοι τὸ Πελασγικὸν Ἄργος ἔναιον, remarks on the "peculiar device" of the passage by which the poet uses a high-flown preface to alert the reader to the fact that he is about to speak of Achilles. He remarks that Madame Dacier had previously made the same observation.]—But who would place any trust in such words, when he sees that elsewhere these scholiasts often report Zenodotean readings unabashedly from report, rumor, and conjecture, not from the inspection of ancient manuscripts?

Aristarchus and the other ancient authors of our text, while some, in my opinion, perhaps deserve to be approved for the future.[81] A fair number of his readings, moreover, seem to derive from the authority of good copies;[82] as a result, we should criticize anyone who rejected them in favor of his own conjectures, however attractive they might be, rather than considering the man who recovered the old readings a rash emender. In due course, indeed, it will become clear that the later critics often departed from fidelity to the manuscripts without justification. Thus everything returns to this: that we should use the remains of Zenodotus to acquire an estimate of the earlier common form of the Homeric text,[83] and that we should recognize how fragile were the beginnings of the

[81] See on 1.169; 2.258, 448; 3.57, 126, 259; 8.304; 12.295; 14.285, 322, 400; 16.188; 23.307, etc. His arguments are sometimes also cited by the scholiasts, as at 7.428; 14.229; 18.198, 499, etc., even if they are occasionally unjustified. We will shortly see how often Aristophanes of Byzantium agrees with Zenodotus, both in readings and in atheteses. Of those readings of Zenodotus which I have at long last recently recalled to the text, tired with the labor of looking, I can remember these four only, at 1.260, 5.227, 12.428, 13.423; with this last compare 8.334, where the schoolmasters are silent, although Zenodotus seemed so ridiculous to them on the preceding verse.

[82] Such, perhaps, are these; or if they were choices from early variants, they will certainly be judged examples of good judgment: 1.34 ἀχέων in place of the vulgate ἀκέων; 1.47 νυκτὶ ἐλυσθείς in place of the vulgate νυκτὶ ἐοικώς (cited on 12.463); 3.152 δένδρει for δενδρέῳ; 4.339 φαίδιμ᾽ Ὀδυσσεῦ: those who object to this have forgotten 1.122, or twisted in that passage the sense of the vocative κύδιστε; 5.898 ἐνέρτατος; 8.166 πότμον ἐφήσω for the unattested phrase δαίμονα δώσω; 9.158 καμφθήτω; 9.660 ἐγκονέουσαι; 9.664 Τῷ δὲ γυνὴ παρέλεκτο Κάειρ᾽, ἣν Λεσβόθεν ἦγε, where the scholiasts forgot the story of the capture of Chryseis at 1.366; 11.841 σεῖ᾽ ἀμελήσω [Villoison's emendation for δὲ ἀμελήσω]; 13.107 ἑκὰς πόλιος; 14.40 ἑταίρων; 16.156 πάντῃ in place of πάντας; 18.565 ἐς αὐτήν; 20.138 ἄρχῃσι. Imagine that the readings which have been put in their place were attributed to Zenodotus: would they not, by the use of that unwelcome name, lose all the charm which they now have? And yet many of the vulgate readings do not seem to be any older than those grammarians who constrained the form of Homeric speech to the requirements of elegance and carefully obliterated anything contrary to their rules. But by luck or chance there remains something, even after many instances of the same type have been removed, to betray the ancient fraud; and later critics marvel at it, and attack it in various ways. As, for example, the phrase Ἴλιον αἰπύ at 15.71, for the sake of which the *diple* is used a hundred times in the scholia in order to make the alleged *sole example* of that noun in the neuter more suspect. But another two verses are marked in the scholia because Zenodotus read Ἴλιον αἰπύ, 16.92, 18.174 [the scholia read ὅτι Ζηνόδοτος . . ., but at 18.174 Villoison supplemented this to read ἡ διπλῆ περιεστιγμένη ὅτι . . .].

[83] Here I will subjoin in a brief table all the remaining passages in which Zenodotus is referred to in the scholia and other writers, with references, in order that I may take account both of the brevity imposed on me and the convenience of my readers. And therefore, let those who wish to know Zenodotus in his entirety, as far as that is possible, consult them themselves: 1.5 (Athen. 1. 12E), 24, 42, 60, 69, 73, 83, 86, 91, 97, 100, 129, 163, 169, 204, 212, 216, 251, 271, 299, 400, 404 (see also Eust. 124.38 and Hesiod, *Theogony* 736), 434, 559, 567, 598, 609, 611; 2.4, 12, 36, 53,

art of correcting early remains, and of grammatical interpretation itself. In fact, however, none of the ancients attributed a commentary to him, so that it seems that he offered an interpretation only where he undertook to emend.[84]

55, 56, 89 [Porph. 26.8], 111, 156, 161, 226, 297, 299, 314, 318, 435, 448, 502, 507 (cf. Strabo 9. 413), 532, 571, 616, 626, 634, 667, 690, 694, 697 (cf. Steph. Byz. s.v. Ἀντρών), 718, 727, 741, 801, 852 (cf. Strabo 12.543, 553); 3.18, 28, 51, 74, 99, 100, 155, 206 (cf. Apollonius *Lexicon* s.v. ἀγγελίην [7.14 Bekker] with Tollius' Excursus 2 [H. Tollius, ed., *Apollonii Sophistae Lexicon* (1788), 735-38]), 211, 244 (cf. Apollonius Dyscolus *De synt.* 215.6 Uhlig and Eust. 410.15), 339 (with reference back to 334) [Wolf's interpretation of this note is incorrect], 361, 364; 4.3 (cf. Eust. 438.12), 88, 137, 139, 161, 277, 282, 478; 5.31, 128, 132, 146, 156, 162, 263, 323, 329, 638, 708, 807; 6.54, 70 [B Dindorf], 71, 121, 135, 226, 266, 514 (reference to 511); 7.32, 153, 451; 8.10, 53, 56 (reference to 562), 139, 207, 213, 290, 349, 378, 448, 503, 526; 9.3, 14, 29 [26-31], 36, 88, 271, 404, 447, 506, 537, 564, 594, 612, 638 (to be referred to the error at 9.131ff. mentioned just before; see schol. 9.131 and 19.246, cf. Eust. 741.5); 10.10, 25, 98, 127, 175 (referring to 19.239), 291, 317, 515, 545; 11.32, 86, 94, 101, 106, 111, 123, 219, 222, 368, 413, 437, 439, 451, 458, 528, 589, 677 (this is one of the few places in which there is little doubt that one should connect this to Zenodotus of Mallos [Bekker, followed by Erbse, reads "Herodotus" here; cf. schol. 14.387]), 754, 782, 831, 838; 12. 59, 66, 79, 127, 231, 296, 340, 342, 346, 348, 359, 368, 423; 13.2, 68, 71, 148, 166, 191, 198 (Eust. 927.33), 222, 229, 237, 245, 257, 315, 374, 450, 485, 546, 551, 643 (Eust. 953.5), 692, 702, 824; 14.16, 36, 40 (Eust. 966.17), 89, 135, 208, 236, 249, 259, 276, 285, 299, 310, 349, 351, 366, 400, 412, 427, 437, 485, 505; 15.86, 139, 169, 192, 207, 301, 307, 333 (Eust. 277.1, 1018.59), 356, 377, 459, 469, 470 [Wolf is wrong; there is a reference to Zenodotus in the scholium on 470 (471 in B), but none on 469], 480, 587, 626, 640; 16.10, 93, 150, 161, 223, 233 (Steph. Byz. s.v. Δωδώνη), 243, 507, 515, 666, 677, 710, 748, 807; 17.7, 15, 54, 103, 149, 171, 173, 215, 268; 18.142, 154-156, 160, 210, 222, 230, 364, 400, 466, 502, 563, 570, 576, 579, 581, 584; 19.26, 118; 20.11, 114, 261 (cf. Apollonius Dyscolus *De synt.* 222.13 Uhlig), 273, 283, 331, 346, 484; 21.95, 169, 335; 23.461, 527, 533; 24.47, 110, 293, 512, 725. Besides these I have nothing in my notes which is relevant to Zenodotus except for a few trifles preserved by Eustathius alone, as at 289.38 on 2.569-80, the reading Ἑλλεροφόντης for Βελλεροφόντης, 1014.60 on 15.256, "that Apollo is the one elsewhere called Παιήων," along with a few readings in the *Odyssey*, 1394.44 (on 1.93; cf. 1470.10 [3.317]), 1478.35 [4.1], 1490.23 [4.15], 1500.40 [4.366], 1773.28 [15.20], 1841.23 [18.130] (cf. Ammonius s.v. οὐδέν [361 Nickau]), 1885.53 [20.105], etc. If there is anything that I should regret having omitted, it will be criticized soon elsewhere.

[84] There is no passage in the scholia in which a ὑπόμνημα or treatise of Zenodotus is referred to, as is the case with Aristophanes and Aristarchus. Rarely, in fact, does anything of his appear which points in that direction; sometimes it arises from the conjectures of grammarians interpreting the readings of Zenodotus, and sometimes, unless I am mistaken, from the book in which Zenodotus had explained more difficult words in the manner of the glossographers. Such a book by Zenodotus is cited by the scholia to Apollonius Rhodius 2.1005; see Athenaeus 1.12C-D and the scholia to Theocritus 5.2, where the reading νάκος ἕλετ᾽ αἰγὸς ὀριτρόφου [ὀρειτρόφου Wendel] is cited from *Od.* 14.530, along with the scholia to *Il.* 2.89, 9.447, 11.106. I have deliberately omitted the passages of the Etymologicum Magnum, of which the majority can be assigned to Zenodotus of Ephesus with no more justice than can the little treatise edited by Valckenaer in his *Animadversiones ad Ammonium*, 228ff. [2d ed. (1822), 173f.]. I would be more confident in ascribing to the earlier Zenodotus the "Epitomes of Myths" referred to by Athenaeus 10.412A.

CHAPTER XLIV

Zenodotus' successor in editing and emending Homer was his pupil Aristophanes of Byzantium, who achieved renown under the rule of Philopator—himself a lover of Homer[85]—and of Epiphanes.[a] Following Callimachus and Eratosthenes, he was the leader in embracing with the greatest zeal the study of the poets and all literature of antiquity.[86] He opened a school of grammar on the model of those of the philosophers and rhetoricians, from which a number of Homerists emerged: aside from the three others known to us today,[87] the most renowned by far was Aristarchus. But the services

[85] Aelian *V. H.* 13.22.

[86] The assiduousness of his studies is shown to have been very great by Cicero, *De finibus* 5.19.50, and Varro *De lingua latina* 5.9, where a *lamp* is attributed to Aristophanes, and even from the silly story at Vitruvius, 7, pr. 5, in which he is said "to have read all books in order daily with the greatest diligence." No one else (for the architect speaks rather clumsily) interprets this to refer to anything other than his constant reading of the classical writers and to the work of teaching. This reminds me of the learned man of overeager talent whom I recently heard announcing that when he was a young man he used to read through the whole Bible between dinner and his drink of hot coffee.

[87] I have elsewhere already referred to Agallias of Corcyra [ch. 42, n. 64]. We know of two of his fellow students: Diodorus, whose inept correction of *Od.* 4.18 καθ'αὑτούς is rejected by Athenaeus 5.180E and, drawing from him, Eustathius, who also praises at 1504.38 [on *Od.* 4.441] a Diodorus the grammarian, who is in my opinion the same as the other and as the one mentioned by the scholia to Pindar *Isthm.* 2.54 [3.219.25 Drachmann]; and Callistratus, who, as cited by Athenaeus 1.21C, violently criticized Aristarchus not for a bad emendation, but because "the draping of his cloak was uneven." He is the same Callistratus as the one whose commentaries on Homer, Pindar, Euripides, and Aristophanes once existed, cited by our scholia elsewhere and for six readings in the *Iliad* (3.18; 6.434; 12.25 [Porph. 174.27]; 21.126; 24.134, 213) from three different works, all of which concerned either the interpretation or the emendation of Homer. His *recension* of Homer is, however, cited "among the most elegant ones" on 3.18. One conjecture of his at 12.25, ἐν δ'ἦμαρ, is more worthy of the gods than of Homer, and, extremely mild though it was, it was rejected, before Callistratus had become known as its author, by Barnes in accordance with Biblical precept. There is an even milder conjecture of his in the scholia minora and Eustathius [1827.57] on *Od.* 17.455. But granted that he played games far worse than this, he and the other two may have served Homer well in other respects which are now completely unknown. For the rest, as I have referred to the *school* of Aristophanes as a novel institution, I do not think that the same could truly be said of Zenodotus. His teaching is nowhere mentioned, nor is anyone ever properly called Zenodotean, unless one wished to include οἱ

[a] *Zenodotus' successor in editing and emending Homer . . .:* On Aristophanes see Pfeiffer, *History,* 171-209 = *Geschichte,* 213-57. The most recent edition of the fragments is that of A. Nauck (1848); a new one by W. J. Slater will be published shortly.

of Aristophanes to the other areas of philology seem to have been much more important than those to Homer; in the forty passages in which he is referred to by the ancients, there are no more than one or two mentions of his recension or illustration of these poems.[88]

Indeed (if I may give a brief account of large matters), aside from the extremely useful choice and evaluation of the best writers of every sort which was undertaken by Aristophanes and completed by Aristarchus,[89] he was the first to investigate with any care the authenticity of the remains of earlier times;[90] he was also the first to pay close attention to the grammar of the Greek language, particularly to analogy and to those areas which, in the modern specialization of subjects, are dealt with by philosophers.[91] He fitted this study with new equipment of various kinds, notably the accents and marks of punctuation that he invented; up to that time inflection and the sound of the voice, without any signs, had been used, and the unbroken and continuous string of letters made

---

περὶ Ζηνόδοτον ["those around Zenodotus"] who are occasionally mentioned in the scholia, as at 7.452 [A Dindorf], 15.86. This formula, however, normally refers to people who share an opinion, not properly followers [in fact, it normally means no more then "Zenodotus" in later Greek]. The scholia would call the latter οἱ ἀπὸ Ζηνοδότου, as the Aristarcheans are called οἱ ἀπ᾽ Ἀριστάρχου (or, as Varro translated it, ab Aristarcho grammatici [De lingua latina 10.42]), οἱ ἀπὸ Κράτητος, etc. This custom of teaching seems to have appealed, before the time of Aristophanes, to Callimachus, who taught Aristophanes. Indeed Hermippus and Ister are called Callimacheans in Athenaeus; the same Ister, in my opinion, two of whose mistakes are refuted in seven passages of the scholia, on 2.110; 8.491; 10.298, 439; 13.629; 15.230; 19.34. Of the thirty passages in which Callimachus himself is cited nothing appears that was written specifically about the emendation or interpretation of Homer. Even if they are relevant to both areas, the citations at 2.825 and Od. 4.1 in Eustathius alone [1478.36; also in the scholia] (on which see Apollon. Lexicon s.v. κητώεσσαν [99.16 Bekker]) come from another sort of work.

[88] See J. Meursius, Bibliotheca Graeca, in Gronovius, Thesaurus Graecarum Antiquitatum, vol. 10 (1701), 1254f. The industry of Meursius and the rest, however, will shortly be surpassed by the learned young man Bredow, in his commentary on the life and writings of this Aristophanes [never published].

[89] So I interpret Quintilian 10.1.54, 59. On this subject, which I mentioned briefly in note 60 above, see the careful discussion of D. Ruhnken at the end of his Historia Critica Oratorum Graecorum [in J. J. Reiske, Oratores Graeci, vol. 8 (1773), 168-73].

[90] See Quintilian 1.1.15 and the ancient scholium attached to the Hesiodic Shield by Aldus and Stephanus [hypothesis, p. 86.2 Solmsen]. In that fragment doubt is expressed, on the authority of Aristophanes, about the Hesiodic authorship of that poem. This suspicion clearly pertained to the whole Catalogue. On the same critic's doubts about the end of the Odyssey, see my comments above, ch. 31 and note 1.

[91] Varro's De lingua latina shows that he had read those works carefully: see 6.2, 9.12, 10.68. The second of these passages confirms what I suggested above, that the grammarians gave priority to the truth of analogy over attested usage.

reading quite difficult.[92] For this one discovery alone, the name of Aristophanes would have been worthy of immortality had not the familiarity of this custom obscured the memory of its discovery. In addition to this, he commented on many important authors; he reviewed and arranged the works, for example, of Hesiod, Alcaeus, Pindar, and Plato.[93] He devoted his particular attention to the dramatic poets, especially the comic poet who shared his name; and he did so not by dwelling on recondite or elegant words, but by explaining the general significance, artistry, and chronology of the plays.[94]

Aristophanes' methods of dealing with Homer, however, and the methods of emendation that he employed, are as obscure as in the case of Zenodotus. For even if we have recently learned of many readings from Aristophanes' recension,[95] the arguments that he

[92] See J. Foster, *Essay on the Different Nature of Accent and Quantity* [2d ed. 1763], 182ff., together with the sources cited by Villoison in his appendix to *Epistolae Vinarienses* [1783, pp. 115-20] or, even better, the long awaited treatise "On the Discovery of the Accents, etc." of Arcadius of Antioch first edited by him in the same place [Ps.-Arcadius, Epitome of Herodian, ed. Schmidt, 1861]. The grammarians throughout cite some of the teaching of Aristophanes on the system of accentuation, above all Apollonius Dyscolus *De synt.* 443.8 Uhlig.

[93] See the scholia to Hesiod *Theogony* 68, Hephaestion *Enchiridion* 74.12 Consbruch, Diogenes Laertius 3.61, and the life of Pindar assembled by Thomas Magister [schol. Pind. 1: 6.14 Drachmann], where we find: "*Olympian* I was placed first by Aristophanes *the arranger of Pindar's works*, because it contains praise of the games and the story of Pelops, who was the first to compete in Elis." I think that we would know similar, and even greater, accomplishments of these critics concerning the lyric poets, especially in metrical matters, had not an immense catastrophe here destroyed all the best works.

[94] This appears from a number of the summaries or arguments of Sophocles, Euripides, and Aristophanes, in addition to occasional mentions in the scholia, as also from Athenaeus 6.241F, where he is said to have devoted attention to Machon, a famous comic poet of the time, in his teachings about the parts of comedy. According to Athenaeus 14.659B, Aristophanes also wrote a separate treatise on masks. See Bentley, *Dissertation on the Epistles of Phalaris*, 25 [R. Bentley, *Works*, ed. A. Dyce (1836), 1:248 on Aristophanes in general].

[95] Ἡ Ἀριστοφάνειος διόρθωσις, ἡ κατὰ Ἀριστοφάνη ["the recension of Aristophanes, the one according to Aristophanes"]. It is clear from Athenaeus and Eustathius that it included both poems. One should not, however, think that it came complete into the hands of our grammarians. For here too, in citing readings taken from it, they use the word "they say," and elsewhere they betray that their source is Callistratus, the pupil of Aristophanes. He therefore had either accepted the readings of his teacher into the text himself, or had preserved them in his books "On the *Iliad*," "On Textual Matters," "Against the Atheteses" (that is, against Aristarchus' use of the obelus). Didymus in turn excerpted Callistratus, and we are extremely often the beneficiaries of Didymus' work in such matters. See on 2.111, 435; 19.76, 327, etc.

gave for them in his commentary are not transmitted;[96] nor the sources from which he drew them. Hence one must be highly circumspect about assigning him praise or blame for them. But scholars will easily concede that in the fragments of this recension, too, most readings should be ascribed to the paradosis and the then vulgate text; that is especially true of the follies that he shared with Zenodotus and others more ancient than he. Thus he cannot be considered the first to have introduced these.[97] Therefore it is not so clear what Aristophanes did approve or think worthy of Homer in such matters, as it is what he did not reject, what he did not delete. In the case of the other readings, where no other earlier authority is cited, even if the excerpts of the scholia do not in my regard deserve to be trusted for their precise language or pressed in their silences, still in those readings which are properly attributed to Aristophanes it is easy to recognize greater learning and moderation. And there are many readings in that group which Aristarchus did not see fit to reject, and some which, even against his judgment, were taken into the vulgate text by later critics.[98] Others,

[96] That he added ὑπομνήματα [commentaries] to his edition is clear for many reasons, even if they are explicitly cited nowhere in the scholia, except perhaps at 2.133 and 21.130, where my pupil Bredow has rightly seen that ποιημάτων should be changed to ὑπομνημάτων [so also Erbse; Wolf is wrong in his interpretation: the commentaries are those of Aristarchus against Aristophanes]. They are the source, I believe, for the comment on the verse of the *Odyssey* [16.49] in Athenaeus 6.228 C-D and the remarks of Porphyry *Q.H.* 8 [287.21] in which "the noble Aristophanes" is cited verbatim [on 21.126f.]. Porphyry had perhaps seen the book with his own eyes; but I am unwilling to believe that the scholiasts had done so.

[97] The following are Zenodotean; yet only a few of them smack of that vulgarity which was the source of our amusement just now. It is enough merely to give the line numbers: 1.91; 2.801; 3.57, 126; 4.137; 6.121; 7.452 [Aristarchus, not Aristophanes]; 8.290, 304; 9.158; 10.306; 12.66, 79, 127; 13.2, 71, 107, 245, 246, 551; 14.36, 177, 208, 229, 259, 276, 299, 310, 400, 412, 505; 15.139, 301; 16.223; 18.198, 400, 466, 502; 23.461. In another nine passages the agreement of Aristophanes with some of the city editions is reported, at 1.298, 423-24, 585, 598; 3.51; 15.44; 19.86; 20.188; 24.30; and twice with the text of Rhianus alone, 19.41 and 23.81.

[98] See on 1.108, 298, 553; 2.53, 164, 436, 447; 3.18, 35 (where there is some doubt as to whether Aristarchus preferred παρειά or παρειάς: for in the text of the Venetus, as in that of the Leipzig manuscript, the reading is παρειά: and it is clear that both critics approved of it, and see also at 22.491), 227; 5.638 (where after ludicrous arguments about the word οἷον the critics finally agreed on the reading of Aristophanes); 6.148; 12.26; 14.40, 45, 236, 285; 15.49, 53, 134, 601 [†ἀριστοφανης† Erbse]; 16.175; 19.76, 77; 21.126; 23.463. In a number of these passages the name of Aristarchus is not found, but I shall shortly demonstrate that they are probably to be ascribed to his authority [i.e. at 1.164; 6.148; 14.45; 15.49, 53, 134; 23.463]. If I prove this to the satisfaction of the learned, then his most famous disciple agreed with Aristophanes in the following atheteses: 8.164-66, 189,

which were later altered or rejected by ancient critics, did not all
give adequate grounds for alteration, at least with respect to the
appropriateness of the sense and Homeric usage; and further than
that we cannot go, since there is no consensus now about the testimony of the ancient manuscripts.⁹⁹ But just as many of those
readings are quite as good as the vulgate, so some of them are
clearly preferable.¹ And if we believe that Aristophanes produced

---

235, 688-92; 10.387, 397-99; 11.767-85 (νῶϊ ... υἱός); 14.95, 213, 317-27; 15.56-
77, 147, 148; 16.261; 18.597, 598; 19.327; 23.824, 825; 24.6-9, 614-17. With a few
exceptions, I believe that these are admirable models for criticism, and that I should
follow some of them with the use of brackets, which I shall defend elsewhere.

Those atheteses should also be added here, in which Aristophanes followed Zenodotus in one of four ways. In the first place, some verses were missing from both
of their texts, as these two (for no other examples are attested): 10.497 and 15.33.
The most ancient texts, therefore, give such verses little authority; and as a result
there is no doubt that, if we had accurate reports about this type of verse in the
scholia, we would have very different and more accurate ideas about the ancient
boldness of athetesis than is now the case. But those few comments which survive
are defective and confused, as in the first of my examples, at 10.497, to which at
least one of the adjacent verses must be added. In the second place, Zenodotus
athetized some verses that Aristophanes completely omitted. Only one such, however, is reported, at 14.114. Third, we have only a single example of verses athetized
by both, 7.195-99 [on 7.198]. The vast majority of verses to which he attached a
mark of deletion were of the sort that Zenodotus had not even included in the text,
οὐδὲ ἐγεγράφει. If we believe the scholiasts, the verses of this type athetized, that
is, marked with a sign, by Aristophanes were the following in particular: 8.284, 385-
87, 557, 558; 9.23-25, 694; 10.253; 11.13, 14, 78-83, 180, 356, 515; 12.175-80, 450.
Finally, in one passage, 21.130, where Aristophanes is said to have marked this and
the five following verses, his authority alone is given.

I have given the total of all the verses suspected by this critic; and it will not be
surprising that he is nowhere criticized by the ancients for excessive atheteses. He
behaved, indeed, with considerable moderation, in as much as he included even
those verses that Zenodotus had deleted or not found in his manuscripts, so as not
to seem fraudulently to have removed anything that another might consider Homeric. For the rest, one must be extremely cautious about this and other matters
because of the shortage of remains of this sort; nevertheless it is highly probable
that the *Zenodotean text* of the Homeric poems, as we say today, was the *basis of the
Aristophanean.*

⁹⁹ Certainly the greater part of these readings are not intrinsically to be rejected:
2.192; 3.373; 7.32, 238; 9.203, 551; 10.306, 349; 11.103, 546, 686; 12.40, 67; 13.8,
12, 51, 364, 613, 733; 14.44; 15.10, 197; 16.25; 18.53; 19.96, 105, 386. There will
be, I imagine, people to whom a number of these readings will still seem worthy
of the text, since it may appear that they have been neglected more through wil-
fullness and meddlesomeness than from the consultation of better witnesses.

¹ I have considered as such, and have accepted, two in particular, μάχην for μάχης
at 15.459 and Ὅσσον δ'ἐννεάχιλοι for ὅσ. τ'ἐννεάχ. at 14.148, as well as a third
which, unless I am mistaken, differs very little from the vulgate, but which I do not
now remember. Perhaps also I ought to have accepted some of those which the
scholia approve with their formulae οὐκ ἀχαρίστως and μήποτε ἄμεινον (that is
perhaps better, I am not sure it would not be better), as at 13.502 πρόσθεν for πρῶτος etc.,
or these not inelegant readings: οὐδὲ μὲν ἰδρείῃ for οὐδέ τ'ἀϊδρείῃ 7.198, τούς for

them by conjecture in place of earlier absurd and false readings, then we must have no small respect for his critical talent. I must, however, confess that even in those readings which can be ascribed to his conjecture with some degree of certainty I do not recognize a more advanced stage of the art of emendation than in the case of Zenodotus.[2] All the more reason, then, why we should expect Aristarchus to produce something worthy of the immense fame that he acquired by the consent of all antiquity for the emendation, and almost for the restoration, of Homer.

δή 12.67, ἵππῳ [†ἵππωι† Erbse] for ἵππων 4.142. I do not believe the scholiast's statement that Aristophanes there read ἵππω in the dual. In these places, however, the vulgate can easily be defended.

[2] At least, careful thought has given me this impression in considering everything together. In particular passages, as I have often said, it is most uncertain what each of them was the first to conjecture. But if conjectures could be separated from earlier readings by our own conjectures, I would particularly consider as examples of the former 3.13 κονισάλου ὤρνυτ'ἀέλλη (if that is in fact what the scholiast means, and not ἀελλής, as is written. The substantive used to be written in that form, not ἄελλα; see the variant on 16.374), 6.148 τηλεθόωντα followed by ὥρῃ in the dative, with many other similar readings. But anyone who is strongly moved can fill up paper with such things at any time. The last reading, ὥρῃ, has been accepted by everyone and the earlier nominative has now been suppressed. I have now brought it back, as the sense is made considerably more pertinent and the construction is Homeric, ἔαρος δ'ἐπιγίγνεται ὥρῃ, *at the beginning of spring*. And now I hear that Buttmann, a man of exceptional intelligence, long ago thought of the same argument and correction.

Furthermore, let us list here the other passages in which Aristophanes' judgment is cited by the scholia: 1.124; 3.42; 4.17; 7.436; 8.10, 513; 9.4; 10.153, 391; 11.26, 94 [here Dindorf reads "Aristophanes," but Erbse reports "Aristarchus" with no comment in the apparatus]; 219; 12.54, 59; 13.29, 60 ["Aristophanes" A, "Aristarchus" Nauck, Duentzer, Erbse], 92, 348, 713; 14.45, 58, 416, 474; 16.188, 313, 634; 17.178, 234, 264; 18.576; 20.306; 21.127, 249, 446. What trivia are to be found in these will be seen by anyone who wishes to make use of my tedious toil. The inconsistency and negligence of the excerptors will also be evident from the fact that they entirely omit the variant of Aristophanes at 1.122, φιλοκτεανέστατε, which is preserved by two sources that almost never supply anything of the sort, Eustathius [1441.18, *Od.* 2.190] and the shorter scholia on *Od.* 2.190 [not in Dindorf, but cited by A. Nauck, *Aristophanis Byzantii Fragmenta* (1848), 20], while the best scholia report accurately that he read σφὶν σταδίῃ, not σφὶ σταδίη at 13.713; Ῥείας, not Ῥείης, at 14.203; etc.

Nothing remarkable survives on the *Odyssey* of the various writings of Aristophanes, except in Athenaeus and Eustathius, who has a great deal of his grammatical material, excerpted from the commentaries, glosses, and other works of the same sort, which seem to have been passed on for a very long time in the hands of the learned. From those sources comes material for the interpretation of seven passages in the Venetian manuscripts, at *Il.* 1.5, 567; 9.378; 10.334; 11.4; 21.126; 23.104; and elsewhere on prosody or accentuation, at 5.289, 15.606, 20.30, 23.419 [the wrong Aristophanes: the citation is from *Birds* 1131], and 24.84 (compare on 15.10).

CHAPTER XLV

It is impossible to convey how great the authority of Aristarchus[3] once was not only among men of his profession but among all men of learning, both Greek and Latin. Indeed the majority of grammarians who taught their subject at Alexandria and Rome, including about forty who were his pupils[4] and others who were theirs, cherished him in the manner of the Pythagoreans with one accord as if he were their god. They even declared that they preferred to be wrong following him than right with the rest.[5a] As a result, his immense reputation filtered down little by little to all those who attended the grammarians' classes and devoted any part of their time to the study of literature and the interpretation of poets— something which in those days was done by everyone who wanted to be liberally educated—and his name was somehow attached to the very art of explaining and correcting texts.[6] So it came about that, although we know his life and books much less well than those of Aristophanes, even today he is more generally known than Aristophanes and all the others who once toiled in this least eminent branch of learning.[7]

[3] Under the reign of Ptolemy Philometor, about the 156th Olympiad [156 B.C.]. See Bayle, *Dictionnaire historique et critique* s.v. Aristarque, and C. L. Matthesius, *De Aristarcho Grammatico exercitatio* (1725).

[4] Precise knowledge of few of them survives, and of many, nothing but unfamiliar names scattered through Suidas, as of Aper [s.v. Ἡρακλείδης, H 463], Dicaearchus the Lacedaemonian [Δ 1063], etc. Those who made observations on Homer will be referred to later. Here and elsewhere we sadly lack the work Jonsius promised on the Greek grammarians.

[5] This is evident from many passages of the scholia, among which the following are the most ridiculous: on 2.316 "Since this is what Aristarchus thinks, we will follow him, as he is by far the best grammarian"; and on 4.235 "We must follow Aristarchus rather than Hermappias, even if he seems to be right."

[6] The praise of Aristarchus by the contemporary philosopher Panaetius is remarkable; as cited by Athenaeus 14.634C, he calls him "a diviner, because he easily divines the sense of the poems." Sextus Empiricus *Contra math.* 9.110, similarly compares him to Plato and the greatest minds in other fields. The passages of the Latin authors are more familiar, particularly Horace *Ars poetica* 450, Cicero *Att.* 1.14.3.

[7] The reason for my calling the teaching of grammar *least renowned* will be understood by those who know the customs and interests of the ancient states, particularly

---

[a] *they preferred to be wrong following him than right with the rest:* A well-known tag derived from Cicero *Tusculan Disputations* 1.17.39: "errare . . . malo cum Platone . . . quam cum istis vera sentire."

Aristarchus is said to have written more than eight hundred grammatical and critical commentaries and, if my understanding of Suidas is correct, nothing but commentaries.[8b] But those works, in which he followed the example of his teacher in undertaking the explanation and criticism of the greatest poets and many areas of grammar, perished long ago so completely that we do not know even the form of any of them. Of the questions which he considered, and which are the subject of a great part of literary criticism even now, we have nothing left but a few scattered and wretchedly mutilated phrases. How miserable today are those little scraps of the books which he wrote in defense of analogy against Crates![9] He also explained Archilochus, Alcaeus, Anacreon, Aeschylus, Sophocles, Ion, Pindar, Aristophanes, Aratus, and others. Some of these authors, along with his commentaries, disappeared in an age hostile to the Muses; and of the majority of those who do exist,

---

the free ones; I have said something on that score in ch. 13, n. 12. But in both peoples, the more subtle any branch of learning was and the more recondite the source it was drawn from, the less favor and honor it had among the common people. Thus those who were learned even in the most useful subjects, geometricians, astronomers, doctors, grammarians, and critics, were all but scorned in comparison with the orator and the man of civic affairs: Archimedes himself is a *low little man* in comparison with Plato and Archytas [cf. Cicero, *Tusc. Disp.* 5.23.64]. This scorn, however, is proper to the Romans who, more than the Greeks ever did, judged the liberal arts by their profit to the republic and popular glory. See Muret, *Variae Lectiones* 6.1, where his remarks on philosophy are even more true of grammatical studies.

[8] The words of Suidas s.v. Ἀρίσταρχος [A 3892] are ambiguous: "He is said to have written more than 800 volumes *of commentaries alone*" [Wolf is wrong about the ambiguity; see editorial note b to this chapter]. But nowhere in all the ancient references is any specific work of Aristarchus named [Wolf is wrong about this and contradicts himself at ch. 48, n.50], with the result that I think particularly relevant the remark of Aristarchus preserved by Porphyrio on Horace *Epist.* 2.1.257, "who, although he had made many criticisms of Homer" (being asked by someone, we are to imagine, why he himself had not composed a poem in accordance with the best laws of the subject) "he said that he was neither able to write as he wished, nor wished to write as he could." The saying is by no means absurd, and it is filled with wisdom and modesty; the statement of the poet [Horace *Ars poetica* 304] is similar: "Fungar vice cotis, etc." ["I shall take the part of the whetstone, which can make the iron sharp although it does not itself cut"].

[9] See Varro *De lingua latina* 8.63, 68; 9.1, 91; 10.42, comparing Gellius 2.25. If you add to those passages Quintilian 1.4.20, Charisius 1.117K = 149B, Priscian 17.61, 175 = 3.144, 198 K, you will have everything of the sort preserved by the Latin writers.

---

[b] *If my understanding of Suidas is correct, nothing but commentaries:* Wolf's understanding is incorrect. The passage means that Aristarchus wrote more than eight hundred commentaries in addition to other works, not that he wrote only commentaries. See Pfeiffer, *History*, 213 = *Geschichte*, 261.

nothing of his survives—at least nothing that is certainly his. There
is a little on the lyric and the comic poet [Pindar and Aristophanes],
but nothing in comparison with what once existed. In fact, until
quite recently we knew so little about his *Homeric recension* that
scholars labored in vain to discover how closely our vulgate resembled it.[c] Even now we cannot resolve this satisfactorily; but thanks
to the Venetian scholia, so great and so many are the materials
concerning Aristarchus that he alone affords us more study than
any of the other Greek grammarians. Given this abundance of
material, I will scarcely try to consider all the most important topics
here. I will be satisfied if in the course of a general survey, and by
making remarks on specific passages of Homer, I can create a firm
foundation.

CHAPTER XLVI

In this connection one must examine carefully the whole method
of ancient criticism, and form a true mental image of it. We have
not yet adequately refuted[10] the common error into which everyone
easily falls, of thinking that the ancient critics are similar to those
of the present day, and in particular that Aristarchus is very like
Bentley or Valckenaer or anyone else who improves the ancient
texts with equal brilliance. And people want to persuade us of this
by citing Horace's tag, "fiet Aristarchus"—a compliment to which
they could have added that of Panaetius as well.[a]

But, to begin from the latter, it obviously concerns not the textual
critic, but the commentator. And the context in Horace is such that,
if our own Ramler, a most fierce critic of others' poems, were
substituted for Aristarchus, those who praise his judgment and
those who reject it would accept the change equally well. From this
it appears that in that passage "critic" is not used in our modern
meaning. Cicero's remark[11] that "Aristarchus denied that those

---

[10] Ch. 38, esp. p. 157f.   [11] *Fam.* 3.11.5; see also 9.10.1, and *In Pisonem* 73.

---

[c] *scholars labored in vain to discover* . . .: E.g. Giphanius and Küster, whose works
Wolf still used and took seriously, though they had not been able to draw on the
Venice scholia. For their views see the Introduction above and Grafton, 114.

[a] *And people want to persuade us of this by citing Horace's tag, "fiet Aristarchus"—a
compliment to which they could have added that of Panaetius . . .:* For Horace see *Ars
poetica* 450; for Panaetius (who called Aristarchus a "seer," so greatly did he admire
the latter's skill at interpreting poetry) see Athenaeus *Deipnosophistae* 14.634 C (cited
by Wolf at ch. 45, n. 6), discussed by Pfeiffer, *History*, 232 = *Geschichte*, 283.

verses of which he did not approve were Homer's" is even less ambiguous, even if it is a joke: it surely does not mean that the prince of critics employed the art of correction in accordance with our present customs and the rules of a precise discipline. Rather, it compels us to believe that he ignored the first law of history and changed and deleted those passages in which Homer seemed to err, to slip, or to sleep.[b] Seneca, indeed, called those verses which Aristarchus had rejected *alieni* [foreign],[12] Ausonius even called them *spurii*,[13] and the ancient commentator on Horace, quite clearly, "verses that he considered not to be Homer's." I do not doubt that for the most part that is how they appeared to Aristarchus—for the various modes of corruption and interpolation which, as I related above, the text of Homer had suffered could much more easily be recognized then than after such a long lapse of time—but I do not believe that that was a matter of great significance to him. Indeed, when I consider the character of those times and those men, and when I carefully compare the clear reports of the ancients, I do not think that Aristarchus treated Homer any differently than Cato did Lucilius, whose "badly made verses he corrected,"[c] or than Varius and Tucca would have treated the incomplete poem of Virgil had not the desire of their dying friend and of Augustus intervened.[14]

[12] *Epist.* 88.39: "Am I to study the signs of Aristarchus, with which he marked others' verses?" Indeed, many people of Seneca's time had done so and were doing so, as we will show below.

[13] *Epist.* 13.29 Peiper = 11.29 Prete. In the verse "and he who placed signs by spurious verses" there should have been no doubt that Aristarchus is being described. It could more reasonably have been doubted whether he is also the person mentioned in the preceding verse of Ausonius.

[14] The story is extremely well known from Donatus' life of Virgil, sections 39-42, and from the allusions of the poets. The verses of Eugenius' preface to the *Hexaemeron* of Dracontius [ed. Vollmer, *Monumenta Germaniae Historica, Auctores Antiquissimi*, 14:27f., lines 20ff.] are also appropriate:

Quodsi Virgilius et vatum summus Homerus
Censuram meruere novam post fata subire,
Quam dat Aristarchus, Tucca Variusque, Probusque . . .

["But if Virgil and Homer, the greatest of poets, deserved after their deaths to undergo a new judgment, which is given by Aristarchus, Tucca and Varius, and Probus . . .].

[b] *To err, to slip, or to sleep:* See Horace *Ars poetica* 359, *quandoque bonus dormitat Homerus*, "whenever good Homer nods," a tag also used by Wolf in ch. 49.

[c] *whose "badly made verses he corrected":* A citation from the spurious verses prefixed to Horace *Satires* 1.10.

To that generation of Greeks, moreover, even though they were highly involved in the details of grammar, it would necessarily have seemed unworthy of the talents of a serious and learned man to be concerned with dividing books into sections, putting summaries at the beginning, collating manuscripts, removing the errors of scribes, marking words with punctuation and accents, and whatever else belongs to the task of the *grammatista* [elementary teacher]. *Grammarians*, the explicators of words and ideas, differed greatly from these, and particularly those who are by some called "more precise" or "more noble" grammarians,[15] the *critics*, whose duty it was to inquire into the authority and authenticity of ancient works, to assign them to their proper author, and especially to review their virtues and vices so that their hearers might learn what in them was to be imitated, and what was contrary to the true laws of writing. It is that which Longinus calls "the judgment of works of literature, the final product of much experience,"[d] not this learning which is concerned with restoring the genuine appearance of a book or snatching after one or two letters. From the former come those who are called "critics" by the Greeks, "judges of writers" by the Latins, and those are particularly to be considered in this number who are never reported to have tried to seek out the hand of the author by collating manuscripts or by conjecture, such as Maecius Tarpa, the hearer and judge of plays to be produced at Rome for festivals.[16]

It is by this sort of emendation, or rather criticism, that all critics once were rivals in Homer, or rather with Homer. They were driven by the very supremacy of the poems to omit nothing by which it might be increased and by which the most perfect polish of language and poetic art might be contrived. And in this area the more ingenious each was, the more immoderately he seems to have behaved, and often to have corrupted the text in correcting it. Certainly he who could emend the greatest poet by his own ability was thought to be supreme in critical judgment. Others, however, put forward such emendations either in their commentaries or in their

[15] "The most renowned grammarians" in Athenaeus 3.116D; "Some of the critics, that is to say of the more precise grammarians" Eustathius 773.29f. [on 9.540].
[16] Cicero *Fam.* 7.1, Horace *Serm.* 1.10.38, *Ars poetica* 387. There the scholiasts call the same Tarpa a critic and emender and, the phrase I just cited, "a severe and learned hearer and judge of poems."

---

[d] *which Longinus calls . . . :* Longinus *On the Sublime* 6, somewhat abbreviated.

classes, from which they were soon gathered by their students. That this whole practice found acceptance at first is shown by the story, mentioned above, of the Athenian schoolmaster who boasted to Alcibiades of his ability and zeal for emending Homer. If I have any understanding of this, he more or less matched what I am describing here. But shortly after the ancient texts experienced the excessive caprice of Zenodotus and the others who attacked the best verses and indeed whole poems, that method justly incurred the criticism of moderate and prudent men, and the "censorious insolence" and "asperity" and the frigid concern for trivia[17] were censured by many; but nowhere is there a charge of "frivolity" or "boldness" which it is customary to level at critics today. Nevertheless, to the best of our knowledge, none of those critics ever behaved in this way with the text of the tragic poets or other more recent authors; only the older poets were the object of every license in alteration, correction, interpolation, deletion.[18] From this it appears that this excess was not new then, and that it derived a certain authority and appearance of justification from the well-known fate of the Homeric poems.

CHAPTER XLVII

I should not wish all this to be construed as a denial on my part that good and careful emenders made use of ancient and choice manuscripts, and that by collating them they sought the genuine form of the text. Rather, for them the genuine form was that which

[17] See the epigrams of Herodicus of Babylon [*Anth. Plan.* 19A = Athenaeus 5.222A] and of Horace's near contemporaries Antiphanes of Macedon [*A.P.* 11.322 = Gow-Page, *Garland* 771ff.] and Philippus of Thessalonica [*A.P.* 11.321, 347 = *Garland* 3033ff., 3041ff.], where sport is made of "Grammarians, the children of Blame, pups of Zenodotus, those around Callimachus, thorn-gathering bookworms descended from Aristarchus, corner-buzzing, monosyllabic Aristarcheans, who are concerned with σφίν and σφῶϊν and μίν and νίν, etc." [a pastiche of phrases from the epigrams referred to above]. Others, later, do the like, such as Lucian, criticizing "the excessive frigidity of the grammarians following Zenodotus and Aristarchus," *Verae historiae* 2.20.

[18] Nor was Homer alone, even if in his case we have far more adequate and certain evidence of this. But anyone who hesitates about Hesiod, and is not swayed by the appearance of his surviving works, should recall that passage in the *Theogony* extended by eighteen verses from the book of Chrysippus cited by Galen, *De placitis Hippocratis et Platonis* 3.8, p. 318 Mueller [= Hesiod, fr. 343 Merkelbach-West; see also West on *Theogony* 886-900 for a different interpretation].

seemed most to suit the poet, and no one can fail to observe that in this respect everything revolves around the talent and judgment of the Alexandrians. In the great and devastating collapse of antiquity it was therefore extremely fortunate that such a man devoted particular attention to the task and received general approval, a man who was certainly not among the most bold, who often checked the rashness of Zenodotus, who understood better than anyone else the true rules of the Greek language. But I shall return to these topics shortly, when I describe with specific illustrations the talent and technique of the most admired of critics.

These illustrations are taken from the remains of the *two recensions* that once were attributed to Aristarchus. I believe that this occurred immediately after his death. For Ammonius, a student of Aristarchus and his successor in the Alexandrian school, wrote a book "on there not having been more versions (ἐκδόσεις) of the Aristarchean recension."[19] Hence it is most probable that even then a twofold edition or twofold copy of the Aristarchean recension had begun to circulate in the libraries. This opinion and report remained constant among the grammarians; as a result, the agreement of the two texts is often reported in the scholia,[20] as elsewhere are the different readings of the two,[21] and more rarely they are given in such a fashion that the prior edition (προέκδοσις) is distinguished from the subsequent one (ἐπέκδοσις).[22] Nor is it intrinsically unlikely that Aristarchus did the same thing as Apollonius Rhodius[a] and a not inconsiderable number of later writers, in pol-

[19] See the remarkable scholium excerpted from Didymus on 10.397. This book is without doubt the same as that cited on 19.365, περὶ τῆς ἐπεκδοθείσης διορθώσεως ["on the additional recension"], and the latter is perhaps the correct title.

[20] With the words αἱ Ἀριστάρχου, αἱ Ἀριστάρχειοι ["the (editions) of Aristarchus," "the Aristarchean (editions)"], as at 1.91, 2.221, 3.292, 5.808, 6.288, 9.580, 12.404, 17.681, and many passages which I will shortly cite for other purposes.

[21] In one place we find ἐν τῇ ἑτέρᾳ τῶν Ἀριστάρχου ["in the second of Aristarchus' (recensions)"], in another διχῶς ["in two ways"], once or twice διήλλαττον αἱ Ἀριστάρχου ["the (recensions) of Aristarchus differ"]. See on 2.131, 517, 579; 3.416; 4.282, 527; 5.132, 181; 6.113, 174; 8.213, 405; 9.657, 681; 10.159; 11.632; 13.359, 627; 14.36, 67, 427; 15.450; 16.430; 18.579; 23.273, etc. To the same source, that is, to the second edition, Villoison ascribes τὰς ἐξητασμένας Ἀριστάρχου ["the (recensions) reviewed by Aristarchus"] at 7.130. For the rest, the report of the two recensions of Aristarchus was already long familiar from two scholia on 9.310 and 653 and from the Leipzig manuscripts; I do not recall reading of them in Eustathius.

[22] As on 16.613, 19.386.

[a] *the same thing as Apollonius Rhodius:* Wolf alludes to the so-called *proekdosis* cited by the scholia on Apollonius 1.285, 516, 543, 726, 788, 801; its significance, and

ishing their works again and publishing them in a better form. Nevertheless, since Ammonius, a responsible source, seems to deny this categorically, it is possible that the new recension, differing in many respects from the previous one that Aristarchus himself had published, was stitched together from the marginalia of a copy left to his heirs, from the volumes of his commentaries, or from the classes in which he revised his opinions in the light of second thoughts. These are the probable conjectures of the very learned Villoison,[23] in which I gladly acquiesce. Nor do I think it worthwhile to dwell on something that Ammonius, or Posidonius the friend and secretary of Aristarchus, or Ptolemaeus of Ascalon, or Didymus, could tell us in a few words, if they were alive, but which, as in many other similar cases, we cannot establish with clarity by either reason or conjecture.

We progress to the description of Aristarchus' recension, to the extent that it can be done from the few bits of evidence that we have by the use of conjecture and close attention to that period. Even if, as I said, we know none of the ancient critics better than Aristarchus, still, with respect to the whole and not to the small particles, our sources are so meager that it is impossible to reconstitute or restore even the shortest section of the *Iliad* from them in accordance with his intention. We possess many admirable readings of his, some which are generally accepted,[24] some which de-

---

[23] Villoison, xxvii.

[24] In countless passages, where we are in fact unaware of it; in others, where by comparison of all available evidence it becomes no more than probable that our vulgate text reflects Aristarchus' reasoning; and in many, in which now at least we know it as a fact. For example 2.397 γένωνται (others wrote γένηται, see p. 178); 4.299 ἔλασσεν (otherwise ἔεργεν); 5.797 τείρετο (otherwise τρίβετο); 7.213 βιβάς (otherwise βιβῶν, which itself is nevertheless attributed to Aristarchus at 15.307); 9.310 φρονέω (otherwise κρανέω); 12.30 ἐποίησεν (otherwise ἐποίησαν), 142 ἐόντες (otherwise ἐόντας); 13.246 θεράπων ἐΰς (otherwise δουρίκλυτος; from the inept reading before Aristarchus, Θεραπωνεύς, like Ἐτεωνεύς, Harles in Fabricius' *Bibliotheca Graeca* [vol. 1 (1790), 369] has given us a grammarian Eteoneus, like Xenodocus from Eustathius on 3.354 [423.21]), 415 ἰόντα (otherwise ἐόντα), 446 δή τι ἐΐσκομεν (otherwise δή τι σ᾽ ἐΐσκ.); 14.40 πτῆξε (otherwise πῆξε), 157, as at 20.59 and elsewhere, πολυπίδακος (otherwise πολυπιδάκου); 15.64 ἀνστήσει ὃν ἑταῖρον (otherwise ἀνστήσειεν ἑτ.), 187 τ᾽ἐκ Κρόνου (otherwise τε Κρόνου), 621 αὐτήν (otherwise ἀκτήν [or ἀκτῇ]); 16.31 αἰναρέτη (otherwise αἰναρέτης), 261 ἔχοντας (otherwise ἔχοντες); 17.637 δεῦρ᾽ὁρόωντες (otherwise νῦν ὁρόωντες); 20.28 τέ μιν

---

even its authenticity, remain uncertain. The effort to reconstruct Apollonius' revisions of his *Argonautica* and to determine whether verses from the first version had been interpolated into the second had occupied Hemsterhusius and Ruhnken. See the latter's *Epistola Critica II* (1751), 49-52 and E. Hulshoff Pol, *Studia Ruhnkeniana* (Leiden, 1953), 134-36.

serve to be preferred to those that are accepted.[25] We watch him for the most part choose, from a group of discordant readings, that one which best suits the genius and custom of Homer and is most appropriate to the passage; we see many wise and learned observations on his part; but the one thing that must be asked first, what novelty he brought to the totality of the poems, how conscientiously he dealt with ancient manuscripts, how he used the recensions of Zenodotus, Aristophanes, and the others whom I mentioned above;[26]—these and other things cannot today be inferred by certain or even probable arguments. Indeed, from the time when the Aristarchean reading became the transmitted text (the common, and satisfactory, terms are *vulgate reading* and *vulgate text*), which seems to have happened fairly early,[27] new emendations and annotations were composed and attached to it in particular, with the omission, in general, of those responsible for the readings, except perhaps when they disagreed among themselves. This custom was preserved by the grammarians above all, from the time when, as a result of the criticisms and observations of Crates and the other opponents of Aristarchus, many readings, either new or

---

(otherwise τί μιν), 114, as at 15.127, ἡ δ'ἄμυδις (otherwise ἢ δε.); 23.18 ἀνδροφόνους (otherwise ἀνδροφόνου); 24.125 κλισίῃ (otherwise in the plural κλισίης), 344 ἐθέλει (otherwise ἐθέλῃ), 546 τῶν (otherwise τῷ), etc. I admit that many of these are slight, and not of the sort one would expect from the Alexandrian Bentley, but they are good and deservedly preferred to the adjoined readings. These samples are random, not deliberate choices.

[25] I have done so frequently, in some cases for the sake of consistency, in others because of their obvious superiority, as 4.235 ψευδέσσι for ψεύδεσσι, i.e. ψευσταῖς for ψεύδεσι, 9.317 and 17.148 [cf. Erbse, ad loc.] ἐπ'ἀνδράσι for μετ'ἀνδράσι; 11.40 ἀμφιστρεφέες for ἀμφιστεφέες, 672 βοηλασίη for βοηλασίης or βοηλασίην; 14.235 ἰδέω for εἰδέω [Wolf is wrong in his report here]; 15.114 δ'ἔπος ηὔδα for δὲ προσηύδα, 450 ἱεμένων for ἱεμένῳ (although this inept reading, now the vulgate, is also given the authority of Aristarchus, perhaps from the first edition), 15.24 θυμόν for θυμός; 16.633 ὀρώρει for ὄρωρεν; 20.35 κέκασται for κέκαστο, 77 μάλιστά ἑ for μάλιστά γε; 23.287 ἄγερθεν for ἔγερθεν [Wolf is wrong in his report here; see Erbse]. There are others, concerning which my main fear is that there will be many a later scholar to marvel at my slowness, as 2.462 ἀγαλλόμενα for ἀγαλλόμεναι, 7.420 ὠτρύνοντο (or ὀτρύνοντο) νέκυς for ὄτρυνον νέκυας, 9.509 εὐχομένοιο for εὐξαμένοιο, 14.173 κατά for ποτί, 19.95 Ζεύς for Ζῆνα, 21.587 οἳ καί for οἵ κεν, 24.241 ὀνόσασθε for οὔνεσθε, etc.

[26] That Aristarchus made use of them is evident both from common sense and from the scattered observations of the scholia. In one or two of them something is reported about the edition of Zenodotus from the notes of Aristarchus, as at 13.808, 14.162; elsewhere he is often said to have "preferred" one of the older readings, as at 6.4, 7.127, 9.212, 20.138, 21.265, etc.; see especially on 9.222. The ancients apparently never worried about our problem.

[27] That is the significance of the phrase in the scholia ἐπείσθη ἡ παράδοσις

resurrected from older texts, were imported into the *then vulgate text*; until, in the third or fourth century, that *recension* emerged from the same sources, by a renewed examination, which, as it is alike in all surviving manuscripts in the most important matters, and derived from a single copy, we consider as the *vulgate today*.

Since this is the case, we will have to be wary of rashly ascribing many mediocre readings which are reported as from the text of Aristarchus, to the warped cleverness of the emender.[28] And perhaps we should have the same opinion about all the inept readings of his, most of which were rejected long ago, and which I at least would rather assign to Zenodotus or one of the earlier editors than to Aristarchus.[29] For it is one thing to keep a reading in the text,

---

Ἀριστάρχῳ ["the transmitted text followed Aristarchus"], as at 4.138, 5.289, 20.357, or ἐπείσθησαν αὐτῷ οἱ γραμματικοί ["the grammarians followed him"] at 16.415, or ἐπεκράτησεν ἡ ἀνάγνωσις αὐτοῦ ["his reading won out"] at 1.572, 5.69, 6.150, 7.289, 22.67, or οὕτως ἔχει τὰ τῆς ἀναγνώσεως ["that is the situation of the reading"] at 11.652, 23.387, compare Apollonius Dyscolus *De synt.* 216.14, 314.11 Uhlig. On the other hand, it is very rare to find the comment οὐκ ἐπείσθη ἡ παράδοσις ["the transmitted text did not follow (him)"], as at 21.162, 24.316, etc. Note also the remarkable passage at *Etymologicum Magnum* 815.16 [s.v. χρῆσις]: "It [sc. usage] differs from 'transmitted text' (παράδοσις): 'usage' is the name for the evidence of the ancient poems, 'transmitted text' is that of the grammarians; for example, the language of Homer is called 'usage,' and that of Aristarchus the grammarian [is called] 'transmitted text.' " And indeed [his is the transmitted text] *par excellence*.

[28] 1.106, 108 εἶπας, 157 σκιόωντα, 241 τότε δ᾽οὖτι, 447 ἱερήν, 522 μή τι; 2.266 ἔκφυγε; 3.352 δαμῆναι, 362 αὐτῇ; 4.170 πότμον, 426 ἰόν; 5.272 μήστωρε for μήστωρι, 881 ὑπερφίαλον; 6.76 μάντις τ᾽οἰωνοπόλος τε, 288 Ἡ δ᾽ εἰς οἶκον ἰοῦσα παρίστατο φωριαμοῖσιν; 7.73 δ᾽ἐν γὰρ ἔασιν, 241 δηΐων, 481 πιέμεναι; 9.36 ἠμὲν νέοι ἠδὲ γέροντες for ἡγήτορες ἠδὲ μέδοντες, 128 and elsewhere ἀμύμονας (Zenodotus read ἀμύμονα; cf. Hesiod *Theogony* 264), 132 Κούρη Βρ[ισηος] ἐπὶ δὲ μ[έγαν] ὅ[ρκον] ὀμοῦ-μαι (because of the construction; see *Od.* 2.120), 322 πολεμίζειν; the other reading, I think, was πολεμίζων, 10.341 Οὗτός τις; 13.384 ἦλθ᾽ ἐπαμύντωρ; 14.223 μέσῳ; 15.252 ἴξεσθαι, 394 ἀκέσματ᾽ἔπασσε; 18.506 ἀμοιβηδόν; 21.126 ἐπαΐξαι [better ὑπαΐξει; but cf. also Pap. 12, col. 4, line 23 Erbse], 265 οἰμήσειε; 22.416 κηδόμενόν περ [κηδόμενοί περ Erbse], 468 βάλε δέσματα; 23.361 δρόμους. I have called these and similar readings *mediocre* because they do not change the sense, and they would certainly be tolerable had they ever been in all the manuscripts. But now some of them are to be found in our vulgate text, and I am ashamed that I too have left them, particularly μήστωρε at 5.272.

[29] I will give a brief conspectus of readings of this type as well: 1.434 ἀφέντες or ἐφέντες, 518 Ἥρη in the nominative; 3.326 ἑκάστον, 348 and 17.44 and often elsewhere οὐδ᾽ἔρρηξεν χαλκός; 4.17 αὖ πως; 5.874 δ᾽ἄνδρεσσι; 7.64 πόντον, 197 ἑλών, 304 εὐκμήτῳ; 8.109 κομείτην [Wolf is wrong: κομείτων Aristarchus, κομείτην Zenodotus], 449 τοῖον; 9.18 μέγας (see Didymus on 2.111), 66 φυλακτῆρας, 214 ἀπαείρας, 297 τιμήσωνται [τιμήσονται Erbse], 580 ψιλῆς, 605 τιμῆς in the genitive; 10.225 εἴπερ τι [τε Lehrs, Erbse]; 11.72 ὑσμίνη ... ἔχεν, 439 τέλος; 14.72 ὅτε, 202 με σφοῖσι [μ᾽ἐν σφοῖσι Erbse]; 15.439 τέκεσσι; 16.638 Σαρπηδόνι δίῳ, 775 ὁ δὲ στροφάλιγγι, which is still to be found at *Od.* 24.39; 17.27 οὐδέ τε, 202 αἲ δή [Wolf follows Villoison's misinterpretation of this passage], 681 ἴδοιτο; 18.485

but another to be the first to adopt it or to place it in the text by conjecture. And everyone can recognize how difficult it is in this area for one person to recognize and remove all the blots, especially in a book that was corrupted in antiquity and often imitated, corruptions and all, by others, and to do so in that period which had scarcely witnessed the birth of grammar and precise criticism.

CHAPTER XLVIII

Amidst the vast obscurity of the text prior to Aristarchus, therefore, it is surely to be marveled at that even a very small amount can still be found in the scholia to provide the basis for a judgment about the virtues and the vices of the first of critics.[30] Among his virtues the first place belongs to his remarkable acumen, by dint of which he established the whole structure of grammar, the principles of accentuation, and the rest of orthography in accordance with the laws of consistent analogy. How great a service this was will appear very clearly to anyone who considers the history of the language (to which I alluded before) and the errors of Zenodotus.[31]

ἐστεφάνωκε; 20.228 ἄλλοτε [B; A has ἀλλ᾽ὅτε δέ; cf. Ludwich 1.453.14], 255 πολλὰ τά τε καὶ οὐκί [correctly πολλὰ τ᾽ἐόντα καὶ οὐκί]; 21.252 μέλανός του (τινός; see on 24.315 [Porph. 274.1]); 22.475 ἤμπνυτο [correctly ἔμπνυτο]. Many of this class too are obviously errors in the text.

[30] I think that we owe our knowledge in particular to Dionysius Thrax, the most devoted disciple of Aristarchus, to Parmeniscus, to Tryphon, and to the other Aristarcheans who indicated in their writings his readings and interpretations, which were gathered from those sources into the collections of scholia. See on 2.111, 662; 5.299 (cf. Eust. 556.38 on 5.329); 8.513; 9.464; 18.207. It seems that we often have the very words of Aristarchus from this and similar writings, as when we find "Aristarchus says" at 1.554, 2.2, 9.401, 15.385, 18.77, 19.81, 21.344, 22.440, 23.523, 824; or "Aristarchus marked this verse" at 1.219, 2.837, 13.237, 15.86. The actual works of Aristarchus—his "Treatises," "Against Philetas," "Against Comanus," "On the *Iliad* and *Odyssey*"—were not available entire for the inspection of the scholiasts, and perhaps not even his complete *recension of the text*. See 1.97, 423, 524; 2.111, 125, 355, 397, 420, 423 [B Dindorf; Porph. 252f.], 435, 798; 9.349; 10.397; 11.40, 391; 17.373; 24.110, etc. In many of these passages the readings of Aristarchus are cited, and there are many more of them in the *Lexicon* of Apollonius, all excerpted from those books and from his commentaries; it is, however, not intrinsically unlikely that Aristarchus had his own collection of Homeric glosses. See the scholia on *Od.* 7.24, 14.29, 19.229, Etymologicum Magnum 509.27 s.v. Κήδω, etc.

[31] See ch. 43. The errors which I pointed out there were almost all corrected by Aristarchus, even if he is rarely named by those who followed his rules, as appears from Apollonius Dyscolus, Herodian, and others. But see in particular the scholia on 2.396, 4.400, 6.434, 10.408, 11.128, 13.617, 14.1 [B Dindorf] (see scholia on Apollonius Rhodius 1.299), 208, etc. Comments concerning prosody or accentuation

Why should I say more? The *beginnings of all subtlety in grammar* are to be assigned to him, a subject previously unknown to the best writers, and not studied with adequate precision by Aristophanes himself. And not only in the more serious parts of grammar was something left for Aristarchus, but even in some very trivial matters, as in the task of making precise distinctions among variable forms.[32] And even though after his time they became so familiar that they seemed to have been born with the Greek language itself, his near-contemporaries and later poets show that these things were neither commonly observed nor in consistent use. And there were once without any doubt people who thought that in the early poet some anomalous forms of this sort should be accepted, and that those which he [Aristarchus] had rigidly altered in accordance with

---

are found at 1.214, 396; 2.262, 592; 3.20, 128, 344; 4.138, 308; 5.269, 656; 6.239, 244, 422, 518; 8.240, 355; 9.150, 236; 10.242; 11.239, 270, 454, 480, 495, 677; 12.20, 55, 158, 193, 201, 337; 13.103, 191, 543; 14.38, 396, 463; 15.10, 302, 320, 365; 16.123, 185, 211, 324, 415, 542, 548, 558, 827; 18.352; 19.357; 20.53, 357; 21.110, 331, 22.67; 24.84, 134, 228, 235, 247, 557; in these there are solid foundations for more accurate prosody. To these should be added a few comments on anastrophe, on 2.150, 523, 839, 877; 3.240; 4.94; 18.191. Note also the comments on orthography properly so called, in which we owe to Aristarchus a great deal which has long been accepted: thus the fact that such words as παλιμπλαγχθείς, παλινόρμενος, ἐπίηρα, Κηρεσσιφόρητος, ὀνομάκλυτος are written as single words, not πάλιν πλαγχθείς, etc.; see on 1.59, 572; 5.178; 8.527; 9.147; 11.326; 22.51; and compare Homeric *Hymn to Aphrodite* 111, 146. On the other hand certain words are written disjointly, as καὶ κεῖνος, καὶ κεῖθι, not κἀκεῖνος etc.: see 3.402, 6.200 [Aristarchus not named], etc., because consonants are generally not doubled in the manuscripts; see my recent remarks in the preface to the *Odyssey*. See also the scholia to Apollonius Rhodius 1.769, 3.37, and the scholia on *Il.* 5.203; 8.423; 9.154, 299, 574; 10.258; 12.26; 15.31, etc. It is also relevant here to point out that, wherever meter permitted, he removed the augment of verbs for the sake of the archaic Ionic, and wrote not πόλλ'ἔπαθον καὶ πόλλ'ἐμόγησα, but πολλὰ πάθον καὶ πόλλα μόγησα, σπλάγχνα πάσαντο, ἄλγεα θῆκεν, Γλαῦκος τίκτε, ἔχθαιρε, ἕλκε, and also νέρθε, κεῖνος, not ἔνερθε etc., at 1.598, 6.157, 9.492, 15.94, 16.648, and frequently elsewhere, occasionally with some disregard for the meter. Finally other grammatical comments of this nature are to be found at 1.364; 4.245, 410; 5.746; 6.432; 8.296 (23.273), 441; 10.332, 513; 11.441; 12.318; 13.103; 15.240; 16.379; 17.20, 95, 688; 19.27; 21.573; 22.431; 24.8, 331. From all these it is evident to what extent that period was concerned with minute details. But we must pass over these topics and more, about which there is no possibility of dilation in the short space available here.

[32] We had scarcely any suspicion of this previously; but now we see it clearly from the scholia. For the fact that nowhere in Homer do we read θέλω, στεναχέω for ἐθέλω, στενάχω, nowhere ἥδυμος for νήδυμος (no one will pay attention to the Hymn to Hermes [241, 449]; nor did any of the learned Alexandrian critics assign those poems to the genius of Homer); the fact that a number of words are regularized to a greater extent than the law of analogy demands, as Κάλχαν, Θόαν, Πουλυδάμα 1.86, 2.1, 12.231, 13.222, 17.688—these and many similar features are to be attributed to the decision of Aristarchus.

his precepts were not unworthy of being recalled. But this whole subject is too obscure to be illustrated here.[33]

We must speak even more briefly about Aristarchus as an interpreter of Homer. Granted that we know nothing about this other than that he rejected the allegorical mode of interpretation and

---

[33] I will briefly consider one subject, the improved precision of the forms and meanings of the pronouns attained by Aristarchus. For this too is to be ascribed to him, that σφῶε is distinguished from σφῶϊ and ἑοῦ from ἕο, that σφίν, σφός, σφέτερος are generally used for the third-person plural, while ἑός is used for the singular, etc. See the scholia on 1.216, 10.546, 11.142, Apollonius Dyscolus *De synt.* 216, 229f. Uhlig, and frequently elsewhere. Indeed, he altered those things which could be altered in poetic texts by a slight correction, but considered as interpolations those which resisted such correction, as at 10.397-99 because of the use of μετὰ σφίσιν to mean "among you." But the use of this pronoun in this meaning does not seem to have bothered Apollonius Rhodius, since he used the same form to indicate even the first-person plural at 2.1278. The decline of proper Greek in the imperial period permitted the use of the accusative σφᾶς αὐτούς for the first person even in prose, to say nothing of the ancient author of the Orphic Argonautica, for whom the form σφίν is a veritable Proteus. Σφέτερος indeed is used as a second-person plural possessive in the proem of Hesiod's *Works and Days* [line 2]; and granted that the authorship of that proem is uncertain, it still has clear indications of considerable antiquity. Such irregular uses, however, were not allowed to pass without some criticism by the ancient scholars, relying, I think, on the opinion of Aristarchus: but they were imitated by the author of poem 22 in the Theocritean corpus (22.67), by Apollonius 4.1327, by Quintus of Smyrna, and others. And what are we to make of the fact that the same pronoun is used to mean "my" in Theocritus 25.163? Since that is the only extant example of this, scholars vie in their wonder at it, even though they are less perturbed by the use of σφέτερος for the third-person singular at Hesiod, *Shield* 90, Pindar, and others. The latter irregularity can perhaps be defended on the analogy of the frequent use in the best authors of ἡμέτερος for ἐμός, and of σφέτερος or σφός for ἡμέτερος, as by Orpheus and Apollonius Rhodius, so that the author of the poem [Theocritus 25] may appear to have proceeded on the basis of that analogy to his own usage, if indeed he was the first to do so.—In a similar fashion the Greeks distorted the use of the third-person singular pronoun ἑός, to such an extent that they adopted it for all persons in both numbers. For the first-person singular there is an example in *Od.* 13.320, criticized by the Aristarcheans, as I suspect, and certainly by Apollonius Dyscolus *De synt.* 272.11 Uhlig. But this use too was transferred to their highly refined poems by Apollonius 4.1015 and Moschus 4.77. The only surviving example of its use in the second-person singular is at *Od.* 1.402 [not printed by modern editors]; there is another less certain instance at Hesiod *Works and Days* 381 [no longer printed], but many more in the *Batrachomyomachia* and the epics of a later age. Aristarchus seems to have accepted the anomalous form ἑῆος, which I once wrongly confused with ἐῆος, the genitive of the adjective ἐΰς; I am still not certain about this problem, especially after consulting Apollonius Dyscolus *De synt.* 212f. Uhlig.—In the third-person plural ἑός is attested once in Hesiod *Works and Days* 58, twice in the *Batrachomyomachia*, frequently among the Alexandrians, and even in the vulgate text of Homer *Il.* 11.76, which I have emended for the sake of consistency. And some epic poets even used that pronoun for the first- and second-person plural: with *Il.* 10.311, 398 and *Od.* 1.117, 402 compare Apollonius Rhodius 4.1327, 1353, and you will recognize that the author of the *Doloneia* did not speak badly; nor will you think that everything marked by Aristarchus should be considered barbarisms and solecisms. The abuse of analogy

confined Homer's learning to narrower bounds, we must still have a good opinion of his sober judgment.[34] And yet there are many arguments to show that this area of his genius was also vigorous, and that from it, as often happens, certain failings of his derived. For he sought out grammatical precision in a more arid manner than was necessary, and he not infrequently corrupted the more daring and noble sentiments of his poet in order to bring them closer to nature and truth. We know few of his emendations and conjectures on Homer and Pindar for certain, and even these include examples of a frigid logic that is totally unacceptable in the emender of a poet.[35] As a result, if we had to judge the genius of

---

in the possessive pronouns was all the easier, if they referred them to the obscure notion of τὸ ἴδιον, as the grammarians do. See Tzetzes on Hesiod *Works and Days* 152, W. Canter, *Novae Lectiones* 5:13 [in J. Gruter, *Lampas sive Fax Artium Liberalium* (1604), 3:627f.], Brunck on Aeschylus *Prom.* 9, Franz Alter, ed., *Homeri Odyssea* (1794), 41ff.

[34] I deduce this from Strabo 1.31 and similar evidence. The remarks in the scholia that concern interpretation are almost all less serious, and many are occupied with easy glosses. See on 2.271, 809 [Aristarchus not named], and often repeated; 4.343 (cf. Apollonius Dyscolus *De synt.* 225.4 Uhlig); 9.90 [B Dindorf = Porph. *Od.* 133.4]; 10.351; 11.632; 12.258; 13.82, 564 [B Dindorf]; 14.216 [B Dindorf = Porph. 154.6]; 16.59 [B Dindorf]; 18.570; 20.357; 21.319, 344; 23.365, 387, 638, 826 [B Dindorf; but see Erbse's apparatus], 870; 24.315 [B Dindorf = Porph. 275.9], 316, etc. There are very few of what are called aesthetic observations in them, as at 16.170 (where he disagrees with Thucydides) and 22.468. It will be necessary to deal carefully elsewhere with Aristarchus' explanations of words, making use of Hesychius, the Etymologicum Magnum, and other lexicographers who assiduously excerpted his commentaries.

[35] No more than three or four of his corrections are cited in such a way that it is clear that they are *conjectures*; see the commentary on 8.235 "Aristarchus says that it would be less scornful, if it were written as follows, Ἕκτορος ᾧ δὴ κῦδος Ὀλύμπιος αὐτὸς ὀπάζει," and at 16.636 "It would be better, says Aristarchus, if it were written βοῶν εὐποιητάων," without the conjunction, which even Eustathius does not recognize. But I do not think that I will be in error if I count the following emendations in this class: 8.233 [cf. Porph. 121]: the Greeks are boasting among their cups that each man of their nation alone *will meet in battle* one or two hundred Trojans. That is the meaning of the words ἄνθ᾽ ἑκατόν τε διηκοσίων τε, i.e., the adverb ἄντα for which ἀντίον or ἀντία is often used. But this seemed too arrogant to Aristarchus, even for drunken men, and by removing only one accent he corrected it slightly to ἀνθ᾽, i.e., the preposition ἀντί, so that the threats would be more modest and merely verbal, *that each would equal the courage of two hundred Trojans,* ἰσοβαρῆ ἕκαστον γενήσεσθαι ἑκατὸν ἢ διακοσίων. This and many other passages of the scholia cast light on Apollonius *Lexicon* s.v. ἀντί [31.9 Bekker]. At 15.417 the plural νῆας displeased Aristarchus, because it had just been said Τὼ δὲ μιῆς περὶ νηὸς ἔχον πόνον, and therefore he wrote νῆα. At 24.636 the same scholar thought that the verb ταρπώμεθα seemed to be ill suited to the fortune of Priam, and he corrected it to παυσώμεθα, which has since been accepted by many. But nothing demonstrates the frigidity of his mind more clearly than that at 5.860 and 14.148 [schol. only at 14.148; cf. Eust. 972.61], which was rejected even by Eustathius, where he wanted Mars and Neptune to shout not as ἐννεαχίλους ἢ δεκαχίλους, but as ἐννεαχείλους

this critic from those examples alone, there would be reason to wonder why he ever achieved so great a reputation among learned men. And in fact the equal number of surviving good conjectures provides no more satisfactory explanation, as none of those that is transmitted stands out with that degree of brilliance which we are accustomed to admire in the more felicitous critics of our age.[36] Therefore let us confess openly that, whatever we scrape up from our sources, it does not have enough cogency to let us give a true sense of Aristarchus' services to Homer by our own judgment rather than by that of the ancients.

CHAPTER XLIX

We have to complain of the same bad luck concerning the evidence for the renowned *obelus* [dagger] of Aristarchus. Antiquity is unanimous in recording that in wielding it he was the most severe of all in exercising his function; and he used it to uproot those verses that were unworthy of the poet's splendor or, as they used to say, were falsely inserted (παρεμβεβλημένοι). And those ancient writers who approach this subject more scrupulously indicate unambiguously that Aristarchus was *the first* to employ the obelus for annotation of this sort.[37] One might think that similar marks of pre-

---

ἢ δεκαχείλους. Extremely similar to this conjecture is that at Pindar *Pyth.* 3.75 [Drachmann], where, horrified by the size of the leap made by Apollo, he corrected βάματι ἐν πρώτῳ to βάματι ἐν τριτάτῳ. I pass over many other verses in which he follows an excessively petty logic, as when at 2.415 and 9.242 he prefers πλῆσαι; 3.406 ἀπόειπε κελεύθου; 4.260 κρητῆρι, 456 πόνος; 9.19 τότε, 401 ἐμοί; 12.161 βαλλομένων; 23.307 ἐδίδαξεν, etc.

[36] It would require a long collection of examples to prove this to readers. Therefore, to shorten it and not to anticipate what is required in a proper commentary, I will cite one out of all the conjectures attributed to Aristarchus, an extremely clever and elegant one, at 18.207. There, although he too had given our vulgate reading in his text, he later either in lectures or in his commentaries is said to have corrected the verse as follows:

Ὡς δ'ὅτε πῦρ ἐπὶ πόντον ἀριπρεπὲς αἰθέρ᾽ ἵκηται.

Thus he gave *fire* in place of *smoke*; if this verse were in the vulgate, made up by an ancient rhapsode, would not anyone who offered us the one now read seem a complete fool? Let this be a specimen of his judgment, one that shows both how respectful he was of his manuscripts and how firm a corrector he could be at times.

[37] In order to avoid repeating passages referred to above, it will be enough to give two witnesses. Galen on Hippocrates *De nat. hom.* 2.18 [15.110 Kühn]: "The sign, which they call the obelus, such as Aristarchus also used against *verses which*

vious critics were obscured and obliterated by those of Aristarchus; but although I am quite willing to concede that, so as not to be improperly stubborn in an obscure matter, I think it highly probable that the most frequent and technical use of the obelus should be ascribed to the authority of Aristarchus. For even if Zenodotus and Aristophanes are frequently said to have athetized something, and the former in fact received great notoriety from that practice, nevertheless there is no clear attribution of that sign of athetesis to either of them by any author, with the exception of a single passage, which for other reasons as well I consider to be corrupt.[38] There is also particular support for this argument in the fact that many grammarians wrote against the obelus of Aristarchus, but not against that of Zenodotus or Aristophanes.[39]

No one will expect me to demonstrate at length that Aristarchus employed the obelus, not so much on those verses that he believed not to be Homer's as on all those that seemed to him worthy of rebuke and less worthy of their place or of the supreme artistry of the chief of poets. And it is my opinion that this latter use of the obelus was both its earlier and its most precise employment. For although that scholar knew, along with the most learned of his contemporaries, that a great many falsely inserted verses were to be found in the early bards, and that the sources of such interpolation arose almost simultaneously with the poems themselves,

---

he suspected"; Lucian *Pro imag.* 24: "The one who marked *spurious verses* in the epics by putting obeli next to them." Here the one who did this is not even explicitly named, so famous was it. For the rest see the learned discussion of Villoison, following others, about this and the other critical signs in general, Preface, xiiiff.

[38] In the fragmentary note once found at the beginning of the Venice manuscript, published by Siebenkees, in *Bibliothek der alten Litteratur und Kunst*, vol. 1 (1786), 69: "We took the obelus from the recension of *Zenodotus*." [A Dindorf, 1.11, reads "he took"]. And the comments which follow concerning two athetized verses, unless I am mistaken, refer to Aristarchus, not Zenodotus.

[39] Such as the younger Zenodotus in his book "against the lines of Homer athetized by Aristarchus," and likewise Callistratus (mentioned above), Demetrius Ixion, Pius, and others "defending against the atheteses (sc. of Aristarchus)" or "against the athetized verses," and perhaps also Cleanthes, the eminent Stoic, in the book "against Aristarchus." See Diogenes Laertius 7.174, the scholia on 1.423, 6.437, 12.175, Servius on *Aen.* 5.735, a passage in which "Pius, the Homeric commentator" [the name is corrupt in the manuscripts of Servius; Thilo and ed. Harv. read *Porphyrius*; cf. Schrader, Porph. 353] (who is cited also in the scholia on 5.638; 11.100; 21.55, 147, 293) is cited, reports that the description of Elysium or rather of the blessed isles, which Sallust had written were renowned in the Homeric poems, was removed (ἐξῃρημένην). I once thought that that referred to *Od.* 4.565-69, but I now think that the passage is not in our Homer.

nevertheless it was not his task in emending the text to consider what Homer sang, but what he ought to have sung. For if there is any impression to be gained from what has been said so far about the manuscripts he employed, they differed no less among themselves for the *Iliad* and *Odyssey*, in the arrangement and appearance of single sections, in the number of verses, than the manuscripts of the *Batrachomyomachia* collected in this century differ from the vulgate text. Examine them, I suggest, and see if you can extract from them that little poem as it first appeared![a] Let us further consider that no people, no matter how acute, is likely to achieve in its youthful verses the combination of subtlety of judgment with divine strength and force of native talent;[40] that everywhere talented poets existed before poetic technique had reached a sophisticated stage of development, and that they achieved a great deal without it. I am unwilling to compare Homer, that is to say the ancient poems of the Ionians, with the Celtic poems of Ossian, which I think are neither the product of a single age nor transmitted to us in their authentic state:[b] but no one can fail to think that Ariosto or Shakespeare should be compared in talent and skill to Homer. But are there not many things in them which Lessing, Wieland, and Voss would think should be altered and pruned, if they wished to practice criticism in the manner of the Greeks? If we had divergent and contradictory texts of those poets, would not that tempt even the great moderation of our day to emulate the rashness of the Greeks? Why then should we be surprised, if from

[40] It was a very different age that produced writers who excelled equally in genius and poetic skill, along with those who "have no faults, except that they have no faults" in the apt phrase of Pliny *Ep.* 9.26.1.

---

[a] *that little poem as it first appeared:* The *Batrachomyomachia* (Battle of the Frogs and Mice) is a pseudo-Homeric mock epic, which has been dated anywhere and everywhere from the early fifth century to the Hellenistic period, and is transmitted in a huge number of manuscripts with a large number of variant (or interpolated) verses. The opening is clearly Hellenistic, but the original form of the poem is as yet uncertain.

[b] *the Celtic poems of Ossian, which I think are neither the product of a single age nor transmitted to us in their authentic state:* For more extended remarks by Wolf on the poems of Ossian, see Peters, 44: "The general ignorance is still complete; some even doubt their authenticity. Men like Johnson etc. In short, the *Ossianea* lie in the same shadows that obscure Homer—How different the ages are! The Greeks didn't doubt that Homer himself made his two compositions in their entirety; we doubters are completely doubtful of the authenticity of Ossian, and pay no attention to the great and obvious counterarguments. No one has said clearly enough—far less has anyone shown—that the Scot really only arranged the components."

the discordant testimony of the singers and scribes Aristarchus could not—even if he had wanted to and had devoted himself to that goal alone—have recovered the genuine and, so to speak, primitive singer? Indeed, no human wisdom could discern the difference between him and a first-class rhapsode or, in reverse, the difference between a rhapsode of average talent and a Homer who sometimes nodded and misused his native talent.

Thus we can see how dubious was the state of affairs at the time when Aristarchus placed the finishing touches on his Homer. Indeed, we can easily believe the commentators and Homeric grammarians that this critic *at length completed this polished and elegant redaction of Homer, in which the middle does not differ from the beginning, nor the end from the middle,*[c] and that it was perhaps he too who divided the two works into their present books.[41] And therefore, if we are considering the general appearance and manner of the poems, there is no doubt that Giphanius rightly conjectured *that our vulgate recension is the very one of Aristarchus.*[d] We will pay more attention to this, but what I will now add concerning his atheteses and erasures will be a prelude to a proper discussion of that question.

There is a considerable difference between the obelus or athetesis properly called and erasure. That Aristarchus in his corrections did not always use that sign, but entirely removed and deleted additional verses, is made credible by the practice of the earlier scholars,[42] and stated clearly by the authority of Ammonius.[43] What

---

[41] The ancient grammarian "On Homeric Poetry" 2 [Ps.-Plutarch *De vita et poesi Homeri* 2.4 (7.338 Bernardakis)]: "He has two poems, the *Iliad* and the *Odyssey*, each divided into the number of letters of the alphabet; not by the poet himself, but by the grammarians *connected with Aristarchus.*" See also Eust. 5.1, and J. Jensius, *Lucubrationes Hesychianae* [1742], 284. The Greek grammarians behaved similarly with regard to Herodotus and Thucydides, and many others; then the Latins, such as Octavius Lampadio in the case of Naevius' *Bellum Punicum.* For the rest, I will explain my reasons for calling Aristarchus "the creator of the revision (διασκευή) which we have," in another volume. It is slightly different from the question *concerning the author of our recension.* Although that question too can not be considered here as it deserves.

[42] See above, chs. 43 and 44.

[43] Scholium on 10.397-99: "Ammonius the Aristarchean says that first Aristarchus

---

[c] *in which the middle does not differ from the beginning, nor the end from the middle:* Here Wolf employs a famous line from Horace's praise of Homer's epic artistry, *Ars poetica* 152: *primo ne medium, medio ne discrepet imum.*

[d] *there is no doubt that Giphanius rightly conjectured . . .:* In his 1572 edition of Homer; see the Introduction above, sect. 2, for the passage in question.

we do not know is his justification for doing one or the other. One might believe that he used erasure or the hook for those verses which he judged either excessive or inconsistent with Homeric metrics, or contrary to the sense or rules of the Greek language, or which he did not find in the best manuscripts;[44] that he used the comma, a moderate sign, for those which seemed unworthy of the poet because of lesser flaws, but were still tolerable. But this conjecture is not of much significance given the infancy of the art. It will therefore be better to stick to the subject, to prove by numerous

---

placed signs (i.e. obeli) *next to them*, and then *completely removed* them, perhaps because σφίσι was used for the second person, and because they were brought in from above [10.310-12]." The note on 5.808 seems to be drawn from a similar source: "the verse ῥηϊδίως κτλ. *is completely missing* in Aristarchus." We learn at 4.390, the passage from which this verse was most awkwardly repeated, that it was placed there by Zenodotus; whether he was the first and only one to do so is not clear. Perhaps the use of the word ἐγκρίνειν in the remarkable note of Aristonicus on 8.535 refers to the same sort of erasure: Ἐγκρίνει δὲ μᾶλλον ὁ Ἀρίσταρχος τοὺς δευτέρους (verses 535-37).

[44] Isidore *Orig.* 1.21.3: "The obelus is placed next to words or sentences that are superfluously repeated." This is also the reference of Horace [*Ars poetica* 447] *recidenda ambitiosa ornamenta* [cut back excessive adornment]. A more weighty passage is Apollonius Dyscolus *De synt.* 5.3 Uhlig where, after giving warnings about unnecessary letters, syllables, and words (λέξεις), he adds that from time to time there is something superfluous in an entire speech: "And words are sometimes redundant, when they refer to nothing; and indeed *many of the atheteses of Aristarchus came about in such a way.*" These passages have been awaiting full clarification from the Venetian scholia. For example, at 18.39-49 *the long list of Nereids* flowing together to the weeping Thetis, a list that Callistratus had said was missing from the Argive copy and was considered excessive first by Zenodotus, then by Aristarchus (*ambitiosum ornamentum*), and was athetized "as having a Hesiodic manner," etc. Notice, by the way, that the *Theogony* is referred to as a genuine poem of the Ascraean bard. Nevertheless, this passage remained in the text of Aristarchus, from which Virgil adopted it for his imitation. For indeed all the Latins derive from that critic. Thus Cicero *Fam.* 10.13.2 and Strabo 1.17 would not have let fall remarks about "Odysseus the sacker of cities" had they not heard as boys in school that Aristarchus had athetized almost all the verses which now have "Achilles the sacker of cities." The scholia on 8.371 and the next verse, as well as on 15.56-77 lead us by a plausible argument to believe that they were marked with an obelus because of *the unnecessary repetitions there* and for other reasons, of which this is the last: "*Aristarchus says that nowhere did he speak of Achilles as sacker of cities* but as swift-footed." And Aristarchus, I suspect, thought that epithet inappropriate for Achilles because he did not bring the Trojan War to its conclusion. He therefore did not know, or rejected, the truer interpretation in Eust. 91.1 [on 1.230] and 220.7 [on 2.278]. But even at 21.550 Achilles is "sacker of cities." And there the scholia have a remarkable note: "Because *sacker of cities* is redundant in the case of Odysseus; but it is now used for Achilles *for the only time.* The *diple* [Wolf follows Villoison's supplement to the manuscript] is *directed at the dividers*; for they make use of such things. *Some people* have Achilles 'son of Peleus,' since they are astonished by the epithet." Those people who felt that way, therefore, ought to have done the same in 24.108 and perhaps at 2.728 and 20.384.

arguments that he treated the Homeric corpus not merely by marking its blemishes, but by cautery and surgery, by putting what he
thought to be dislocated back in its place. First of all, who could
believe that the verses which Eustathius and the scholiasts add from
other recensions were all later than Aristarchus,[45] not to mention
those which the vulgate scribes add to our text? Why should I
mention those which are found in Hippocrates, Plato, Strabo, and
others, as if once found in their proper place?[46] And yet every trace

[45] A number of these verses might, with equal or greater probability, be attributed
to the rhapsodes rather than to other authors, such as these four in Eustathius,
which Ruhnken mentions on *Hymn to Demeter* 108 [*Homeri Hymnus in Cererem*, ed.
D. Ruhnkenius; p. 16 of 1808 ed.], added after 13.433, and the two after 15.21,
fairly similar to Hesiod *Theogony* 498 and other tales. So also the three wretched
verses after *Od.* 11.438 [better after 437], preserved by the scholia on Euripides
[*Orestes* 249. Homer's name is interpolated here; the verses in question are Hesiod
fr. 176.5-7 Merkelbach-West]. More verses of this sort, even those attested on the
sole authority of nickel-and-dime manuscripts, were accepted by Barnes, and those
in books 13 and 15 even by Madame Dacier, who complains of the negligence of
scribes who omitted whole verses and of the bad judgments of critics. Both are
right; except that the evidence looked at all together should turn the suspicious
mind in another direction. I would like to hear what that learned woman would
have thought, if all the interpolations once rejected by the critics were now in the
text. And yet she was seeking the *complete poet*, whom now we seek. And when she
blames the scribes, which ones does she mean? At which periods? For those omissions
are much older than the scribes of our manuscripts, of which not one, even if they
are all gathered together, has brought forth a single new verse that a reliable witness
ascribes to the recension of Aristarchus, even though the verses added are in some
cases good, and in others tolerable. Their poetic play was occasionally not without
luck when they added verses, although their errors in omission, one in this passage,
one in another, were more frequent; they did not do such things as a group. Thus
the verse which Barnes, following a grammarian of late date [*Herodoti Vita Homeri*
357f. Allen], stuck in after *Od.* 1.153, might seem to be omitted in all manuscripts
because of the similarity of its opening to that of the next verse. Such errors are
extremely frequent in the case of homoeoteleuton, particularly in the Vienna manuscripts. Nevertheless, Clarke and Wesseling, 756 [P. Wesseling's commentary on
Herodotus, reprinted in J. Schweighaeuser, ed., *Herodotus*, vol. 6, pt. 2 (1816), p.
327], are probably right in criticizing Barnes. The whole squadron of the grammarians serves as my witness to the fact that none of the ancients read that verse
there; they consistently and with one voice say, concerning the figure of epanalepsis
or palillogia "that in the *Iliad* he constantly uses epanalepsis, but only *once* in the
Odyssey, at 1.23, Αἰθίοπας"; see also the scholia and Eustathius on *Il.* 6.154 [Eust.
631.28], 20.372 [Eust. 1211.43], etc. The commentators who were concerned with
Aristarchus' Homer made this observation with the care of a Masorete, unless I am
mistaken, because of the "dividers," who did not reject such arguments even though
more serious ones were available. For the rest, no one can tell why Barnes considered
this verse [the spurious verse after *Od.* 1.153] to be *necessary because of economy*. Is it
because the poet, by repeating the name of Phemius, wishes to bring us early to
some sympathy with the singer, who he says was forced to sing by the commands
of the suitors? I suppose it is "so that he might be saved in the slaughter of the
suitors" as the shorter scholia say [on this passage]. Here are the economy of the
poet and the keen noses of the decadent Greeks!

[46] Certainly it is because of the acceptance, or rather the fabrication, of Callis-

of these verses has been removed in the most learned scholia which are arranged with particular regard for the recension of Aristarchus. One should further consider that passage of Plutarch in which he reports that four verses in the speech of Phoenix, removed by Aristarchus, ought to be restored;[47] not even these are recorded in Eustathius or our scholia. With the assistance of all who are considered to be explainers or interpreters of remote antiquity and buried legend, let us consider this, if you care for the truth. Here is a man who removed from their places so many verses which by luck or chance have been transmitted to our time; or (as it is possible that in some of these cases Zenodotus or others had done this before him)[48] here are men who treated Homer as if chopping and polishing: can they be seen to have produced a complete text of his works, or did they remove something more than those verses which we know, something which no longer survives? And then, finally, ask yourself whether we either have or even know of a text earlier than that of Aristarchus. The careful examination of every important piece of evidence shows that he is the principal author of those deletions. But granted that all those deletions might be defended (and I at least would think those verses of Phoenix worthy of brackets, if the consensus of sober and intelligent men[e] did not dissuade me)—still, Aristarchus' reasoning is singularly improbable

---

thenes, whom we linked above with Aristotle, that Strabo cited at 12.542 a verse after 2.855 in the Catalogue. It was created, I believe, *for the sake of economy*, so that the Cicones [correctly Caucones] might not be missing, as they are mentioned at 10.429 and 20.329. Indeed, later commentators wondered at the omission of that people. But those who were able to solve all problems either lightly removed this trifle or cleverly concealed it: see the scholia on those passages and Eustathius 362.17. Another verse cited by Strabo 13.626, added in the Catalogue after 2.866, seems to be even earlier. Strabo, indeed, says that "some people added it," and Eustathius 366.12, drawing on his scholia, which are here rather full, ascribes it to the recension of Euripides (τὴν κατ᾽ Εὐριπίδην ἔκδοσιν); this Euripides is clearly the one whom I discussed above, ch. 41. One may also doubt whether the verses replacing 2.558 (cited by Strabo 9.394) that were used by the Megarians in the famous dispute to refute the fraud of Solon, ever appeared in written copies. But the fact that we do not today read them in the text is scarcely owed to any critic except Aristarchus.

[47] *Quomodo adulescens poetas audire debeat* 26F: "Phoenix, who was cursed by his father because of his concubine, said 'Τὸν μὲν ἐγὼ κτλ.' Aristarchus *removed these verses, fearing*, etc." *Il.* 9.458ff.

[48] This was Küster's reply to Giphanius, *Historia Critica Homeri* (1696), bk. 2, ch. 5.3. But neither of them could know the reason at that time because of the shortage of evidence.

---

[e] *the consensus of sober and intelligent men:* E.g. Giphanius and Valckenaer; see the Introduction above, sect. 2.

when, if we can trust Athenaeus, he destroyed the sense of a passage in the *Iliad* by the deletion of a verse, and then moved that verse with four others to a totally different context in the *Odyssey*.[49] But we will not consider here the logic of this whole method of criticism; and the material for such consideration does not exist. For here too in some fashion *even the ruins have perished*.[f] The Homer that we hold in our hands now is not the one who flourished in the mouths of the Greeks of his own day, but one variously altered, interpolated, corrected, and emended from the times of Solon down to those of the Alexandrians. Learned and clever men have long felt their way to this conclusion by using various scattered bits of evidence; but now the voices of all periods joined together bear witness, and history speaks.

[49] Athenaeus 5.180-81, than which there is no more memorable passage concerning Aristarchus. For that reason I have often wondered why, although this passage was adequately known to the learned editors, and was well explained by Casaubon (Clarke even quoted the passage), nevertheless it was adduced by none of them for the emendation of the vulgate text. Did they think Athenaeus less trustworthy than Plutarch? And yet each one was citing material from the commentaries of earlier scholars, Plutarch perhaps from those of the Stoics, Athenaeus from the grammarians. It is not remarkable that the scholia are silent here too, as they are so maimed and interrupted by the fault of the manuscript in this (18) and the succeeding book. To elaborate briefly, Aristarchus on the Shield, 18.604, after the word τερπόμενοι or τερπόμενος deleted the mention of the *singer*, μετὰ δέ σφιν ἐμέλπετο θεῖος ἀοιδὸς φορμίζων, but he left the verse in the *Odyssey*, when he transferred all three lines, τερπόμενοι . . . μέσσους, to the opening of the fourth book with the addition of two more from an unknown source, which are now numbered as lines 15 and 16. Athenaeus, or the source he was following, perhaps made an error in this. The critic then substituted in place of the genitive ἐξάρχοντος, the universal reading that referred to the singer, the nominative ἐξάρχοντες—as if acrobats could be said to "begin the song." That is only appropriate to someone singing with a lyre or flute, or the leader of the chorus. As now in Pindar we find the phrase ἀναξιφόρμιγγες ὕμνοι ["songs ruling over the lyre"; *Ol.* 2.1], so once the same poet refers to ἀγησίχορα προοίμια ["proems leading the dance"; *Pyth.* 1.4] and Stesichorus has ἀρχεσίμολπος Μοῦσα ["Muse beginner of song"; fr. 73 Page]. Even if Aristarchus might have defended his conjecture by means of the more learned meaning of μολπή (see Apollonius *Lexicon* s.v. μέλπεσθαι [110.35 Bekker]), for many reasons I have no hesitation in agreeing with those who criticize him. In the *Odyssey*, moreover, there is scarcely a place for those verses for the reasons very correctly given by Athenaeus 5.181E. As for the fact that he removed the song from the Cretan chorus, I can suggest no plausible reason, but there is no one who does not see that his daring in correction and improvement is astonishing. Even greater is that shown by Diodorus the Aristophanean, since he threatened more, and very beautiful, verses by deleting the whole wedding scene, *Od.* 4.3-20. But Casaubon's interpretation of this passage in Athenaeus [*Animadversiones*], 327, is different, where he rightly says that "we must infer from this passage that our present manuscripts of Homer were to a large extent emended in accordance with the edition of Aristarchus." I shall offer further comments on both passages at another time.

---

[f] *Even the ruins have perished . . .:* Cf. Lucan 9.969.

CHAPTER L

But the bard himself seems to contradict history, and the sense of
the reader bears witness against it. Nor indeed are the poems so
deformed and reshaped that they seem excessively unlike their own
original form in individual details. Indeed, almost everything in
them seems to affirm the same mind, the same customs, the same
manner of thinking and speaking. Everyone who reads carefully
and sensitively feels this sharply; and to know the reason for it
rather than merely to sense it, you must switch from these poems
to Apollonius of Rhodes, to the other Alexandrians, and to Quintus
of Smyrna, who is commonly thought the image of Homer. Does
it matter if we owe the restoration of that miraculous harmony
above all to the exquisite talent and learning of Aristarchus? If he
himself removed interpolations of Zenodotus and those more ancient as well as many discordant verses? I refer to those which I
mentioned above;[50] and if some new editor wanted to restore from
exile those verses which I have uprooted, I believe that he would
be laughed at by just those people who now laugh at the talent of
Aristarchus. What does it matter if Aristophanes and Aristarchus,
by gathering all the remains of antiquity, became connoisseurs of
the language appropriate to each age and of the legitimate forms
of primitive language, that those same men expelled from the Homeric family as illegitimate the *Hymns* and the other books that
were once hawked in great numbers under the name of Homer,
and that they set a glorious precedent as the first men to excel in
this area, an area of deep and subtle judgment, but an area that
was less difficult for Greeks?[51]

[50] In [ch. 49] nn. 45 and 46. To these should be added the greater part of those
verses, still to be found in our vulgate text but bracketed by me, which are completely
missing from our best witness the Venetus; there are 46 of them. Nor is there any
more evidence in our scholia of these than of those preserved by Eustathius.

[51] And not only in the *Hymns*, in my opinion. For it is to those critics or their
disciples that I would ascribe the fact that no "written work agreed to be older than
Homeric poetry," as Josephus says [*Against Apion* 1.2.12], was ever cited by more
learned ages [cited ch. 18, n. 38]. But as far as the Hymns are concerned, I am
virtually certain, as I said just above, that none of the Alexandrian scholars considered them Homeric. And even here it is silence that speaks. I do not give much
weight to such comments as that in Apollonius *Lexicon* s.v. Φιλομηλείδης [163.21
Bekker]—although they are not without their value. But nowhere in the large

I admit that the paucity of sources makes it impossible for us to prove all this; and in awaiting the light of a brighter day we are gradually overcome by a surfeit of conjecture. I should not, however, omit one subject of the greatest significance for our judgment of this Homeric vulgate. For although Aristarchus is accused by a great many ancient authorities, some openly, some indirectly, of the greatest rashness in correcting and in removing and sifting out perfectly good verses,[52] nevertheless no one reports that he foisted anything significant on the poet or that he inserted verses of his own composition. That he did not do so, moreover, is made probable by what we have said about his genius, which was suited for, and practiced in, the judging of verses, not writing them. To sum up the whole matter briefly, Aristarchus made the mistakes that he did through a daring that was common to his age and also appropriate to his task, and through excessive seriousness of mind; but he seems to have weighed his task with scrupulous care, taking every precaution to avoid admitting to his text anything but what was of Homeric, or at least archaic, coinage.

Let us return to our subject. It remains for us to speak directly of Aristarchus' athetesis. Macrobius indeed writes that these three

---

quantity of scholia on the *Iliad* and *Odyssey*, not even once, is the authority of the Hymns cited, although there was occasion for it. Indeed, the usage of the Hymns is often clearly similar to that of the examples of "the newer poets" or "those after Homer" that are cited by them. If these observations are true, it is an easy conjecture that in early times there was no famous collection of Hymns by a learned grammarian. If such a thing had existed, either I have no understanding of the habits of scholiasts, or somewhere at least its name would be extant. And now the Hymns, neglected by the best writers of antiquity with the exception of Pausanias and similar antiquarians, would not even excite our regrets had not rare good luck spared a few pages of manuscripts.

[52] See above, chs. 46 and 49. Some people, perhaps, would include erasure under the term *athetesis*. For the two seem occasionally to be confused; and it was easy to make that confusion, especially in the case of the words περιγράψαι and ἐξελεῖν. A clear example of this is given by Eustathius on the *Odyssey*, 1480.19 [on 4.18, reading παραγράψαντες], in comparison with the passage of Athenaeus [above, ch. 49, n. 49]. For the rest, the ancients very rarely criticized Aristarchus for an excessive desire for correction, which is the proper term in the case of words and single thoughts, even though they frequently disregard his commands. Besides these there are two singular passages in the scholia, one on 9.222, the other on 16.467; in the former, Aristarchus is credited with reverence for the old recensions and "excessive caution," and in the latter, with consistency in emending those things that he thought contrary to his teaching. And since there is something of the sort in that passage, the commentator conjectures that his [Aristarchus'] exemplar had once had a different reading, "for Aristarchus would not have let it pass unimproved." This is a learned and ancient scholium, but one whose author had not seen the text of Aristarchus.

things are judged equally impossible: to steal the thunderbolt from Jupiter, his club from Hercules, or a verse from Homer.[53] In the way in which he meant it, he was correct; but it cannot be applied to textual matters. Nor am I speaking of those verses which the recension of Aristarchus long ago obliterated. They were removed; Homer endured it; no one notices it. But there is no writer of any kind from whom something can be removed with greater ease or less loss of sense than from these poets; their thought, in its youthful exuberance, takes long detours, and in their works there are often vivid descriptions of what appear to us to be trivial and unimportant things. Nor do they use periodic and artfully arranged sentences whose continuity would be destroyed by the removal of a verse; on the contrary, the resulting thought often runs more smoothly to the learned ear. I do not wish to pursue here the causes of this manner of emendation; I will briefly and simply report what Aristarchus approved of.

Our first task is to investigate the source for examples of athetesis. Of that renowned obelus so few surviving traces are attached to the name of Aristarchus that from the scholia, from Eustathius, and from the remaining sources there are barely thirty verses on which doubt is cast. That fact has led me gradually to the conclusion that there are many more atheteses of that critic to be read today than are attached to his name, and that much the greater portion of the annotations of this sort which are reported in the scholia without an author[54] should be ascribed to his authority. I will demonstrate briefly the arguments on which I base this judgment; I leave it to the reader to decide whether or not they are probable.

---

[53] *Saturnalia* 5.3.16.

[54] Either with the word ἀθετεῖται "it is athetized," written alone in the scholia next to those verses which in the text of this most excellent manuscript are marked with a critical sign, as in 1.29-31, 110, 133, 139, 192, 424, 444 [the word ἀθετεῖται "it is athetized" is found in the scholium on 443, with a *diple* in the margin; 444 has an obelus, but no explicit statement of athetesis], 474; or with the addition of the word "obelus," as at 8.235 [the word "obelus" is Villoison's addition]; but that is very rare. There are, however, passages that have in the text a mark or obelus, but where there is no indication in the scholia; see on 1.96 [Wolf is wrong; there is a note], 493 [obelus and *diple*]; 2.603 [not recorded by Erbse], 631, 874, 875; 4.149 [Wolf is wrong; there is a note but no obelus in A]; 10.51, 52 [there is a note but no sign recorded by Erbse]; 12.371 ("because it has been revised") [daggered by Erbse]; 19.125 [no sign recorded by Erbse]; 23.259-61; 24.677 [not recorded by Erbse], 778 [*diple*]. In a number of places the obelus is used in confusion or wrongly, to such an extent as must be explained in detail in the description of the manuscript.

In the first place, it appears that this entire corpus of scholia was compiled with particular reference to the recension of Aristarchus. That is shown by the subscriptions in the manuscripts,[55] by a great many readings and corrections, and by all else. So great was his reputation among grammarians of every school that even when his name was omitted, the reader understood that he was being referred to. To these arguments can be added one very important one, that a number of verses are reported in the scholia simply as athetized, and in the text are marked with an obelus, which others clearly report to have been marked by Aristarchus.[56] And what are we to make of the fact that we read with great frequency in these remarkable scholia, that Zenodotus and Aristophanes *made a prior athetesis*, that is, *marked previously, used the obelus in advance?*[57] Of

[55] Where in the first place the scholia promise "the signs of Aristonicus and the comments of Didymus on *the recension of Aristarchus.*"

[56] It will be enough here to examine three examples. The verse *Od.* 11.584 is assigned in the Venice scholia on *Il.* 2.597 to "those deleted in the Nekuia," and next to that whole passage about Tantalus is found in some manuscripts "it is spurious" [schol. *Od.* 11.568]. Long ago, it was clear from the scholia to Pindar *Ol.* 1.97 [1: 37.21-22 Drachmann] that "according to Aristarchus these verses are spurious." On 2.529 we find in Eustathius [276.35] and the scholia edited long ago [the so-called *Scholia Didymi*, ed. J. Lascaris (1517)], that this and the two following verses were athetized by some; and among the athetizers Zenodotus is named [cf. schol. 2.528]. But on 9.395 [A Dindorf] the same scholia give the authority for the judgment on one of those verses to Aristarchus, as if following Thucydides (1.3). We also read that the essential verse *Od.* 1.344 was marked by him, and 4.726 and 816 are clearly to be added to this group [A Dindorf on 9.395; cf. Ludwich, 1:516]. A third, more illustrious witness, is Athenaeus 2.39D on *Il.* 8.231, in which he writes that Aristarchus marked or deleted (his word is περιγράφειν [circumscribe]) it because it was foolishly superfluous, and Athenaeus approves that judgment, that it is drinking, not eating, which gives courage. But it is even better with both, and it would be remarkable if Aristarchus had not thought so too. What then, if the next verse, beginning with "drinking," were more recent than the other, and added by a new corrector? Indeed that verse suffers badly from asyndeton, and I doubt that any other example, involving two participles, could be found. Aristarchus, however, liked that figure, and in a number of cases can be seen to have introduced it into the text, as at 4.238, 21.191, and other more appropriate instances which I do not now have at hand. But the new manuscript gives no evidence about the author of that athetesis; it has an obelus in the text, and a scholium *the line is excessive*: vaunting arises from drinking, not from eating."

[57] See on 11.356, 515; 14.95, 213, 317-27; 15.147, 148; 18.39-49; 19.327; 23.824, 825; 24.6-9, 614-17; in these, it should be noted, the usual word ἀθετεῖται ["it is athetized"] is normally preferred to the word προηθέτηται or προηθεῖτο ["it was athetized in advance."] Of the same sort and meaning are the passages where we find "it was athetized also by Zenodotus" "and in Aristophanes as well" or "it was not even present, it was not even written, it was not even reported in Zenodotus, in Aristophanes." See 8.164, 189, 235, 371, 528; 9.23, 416; 10.240, 387, 397, 497; 11.78, 767, etc. See also 9.688-92, 10.253, 11.180, 18.597f., 21.130. In four or five passages the name of Aristarchus appears after theirs, as at 9.688. Anyone who

whom, I ask? Could it be any other than he, who alone was believed most zealously *to have sought out the style of Homer*, and virtually to have invented *the obeli, the brands of spurious bards?*[a] I do not fear that I have erred in my conjecture, therefore, if I say that the vast majority of those obeli belongs to Aristarchus. A number of them might of course seem to belong to Aristonicus or perhaps to older critics whose memory our transmission has overwhelmed. And anyone who would flatter a great man may desire this to be the case: so many are the examples of the worst sort of daring among them.

In the manuscript [Vetetus A] there are some 470 obelized verses; the number would perhaps be greater, if it survived complete. But I should not think even that number excessive given the fame of the obelus of Aristarchus. But in order to understand it, we must seek out such examples as are definitely ascribed to Aristarchus. Nor do we lack instances which must seem to us, who know neither his sources nor all the causes for his corrections, both rash and the result of remarkable self-assurance. It is not, however, appropriate here to speak in detail of this subject: and so we will examine a few of the more notable instances briefly.

Let us begin from the end, *à la façon d'Homère*, as they say. Eustathius and other sources long ago provided information about the athetesis of the verses about the judgment of Paris, 24.24-30 [better 25-30], although the author of the athetesis, whom we now know to be Aristarchus, was then unknown. He, then, is the source of the remarks on that passage, some of which are not very significant, but include the observation that Homer would not have reported that most serious cause of the war in one place only, since there would have been many occasions to refer to it, if the story actually belonged to the Homeric period. Several people referred to many things that are mentioned only once in Homer, but which the critics nevertheless left alone; in vain. He does not keep silent at 5.63 about the νῆας ἀρχεκάκους ["ships that began the trouble"], the departure of Paris for Sparta, where, following the custom of his age, he would no doubt have gone back to the fatal cause, which

---

goes over all this, as I have, will have no doubt that almost everywhere the scholiasts are referring to *the founder of the vulgate recension and transmission* [παράδοσις], Aristarchus.

---

[a] *the obeli, the brands of spurious bards:* The source of the phrase, *obelosque, spuriorum stigmata vatum*, is Ausonius *Ludus septem sapientum* 1.13.

would bring the fault back to the gods. And therefore the ancients[58] and a few more recent critics (among whom Hemsterhusius is worth all the rest) voiced their approval of the judgment by which the judgment of Paris is annulled. Nor would I disagree with such an authority, did I not (as I have said elsewhere) seem to hear another author in these last books from that of the earlier ones. But now I am not particularly troubled by that, and by the Hesiodic μα-χλοσύνην [24.30],[59] even if that word was removed already in the copy of Aristophanes and some of the city manuscripts by the alteration of the whole hemistich to ἥ οἱ κεχαρισμένα δῶρ᾽ ὀνόμηνε ["who named to him pleasing gifts"]. How properly and scrupulously that was done, I should not care to say. In fact, I consider that all those conjectures and obeli with which they wanted violently to reshape the end of the *Iliad* to match Homeric usage are improbable.[60] In other places, Aristarchus' opinion is frequently more unclear. For example, at 16.613 it is not clear whether this particular verse or the next two, which are excessively redundant, were missing from his second recension. Likewise at 9.688-94, it may seem unclear what Aristarchus was the first to do, and what he marked at all, although he is clearly included in the phrase "they athetize." And if he was the same person, as I suspect, who "cut up" that passage, then he wished to delete these six verses and write the passage in such a fashion that χεῖρα ἑήν be the end of Ulysses' speech; he added two verses to that one, Ὣς ἔφαθ᾽, οἱ δ᾽ ἄρα πάντες ἀκὴν ἐγένοντο σιωπῇ ["so he spoke, and they all fell silent"; 9.693] and δὴν δ᾽ ἄνεῳ ἦσαν τετιηότες υἷες Ἀχαιῶν ["for a long time in silence the sons of the Achaeans were troubled"; 9.695], deleting the verse which is commonly inserted [9.694], but which I have bracketed. For this last verse has always seemed to me to be inopportunely repeated, while the earlier ones, granted that they are troublesome, still seem to me to be tolerable for the sake of the thought. The defense of our (that is, Aristarchus') daring against Pius at 12.175-81 is more difficult, as he has made some excellent

---

[58] Macrobius *Sat.* 5.16.10 and [Plutarch] *De vita et poesi* 1.6 [7.333f. Bernardakis].

[59] Compare Suidas [M 307] and Apollonius *Lexicon* s.v. μαχλοσύνη [110.9 Bekker] and Villoison, ad loc. [ed. Apollonius (1773), 2:537]. At the same time we learn from this that Aristarchus gave a later date to Hesiod or the author of the Catalogues than to Homer.

[60] That it was done in that way is clear from the scholia on books 20, 21, and 23. In those books the ancients vied in removing the distinctive signs of supposititious poetic talent.

objections, but has not succeeded in giving me more faith in those verses than I have in the similar ones at 18.356ff.[61] Other atheteses of his are reported for 4.117, 14.500, 15.449-51 and 712, 18.444-56, 24.556, 557. And it is particularly remarkable that at 17.172 the grammarians wonder that the verse is transmitted without any mark of his, since *he was accustomed* to mark with the obelus such things as reduced the force of a thought by limiting it.[62] Even if all the rest were missing, that one passage alone would show that Aristarchus athetized many more verses than those to which his name is attached. And for the *Odyssey*, in fact, I remember only one verse athetized specifically by him, 2.137, which is certainly not defended by the rather harsh ellipse of the substantival verb [ἔσσεται]. This itself could certainly have been the cause of the interpolation, as at *Il.* 7.353, 9.416, and elsewhere. For the rest, he also used the obelus combined with the asterisk, indicating by the double sign that the verse was fine in its original place, but was improperly repeated where it did not belong. That is partly the reason why twenty-seven verses, 1.366ff., were considered to be interpolated; that judgment was wrong, as are many others connected with the same sign. Nor can it be doubted that some similarity between passages occasionally gave an excuse for the inept repetition of verses; but I will discuss this and other topics in more detail in the second part of this book, in which I will have to defend my own deletions.

CHAPTER LI

There is only one of the greater critics remaining, Crates of Mallos, who was called *Homericus* because of his singular interest in the poet, and who was both the rival and the fiercest adversary of Aristarchus.[63] He appears to have founded the school of Pergamum, similar to that of Aristarchus and no less renowned for its

---

[61] See above, ch. 30.

[62] "He lessened the emphasis. *And Aristarchus was accustomed to athetize such things.*"

[63] Suidas, s.vv. Κράτης [K 2342] and Ἀρίσταρχος [A 3892]. There he is credited with "correction [διόρθωσις] of the *Iliad* and *Odyssey* in 9 books, and other writings." Among these "other writings" there were, in my opinion, a number that concerned the history and learning of the poets and a work "on the Attic dialect" (i.e. diction), whose fifth book is mentioned by Athenaeus 12.497E.

pupils.[64] For just as those of Aristophanes were called Aristopha-neans, and those of Aristarchus were called Aristarcheans, so a num-ber of people are called "those of Crates," who themselves engaged in rivalry and contests with the Aristarcheans.[65] For after the kings expelled the more spirited activities from the Greek states, the love of contention passed to the schools of the rhetoricians and gram-marians; and just as once they contended about the leadership of the state, so now they had serious disputes about small grammatical problems. Crates, indeed, seems to have yielded little to Aristarchus in the opinion of their contemporaries—they are listed together among the leaders of this profession[66]—and he acquired a new glory from the fact that he was the first to bring the teaching of letters to the Romans.[67]

It is most remarkable that among the few remains of Crates there is enough left to allow us to suspect what the subjects of his strife with Aristarchus were, and how much inferior he was to the latter.[a] In fact, we seem to know the mind and learning of none of the ancient critics so well as that of Crates. In the first place, while Aristarchus undertook to interpret Homer in accordance with the simplicity of primitive times, not in accordance with new ideas rashly applied, Crates the Stoic thought that the glory of the bard would be badly served unless he smeared him with the various Pergamene arts and transformed him into a philosopher, mathe-

[64] Ptolemy of Ascalon had written about it in the book "On the Cratetean Sect" cited by the scholia on 3.155. To the authority of that same school or sect alone I refer "the grammarians from *Pergamum*" and "the *Pergamene* pinakes" (*catalogues of classical writers*) in Dionysius of Halicarnassus *On Dinarchus* 630, 661 [5.297.16, 317.3 Radermacher], where Sylburg had wrongly thought of Aristarchus.

[65] Such as Herodicus of Babylon, on whom see Jonsius, *De Scriptoribus Historiae Philosophicae*, 2:13 [p. 217]; compare the scholia to 13.29, 20.53, if this is the same Herodicus, to be distinguished from the well-known doctor Herodicus of Selymbria, cited at 9.453, 11.515. I have offered my own conjecture about Zenodotus the Cratetean at ch. 43, n. 69. Sextus Empiricus *Adv. math.* 1.248 adds Tauriscus, and Suidas [A 1129] adds Alexander Polyhistor. On the other side, the books of Dionysius Thrax and Parmeniscus "against Crates" are cited on 8.513, 9.464.

[66] Strabo 1.30, Sextus Empiricus 1.44.

[67] Suetonius *Gram.* 2, where the Attalus referred to is clearly the second, called Philadelphus, who began to rule at Pergamum in Olympiad 155.2 (159 B.C.).

[a] *how much inferior he was to the latter:* Although there is no modern discussion devoted solely to Crates as a textual critic, most of the observations mentioned in this chapter are discussed by H. J. Mette in two monographs, *Parateresis* (Halle, 1952), and *Sphairopoiia* (Munich, 1956), devoted, respectively, to Crates' theory of language and his cosmology. For a more general discussion of Crates' scholarship, see Pfeiffer, *History*, 238-45 = *Geschichte*, 290-99.

matician, astronomer, geographer, and anything other than what he himself had wanted to be. Many things of this sort are to be found excerpted from his commentaries in Strabo, Geminus, and the grammarians, concerning the Homeric Ocean, the nonsetting of the Great Bear, the two divisions of the Ethiopians, the circumnavigation of Cádiz by Menelaus, the Laestrygonians' living under the constellation Draco, the Eremni, one of the peoples of India, the interpretation of νὺξ θοή.[68b] There are also similar follies about the allegorical interpretation of stories, about the identification of Apollo with the Sun, about Vulcan's having been dropped on Lemnos as an experiment in physics, about the haute cuisine of the heroes, et cetera.[69] And if he did not give better instruction about these things than those which I have mentioned in passing, let our friend Voss instruct us concerning them, and let us not seek the wisdom of Crates. Nor do I find that he did better in grammatical interpretation when he differed from Aristarchus, which I think happened much more often than we find reported.[70] It must, how-

[68] See Strabo 1.3, and compare Apollonius *Lexicon* s.v. ἄμμορον [29.14 Bekker] with the Excursus of Tollius [ed. Apollonius (1788), Excursus 5, pp. 743-48] (who was, however, deceived by both the emendation of the comment of Crates and the astronomy), and Strabo 5, 31, 38, Geminus *Elem. astron.* 6.10, 16; 16.22f., 27, the scholia on *Il.* 15.496 [B Dindorf], Eustathius on 10.394 (814.20); on *Odyssey* schol. 2.1 and Eustathius at 4.84 (1485.1), 10.86 (1649.33), 20.299 (1893.1), Etymologicum Magnum 370.43 [s.v. Ἐρεμβοί]. You will have a clear idea of the man if you compare to these passages Strabo 3.157, where he is referred to as the leader of those who "turned Homeric poetry to *scientific topics*." In passing, let us offer the one surviving example of a "solution" belonging to him, at *Il.*18.192. There, because Achilles declares that he cannot fight, because his own arms have been taken away, and that those of no other hero, except perhaps Ajax, would fit, the "questioners" asked why he did not take the weapons of Patroclus, and various others used other means to solve this grave difficulty. Here Crates pretended (I use the word deliberately: for where does Homer use this trick in such a manner?) that Automedon had already put on Patroclus' weapons. That clever fellow did not see that the whole problem begins anew, why Achilles did not put on Automedon's arms, if they would fit him equally well.

[69] See Heraclitus *Alleg. Hom.* 27.2, the scholia to *Il.* 18.240, Eustathius 1140.47 [18.239], 1893.1 [*Od.* 20.299].

[70] See Strabo 9.439, schol. on *Il.* 1.591 [B Dindorf] with Eustathius 1003.38, scholia to 9.169, 13.358 [B Dindorf], 14.31-32, 23.679, Apollonius *Lexicon* s.v. πλωτῇ on *Od.* 10.3 [132.18 Bekker], scholia on 12.61 and Eustathius on 14.12 [1748.57], 19.229 [1863.43], Etymologicum Magnum 634.8 [s.v. ὀρσοθύρη], etc. Crates' *Homerica* are cited once in the scholia, on 15.193 [A Dindorf].

[b] νὺξ θοή: The meaning of this phrase (which is found in *Il.* 10.394, 468; 14.261; 24.366, 653; and *Od.* 12.284) was much discussed in antiquity, and interpretations of θοή include "cone-shaped" (because of the shape of shadows), "putting cattle into their stalls" (deriving it from τίθημι, "to place"), as well as the normal classical translation "swift." Crates accepted the last, and took it to refer to the equal speed of the sun and the night; see Mette, *Parateresis*, 55f.

ever, be noted that there is a certain amount of this sort of thing which has been received and is now in favor, and is defended by the best interpreters.[71] Finally, we know less about his manner of dealing with the various parts of the critic's task, which he undertook for Hesiod as well, because of the lack of examples.[72] But I at least would not ask for more in order to wonder at the twisted cleverness of the man and his unlearned rashness.

END OF VOLUME I[c]

[71] See the scholia on *Od.* 1.320, with Etymologicum Magnum 111.21 [s.v. ἀνόπαια], the scholia on 22.188 with Eustathius 1924.11, etc.

[72] The readings of Crates, not all his own conjectures, that are cited in the scholia, Eustathius, and the Etymologicum Magnum are the following: *Il.* 3.155 ὦκα connected to ἰοῦσαν; 11.754 δι᾽ἀσπιδέος, the common reading today; 12.25 [Eust. 890.35] ἐν δ᾽ἦμαρ (on which see above, ch. 44, n. 87); 21.323 τυμβοχόης for the infinitive τυμβοχοῆσ᾽ or the vulgate τυμβοχοῆς, 558 Ἰδήϊον, which is perhaps his best; 23.361 μεμνοῖτο [Etymologicum Magnum 579.1; see also Erbse's apparatus]; 24.253 κατηφέες; *Od.* 3.293 Βλισσήν [correctly Λισσήν]; 11.14 Κερβερίων for Κιμμερίων. See also the scholia and commentators on Hesiod *Works and Days* 529-31, *Theogony* 142.

[c] *End of volume I.* So Wolf, optimistically.

PART II

CHAPTER I

Now, thanks to my previous arguments about the changes and vicissitudes of the Homeric text and the sources of its variants, the way seems to be cleared to the second section of this essay, in which I shall set out the chief general precepts and examples for this sort of emendation. And in fact several have rightly pointed out that the method of the art of criticism must be varied and changed in many ways to fit the variety of talents and subjects on which it works. How great, then, will we think that the difference must be in Homer? Not only is he very different from the other poets, but his poems were also transmitted to posterity in a different way. This fact must not infrequently lead to changes in the laws that are justly considered the most important ones in other cases.

For since it is quite impossible to restore this poet to his original state, we must first relax to some extent the severe rule according to which, in other cases, we try to give nothing that did not come from the [writers] themselves; and we must be content if we can restore him to the form of which learned antiquity most approved.

The manuscripts now available for our use in establishing the text of the *Iliad* are these (I say nothing of those mentioned in the scholia and Eustathius, in the Etymologicum Magnum and other grammarians, or those which were of old the authorities for the readings they have transmitted. For we would then have to admit into the list even the Sinopic and Argive texts, and those of the other city-states, and almost all the recensions of the grammarians): Venice MS 454, the Leipzig and Breslau manuscripts that Ernesti excerpted carefully enough, Barnes's three, Alter's five, among which ρ and 117 stand out; the other manuscripts from which scholars occasionally produce a reading, such as the other Parisini; Bentley's Harleian and Italici, which have not been collated through the whole work; that of Stephanus, the variants from which he scattered in both his edition and the *Thesaurus Linguae Graecae*; the manuscripts of the old editors from Chalcondyles on. Since they, after the custom of their time, did not record what they thought should be removed and what accepted, it can rarely be declared for certain what readings appeared there. One can only recover them by conjecture, and not in all passages. I would say with more assurance that more of those editors of the fifteenth and sixteenth centuries than Ernesti thought had access to manuscripts. I realized that from the substantial number of their readings which they could not have had from Eustathius or any other source. There is no point in a digression about these. Once I had scrutinized the readings of these manuscripts and reduced them to their classes, I readily understood that none survived which could represent the recension of any ancient grammarian for us. Even the worst ones, those drawn from the worst exemplars, sometimes offer a fine old reading. The good ones on the other hand, even the best, sometimes have worse readings mixed in. I do not refer only to such slips of the pen as normally deform the best recensions. In this regard the Venice manuscript would have enjoyed a singularly good fortune if—as was only to be wished—it had been printed with simple accuracy. I refer to the recensions . . . We would have them entirely jumbled together if the scholia did not come to our aid in such cases.

The readings drawn from all these sources, themselves from almost all the centuries, make up the resources for restoring the text to the standard of the ancients. In this one must conduct oneself so as not to accept any word, so far as possible, that cannot be supported by a good witness or authority. And in many passages it is clearly possible to attain this virtually diplomatic level of accuracy. For to prove the point by a single example, the follies of Apion (see Seneca *Ep. mor.* 88.40) and of others, whom Lucian mocks (*Ver. hist.* 2.20) are enough to show that the ancients' *Iliad* began from the word Μῆνιν. Just after that the words ἄειδε and οὐλομένην have an even older authority, that of Protagoras, in Aristotle (*Poet.* 19 [1456 b 15-17]). The two final words in the first line also have sufficient attestation from the ancient observation of a metrical difficulty, which was an irresponsible invention. And the whole number of syllables in the verse, which was observed long ago, would give authority to the noun θεά as well, if that were not certain from other sources. But since Μοῦσα would not fit in its place, the nature of the case is enough to support the vulgate. So far in this enquiry into the trustworthiness of the old [text] we have not had to cross-examine the scholiasts. But we learn from them that some found the nominative ἥ in the second line unsatisfactory and preferred the dative ᾗ, so that even the grammatical construction would refer to Achilles the event described by the next few words. One must decide from ancient usage and ways of forming sentences whether this correction or the older reading is preferable. For the text is certainly not to be made worse by conjectures, when it should not be changed in this way without sufficient cause even when the change is plausible. For who could bear the change of ἰφθίμους to ἰφθίμων in the third line, on the ground that the word is in general used in other passages in the poet for persons rather than things, and that that form never appears in the feminine gender anywhere else? Or if someone should replace the fourth line with this feeble one, Τρώων, αὐτοὺς δὲ ἑλώρια τ. κ., where ἑλώρια would have to lengthen its first syllable without any authority? For the fact that the same thing commonly occurs in Ἀχιλεύς and many other words does not mean that it can necessarily be transferred to another if there are no examples. But ἕλωρ does not lengthen its first syllable or duplicate the consonant, any more than does the verb ἑλεῖν, in any poet. Or if someone should transpose the words and write ἄλγε᾿ ἔτευχε and θῆκε κύνεσσιν? For that vulgate ἄλγε᾿ ἔθηκε is supported by Apollonius of Alexandria (s.v. ἔθηκεν [63.14 Bekker]), Fulgentius de allegoria Virgilii (ed. Munker p. 146 [= ed. Agozzino-Zanlucchi p. 46]) and others. So, finally, the prosaic conjectures of Apollonius Rhodius and Zenodotus, κεφαλάς for ψυχάς, δαῖτα for πᾶσι, only confirm the antiquity of the vulgate readings. In punctuation, I would wish that one could simply follow the custom of the ancients who added it, not to reveal the construction, but solely to aid in the pronunciation. We commonly wish to give the impression of making a judicious combination of the two. Because of this, more marks of punctuation than is reasonable, and in some cases absurd ones, have been introduced. These I have often left untouched in passages where they were not completely useless. But in other cases I have consistently removed them, where they actually hindered good pronunciation. For nowadays many often use them even where they are quite unsuitable and unreasonable—for example,

the completely unsuitable ones before enclitic words, the essence
of the pronunciation of which is that they must be taken along with
the preceding word without any interval—as in the Hymn to Demeter, 338 and 349, ὄφρα ἑ μήτηρ. That is all the more absurd,
since there used to be those who gave a double accent to a paroxytone with a long first syllable, and in this class of cases put an
acute accent on the final syllable of the preceding word. I think it
right to imitate this practice, which was commonly followed in the
Roman Eustathius and some other old books, where it might seem
necesary to counteract an ambiguity in some way. For example,
where οἱ follows the paroxytone ὄφρα, for only the play of voice
makes clear whether it is the article or the dative of the pronoun.
See, for example, ἔσαν οἱ πέπλοι Od. 15.105; also Il. 22.196 εἴ πώς
οἱ, like Ἄνδρά μοι ἔννεπε——ἄλλό τι.

CHAPTER II

Now thanks to my previous arguments about the alterations and
vicissitudes of the Homeric text and the sources of its variant readings, the way seems to be cleared to the second section of this essay,
in which I shall set out the more useful general precepts and examples for this sort of emendation. And in fact several have rightly
perceived that the method of the art of criticism must be varied to
fit the variety of talents and subjects on which it works, and can
not be confined to one single set of rules. If that is true for the
writers of later periods, it must apply even more to the early bards,
who are rendered very different from the rest by their fortunes
alone, and by the manner in which their texts were transmitted.
To that extent the fortunes of Homer resemble those of our Scriptures, especially the Jewish ones—though the critical history of
these has been remarkably obscured by the loss of the books older
than the Masorah that pertained to it, and by the way in which that
farrago itself is organized. But to omit conjectures about their original form that are slightly overbold and supported by weak arguments, I nevertheless do not think there is any doubt that several
parts of that work, specifically the Pentateuch, were first published
separately, and that a sort of corpus and, so to speak, sacred library
appeared when different parts had been joined together and new

books added to them in turn. But apparently even at the time when the people, on its return from the Babylonian exile, gave attention to the better ordering of its public or holy remains—whether Esdras or someone else was responsible for that enterprise—only an obscure report about the authors was repeated, and that took on more strength after the collection was made. For there is no doubt at all that this collection was deliberately made, even though the conflation of older and newer songs and prophecies of different kinds in the Psalms and in some of the Prophets reveals a structure that was the product of chance rather than skill. The fortunes of the text itself make up the other area in which the great similarity between these sacred volumes and Homer is clear. For there could not have been one fixed paradosis of the text when they were first collected, certainly not in the older parts. For it is certain that the Alexandrian translators rendered some things from a recension different from the one now in circulation. And it is likely that some new work was performed precisely in the centuries nearest to Christ's birth, whether the nature of the case brought that about, or a sort of rivalry with Greek learning, as a result of which other additions were made to both the treatment of the Scriptures and the fabric of the Christian religion. Certainly the surviving vestiges of Talmudic criticism are such that certain scholars must have occupied themselves with the choice of variant readings even somewhat before the Masorah was created.[a] But given that the Masorah itself consists of a mass of different glosses and notes, it doubtless includes many older notes, the omission of the authors of which has cast the whole affair into darkness. But the Hebrews were earlier than the Greeks to cease devising new readings and to treat as sacred the paradosis that was clearly corrupted as soon as it was introduced. By far the greatest part of the blemishes that infect the sacred text had already come into existence in the earliest times, when the Jews thought they had no less license to deal with it than with any ancient human book.[b] For the error of imagining that a divinity had dictated the individual words to the writers was late

[a] *certain scholars must have occupied themselves:* See J. Weingreen, *Introduction to the Critical Study of the Text of the Hebrew Bible* (Oxford, 1982), 11-24 for a study of "Rabbinic antecedents of textual criticism" preserved in the Talmud and elsewhere.

[b] *By far the greatest part of the blemishes:* Wolf's debt to Eichhorn is clear here; see the Introduction above, sect. 6.

to arise; the different forms of the text transmitted in many passages were enough to stop it. Moreover, even afterward scholars set about reworking the translations of the Old Testament with equal license, though they ascribed almost as much divinity to these as they did to the Hebrew texts. One who considered all these facts thought that the holy Masoretic text had taken on its complete form even before Christ's birth, and it is not surprising that almost all the ancient witnesses agree in their worse errors, lacunae, and interpolations. Nor can we justly feel indignant at the Masoretes for passing on to us a text riddled with errors, unless we wish to blame Herodian or Porphyry for not restoring the pure Homer. Finally those who practiced criticism on the Bible were no more expert in grammatical principles . . . in the way in which Zenodotus and Origen were.

Given the great obscurity of all these points, no one can say for certain whether one or more vulgate texts preceded ours. Yet it is likely that ours was not the only one, especially in the greatest books of the Old Testament. But ours by some chance caused the rest to disappear. And the Alexandrian translators certainly rendered some books from a recension different from that of the Masoretes.

This is also more or less how our vulgate text of Homer [came to be].

But many who misapplied their wits later reworked this other vulgate text in different ways and infected it with conjectures. The serious (no more appropriate word comes to mind) Jews were more or less content with what was furnished them, even if it was grossly corrupt. Yet it would be surprising if there were no conjectures in the sacred text, from the earliest times when superstition had not yet become so strong. Though in the earliest times both peoples thought these works divinely inspired, neither was so foolish as to think the individual words to be completely valid. Hence they always thought they had some license to change, sift, and add to these. The same was then freely done to the translations, though they ascribed almost as much authority to these. In general, they thought quite freely, and could not do otherwise if they still had several versions of the divinely inspired discourse that were not identical. But there is this similarity above all: that throughout both works there are clear traces of their earliest form, such as seams that are by no means fully concealed. These, I think, are such that they must be ascribed to the primitive inconsistency of those who revised the works rather than to deliberate and precise choice. Thus no one may infer from these examples that they worked with equal accuracy on the rest.

Our Hebrew text derived from a paradosis; so, clearly, did our Homeric vulgate. In each paradosis a choice was made among readings, which we may nonetheless rework. In each text the paradosis itself has undergone some mutilation and corruption.

Thus the Masorah very often harmonizes with the corruptions in our vulgate text. The same thing sometimes happens in Homer, so that the authority of all the scholia and the paradosis defends doubtful passages and readings.

The Masorah is full of all sorts of absurdities and feeble, superstitious inventions; this mass of scholia has no lack of similar contents. True, Greeks rave in one way, Jews in another; and one who is master of the grammatical system of a language in one way, an ignorant man who takes no interest in it in another.

The Masorah and the Homeric scholia are bodies of material that were finished off by different processes of sifting at different periods.

SUBSIDIA

1. J. G. EICHHORN'S EINLEITUNG INS ALTE TESTAMENT

Some specimens follow of Eichhorn's *Einleitung*. Chapter 12 and parts of 14, in Gollop's translation, will reveal the general tenor of his approach. A section of chapter 152, on the Masoretic marginal direction *Qerē velo Kethib* (literally "Read and not written"), which directs the reader to insert a word into a given passage of the Bible when reading it aloud or analyzing it, but not when copying the text proper, will show how he worked through the Masoretic evidence. And some sections of chapter 426 will show how he used the occurrence of two different names for God (Jehova and Elohim) and other stylistic features to locate and reconstruct the underlying sources of Genesis.

Chapter 12: Genuineness of the Scriptures of the Old Testament

I.—*They Come to Us from no Impostor.* He who with knowledge and impartiality examines the question whether the writings of the Old Testament are genuine, will certainly be compelled to answer it in the affirmative.

They cannot all be the invention of one impostor—this every part of the Old Testament declares. What a variety in language and expression! As Isaiah writes, so does not Moses, nor Jeremiah like Ezekiel, and between these and each of the lesser Prophets a wide cleft of style is established. The grammatical structure of the language in Moses is very peculiar; in the book of the Judges provincialisms and barbarisms appear; Isaiah casts the store of words into new forms; Jeremiah and Ezekiel are full of Chaldaeisms; in short, as we proceed from the authors placed back in the early times onwards to the later, we find the language in a gradual decay, till finally it settles down into a shape absolutely Chaldaean.

Well then, what variety in the movement of ideas and extent of imagery! The harpstrings of Moses and Isaiah give a rushing sound, but their chime is soft beneath the hands of David. The muse of Solomon glitters in the pomp of the most voluptuous court; but her sister, clad in careless array, wanders with David by brooks and banks, on plains and with flocks around. One poet is original, like Isaiah, Joel, and Habakkuk; another a copyist, as Ezekiel. One wanders along the untrodden paths of genius, whilst another steals by his side over beaten ground. From one stream forth rays of erudition, whilst from his neighbour a spark has never issued. In the oldest author strong Egyptian colouring glitters throughout, in his successors it grows fainter and fainter, and becomes quite extinguished in the last.

Lastly, also, in the manners—the finest gradation! At first everything single and simple, as in Homer, and still with the Bedouin Arabs; this noble simplicity becomes gradually lost in luxury and effeminacy, and vanishes at last in that most voluptuous court of Solomon.

Nowhere a leap; everywhere a gentle gradual progress! Only ignorant or thoughtless sceptics can affirm the Old Testament to be the work of one deceiver.

Chapter 14: Marks of Genuineness

Moreover, the Old Testament bears all the marks of genuineness in itself. Just the same grounds which are alleged in defence of Homer, support also the genuineness of each separate book of the Old Testament. Why should the justice which is granted to the former be withheld from the latter? If a particular age be assigned to a profane author, and all the circumstances of his book both internal and external coincide therewith; doubts upon the point will be entertained by no impartial inquirer after truth. Nay, where the age of an author is unfixed, is there the least hesitation felt in deciding his date upon the internal evidence afforded by his works? Why, then, should the critical inquirer hesitate to take this very road only with regard to the Bible? . . .

It is, however, to be taken for granted, what for other reasons was to be expected with regard to such ancient books, that most of the writings of the Hebrews have passed through various hands, before acquiring their present form, and that in them sometimes old and new are found mingled; this will, however, not induce an impartial judge to throw doubts on their genuineness.

There is no instance of any surviving ancient author, of what nation soever, whose text has not undergone many alterations and interpolations. Sometimes intentional glosses were made, and old words and expressions and geographical names exchanged for new, in order to clear the sense to the modern reader; sometimes remarks were made on the margin, for the writers' or others' use, without any intention of their introduction into the text, but which have been subsequently interpolated by the excessive zeal of posterity. Before, then, the genuineness of a book can be affected by such passages, a careful previous critical examination must be made, as to whether they originally stood where they now are, and really flowed from the author's pen.

2. The intermingling of old and new passages and sections arose by necessity from the very mode of origin of many of the writings of the Old Testament. The smaller number came to us in the form in which we now possess them, from the hands of their author. With regard to many, the substance was already extant in separate works, before being bound up together, with certain parts now added to them. Supposing the Mosaical books in their present disposition not to be the work of Moses, still they are composed of Mosaical materials, merely put into form by a later hand. It will be demonstrated in its proper place that the chief foundation of our present 'Samuel' and 'Chronicles' (particular lives of David and Solomon) attained its actual form by passing through at least the hands of two very different editors, of whom each increased and enriched it with his own peculiar additions. . . . Our Isaiah is a collection of various anonymous prophetical poesy, of which much appears to belong to the time of the Babylonian captivity, and to which the name of Isaiah was given that no part might be lost. Our Psalms, according to their actual arrangement, attained their present extent after the exile, by the junction of several larger and smaller Books of Songs. . . .

In short, it was the custom to arrange old and new together, and to connect with one another what was capable of such disposition—sometimes to increase the extent of separate books and suit the rolls in size to one another, sometimes on account of similarity of matter, and so on. And this, in all probability, was the mode of proceeding in the old times before the captivity, but chiefly afterwards on the occasion of founding the new temple-library.

Were it now resolved to describe as forgeries all books whose every part and passage fell short of congruity in point of time, then truly very few genuine writings of the Hebrews would survive such a sentence; but at the same time this would be a great blow to the classics of both Greek and Roman antiquity. As with regard to the latter so in the case of the former, it behooves the higher criticism only to exercise its office and pronounce sentence after separating, from internal evidence, what belongs to different authors and times. He who blames a Biblical scholar, or even sighs with pious apprehensions, when he beholds him instituting with critical precision and judicial severity an examination into each book of the Old Testament with this object in view, such a person must be either altogether unacquainted with antiquity, profane literature, and the usual mode of dealing with it, or be so entirely destitute of strength of mind as to be incapable of perceiving the serious consequence of omitting to apply a test of this nature and also the otherwise invincible army of doubts, which only by the method proposed can be driven from their intrenchments. And he who, holding such proof to be alike useful, important, and necessary, should from sensitive and over-anxious piety wish to prescribe a law to the critical inquirer, only to separate where external marks afford occasion or compel to such division: such a person in the realm of criticism must still be classed among the weak and would still endanger the character for genuineness of the greatest number of Hebrew writings.

Chapter 152: Qerē velo Kethib . . .

The Talmud already knows seven instances of the Qerē velo Kethib: the Masorah lists ten of them at the beginning of the fifth book of Moses. Our editions, finally, note a still greater number, but they deviate from one another in the passages where they omit the Qerē velo Kethib. The passages in the Masorah are: Judges 20.13; Ruth 3.5, 17; II Sam. 8.3; 16.23; 18.20; II Kings 19.31, 37; Jerem. 31.38; 50.29. In our editions cf. II Kings 20.13; Ezech. 9.11; Is. 53.4, 9; Ps. 96.2; Jos. 22.24 . . .

The Qerē vero Kethib are not variants, as they have been previously presented, but exegetical glosses. . . . For all the words added in the Qerē could be omitted without harming the sense. An interpreter presumably added them for the sake of clarity in meaning. Further, in the passages that I checked by way of trial, there is no evidence that the ancient translators read them. In sum, they are simply exegetical glosses.

[Ed. note: The basic list of instances is that attributed to R. Isaac in the *Babylonian Talmud*, tractate *Nedarim*, 37b. Eichhorn's treatment is much too sweeping. Some of the cases he mentions do support his thesis. The Qerē in Ruth 3.5 and 3.17, for example, supplies a preposition with pronominal suffix (the same in both cases) to serve as the indirect object of a verb of speaking. In each case the verse can be construed without the Qerē, which could reasonably be called an exegetical gloss. In Judg. 20.13 and 2 Sam. 18.20, however, the consonantal text is apparently defective unless the Qerē is supplied, and the omission of the Qerē can be explained in both cases as the result of haplography, a normal scribal error. See on the latter cases J. Weingreen, *Introduction to the Critical Study of the Text of the Hebrew Bible* (Oxford, 1982), 58-62.]

Chapter 426: Separation of the Two Sources

I now venture an attempt to separate the two sources from which the first book of Moses was composed, and to set them out, apart from one another, with the proofs why I separate the interwoven pieces just in this way and not otherwise—an attempt [meant] to stimulate others to similar attempts, or at least to the improvement and completion of mine.* True, I have not in my own been lacking in energy and repeated testing; but works of higher criticism, by their nature, cannot be brought all at once to their highest completion.

[Ed. note: A chart of Genesis chapters and verses, set out in columns by J-source, E-source, and Einschaltungen, follows. Eichhorn's arguments follow:]

1 Moses 1-2.3 The picture of Creation is represented in advance—a masterpiece of art! Up to Cap. 2.3 there is a coherent underlying plan, and up to that point the use of the name Elohim for God continues uninterruptedly. . . .

Cap. 5.1-28 To be quite precise, the source with Elohim begins really with this chapter. The author had already sung as a poet the origin of the Universe, and considered it not inappropriate to place "this shield of Achilles, full of living creative power" before his reports of the *Urwelt*.

After it, it would be reasonable for a new title and a short account of the origin of man to open the History itself. . . . Not only similarity of language, but also the use of the word Elohim for God . . . characterizes this chapter as part of our source. Finally genealogy, combined with dates or chronology, is also a practice in other parts of this source.

Only 5.29 disrupts the entire economy of this chapter. Here is the name Jehova, and nowhere else; here is an etymological explanation of the name Noah and nowhere else in this family list a similar derivation for a name. The whole verse probably belongs to the source with Jehova. It loves this kind of etymology; to it belongs to a degree not only the name Jehova but the rest of the phrasing of this verse.

---

* So far I have not been made acquainted with any serious doubt as to this idea and treatment of Genesis. I at least cannot find the objection relevant that "It's a poor occupation to patch a Book together from such fragments." Did the oldest Greek historians before Herodotus work any differently?

2. WOLF'S CORRESPONDENCE WITH C. G. HEYNE

The following texts are excerpted from Wolf, *Briefe*, 229-307. The page numbers of Peppmüller's edition are given in brackets at the beginning of each selection.

Letter I. Wolf to Heyne, 18 November 1795

[Wolf's purpose in this letter is to ask Heyne to produce a review of the *Prolegomena*]:

[230] In the year 1779 you were the first person to whom I presented my unorthodox thoughts on Homer. I did this in an essay which I gave you at the time of my departure from Göttingen in order somehow to earn the confidence with which at that time you showed me the prospect of a first job, on your own initiative and even though you knew me only through a few friends. Doubtless you still have some recollection of this matter. It was the only essay you received from me in Göttingen, and the ensuing conversation the only one I had the honor to conduct with you about a literary topic. For me these memories are fresher than most others from that time: they were connected with the destinies of my life, which concern me more intimately than Homer and all his scholiasts. I still preserve that essay, too, together with the refined criticisms which I jotted onto it as you uttered them.

Never since then have I found a more stubborn opponent of my ideas, or rather one who has dismissed me more peremptorily, though I have never avoided an opportunity to find one. But after I first got over the pain of this dismissal, it made no further impression upon me than what it could, and perhaps was intended, to make. I became more cautious in my claims and more attentive to the hidden difficulties of the matter; I continued to work on and brood about them as well as I could. The small crop of the next years I kept to myself: anyway a conversation or a letter was not an appropriate place for gathering together the threads of so complicated an investigation. But at the time when I was a novice—and only a novice who had not even once read Aristotle's *Poetics* properly could stumble upon doubts and difficulties which might have elicited a smile from an older scholar—and was nibbling at these subjects, my doubts were small compared to what they subsequently became. At first I only thought I had noticed that the real *writing of books* had not appeared in Greece before the Seventh Century B.C., and on the basis of historical considerations I believed that *Wood*, that inspired guesser, had only erred by a century and a half; I thought I had a truer sense of the business and art of the Greek *Rhapsode* than that suggested by the bald concept of declamation and ῥαπτὰ ἔπη, *composita, facta carmina* ["stitched songs, composed, made songs"]. I began to consider both points, the late appearance of the *writing of books* and *rhapsody*, as important for *the philosophy of the history of human nature in Greece* as well. I suspected here and there the obliterated, dilapidated traces of a later *cementing together of the rhapsodies*; but for a long time I could make no progress in this matter. In general, all that stood in my papers at that time was a crude outline and sketch of the present study. Some time later, my frequent re-readings of Homer brought me nearer to the difficulties I had suspected and to their solution by simultaneously distancing me all the more from traditional notions. In the course of an intensive uninterrupted study of the *Iliad*, I now saw in the *Nineteenth* Book and the *four following* ones just as many signs of a mental and linguistic tone and character which were new and foreign to the preceding books, as in the *final* book, which others had already rendered suspect, but on rather trivial grounds. Furthermore I noticed that my original feelings could be put into words and that the dissimilarity between the first and last books in both works could be conceptualized; I found what seemed to me unmistakable traces of the cement which had served to combine large rhapsodies, *and this starting as early as the Eighth Book of the Iliad*; finally I found the *Odyssey* to be just as inconsistent in itself and divergent from the *Iliad* in many things, modes of thought and customs, as the last books of the *Iliad* were from the first ones. In this way I gradually reached the result that the *Odyssey* too, despite its current form, which is harder to disassemble, had been put together out of parts which were not originally joined with precision, and that it was either not composed by the original author of the *Iliad*, or was so only in very small part.

If need be I could use documentary evidence to prove which of these discoveries I made before Villoison's scholia were published and in which years I made them. I will recall a single circumstance. In completely distinct periods, every time I came in my reading to *Od.* 4.620, where no one had ever expressed the slightest suspicion, I wrote down approximately the same thoughts as appear on p. 131 [ch. 30] of my book about that peculiar, strikingly harsh juncture. It was only when I was organizing my papers to write the *Prolegomena* that the note cards with similar contents unexpectedly flew together; even now they betray the difference in their ages, through ink, paper, and handwriting, more clearly than the Homeric songs do. I encountered the same thing with regard to a number of other passages in the last books of both works with which I was satisfied at first, when making a superficial review. It is only natural that such unexpected chance occurrences gave me courage and were a sign that I was not wasting my time on empty feelings and fancies. For in the meantime I always occupied myself with entirely different sorts of reading and work, and did not rush my Homeric matter to the public. Certainly it was not impossible that an attachment to old sentiments (which otherwise tends to be characteristic only of madmen and quiet country folk) was for once playing a trick upon that careful criticism which is indifferent to the results of its investigations. For that reason, and because I heartily detest affectation, in writing I seldom distinguished my own perceptions from what I had just learned from the *Venetian scholia*. Moreover, this seemed to be of no use whatsoever for my readers or for the few connoisseurs of the scholia. The latter know anyway that *nothing* appears there about the unhomeric quality of the last books of both works, about the junctures of the *Odyssey*, and about several other similar matters; and the hints that really do appear in the scholia would of necessity have been entirely wasted upon anyone who had not already come upon the traces of the thing by other paths. I believe that *Villoison's Prolegomena* make the best proof of this. I think that that unselfish scholar must himself be struck now by amazement when he realizes how much his book contains. . . .

[234] But why did I hide the most difficult questions in a pile of things which are primarily directed to the reconstitution of the text? Why did I not even provide a table of contents at the front or a subject index at the back so the public would know what the book contained? Perhaps you ask these questions; others have asked them already.—Between ourselves: I have no truck with what is called the public. It is too fine, too spacious, too big for me; I cannot think my way up to it: I only wish not to be exposed to its smile of contempt. It was always my wish to be accompanied only by learned, calm researchers, by men who are interested in the history of the most ancient poetry and human culture, who know the attraction of doubts which no *locus probans* resolves, and who, finally, are expert in a way of treating historical objects which does not make guesses left and right (I had almost written, "make messes") and play hocus-pocus with *Certainty*, *Probability*, and *Possibility* so as to transform hypotheses into facts and facts into hypotheses at whim. . . .

[236] Up to now I have especially tested the strength of the *external grounds*. Since this is generally understandable, it seemed most helpful for the majority of readers and for the first step without being detrimental to the subject itself. But, as I said, one can get around the *external grounds* if necessary, should the *internal* ones not stand up to examination. And few

are willing to consider the point I briefly touched upon on p. 137 [ch. 31]. Hence the questions remain: *What discrepancies* are found among the books of the *Iliad*, which were gradually united for a variety of reasons; and likewise in the *Odyssey*? *Which* are the *internal traces* that compel one to conclude that both works were originally not conceived on the plan of large and spacious epics, just as a *trilogy* of plays is not conceived on the plan of *one tragedy*? Furthermore, *why* can we no longer assume that both works have the same author?

I certainly need not tell you that these questions must be treated *without any regard for the customs of rhapsodes and the history of the writing of books.* They are of exactly the same sort as the questions whether a *Platonic* dialogue or a speech of *Demosthenes* or *Lysias* be genuine, i.e. whether it belong to the person to whom it has been ascribed since antiquity. In short, we must try so far as possible to do for Homer exactly what Dionysius of Halicarnassus did for the orators. . . .

[238] I would also wish that you might protect me against a couple of misunderstandings which I have noticed among some of my better readers. Here and there, people have read into the book that I sought to make one man responsible for the composition of the Homeric songs, one who had made the *Iliad* and *Odyssey* for us *out of scattered fragments*: they thought that I wished to seize upon *Lycurgus, Solon*, etc. for this purpose. I do not quite understand this; at least I do not know how I could ever have given rise to this bizarre opinion, which has long been the object of ridicule. Nevertheless I have heard that it is pointed out with benevolent forbearance as a new error in my own little book.

Not all the readers of Homer can have felt strongly enough how equably and uninterruptedly the thread of the events and actions proceeds in the whole of both works. Otherwise no one would have doubted that the arrangement of the books, with the exception of two or three, bears the obvious traces of an *intentional continuation* by the original author himself. I have indicated just this in several passages, most clearly in the *Preface to the Text*. The last decisive question was simply left *undecided*: Is *Homer* (the first and best singer of Trojan legends), or are the *rhapsodes* by their ῥαφή ["stitching"], or the *collectors, organizers, revisers*, or the later *correctors* and *critics* the *principal* creators of the great artistic compositions that lie before us? Whom do we have to thank for the greater part of this artistry? . . .

Heyne's Review of Wolf's Prolegomena (*GGA*, 21 November 1795)

[240] So then, here we would have received the first fruits of the unparalleled industry of Monsieur D'Ansse de Villoison, who has deserved so well of literature but for whom we have often felt sorry, since it was his

fate merely to do the preliminary work for others, and not to harvest the fruits himself.

It is well known that a critical edition of Homer has been delayed by many difficulties, and especially by the fact that none of the older manuscripts equipped with the old commentators had yet been collated. This could have been done in Leiden, Leipzig, Paris, Rome, where such old codices are located; this wish was finally fulfilled by M. de Villoison with an edition of the Venetian codex, which appeared in 1788 after long anticipation. Here he had gathered together so much material for criticism in his Prolegomena that only a reworking of it was now necessary; and we have now received a treatment such as could have been expected only from a scholar who devotes himself and his acuity entirely to criticism. Since, as he himself says, these Prolegomena are intended above all to provide a correct conception of Homer's poems and the genuine and true criticism of them, we intend to follow him and give an account of these to begin with.

Since the reviewer, as Prof. W. himself knows, has been occupying himself for more than twenty years with a new recension of Homer (admittedly with many interruptions and seriously only since the appearance of Villoison's Homer) and has done his part to bring many better conceptions of Homer into circulation for the first time, he is in a position to evaluate what has been achieved here. Hence, when he declares that this work is learned, thorough, and excellent, such a judgment cannot be a matter of indifference to Professor Wolf. He regrets only that Prof. W., who knows quite well how highly the reviewer values his erudition, did not inform him openly that he had laid aside other works in order to occupy himself with Homer; [the reviewer] would gladly have entrusted to him the whole critical part of the work, since this could come into no better hands. But the reviewer is willing to resign himself to the fact that every man has his own way of acting; it is a pleasure to him to work together to one end with Prof. W. even in this way; "this threshhold will receive both," as Homer says [cf. *Od.* 18.17]. Perhaps it will be of some value for literature itself for two scholars to work simultaneously on one object, one which furthermore is such that, even after both of them, there will be material enough for future workers. And the whole interpretation [of Homer], like the criticism of details, is still a great unworked field. But let us turn to the content of the Prolegomena, which we intend to impart in excerpts. [What follows is largely Heyne's epitome of the *Prolegomena*:]

A new recension of a classic author is more difficult and laborious than merely individual improvements; in Homer, for several reasons, even more so, since he was previously so neglected. Short survey of the editions (no genetic history). A critical recension is made possible now by Villoison's edition of the old scholia; from the newer manuscripts, as it is well known, there is not much more to hope for (to page xvi [ch. 4]). Now he tells us everything he read with an eye to the criticism of Homer, before and after the time Villoison's edition reached us in 1789. The reviewer went along the same road and knows full well all its difficulties, but he consoled himself with the well-known "a book is not made in any other way" [Martial 1.16]. W. intends now to supply a text of Homer, so far as the words, the punctuation, and the accents are concerned, in the form that a Longinus or another ancient critic would have demanded it according to the best Alexandrian recensions (p. xxi [ch. 7])—with the restriction that W. himself is finally required to make: "as far as we can go." To explain everything, he says, belongs in a commentary; but just to show in general the rules according to which the emendation of Homer must be performed, he wishes to present in a summary fashion the history of the Homeric text and to divide it into six ages: I) from the origin of the poems themselves (950 B.C.) to Pisistratus, to whom the collection of the two poems, the *Iliad* and the *Odyssey*, is assigned; II) from then to Zenodotus, who prepared the way for the criticism of Homer; III) to Apion; IV) to Longinus and Porphyry; V) to Demetrius Chalcondyles; and VI) the last three centuries. At the moment the author, as far as we can tell, has stopped while still in the third period with Aristarchus and Crates.

Prof. W. complains that there is so much material which he is working on everywhere according to his own method: nevertheless he inserts a long justification of criticism on Homer. Upon this follows an even longer digression and treatise (pp. xl-cix [chs. 12-25]) upon the first invention and introduction of writing in Greece. After everything that has been written on this subject, there was nothing new to say; but for the question whether the *Iliad* was composed in writing exactly as we have it, the one remark was helpful, that the *use of writing* was much later than its *invention*; and this is so for the quite simple reason that the spread of its use depended upon more convenient writing materials than were known at first. When doubt is expressed—and indeed it has been—whether Homer composed his *Iliad* in writing, the reason for the doubt could not be whether the letters of the alphabet were known to the Ionians at that time or could have been, but instead whether the use of writing at that time had already progressed to the point that large works like an *Iliad* were written down. Historical evidence is entirely lacking, and cannot even be expected from those times; hence the question can only be decided by probabilities. But there are more arguments of probability for the negative side, so that it can now be considered practically the general opinion that Homer did not compose his poems in writing—especially as Mr. Merian has just now worked out this hypothesis.

Prof. W. now provides this hypothesis with support in a careful investigation which is full of scholarship, erudition, and acuity. He makes a number of good observations in passing, as p. lv [ch. 14] on ἀνέθηκεν ἐών [ἰών], and on the spuriousness of the well-known inscriptions in the temple of Apollo Ismenius. It is also an excellent insight that there must have been a certain connection between the spread of writing and the coming into fashion of prose, as well as of the literary activity which now followed. It is also extremely probable that the use of writing became more general in Ionia, then in Sicily and Magna Graecia, perhaps as early as the eighth and seventh centuries B.C., but in Athens not until the sixth and fifth centuries B.C. Hence the songs were preserved sufficiently at first in the memory of the poets. But one will reply at once to this that it is still not at all probable that *one* ancient bard could have taken so many songs as the *Iliad* and *Odyssey* contain, which he had conceived in memory alone, and turned them into one such whole as the two poems make up: for this, recording in writing was necessary.

To the author, the expression of this consideration seems new and daring; he demonstrates the improbability that Homer might already have composed a unified epic, on pp. cix-cxxxviii [chs. 26-31], in a long-winded, but learned and acute manner. To the reviewer the matter seemed *quite simple*, and he has always so presented it in lectures. Historical evidence for Yes or No is lacking; hence historical probability must decide; and for this the rules have been better worked out in our time than the ancient grammarians knew them; these latter, just like us, only conjectured, or affirmed a conjecture. What is more, all the ancient legends tend in the same direction: that in the beginning only *individual rhapsodies* were sung; this corresponds precisely with what we know about the ancient songs of the bards, even from Homer: everywhere it is only individual heroes, actions, and events which are the subject of a song. The natural course of events and of the human spirit gives just about the same result as well; and the Cyclic poets, and in more recent times the poems of Ossian, illustrate how such individual songs can be combined later into a whole, more or less artistically and with genius.

The few historical facts about Homer's poems, about their transmission to Sparta, and to Athens, at the time of Pisistratus and Solon, where in all probability the poems were put down in writing for the first time and divided into the two corpora (pp. cxxxviii-clix [chs. 32-35]). The age of Pisistratus up to Zenodotus. (Here the reviewer would make several breaks, both before Pisistratus and after him; in this period there must have been quite large changes in the Homeric poems; among these was one which the author did not notice but which is of the greatest importance for Homeric meter and criticism, namely the omission of the so-called Aeolic digamma; but to this subject the reviewer will return in the next issue: here we are limiting ourselves to what we owe Prof. W.)

Eight recensions before Zenodotus have become known, according to the introduction to Villoison's collections. About Zenodotus (p. clxxxviii [ch. 41]), as a critic about whom we must certainly have a different conception than about a Bentley. Concerning the way in which he treated the text of Homer there is still much obscurity; about Aristophanes we know even less, and nothing satisfactory about Aristarchus either. Prof. W. has listed with admirable scholarly industry the passages in the scholia where their names or readings, improvements or criticisms of them are indicated. He has placed the services Aristarchus rendered Homer in a very favorable light. A bit more about Crates. By the way, Prof. W. has posed most matters as problems; hence he requires a reader who works with him through all the roundabout paths of Pro and Contra and at the end is in a position to decide for himself.

Since Aristarchus' recension is the one upon which the whole Homeric text, as we have it, is based, Prof. W. has attempted to reconstruct it in the new edition—to be sure, only *so far as is possible*; for no codex presents it with total purity, not even the Venetian, which does not even observe analogy, the principle which Aristarchus must have followed if he was self-consistent, e.g. in the Ionic omission of the augment. Already in the first edition, W. performed a great service by leaving out the nu-movable; it certainly does not come from the age of Homer; but what if Aristarchus approved it?—W. himself recognizes that a number of incorrect readings remained in Aristarchus' recension, and that for their improvement one must go back even further. The reviewer compared *Iliad* 16 and 17; but it would be quite improper for him to go into detail and to indicate passages in which his opinion differs from that of Prof. W. or to list verses in which metrical mistakes are still to be found. Enough: Prof. W. has provided something which we did not have before and which goes far beyond the services rendered Homer by Barnes, Clarke, and Ernesti; no age will fail to appreciate this beautiful memorial of his critical spirit. We now await from him the Aristarchean *Odyssey* and the second part of the Prolegomena, which are certain to give us elucidation and information on many confused and obscure matters.

Letter III. Wolf to Heyne,
14 December 1795:

[259] I would be glad to leave aside one passage of your review which concerns me *personally*, if it were not written so very benevolently. You regret that I did not candidly give you a report of my studies in Homer.

Indeed, you add, you would have been delighted to entrust me with the whole critical part of your work. To put it in a nutshell, this statement—unintentionally, without question—made a disheartening and shaming impression upon me. My only solace is that *lack of candor* perhaps means negligence in letter-writing here. And I have finally gotten used to being reproached for this: but no one who knows me has ever yet blamed me for any other failure to act directly and candidly. I also think that I was acting candidly when I publicly announced that I was undertaking the new edition of Homer. The undertaking itself became necessary when the first school edition sold out; it came several years sooner than I wished or than my other literary projects made convenient. Moreover, had I been able to go to work following a predecessor like yourself, then my progress would have been different from the very beginning, since I had no lack of the necessary materials. But forgive my uncertainty. I never knew or believed that you yourself were occupied with a *critical* work on Homer. The general public had always expected an *explication of the poet*, a so-called *continuous commentary*, although in the *Gött. Gel. Anzeigen* for 1783, p. 1387, you were so stern that you destroyed this expectation almost completely. Later I heard, to be sure, that you had really decided to satisfy the increasingly urgent public desire, and that you had already collected all sorts of contributions for this purpose. Nevertheless, in my situation I could not act differently than I did if I did not wish to violate the publisher's interests and my own. Incidentally, in undertaking my new edition I did not have to fear collisions except those of the sort that arose from my other occupations. One comes to terms with such collisions most easily if one works as a pastime as I do, that is, if one does now this now that in order to fill his time properly.

Heyne's Report of his lecture on 1 August 1795 at the
Royal Göttingen Scientific Society
(GGA, 19 December 1795)

[262] "On Seeking Out, Judging, and Reconstituting the Ancient Text of Homer" was the title of a lecture which Privy Councillor Heyne held at one of the meetings of the Society, which has already been reported. Since he has never been a friend of preliminary announcements of what he intends to do in the future, his intention had not been to speak of this and similar matters until a more immediate occasion to do so would be provided by his completion of a certain work. Even now he does so unwillingly, since it comes too early for him. But since he sees that the question has been broached sooner [i.e. by Wolf], he feels himself justified in speaking his part too, particularly since it concerns an object about which he

already had a certain way of thought thirty years ago. He has expressed this in lectures, writings, and in these *Anzeigen* as well, whenever the subject demanded it. Much of this has already been applied to the most ancient writers of the Hebrews.

The common opinion concerning a single Homer and his epic has always been subject to serious doubts, and it is easy to doubt once one is directed to test common opinions (if only it were just as easy to put something certain in their place!). Hence the Privy Councillor never believed that his own divergent opinion could cause a sensation; and he sees himself further confirmed by the fact that this opinion agrees in many respects with what Professor Wolf has presented at length in his *Prolegomena* reviewed above (in number 186). As he already said then, the matter seemed quite simple to him: we have no *valid historical testimony* about Homer and the earliest condition of his poems; we have only *legends*, and *opinions* based on those legends; but even these legends we do not possess in their *primitive purity*, but instead mingled and embellished with various *additions*. Even the first man who collected them, *Theagenes of Rhegium* (hence not an *Ionian*), lived *400 years* later than Homer is supposed to have lived. Hence what can be done here is, without a preconceived opinion, without presumptuousness and obstinacy, to discover the earliest form of the legend, to compare it with the ancient condition of literature, and to see what results these two processes can yield in accordance with the rules of historical probability; if we then find that no theory is entirely free of difficulties and objections but that some theories have stronger arguments in their favor, then we may choose these and let others build their own houses of cards. The Homeric poems themselves gain and lose no value, whatever opinion one adopts.

Letter IV. Wolf to Heyne,
9 January 1796:

[271] I had thought I could end this business with the two previous letters. These two were already heartily unpleasant for me. You must have noticed that. The tone you set me by your *elegant* review was not my own. And what is not ours does not fit us well, or turns out poorly. But in truth you know how to give your correspondents a second wind. Thus the fact that I am writing once again and perhaps yet again is *your* responsibility; how I write is *mine*. . . .

[288] We still lack much of what we need to elucidate the history of the rhapsodic art, an indispensable part of Greek literature. What was immediately relevant to my purpose was first of all determining the nature of ῥάπτειν ἔπη ["to stitch verses"], an expression which points not towards

finishing but towards *artificially combining* and *arranging*; secondly, that this art, like rhapsodic performance in general, had to be learnt and practised in *schools* of some sort (poetry had these earlier than philosophy), in a way not too detrimental to the preservation of the songs; finally, how the *mode of singing* of these representatives of the older bards quite naturally confused, obscured, and totally destroyed many other *Homers* whose names were once famous. Most of this, admittedly, is based upon reasoning by analogy; but you will concede that sometimes in the series of secure historical data this achieves a degree of certainty such as the twenty-three dagger thrusts which killed Julius Caesar scarcely have. And brief as I was, especially here, nevertheless the general direction of the whole is so easy to perceive that every thoughtful reader should be led as far as the matter allows.

You were among these thoughtful readers. I am also willing to believe that, in certain points concerning the rhapsodes and other Homeric issues, you saw further than *Dresig* and his like. I myself find *one* good and true remark in the *Introduction to Homer* composed of notes from your lectures. You gave a hint about how the rhapsodes mocked by *Plato* were to be distinguished from the older ones. But about those central matters you said nothing, or something false: e.g. about the name of the rhapsodes, on which everything hangs. I repeat to you your own words on this subject, as I find them; they are a paradigm of cautious philological reasoning: "People tend to speculate a lot about the derivation of the word ῥαψῳδός ["rhapsode"]. The grammarians made a false derivation, as though it meant the *Staff-singers*, from ῥάβδος ["staff"]. For they held a staff while they declaimed. But such a derivation is grammatically impossible. [Is it? FAW] It must come from ῥάπτω τὴν ᾠδήν, i.e. *to sew together*, that is, one who puts verses together rather than making them. But this too does not fit. Hence *to make or compose songs or verses*: in the oldest period of the language, ῥάπτειν ["to stitch"] means the same as ὑφαίνειν ["to weave"]: but this too is not quite right, although it is already better. The rhapsodes did not actually make the verses, but only declaimed. Consequently the most correct seems: ὁ ἀείδων ῥαπτά, *singing composed verses.*" So that's it! *Singing composed verses: he who sings* made *verses!* And what then was the term for those who sang *unmade* verses?—More or less the same result of this cautious scholarly reasoning you bestowed upon the general public in 1791 on p. 109 in the addenda to your Pindar edition, after you set out a sequence of words that certainly, even without my note on p. 107 of the *Prolegomena* [ch. 25], would remain forever new. Then you continue, *"The words* ῥαπτὰ ἔπη ["stitched verses"] *seem to be used in various ways: first, since* ῥάπτειν ἔπη *is to make or compose verses* (where ever might it mean that?); *second, since they used to recite the different parts,* ἔπη ["verses"], *of the* Iliad *which they had memorized one after another*," that is, according to Solon's rule. That is all. You seem nowhere to have taken the slightest notice of the other points mentioned above.

On the other hand I cannot tell whether you interpreted the reports of *the collection of Homer by the Pisistratids* in the same sense as that to which I was accidentally led at first glance. Apparently not. At least in that case you would, by an inevitable association of ideas, have hit upon notions about the *Cyclic poets* different from those you presented in the Excursus to your *Virgil* edition and repeated in the notes on p. 45 of your edition of *Proclus' Chrestomathy*. In both places you speak of the *epic cycle* as a collection made by *grammarians*, hence not until the *Alexandrian* period. But about the *Homeric arrangement* you did not utter a word anywhere, neither in your writings, so far as I know them, nor in your lectures. Hence everything sounded just as it did in *Küster's* well-known little book. Instead, you provide us with introductory observations concerning the whole of *Homer's epic poems*, dealing with *great action, great designs, great passions, great dangers, great obstacles, great sentiments,* about *astonishment* and *admiration, knots* and *illusion* and *beginning* and *middle* and *end of the epic poem;* where I found your first *Disquisition* before the *Aeneid* and dear old *Batteux* in person; together with an appendix on the duration of the actions in the *Iliad,* according to a *Mémoire* of the *Academy of Inscriptions;* also a work about the *topography of Troy,* one in which one could still see the trouble it had cost you. In short: we have never read a syllable of yours in writings or heard one in lectures about how the rhapsodies and so-called poems might have looked before *Pisistratus.*

It is also possible that you presented other ideas at another time, perhaps ones that contradicted one another; or certain *modes of thought* were expressed precisely in those sessions from which I was absent. Fortunately, your recent writings do not leave us in the lurch. Throughout the most recent one, *Lechevalier's Trip to Troy,* there are many things which one would not expect from your present explanations to find in 1792. In this book you speak, just as before, about the *epic poet Homer*—once, in fact (p. 269), about him as *high epic,* and that à propos of a point that has enough similarity with the story of the *Tower of Babel* to make Moses too into a high epic author. But what I cannot understand at all is how you could seek a self-consistent topography in the *Iliad* until 1792 and—according to your own testimony—make so many fruitless attempts in this matter, when you discovered in that work, according to your current expression, interpolations of whole rhapsodies by different singers. One who has discovered the latter *absolutely* cannot seek the former, at least in the way that you did. Only after I had convinced myself, by an incessant study of the connected complete songs and of the history of the text, of the existence of *interpolations of whole rhapsodies* (not merely of the last book of each poem) was I able to draw the firm conclusion that much larger discrepancies than now remain about the locale must have been effaced by the smoothing hands of the revisers. Only then was I able to express (on p. 134 [ch. 31, n. 99]) the well-intended wish *that no one should any longer trouble himself to go to Troy on account of the Iliad.* The remark is *simple*, and, if made earlier, would have left many wanderers and researchers in peace.

The *high epic poet Homer* brings me back to the subject of your *Virgil* edition, from which nevertheless I remind you of only one passage, which I really had *before my very eyes.* It is the one in which, both in the larger editions and in the smaller ones, in all four impressions (pp. xxi, xxviii, 360, 355), you speak of the elegance and the beautiful weaving of the *episodes* into the main action. You add concerning Homer: *Out of the whole course of the Trojan War he selected one hero, one action, and in this way he was able to make the right use of countless other things drawn from the history of that war to adorn and amplify his plot.* Do you now understand my passage on p. 117 [ch. 27], *one act, one hero selected, everything else* I suppose *shrewdly interposed for the sake of ornament?* If at that time I had had available your *Letter on a New Edition of Homer*, pp. 15 and 19 could easily have tempted me into several similar *I suppose*'s. For there too you enjoin the future editor of Homer to pay attention to the *epic poem's nature, plan, rules and concentration on a single main action.* But how can all that agree with the lecture you just recently laid away in the archive, in which you find it most improbable *to see in such old poems so many individual actions, subordinated, introduced as episodes, parts that do not belong to the main action, that can be placed in groups* etc.? In which you say: *Everything inclines to the side of the hypothesis that the great poem, the Iliad, only grew later out of individual songs?* By this duplicity you put your readers and adherents into extraordinary confusion. Should they now trust your most recent lecture, even before it has been printed, or the *Virgil* that has been reprinted several times? Certainly, many people will find your real opinion on this subject crucial to their peace of mind.

I add to this a passage from your *Göttingen Gelehrte Anzeigen* (for you refer to this too), a passage which I may at least have had vaguely in mind when on p. 119 [ch. 27] I pointed to the absence of an *announcement of the contents* which covered the plan of the *Iliad* more fully. I wrote: *It would be absurd to claim that such accuracy was too meticulous for the age of Homer* etc. The momentary censure is, as you see, meant in general for the reader; but perhaps it refers to the words with which you answered a scholar who solved the aesthetic doubts about *Iliad* 24 with a new explanation of the first verses: "One should not expect or require of poets to indicate the contents of an epic narrative with the exactitude of an epitomizer. Homer merely expresses himself in general terms: he says that he wishes to sing the wrath of Achilles with the defeats that resulted after his withdrawal from the army. Let one twist his words as one will: more than that he does not say. Here too one expects from Homer the artistry and exactitude of an Alexandrian poet, which he cannot and should not have." So you wrote—when do you think?—in May 1792 on p. 843 of the *Anzeigen*. In December 1795 of the same *Anzeigen*, pp. 202ff., the common opinion that one man designed two poems of this compass in the most artistic possible manner seems to you *most improbable*; and the large-scale plan of the *Iliad* seems improbable; the unity of this plan itself seems *capable of enormous restrictions and exceptions*; and you mention as a reason not only the inartistic plans of the *Cyclic poets* and the like but also *this*: "that now not even the first *announcement* fits it any more; *for far more things are now contained in the Iliad than are announced*." Now indeed! But this is precisely how things stood in May 1792.

But we have not yet reached the limit. It would be strange if you had not laid claim to the elegances of the *episodes* from your *Virgil* edition for the longest time. You did this, perhaps for the last time, in an *Anzeige* of 1793, p. 1143, which led you to the historical plan of *Herodotus*. "Herodotus' way of arranging the manifold material of history *episodically* led, by its similarity to *Homer's epic poetry*, early to the remark that *Herodotus* had followed *Homer* in this." But here by *Homer's epic poetry* you presumably mean the later Διασκευή ["revision"] which the historian had available in his own age. For by this time the *Venetian scholia* had already reached us; by now it was gradually becoming high time to accept the *opinion diverging* from all your earlier statements. Since the middle of 1793 you have gone about this as can be seen; two years before the oft-mentioned lecture before the Society!—I do not contradict this: I am only pleased that at that time my edition was already being printed and that its introduction had already been written in its present form. I say *in its present form*. I should like to have seen how the *Prolegomena* would have been received in the earlier German version in which the editor of the *Journal von und für Deutschland* in the fifth issue of 1784 had promised it, or in which four years earlier a *Berlin scholar*, to whom I had offered a single manuscript about it for publication and who by a negative answer on 16 May 1780 became the first occasion for a lengthy delay, had become acquainted with its outlines. This will provide you with an explanation of the note on p. 113 [ch. 26, n. 84], where however the two figures should read 1779 and 1780.

But for a long time already I have become disgusted with these figures and dates. Yet they were necessary here. It would be more pleasant to take a stroll into the so-called *higher criticism*, if only my business with this *lower* one had not so exhausted me. Indeed, it would be a higher problem to consider whether you have been *able* to progress to the firm modes of thought of the lecture. It is not as though an extraordinary exertion of the spirit and distance from all those preoccupations, the quantity of which you always complain about, were necessary for this: as far as I know, you have never given any illustration of such matters anywhere, even before your preoccupied period. With regard to the interpolation of Zaleucus' and Charondas' fragments you came almost a century too late to—part of the explanation. In this matter the old grammarians seem to have gone further, even though in their age the rules of historical probability had not been elaborated so well as in the last thirty years.

In the history of the arts and sciences of antiquity, as in dogmatic theology, certain points of view thoroughly obstruct the path to genuinely historical research. The most pernicious of such opinions are those which attempt to adapt antiquity to our taste, our scholarly desires and artistic ideas. It does not seem that this was your mistake with Homer. For you have often reminded us that ancient poets must be read *as ancient poets.* Some people indeed consider this reminder to be one of the greatest services you have rendered, although you yourself rightly remark in the *Göttingen Commentationes* (8 [1777] 34) *that it is self-evident and has been sufficiently pointed out by many. It becomes harder when it is a question of how.* Here, precisely with regard to the how, you made a couple of false steps at the very beginning which by necessity led you constantly astray from the correct viewpoint later on. *One was* that you supposed that the crude singers after *Linus, Orpheus*, etc. had by their shorter songs as it were prepared the way for the great prophet of the true epic poem, *Homer.* He too, admittedly, had not quite understood the essential rules of the art, but had by mere feeling or clear-sightedness progressed to the point of artistically interweaving main and secondary actions and of creating the two works from which Aristotle had derived the most perfect theory and all later poets of the same genre had derived the model for their poems.— Perhaps you did not use these precise terms; but your *Virgil* edition, wherever one opens it, breathes forth exactly the same spirit.

Second: you supposed that this same Homer "for the purpose of poetic artifice, *in accordance with the essence of epic narrative*, made a felicitous change in mythology. He took the fables, that earlier had served as the veils for philosophical doctrines, the symbolical modes of thought of the earlier poets, and let them appear as real facts and old historical events, in order to keep the marvellous and the imagination in tension." You praised this everywhere, in writings and in lectures, and called it a *splendid, pleasing, thoughtful invention.* You thought knowledge of it very useful in all interpretation, even including the oldest Hebrew authors. I would have called it only a *great change*. It is so great that no bard could ever have thought of it—far greater than when nowadays, inversely, interpreters make *phil-osophical doctrines* out of old events; so great that, if Homer had made it, he would have had to be a giant who surpassed the whole mode of thought of his age. How can it be called a *pleasing, thoughtful invention* to present the old national fables in a different sense than earlier singers had done, as though they were new? It would be easier to call such a trick *unpleasant* and *thoughtless: thoughtless*, inasmuch as Homer either had not seen the deeper philosophical thought of his predecessors or had sacrificed it out of a mania for his beloved epic poem; *unpleasing*, for he thereby imposed upon his good-natured contemporaries a series of tall tales and bugbears which supported nasty pagan antiquity for so many centuries. Hence the invention ought to have been called *unhappy*: though, to be sure, *unique of its kind*. Because of this last circumstance you seem in the last *Virgil* edition (Disquis. I to the *Aeneid*: p. xxvi in the large edition, p. 353 in the small one) to set the attention of the student more strongly into motion with that SUCCESSIT ECCE HOMERUS [AND LO THEN CAME HOMER]. But you have recounted the same thing to us in the *Comment. de origine et causis fabularum Homeri* in the eighth volume of the *Novi Comment. Soc. Reg. Gött.*, in the *Preface* to *Heraclitus' Allegories*, in the *Anzeigen* of these and other writings and in so many other places that I am too exhausted to list them all now.

I am—

W.

BIBLIOGRAPHICAL ESSAYS

1. Wolf and His Context

Wolf's attack on the unity of Homer was only one episode, though a central one, in the creation of modern classical scholarship in Germany between ca. 1770 and ca. 1830. The reader who wishes to explore the wider context within which Wolf did his work can begin with the standard surveys of the history of classical scholarship: J. E. Sandys, *A History of Classical Scholarship* (Cambridge, 1903-8); U. von Wilamowitz-Moellendorff, *History of Classical Scholarship* [1921], tr. A. Harris, ed. H. Lloyd-Jones (London, 1982); and R. Pfeiffer, *History of Classical Scholarship from 1300 to 1850* (Oxford, 1976), best consulted in the revised German edition, *Die Klassische Philologie von Petrarca bis Mommsen* (Munich, 1982). For the history of textual criticism and editorial technique before and after Wolf see E. J. Kenney, *The Classical Text* (Berkeley, 1974); and S. Timpanaro, *La genesi del metodo del Lachmann*, new ed. (Padua, 1981). And for the specific cultural, political and institutional setting within which the German philologists worked, see in general H. Butterfield, *Man on His Past* (reprinted Boston, 1960); P. H. Reill, *The German Enlightenment and the Rise of Historicism* (Berkeley, 1975); C. Diehl, *Americans and German Scholarship, 1770-1870* (New Haven and London, 1978); and C. E. McClelland, *State, Society and University in Germany, 1700-1914* (Cambridge, 1980). More penetrating than Diehl and more attentive to the problems of the philologists than McClelland is R. S. Turner, "The Prussian Universities and the Concept of Research," *Internationales Archiv für Sozialgeschichte der deutschen Literatur* 5 (1980), 68-93; a recent monograph of critical importance on the content of German scholarship is A. D. Momigliano, *New Paths of Classicism in the Nineteenth Century (History and Theory*, Beiheft 21, 1982).

The history of the other scholarly disciplines that Wolf drew upon can also be followed up in standard works. E. S. Shaffer, *"Kubla Khan" and the Fall of Jerusalem* (Cambridge, 1975), and J. L. Kugel, *Parallelism in Biblical Poetry* (New Haven and London, 1980) offer informative and insightful discussions of eighteenth-century Old Testament scholarship. W. G. Kümmel's *The New Testament: The History of The Investigation of Its Problems* (London, 1973) is a rich survey, supported by lavish quotations from the sources. B. M. Metzger, *The Text of the New Testament: Its Transmission, Corruption, and Restoration*, 2d ed. (Oxford, 1968), though detailed and sensible, must be supplemented and corrected from Timpanaro's *La genesi del metodo del Lachmann*.

These works provide an adequate orientation into theology, the field that was crucial for Wolf. Many other areas of eighteenth-century learning may also have had an impact upon him. For the general development of historical thought and method, Reill and Butterfield (cited above) are excellent. For a perceptive and erudite study of medieval scholarship—including the earliest serious work on medieval poetry—see L. Gossman, *Medievalism and the Ideologies of the Enlightenment* (Baltimore, 1968). And for the growth of interest in the *carmina* that supposedly transmitted the early history of Rome—an area of scholarship that probably affected, and was definitely affected by, Wolf—see A. D. Momigliano, "Perizonius, Niebuhr and the Character of Early Roman Tradition," in his *Essays in Ancient and Modern Historiography* (Oxford, 1977). Finally, for the study of Roman Law—a discipline in which the creation of a history of one central text, the *Digest*, was a vital concern of eighteenth-century scholarship—see B. H. Stolte, Jr., *Henrik Brenkman (1681-1736): Jurist and Classicist* (Groningen, 1981).

Wolf himself has never ceased to attract attention. Mark Pattison's 1865 essay on his life and work remains unsurpassed as an evocation of Wolf's personality and impact (*Essays by the Late Mark Pattison* [Oxford, 1889], vol. 1, pp. 337-414). Three rich and well-documented recent essays illuminate the tension between historicism and classicism in Wolf: M. Fuhrmann, "Friedrich August Wolf," *Deutsche Vierteljahrsschrift für Literaturwissenschaft und Geistesgeschichte* 33 (1959), 187-236; A. Horstmann, "Die 'Klassische Philologie' zwischen Humanismus und Historismus. Friedrich August Wolf und die Begründung der modernen Altertumswissenschaft," *Berichte zur Wissenschaftsgeschichte* 1 (1978), 51-70; and D. Lanza, "Friedrich August Wolf: L'antico e il classico," *Belfagor* 36 (1981), 529-53. B. Hemmerdinger has stressed Wolf's originality in tracing the history of a text in "Philologues de jadis," *Belfagor* 32 (1977), 496-506; G. Broccia has denied Wolf's originality in analyzing Homer in *La questione Omerica* (Florence, 1979), 22-31. For efforts to set Wolf's Homeric scholarship into a wide context without denying its considerable novelty, see M. Murrin, *The Allegorical Epic* (Chicago, 1980), 189-96; and A. Grafton, "*Prolegomena* to Friedrich August Wolf," *Journal of the Warburg and Courtauld Institutes* 44 (1981), 109-29. And for a vast fund of texts and information, still in part unstudied, see the great edition of Wolf's correspondence by S. Reiter, *Friedrich August Wolf: Ein Leben in Briefen*, 3 vols. (Stuttgart, 1935; supplementary volume, 1956).

2. The Homeric Question

Wolf, of course, was only one of the legion of scholars and critics who have taken a passionate interest in Homer. In particular, during the seventeenth- and eighteenth-century debates usually referred to as the Quarrel of the Ancients and Moderns, Homer had served as a sort of litmus test; views about the sort of poetry he wrote and the sort of society he wrote for tended to define a critic's stance on a much wider and deeper range of intellectual issues. These debates are summed up in K. Simon-suuri's well-informed if unexciting *Homer's Original Genius* (Cambridge, 1979), which helpfully assembles the vast secondary literature that has appeared since G. Finsler wrote his classic survey, *Homer in der Neuzeit* (Leipzig and Berlin, 1912). Two detailed and incisive monographs are N. Hepp, *Homère en France au XVIIᵉ siècle* (Paris, 1968); and Th. Bleicher, *Homer in der deutschen Literatur (1450-1740)* (Stuttgart, 1972).

After the *Prolegomena* appeared, the Homeric question became the most contentious of all philological problems, as it had long been the most contentious of critical ones. The German philologists who grew up in Wolf's shadow tried to carry out the analysis of which he had stopped short. They cut the *Iliad* and *Odyssey* up into dozens of hypothetical shorter source poems, agreeing on the validity of the method as strongly as they disagreed on its specific results. Some English scholars agreed. Others, innocent of historical method but trained to a high level of linguistic and poetic sensitivity, fought to save the unity of the poems. After Schliemann's discoveries in Greece and Asia Minor, which seemed to confirm the historicity of the Trojan War, and World War I, which seemed to some to cast doubts on the validity of German culture in general and German scholarship in particular, unitarian views became more prominent within the philological profession and found some assent within Germany. Since the 1920s, finally, Homeric scholarship has been enriched by the discoveries of Milman Parry and his students. Developing an insight of Gottfried Hermann and studying the oral poetry still composed in Yugoslavia, they showed through Homer's repetitive use of formulas in given metrical positions that he came from a tradition of oral composition of verse. We now have a far clearer understanding than Wolf could of the problems involved in reconstructing the historical background before which Homer must be set, the social world portrayed in his poems, and the very different social world for which they were composed.

Yet disagreement persists on crucial points. Reputable scholars disagree sharply on whether the authors of the *Iliad* and *Odyssey* were literate, on the extent to which both poems draw on earlier sources, and on the extent to which they have suffered interpolation and corruption. Unitarians and analysts still devastate one another in the classical journals. And some points that seemed obvious in earlier times—like the spuriousness of *Iliad* 10 or *Odyssey* 24—are once again the subjects of dispute.

The development of opinion on these and other points can be followed in a number of attractive surveys: R. C. Jebb, *Homer* (5th ed., Glasgow, 1894); E. R. Dodds, "Homer," in *Fifty Years (and Twelve) of Classical Scholarship*, ed. M. Platnauer (Oxford, 1968); H. L. Lorimer, "Homer and the Art of Writing: A Sketch of Opinion between 1713 and 1939," *American Journal of Archaeology* 52 (1948), 11-23; J. L. Myres, *Homer and His Critics* (London, 1958); Broccia, *La questione Omerica* (cited in sect. 1 above). The best general introduction to the field remains *A Companion to Homer*, ed. A. Wace and F. Stubbings (London, 1962). For Milman Parry see especially his Homeric papers, collected in *The Making of Homeric Verse* (Oxford, 1971); the introduction, by A. Parry, is one of the best surveys of the Homeric question in general as well as a fine introduction to M. Parry's work.

3. Ancient Scholarship in Modern Scholarship

The persuasiveness of Wolf's analysis of the Venice scholia seems at first to have deterred anyone else from retracing his steps. In the 1830s, however, his admirer Karl Lehrs worked through the A scholia anew. He resolved them, far more consistently than Wolf had done, into their constituent elements; and he inferred from them that Wolf had misjudged the Alexandrian critics. Aristarchus, he suggested, had not been the elegant man of letters Wolf described, bent on improving the Homeric poems, but a diligent and systematic textual critic, engaged in collation and emendation at a professional level. This view was more attractive than Wolf's: insofar as it implied that Aristarchus had systematically relied on the oldest available manuscripts and honestly reported their readings, it also implied that modern textual critics could reconstruct the text as it had been before Aristarchus and his cohorts went to work. Such helpful and optimistic views held the field—especially in Homeric studies—from Lehrs's time until fairly recently, and still have competent adherents.

Since late in the nineteenth century a reaction has been growing. The new evidence of Greek papyri, though multiplying the sources of information about the textual history of Homer, has tended to contradict Lehrs's view of the Alexandrians. And the reevaluation of Hellenistic culture brought about by Rudolf Pfeiffer and others has tended to support Wolf's view of the nature of Hellenistic textual criticism. The Alexandrians, though diligent workers and original scholars, were basically men of letters (and sometimes poets) rather than professional researchers. They corrected Homer's errors of taste and language against their own up-to-date standards of refinement as eagerly as they emended the blunders of his scribes.

These difficult subjects can be pursued in a number of recent secondary works. L. D. Reynolds and N. G. Wilson offer a concise and judicious survey in chapter 1 of *Scribes and Scholars* (2d ed. Oxford, 1974), now available in a revised French translation (Paris, 1984). E. G. Turner weaves an eloquent description of Alexandrian techniques of textual criticism into his standard work, *Greek Papyri* (Oxford, 1968); P. M. Fraser builds a full and original history of Alexandrian scholarship into his great re-creation of its social and institutional setting, *Ptolemaic Alexandria* (Oxford, 1972). Rudolf Pfeiffer focuses his *History of Classical Scholarship from the Beginnings to the End of the Hellenistic Age* (Oxford, 1968) on the study of Homer; and N. G. Wilson traces the afterlife of Alexandrian methods in the age of the scholiasts and Eustathius in *Scholars of Byzantium* (London, 1983).

The central question addressed by Wolf in the last third of the *Prolegomena*, the nature of Alexandrian criticism, is in many ways inextricably linked to two other questions, that of the formation of the extant collections of Homeric scholia and that of the transmission of the text of Homer itself. A vast amount of information on ancient (and modern) Homeric scholarship is helpfully synthesized in H. W. Clarke, *Homer's Readers* (Newark, Del., 1981). The transmission of Homer is discussed in a number of works. J. A. Davison's chapter in *A Companion to Homer* (cited in sect. 2 above) provides a useful introduction. The earliest surviving texts of Homer are assembled, with an excellent introduction, in S. West, *The Ptolemaic Papyri of Homer* (Cologne, 1967). The sources for the history of the text are conveniently collected in T. W. Allen, *Homer: The Origins and the Transmissions* (Oxford, 1924). The best account of the relationship between Alexandrian scholarship and the subsequent transmission of Homer is that of G. Pasquali, *Storia della tradizione e critica del testo* (2d ed. Florence, 1962), 201-41. Two recent articles, more technical in nature, should also be mentioned here. M. Haslam, "Apollonius Rhodius and the Papyri," *Illinois Classical Studies* 3 (1978), 47-73, discusses the relationship between the papyri of Apollonius and the medieval tradition; his comments are equally relevant to the transmission of Homer. Nigel Wilson, "Scoliasti e commentatori," *Studi classici e orientali* 33 (1983), 83-112, provides an excellent brief introduction to the nature and transmission of Greek scholia.

The problems regarding the extant scholia to the *Iliad* are extremely complex and not easily accessible to the nonexpert. The recent edition by H. Erbse, *Scholia Graeca in Homeri Iliadem* (Berlin, 1969-83), against which we have corrected Wolf's citations, could have been improved by adding the so-called *Scholia Didymi*, some of which are in fact found in all the major Byzantine collections of scholia; for the problem, see the brief discussion in N. G. Wilson's review of Erbse's first volume in *GGA* 224 (1972), 1f. The scholia omitted by Erbse are most readily found in the nineteenth-century editions of the three major manuscripts (known generally as A,

B, and T) made by Dindorf and Maass. Some of the problems regarding the origins of the A scholia and their relationship to Alexandrian scholarship are discussed by Pfeiffer at various points in his *History*; for more detailed analysis, see H. Erbse, *Beiträge zur Ueberlieferung der Iliasscholien*, Zetemata 24 (Munich, 1960); and M. van der Valk, *Researches on the Text and Scholia of the "Iliad"* (Leiden, 1963-64).

The reader in search of further information about the Jewish scholarly tradition that so interested Wolf will find helpful introductions to the field in the articles by S. Talmon, in *The Cambridge History of the Bible*, vol. 1, ed. P. R. Ackroyd and C. F. Evans (Cambridge, 1970), 159-99; and B. J. Roberts, in *The Cambridge History of the Bible*, vol. 2, ed. G.W.H. Lampe (Cambridge, 1969), 1-26. J. Weingreen discusses the assumptions of the Masoretes as well as many specific examples of their work in his *Introduction to the Critical Study of the Text of the Hebrew Bible* (Oxford, 1982). No one has yet carried out the comparative study of Masoretes and Alexandrians that Wolf called for. For some helpful remarks see S. Lieberman, *Hellenism in Jewish Palestine* (New York, 1950), 28-37, and M. Greenberg, "The Stabilization of the Text of the Hebrew Bible . . . ," *Journal of the American Oriental Society* 76 (1956) = *The Canon and Masorah of the Hebrew Bible: An Introductory Reader*, ed. S. Z. Leiman (New York, 1974), 317-18, 325-26.

INDEX NOMINUM

This is a highly selective index of names of individuals, historical and mythological, to whom Wolf devotes some attention in the text or the notes. Dates are given (A.D. unless otherwise noted) and unfamiliar names are briefly identified, with a view to clarifying Wolf's allusions. References are to Wolf's chapter and footnote numbers.

INDEX LOCORUM

This is a highly selective index of passages that play a substantial role in Wolf's argument or receive a substantial amount of attention from him. References are to Wolf's chapter and footnote numbers.

LIBRARY OF CONGRESS CATALOGING IN PUBLICATION DATA

WOLF, F. A. (FRIEDRICH AUGUST), 1759-1824.
PROLEGOMENA TO HOMER (1795)

TRANSLATION OF: PROLEGOMENA AD HOMERUM.
BIBLIOGRAPHY: P.
INCLUDES INDEXES.
1. HOMER—CRITICISM AND INTERPRETATION.
I. GRAFTON, ANTHONY. II. MOST, GLENN W.
III. ZETZEL, JAMES E. G. IV. TITLE.

PA4037.A2W6813 1985   883'.01   84-42907
ISBN 0-691-06639-6 (ALK. PAPER)